CRUSADERS, GANGSTERS, AND WHISKEY

CRUSADERS, GANGSTERS,

AND

WHISKEY

PROHIBITION IN MEMPHIS

Patrick O'Daniel

University Press of Mississippi / Jackson

The University Press of Mississippi is the scholarly publishing agency of the Mississippi Institutions of Higher Learning: Alcorn State University, Delta State University, Jackson State University, Mississippi State University, Mississippi University for Women, Mississippi Valley State University, University of Mississippi, and University of Southern Mississippi.

www.upress.state.ms.us

Designed by Peter D. Halverson

The University Press of Mississippi is a member of the Association of University Presses.

First printing 2018

∞

Library of Congress Cataloging-in-Publication Data

Names: O'Daniel, Patrick. author.
Title: Crusaders, gangsters, and whiskey : prohibition in Memphis / Patrick O'Daniel.
Description: Jackson : University Press of Mississippi, [2018] | Includes bibliographical references and index. |
Identifiers: LCCN 2018016621 (print) | LCCN 2018018647 (ebook) | ISBN 9781496820051 (epub single) | ISBN 9781496820068 (epub institutional) | ISBN 9781496820075 (pdf single) | ISBN 9781496820082 (pdf institutional) | ISBN 9781496820044 (hardcover : alk. paper)
Subjects: LCSH: Prohibition—Tennessee—Memphis.
Classification: LCC HV5090.T2 (ebook) | LCC HV5090.T2 O43 2018 (print) | DDC 364.1/33209768109042—dc23
LC record available at https://lccn.loc.gov/2018016621

British Library Cataloging-in-Publication Data available

FOR MY FATHER

CONTENTS

ACKNOWLEDGMENTS

I would like to thank the staff of the History Department and Memphis Room of the Memphis Public Library and Information Center, the Shelby County Archives, the University of Memphis Special Collections, and the Memphis Police Department Photo Lab for their assistance. I would like to thank Dr. Charles Crawford, G. Wayne Dowdy, Gina Cordell, Dr. James R. Johnson, Mark Greaney, Tom Colgan, Bill Dugger, Dr. Michael Bast, and Karen Campbell for their advice and encouragement. I would also like to thank my family, Uncle Frank, Sean, Rowan, Baba, Marcy, Ajna, Jeri, Mac, Kathy, and Kelly for their support.

ABBREVIATIONS

ASL	Anti-Saloon League
CA	*Commercial Appeal*
EA	*Evening Appeal*
ES	*Evening Scimitar*
NARA	National Archives and Records Administration
NS	*News Scimitar*
PS	*Press-Scimitar*
WCTU	Woman's Christian Temperance Union

CRUSADERS, GANGSTERS, AND WHISKEY

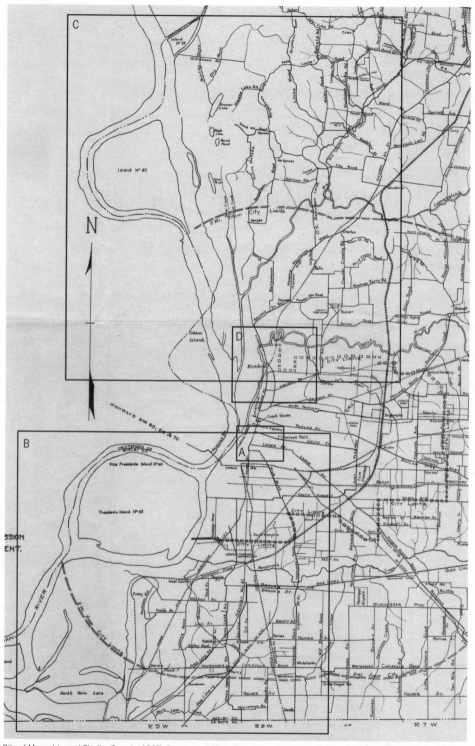

City of Memphis and Shelby County, 1927. Courtesy of Memphis Room, Memphis Public Library and Information Center. A) Figure 3.1, B) Figure 14.1, C) Figure 15.1, and D) Figure 16.4

INTRODUCTION

No political, economic, or moral issue has so engrossed and divided
all the people of America as the prohibition problem, except the issue
of slavery.
 —Mabel Walker Willebrandt, US assistant attorney general

The night air was hot, humid, and filled with the sound of cicadas. Deadly water moccasins lived in the woods by the creek, and anyone walking through them had to watch where he stepped. The lookouts hid in the trees and undergrowth and settled in for a long night. The men swatted away the swarms of bloodthirsty mosquitoes as they kept careful watch over the moonlit trails leading to the still. They stood ready to fire off warning shots from their rifles at the first sign of Prohibition agents, sheriff's deputies, or hijackers. They knew that if any raider made it past them undetected, their comrades could lose their freedom or their lives.

A short way up the trail, the moonshiners poured foul-smelling mash into a copper still. The mixture of water, cornmeal, sugar, and yeast had been fermenting in a buried vat for weeks. With the still full, they prepared a fire and stoked the flames until the boiling mash released its alcoholic vapor. The mist rose into the cap, moved through a copper line, and filtered through water in a barrel called the thumper. The fumes drifted through the worm, a coiled copper tube submerged in another water-filled barrel, where it cooled and liquefied. They discarded the toxic methanol-laced first drops, and filled bottles with the rest of the clear liquid as it dripped from the copper coil. It was the night's first batch of corn liquor, or as they liked to call it, white mule.

Some dismissed moonshining as just a gimmick to make easy money, but for bootleggers during Prohibition, it was a high-risk venture with a

tremendous profit potential. Capitalism, like nature, abhors a vacuum. Prohibition took legal liquor away, but the desire for alcohol remained and
bootleggers gladly stepped in and filled the demand.[1]

Statewide Prohibition took effect in Tennessee in 1909 after years of agitation by temperance organizations. Even after the National Prohibition Act
ran its course from 1920 to 1933, Tennessee's antiliquor laws remained in
effect until 1939. Prohibitionists believed outlawing alcohol would make the
country safer and more productive and improve the lives of women and children. They succeeded in the legislative arena, but in their naïveté, they did not
understand that passage of a law did not guarantee its enforcement. Despite
harsh penalties, bootlegging flourished and the country entered a period of
unparalleled illegal drinking and lawbreaking. In the end, everything that
could go wrong with Prohibition went wrong, and few places illustrate that
failure better than Memphis.

Prohibition was one of the most important issues to affect Memphis after
the American Civil War, and at the same time, it is one of the least understood
in the city's history. Few events other than the civil rights movement had a
more significant and longer-lasting impact. Even so, few written accounts
were kept, and most oral histories were little more than conjecture.

The lack of adequate source material has led to shortcomings in the historiography of Prohibition in Memphis. Historians pulled information from
the same small pool of stories and repeated them until readers no longer
questioned their authenticity, accuracy, or thoroughness. Making this observation is not to say that any history of Memphis is flawed, but rather it
is to say that previous accounts only provide a limited explanation of this
critical period.

Bootlegging defined the failure of Prohibition in the 1920s and 1930s, and
many historians maintained that bootlegging was an extension of Edward
Hull Crump's political machine and functioned under its protection to support it financially. Sharon Wright wrote, "Crump soon created a machine
which sustained itself on corruption. During the age of Prohibition, his
administration accepted bribes from brothel, gambling houses, and saloon
owners."[2] Roger Biles wrote, "The necessary funds [for Crump's organization]
materialized in the form of protection payoffs collected from gamblers, prostitutes, and liquor dealers operating in blatant violation of Tennessee prohibition statutes."[3] Michael Honey wrote, "[Crump] built his political machine
by collecting money from illegal gambling dens, houses of prostitution, and,
during Prohibition, from illegal liquor joints."[4]

Crump was ousted as mayor in 1916 for nonenforcement of statewide Prohibition but regained control of the city's administration in 1927. When law enforcement under Crump did not bring down bootlegging, many assumed that it was not because of ineffectiveness but rather because the powerful urban boss deliberately allowed bootlegging to continue. In 1936, *Time* published an article that claimed, "The Crump dynasty is supposed to be financed by various forms of protection money from bootleggers, gamblers, et al."[5] The notion of collusion continued to appear in subsequent histories of Memphis. David Tucker wrote, "With Crump back in power, Memphis once again developed a powerful underworld. Bootleggers, gambling houses, pimps, prostitutes, and policy men thrived under the protection of the machine."[6] William Worley and Ernest Withers wrote, "When Tennessee prohibition ended in 1939, Crump's ability to control aspects of city life through the bootlegger network came to an end."[7]

Bootlegging, however, was a much more complex phenomenon. A day-by-day study of news reports and documents of the period brings into question the assumption that bootleggers operated with the consent of the machine or for its benefit. No one can say to what extent Crump's political machine, the Shelby County Organization, accepted money from criminals; however, Crump's men did not, and could not, force every bootlegger to pay tribute to the organization. Furthermore, Crump became politically powerful, but not powerful enough to protect bootleggers from the federally controlled Prohibition Bureau.

Contrary to rumors spread by critics, Crump became wealthy and powerful without the help of bootleggers. He married into a well-to-do family, invested in the Coca-Cola Company, and started a leading real estate insurance company. Crump built political support by developing relations with business elites and business-oriented progressives with the goal of making Memphis the most important commercial center in the South.

Considering these findings, we must ask ourselves how much we truly know about the failure of Prohibition in Memphis. If the Crump machine was not behind bootlegging, who was?

This book offers a fresh look at those responsible for the rise and fall of Prohibition, its effect on Memphis, and the impact that events in the city had on the rest of the state and country. The first chapter covers the rise of local chapters of the Woman's Christian Temperance Union and the Anti-Saloon League and their campaign for a ban on alcoholic beverages. It includes the city's role in state efforts and the violent death of the movement's beloved martyr.

The next chapters deal with fall of the saloons and the city's gangsters who inspired the local Prohibition movement. Chapters 2 and 3 cover the efforts to enforce statewide Prohibition in Memphis and the resistance to the law. They include the relationship between saloons, politicians, and the ouster of Mayor Crump. Chapter 4 examines the more notorious saloon owners and gangsters who embodied the lawlessness and moral decline described in temperance rhetoric.

Chapters 5, 6, and 7 explore the rise of bootlegging and the corruption of law enforcement. Newly appointed administrators struggled to enforce the unpopular law and bring down a shadowy criminal organization led by one of their own. The country faced the first assessment of Prohibition in the federal courts in Memphis in what Americans should have seen as a test case for national Prohibition.

Chapter 8 covers the attempts by federal, county, and city law enforcement to combat bootlegging. It includes the arrival of the US Bureau of Internal Revenue's Prohibition Unit (the federal entity created to enforce the liquor law that became the Prohibition Bureau in March 1927), the reorganization of the police department, and Shelby County sheriff Will Knight's efforts to stop moonshining. Some officers gave in to temptation and took bribes from bootleggers. Others, frustrated by the inadequacies of the law, found extralegal means to mete out rough and ready justice on local gangsters.

Chapters 9 through 12 look at problems resulting from the uneven enforcement of Prohibition. The brunt of enforcement fell on African Americans, immigrants, the working class, and the poor, while the wealthiest used their influence to skirt the law. Others used medical and religious exemptions as means to circumvent the law to acquire alcohol, while the poorest people risked injury and death by drinking industrial alcohol laced with toxic additives or tainted moonshine. The Ku Klux Klan used the Prohibition issue to veil their attempts to intimidate immigrants and African Americans, and youthful rebellion against the hypocritical liquor law grew into a disregard for all laws.

Chapters 13 and 14 explore the places that took on the role of the saloon and their clienteles' steadfast resistance to Prohibition. Social drinking in defiance of the law gave rise to new gathering places. Restaurants transformed into roadhouses and nightclubs with crowds of scofflaws dancing to the music of jazz orchestras. Corn whiskey and home brew beer flowed freely in brothels and gambling halls as their proprietors became a new kind of bootlegger.

Chapters 15 through 17 cover the gangsters, scandals, and warfare among the bootleggers. Joe Sailors ran a moonshine operation, protected through bribery, intimidation, and murder, out of President's Island, a seventy-five-hundred-acre island in the Mississippi River just south of Memphis. John Belluomini oversaw a gang that produced thousands of gallons of liquor a week. A misplaced ledger with the names of bribed police officers discovered by Prohibition agents set in motion a series of events that brought down his empire and shook the public's faith in law enforcement. Violence broke out among rival bootlegging gangs after Ed Crump's political machine, the Shelby County Organization, inadvertently interfered in the corn liquor market. The resulting war brought about the demise of the Liquor Barons and a purge of the old liquor interests from the organization.

The final chapters deal with the roles of Memphians in Prohibition repeal in 1939. They explore the rise of the repeal movement and the desperate attempts to save Prohibition by the Woman's Christian Temperance Union and the Anti-Saloon League. Law enforcement's inability to bring leading bootleggers to justice helped build the case for repeal. The police department all but gave up its fight against liquor traffickers as politicians gave in to the demands to use liquor as a new revenue source. As the ban on liquor faded, a new bootlegging stood poised on the horizon.

Prohibition, with all its crime, corruption, and cultural upheaval, ran its course after thirteen years in most of the rest of the country; but in Memphis, it lasted from 1909 until 1939. *Crusaders, Gangsters, and Whiskey* explores those tumultuous decades. The failure of Prohibition in Memphis deserves a careful study because of its impact on the city, state, and country. How did Prohibition affect Memphis? Why did it fail and how was that failure important? The answers lie in the lives of the people involved: the people who fought for Prohibition, the people who fought against it, and the people who profited from it. And their story begins with a gunfight.

1

RISE OF THE WHITE RIBBONS

Temperate temperance is best. Intemperate temperance injures the
cause of temperance, while temperate temperance helps it in its fight
against intemperate intemperance. Fanatics will never learn that,
though it be written in letters of gold across the sky.
—Mark Twain, 1896

Edward Ward Carmack was about to become a martyr. Of course, he
had no idea this was about to happen; it was just the end of another
typical day at the office where he worked as the editor of the Nashville
newspaper *The Tennessean*. He finished up, locked his door, and began to
walk home along the crowded streets on an otherwise pleasant afternoon
on November 9, 1908.

The tall, red-haired Carmack had begun his law career in Columbia, Tennessee, and served as a member of the lower house of the state legislature
in Nashville in 1885. He found an outlet for his political opinions as editor
of the *Columbia Herald*, the *Nashville American* in 1888, and the *Memphis
Daily Commercial* in 1892. Carmack's caustic personality and no-holds-barred
approach caused many hard feelings, including those of W. A. Collier, editor
of the rival Memphis newspaper the *Appeal-Avalanche*.[1]

Carmack's stand on the issue of silver cemented his reputation as a firebrand. He joined the crusade to increase the money supply through silver
coinage to offset the panic and depression. In 1896, he resigned from the
recently merged *Commercial Appeal* because three of the five owners of
the newspaper swayed the local Democratic Party to nominate pro-gold-
standard Josiah Patterson to US Congress for a fourth term. Tennessee's so-
called Silver Democrats withdrew from the party and nominated Carmack.

8

Fig. 1.1. Edward Ward Carmack. Courtesy of the Library of Congress.

After a long battle, Carmack eventually won but made an enemy of Patterson's son Malcolm, who became governor. Carmack served two terms in the US House of Representatives and began a term as a US Senator in 1901.[2]

Carmack challenged Malcom Patterson in his 1908 re-election campaign, so the Democrats took the unusual step of holding a gubernatorial primary. Prohibition became the deciding factor, and each candidate stood firmly entrenched on his side of the issue: Carmack represented the rural Prohibitionists and Patterson represented the urban opposition. Patterson won the nomination and the election, while Prohibitionist candidates won the state legislature. Carmack remained editor of *The Tennessean*, where he continued his attacks on Patterson and his advisor Col. Duncan Cooper.

Cooper had hired Carmack as editor of the *Nashville American* in 1888, but the two became political opponents after Cooper sided with Patterson. Carmack, true to form, used his newspaper to attack Cooper's integrity and influence over the governor. He then accused Patterson of fraud and Cooper of secretly orchestrating an alliance with former governor John Isaac Cox to sway the election. The blatant attack on his honor infuriated Cooper and made him a bitter enemy.

On the afternoon of November 9, 1908, Carmack lit a cigar and left his office headed north on Seventh Street with the evening paper under his arm. He stopped in front of the Polk Apartment House to speak to friends Charles and Catherine Eastman. He had just tipped his hat to the lady when he noticed Duncan Cooper and his twenty-seven-year-old son Robin across the street. Cooper yelled, "You're trying to hide behind a woman, you coward!" Carmack stepped away from Mrs. Eastman, and Robin Cooper stepped in front of his father. Robin Cooper and Carmack both drew revolvers as Mrs. Eastman screamed, "For God's sake, don't shoot!"[3]

Both men opened fire. One bullet struck Robin Cooper in the shoulder and another missed. Two bullets struck Carmack in the chest. The third bullet from Robin Cooper's pistol hit Carmack in the back of the neck and exited through the mouth as he spun around from the impacts of the first two shots. Cooper staggered to the ground wounded, and Carmack fell into the gutter. Dr. McPheeters Glasgow rushed to the scene, examined Carmack, and pronounced him dead. Colonel Cooper rushed his wounded son to Dr. R. G. Fort's office to call for an ambulance.[4]

Police arrested the Coopers on charges of second-degree murder and former sheriff John Sharpe with aiding and abetting. The Coopers claimed they met Carmack by chance while walking to the state capitol in response to a telephone call from Governor Patterson. Vengeful Carmack supporters insisted the Coopers were guilty of premeditated murder. The Memphis *News Scimitar* accused Patterson of complicity and suggested he had promised Cooper a pardon in advance.[5]

The jury acquitted John Sharpe in March 1909 but, after much debate, found both Coopers guilty. The judge sentenced each to twenty years in the state penitentiary. Duncan Cooper appealed, but the state supreme court upheld the decision. Patterson, however, issued a pardon within the hour. He maintained that the elder Cooper, who never drew his pistol during the fight, did not receive a fair trial.[6]

A second jury acquitted Robin Cooper on November 15, 1910, despite the uproar from temperance supporters who wanted him imprisoned. He won his freedom, as well as many enemies. He made the news again on August 19, 1919, when unknown assailants beat him to death and left his body in his car.[7]

Carmack supporters held memorial services across the state the Sunday after his death. Seven thousand people crowded into Ryman Auditorium in Nashville to sing hymns, listen to speeches, and solemnly resolve in Carmack's memory to "drive the liquor power from the State of Tennessee." Mourners claimed the liquor interests assassinated their champion and his death was a call to arms. Charles D. Johns conveyed the meaning of Carmack's death in his book, *Tennessee's Pond of Liquor and Pool of Blood*:

> There is not a day that passed since the blood of the peerless Carmack, made flow by an assassin's bullet, dampened the ground on that now hallowed spot on Seventh Avenue, Nashville, Tennessee, that many interested and grieving strangers do not visit the scene of the lamented senator's last moments on Earth, where he was shot down almost without warning in the prime of his manhood and in the midst of his usefulness to his state and country as a leader and statesman. . . . Do you not feel the presence of his great spirit as you stand there and recall the whole affair? Do you not experience the peculiar sensation of being on sacred ground when you remember the greatness of the man whose life ebbed away there on that spot, while the pistols of his assassins were yet smoking . . . ?[8]

Carmack's violent death caused outrage across Tennessee and the country. Prohibitionists labeled the shooting an assassination and framed Carmack as a slain martyr. Public opinion in Tennessee, incited by temperance propaganda, shifted in favor of Prohibition.

The temperance movement in the United States originally aimed to curb excessive alcohol consumption, but after decades of unresponsiveness from the government and the public, members shifted their focus to building enough support to force a legal ban on all alcohol consumption. Temperance workers had a genuine cause for concern. In 1830, the average fifteen-year-old boy consumed nearly seven gallons of alcohol a year, three times the average of modern Americans. Adults drank far more. Alcohol played a role in missed work, on-the-job injuries, workmanship, higher crime rates, and domestic violence. Women suffered the most since they had few legal rights and depended on drinking fathers and husbands for support.[9]

The rising indignation of wives and mothers across the country gave rise to the Woman's Christian Temperance Union (WCTU) in 1874 in Cleveland, Ohio. Members chose the white ribbon bow to symbolize purity and took pledges of abstinence from alcohol, and later tobacco and narcotics. The

Fig. 1.2. Wayne B. Wheeler. Courtesy of the Library of Congress.

WCTU, under Annie Turner Wittenmyer, opened chapters across the country with the slogan "Agitate—Educate—Legislate."[10]

The WCTU became a formidable force, especially after its members allied with Susan B. Anthony, Elizabeth Cady Stanton, and other women battling for women's suffrage. The organization, later led by Frances Willard, lobbied to restrict alcohol sales, created antialcohol programs for children and campaigned for state legislation against alcohol. Under pressure from the WCTU, North Dakota, South Dakota, Iowa, and Rhode Island adopted Prohibition laws, and Kansas legislators wrote Prohibition into their constitution in 1880. Georgia passed statewide Prohibition in 1907, followed by Oklahoma in 1907, Mississippi in 1908, North Carolina in 1908, Tennessee in 1909, and West Virginia in 1912. The WCTU claimed significant successes, but its goal of a nationwide ban remained just out of reach.

The campaign for a Prohibition amendment to the United States Constitution gained momentum with the formation of the Anti-Saloon League (ASL) in 1893. Under the shrewd and ruthless leadership of Wayne Wheeler, the ASL became the country's most successful single-issue lobbying organization intent on destroying the saloon's influence on society and politics. An ASL member wrote, "A Prohibitionary law puts the saloon where it can't fight back. It removes the saloon from politics by removing it from existence."[11]

The ASL harnessed both morality and patriotism for its cause. ASL propaganda took advantage of the rising anti-German fervor and framed beer brewers as German sympathizers. Thinking ahead, Prohibitionists supported the income tax amendment in 1913 to cover revenue expected to be lost when the breweries closed. Most politicians dared not defy the ASL as the proposed Eighteenth Amendment to the US Constitution, the ban on alcohol consumption, stood on the verge of ratification by both houses of Congress.[12]

In Tennessee, the battle over alcohol began with the founding of the state in 1796. The first laws limited amounts sold, limited sales to African Americans, and outlawed drunkenness. More laws followed as the temperance movement begun by Quakers and Congregationists spread from the Northeast into Tennessee in the 1820s. Legislation following the Civil War introduced high taxes and local option laws and outlawed the sale of alcohol near schools and churches. The effort by the Tennessee Temperance Alliance nearly succeeded in enacting a Prohibition amendment to the state constitution in 1887.[13]

Prohibitionists despised Memphis's saloons, with their stand-up bars with big mirrors, polished mahogany, brass rails, and spittoons. The city had over 150 such places by 1899, for a population of just over one hundred thousand. Even groceries sold ten-cent cups of whiskey from a barrel kept behind the store counter or in a back room.[14]

Saloons played a big part in the business life of the city in the nineteenth century, and many of the city's elite invested in the liquor trade. For example, Robert R. Church Sr. became the South's first African American millionaire after coming to Memphis during the Civil War. He invested in real estate and founded the Solvent Savings Bank and Trust in 1906; however, his first business successes came from running some of the busiest saloons and brothels on Beale Street.[15]

Elizabeth Fisher Johnson established Tennessee's first WCTU chapter in Memphis in 1876 and collected six thousand abstinence pledges. Membership flagged because of the yellow fever epidemic in 1878 until Frances Willard's visit to the city in 1881. In 1882, Johnson joined forces with a newly formed Nashville chapter to create a statewide organization. The Tennessee WCTU then became the most powerful component of the Tennessee Temperance

Fig. 1.3. Frances Willard of the Woman's Christian Temperance Union.
Courtesy of the Library of Congress.

Alliance, an organization of Methodist, Baptist, and Presbyterian churches
that rallied support for a Prohibition amendment to the state constitution
in 1887.[16]

Lide Meriwether, wife of Memphis civil engineer Niles Meriwether, became president of the seventy-five-member Memphis WCTU after Johnson
died in April 1883. Meriwether had joined only four months earlier and had
never spoken in public until attending a WCTU convention in Arkansas. To
her surprise, she became a powerful speaker and leader. She created an effective propaganda tool by organizing children into "Bands of Hope" in Memphis and other communities in Tennessee to carry the message about the
"evils of strong drink." With her encouragement, African American women
formed chapters and later organized the Sojourner Truth of Tennessee State
Union at the state convention on September 21, 1886.[17]

Prohibition divided African Americans as deeply as whites in Tennessee during the 1887 campaign. Those who supported Prohibition organized
within churches and colleges, especially Fisk University, Roger Williams

University, and Tennessee Central College. Many black Tennesseans heeded
the appeals of Fisk University founder Gen. Clinton Fisk and Frederick Dou-
glass to join the cause. Many in Memphis, however, proved harder to sway.
"Prohibition is a slave law, as it puts some in bondage and leaves others to do
as they please," wrote an editorialist from the African American newspaper
The Watchman. Another black Memphian said, "I fought the rebels for my
freedom, and I'll fight again before I will let the Prohibitionists take away
my rights."[18]

The Memphis WCTU continued to meet and even opened a lunch room
for shop girls in 1887, but interest began to fade by 1900. Ada Wallace Unruh,
president of the Oregon chapter of the WCTU, spoke at the Court Street
Presbyterian Church in Memphis in 1898 to an enthusiastic crowd. She returned to the city two years later and spoke at the Central Baptist Church.
The meager reception left Unruh disappointed. She said it was the smallest
audience she had addressed in her twenty years of temperance work.[19]

In 1902, Rev. John Royal Harris, state ASL superintendent, announced in
Memphis, "We have arrived at last!" The Tennessee branch of the ASL revital-
ized the antiliquor movement by recruiting members of both political parties
to force passage of increasingly stricter laws. Pro-ASL legislators began by
outlawing alcohol sales within four miles of any school in rural Tennessee.
They next enacted bans on alcohol sales in towns with populations less than
two thousand people in 1887 and on the state capitol grounds in 1901.[20] The
1903 Adams Act extended the four-mile law to towns with populations of five
thousand, banned liquor sales within four miles of soldiers' homes, limited
liquor to inmates of public institutions, and made nonpayment of US internal
revenue tax or nonpossession of an internal revenue stamp evidence of guilt
in all prosecutions.[21] In 1907, Sen. Isaac Louis Pendleton introduced a bill to
extend the four-mile law to cities of more than 150,000 people. It passed the
Tennessee Senate by a vote of twenty-six to five and the Tennessee House of
Representatives with a vote of seventy-one to twenty-four.[22]

Prohibitionists held a mass meeting in Memphis beginning January 17,
1908. WCTU vice president Mary H. Armor arrived two days later to speak
at the Central Baptist Church. Unlike the earlier visit by Ada Unruh, Armor met with an enthusiastic response. The meeting ended with a rousing
rendition of "Tennessee's Going Dry," a popular temperance song sung to
the tune of "Bringing in the Sheaves," that reportedly left the left the whole
church trembling.[23]

A series of debates between Edward Carmack and Malcolm Patterson
drew enthusiastic crowds who turned out to cheer and heckle the celebrity

candidates. The two squared off at Ellis Auditorium in Memphis on May 30, 1908, in front of a rowdy crowd of eight thousand people. Carmack argued for state Prohibition while Patterson argued for the local option, the more moderate stance of allowing individual communities to decide whether to allow alcohol.[24]

Meanwhile, Prohibitionist newspaper editorialists appealed to white racism by blaming saloons and distillers for supposed sex crimes committed by African Americans. Methodist clergyman Horace Mellard DuBose wrote in the Nashville newspaper *The Tennessean* about the death of a Texas woman at the hands of a black "saloon lounger." In June 1908, the minister seized upon an article by Will Irwin in *Collier's* magazine about the rape and murder of a fourteen-year-old girl by a drunken African American man in Louisiana. Irwin accused the Lee Levy Gin Company and other liquor producers of marketing to black men with suggestive pictures of white women on their labels. DuBose called upon Tennesseans to "set aside all other reasons for the crusade against the saloon and consider this one—the Negro problem." DuBose said, "The effect of the saloon upon the Negro is disastrous to his industry and good citizenship. And more, the Negro, fairly docile and industrious, becomes, when filled with liquor, turbulent and dangerous and a menace to life, property, and the repose of the community."[25]

Patterson won the election, but Carmack's death galvanized Prohibitionists, who "determined that his death should not be in vain." Texas WCTU leader Nancy Curtis traveled to Memphis to urge women, in defiance of their husbands if necessary, to march in support. WCTU members, known as "white ribboners" because of their white ribbon symbol, paraded at polling places carrying banners and singing songs like "Give Us Prohibition" sung to the tune of "Old Time Religion," while their children carried banners proclaiming, "Tremble King Alcohol for We Shall Grow Up!" Memphis members served lunch to poll workers and instructed the poor how to vote "the right ticket."[26]

The Prohibition campaign overwhelmed proliquor interests in Memphis. Brewers and distillers organized a chapter of the Tennessee Model License League in February 1908 to eliminate objectionable practices of the retail liquor business and quiet the complaints from critics. They advocated limiting licenses to only men of good character, allowing only one saloon for every five hundred people, and revoking licenses of violators.[27]

Prohibitionists, however, had no interest in compromise and pushed for more legislation. On January 8, 1909, the editors of the *Commercial Appeal* and local businessmen held a "monster mass meeting" at the Memphis

Merchants Exchange in a last-ditch effort to fight the new four-mile law. Their delegation went to Nashville to make a case against the proposed bill, only to be forced back by a mob of Carmack supporters.[28]

On January 19, 1909, the state legislature passed two pieces of Prohibition-related legislation. The first, Senate Bill No. 1, banned alcoholic beverages from a four-mile radius of any school whether in session or not. This bill did not explicitly ban the sale or consumption of alcohol, but the practical effect of it did just that since most communities fell within four miles of some school. The second piece of legislation, Senate Bill No. 11, banned alcohol manufacturing and gave brewers and distillers until January 1, 1910, to sell off inventories. Patterson opposed both bills, but the assembly promptly overrode his vetoes. More legislation followed to set expiration dates on liquor licenses, refund money for licenses extending beyond July 1, 1909, forbid solicitation of Tennessee-made alcohol, and allow investigators to use records from the Internal Revenue collector as evidence of selling liquor.[29]

On June 30, 1909, a reporter wrote, "We'uns of Tennessee will awaken tomorrow to find ourselves riding the water wagon!" Sen. Oscar Holladay's four-mile law went into effect after midnight despite protests from Memphis and Chattanooga. In theory, this shut down every saloon in the state. The euphoria of legislative victory, however, did not last long.[30]

A decade later, Prohibitionists still had not rid the state of liquor, so the ASL decided to create a memorial to Edward Carmack to reinvigorate their followers and quiet their critics. The ASL unveiled the statue, along with a plaque provided by the WCTU in a grand ceremony in 1925. Ironically, the placement of the statue illustrated the Prohibitionists' relation to the foe it could never defeat. The majestic, larger-than-life figure of Carmack stands proudly on the grounds of the state capitol, just to the right of equally majestic Motlow Tunnel, the grand passage to the capitol built with money provided by the estate of whiskey distiller Jack Daniel.[31]

2

FALL OF THE SALOONS

The saloon has sinned away its day of grace.
—Edward Ward Carmack

hurch bells and clock steeples rang out at midnight July 1, 1909. The moment had come when the four-mile law went into effect. Only two saloons remained near the Mississippi border, but the WCTU promised to open a new school near them to force them to close. While some celebrated the coming of statewide Prohibition, others rushed to the nearest saloon for their last drink. Silas Bent, a *St. Louis Post-Dispatch* reporter covering the events in the city, wrote, "The night before the law became effective, Memphis got drunk. Men, who had never before been seen publicly intoxicated, reeled through the streets. Others who had never before bought whiskey in bottles bought quarts of it. The town had never witnessed such an orgy. Many saloons sold out their entire stocks."[1]

Once the excitement settled, Memphians realized having a law and enforcing a law were two different things. Memphis historian John Preston Young wrote, "But it was whispered, then spoken aloud, that this law was not a popular law and that therefore the saloonkeepers should not be forced to obey it." Bartenders hung out signs advertising only the sale of soft drinks, but with a wink of the eye or knowing look, supplied the genuine article.[2]

The saloons stayed closed for a day or two until word spread that the staff of the Peabody and Gayoso Hotels continued to sell alcohol. Bartenders removed the labels from bottles and filled glasses behind the counters so customers could claim they did not know what was in their drinks. Crowds flouted the law and filled the saloons as the city became once again "wide open." Most Memphians showed little surprise at the flagrant violations since few had any confidence in the law anyway.[3]

Fig. 2.1. Gayoso Hotel and Bismarck Saloon. Courtesy of the Library of Congress.

Silas Bent returned on October 2, 1910, and reported, "Saloons in increased numbers sell drinks with no pretense at secrecy. Gambling goes on in most of them, policemen enter them openly and are served at the bars without cost. The city authorities declare that, 'Prohibition having been thrust upon Memphis against its will, they propose to continue ignoring the law.'" Rowe "Deacon" Jones, who had a saloon at Third and Gayoso, remembered, "When the prohibition law first went into effect I thought at first they were going to enforce it. I shut up the place, took my bartender with me and went for a fishing trip. We came back in about a month and opened up, and I haven't closed since. My wine rooms are never closed."[4]

Downtown drinking establishments had plainly visible electric signs displaying words like "bar" or "saloon." Strong's Saloon at Third and Union Avenue even had placards out front advertising its wine room. Many had staff standing outside inviting in those walking by their businesses. The Climax Bar and Chop Suey Restaurant at 44 South Second displayed a brightly lit sign. An African American man played piano to guests in the restaurant upstairs, while customers downstairs played poker and drank with a police officer called "Mac."[5]

Fig. 2.2. Main Street, north from Gayoso Avenue. Courtesy of the Library of Congress.

Police ordered saloons to close at midnight and remain closed on Sundays, but even these small concessions met with resistance. Bob Carruthers, a part proprietor of a bar at 158 Monroe, had wine rooms upstairs and permitted gambling. He kept the place open as long as customers continued to drink but used a side door instead of the front to make the bar appear closed after midnight. Sam Baumgarten, who also had a wholesale liquor business, operated his saloon at 8 North Main Street on Sundays but had his customers enter through a hallway from the restaurant in the rear. Harry A. Smith, the owner of the Bismarck Saloon attached to the Gayoso, never bothered to route customers to a side door since he did not have one.[6]

The Garden Theater drew capacity crowds with Friday night boxing matches, a dancehall, and a stage for movies. Between shows, risqué vaudeville acts entertained the audiences. Afterward, prostitutes, "wearing skirts barely to their knees" walked among the tables soliciting men to drink and dance with them on floors sprinkled with sand. Men and women drank together at the bar and in the more private boxes overlooking the main room. Bent watched a "stout blonde woman" take the tasseled cord of the night-stick held by a police officer, turn and hold it over her shoulder, and lead him to a table for drinks amid the laughter and jokes of the other customers.[7]

Rev. William E. Thompson, of St. John's Methodist Church, and the Law Enforcement League finally lost patience. The lack of enforcement and stories of men and women drinking together infuriated the fifteen-hundred-member league. To make matters worse, the police headquarters occupied the southwest corner of Second Street and Washington Avenue, while saloons operated openly within sight on the northeast and northwest corners. Field secretary James C. Penn hired private detectives to gather evidence of illegal activities over a three-month period.[8]

The league presented Mayor Crump its findings along with a petition to close 126 establishments. The league claimed, "Illegal drinking saloons are being openly, publicly, continuously, and notoriously conducted both daily and on Sundays." Members complained of electric signs, women drinking with men, the sale of alcohol to minors, under-aged girls tending bar, gambling, accommodations made to prostitutes, unpaid back taxes, and the monthly fifty-dollar state license fees that never reached the capitol.[9]

The league demanded law enforcement take action. They claimed that police officers ignored violations, drank for free in the saloons, and provided protection for gambling. They complained the Shelby County Grand Jury had not taken advantage of legislation allowing the use of federal liquor licenses as evidence against liquor dealers and jurymen refused to return indictments. Thompson said juries also "utterly ignored such evidence and laughed at it, joked and made fun of the witnesses who appeared before them to submit evidence."[10]

Crump said, "I can do more good by stopping gambling and closing dives than by trying to enforce a law to which the people are opposed. The state passed the law and should enforce it. There is not city ordinance against the sale of liquor." Chief of police William C. Davis explained, "Under Mayor Malone, I made some arrests for violation of the law, because he was in sympathy with prohibition, but the present mayor opposes it. I have had no instructions to make arrests and do not expect to make any. Memphis does not want prohibition."[11]

The Shelby County Grand Jury, at the request the league, investigated the illegal liquor trade and reported a year later conditions had worsened under Prohibition. They found over a thousand saloons operated openly in the city, up by three hundred from 1909. Shelby County attorney general Z. Newton Estes, who had the endorsement of the Law Enforcement League, said, "I stand ready to prosecute any man in Memphis who sells liquor illegally, and

I am ready to do all in my power to get indictments, but I can't get them. You cannot enforce an unpopular law."[12]

Thompson acknowledged the worsening conditions but stubbornly demanded Prohibition enforcement. "The main value of this [law] is that it removes the saloon as a political center," claimed Thompson. "If there are nine hundred saloons in Memphis that means a saloon vote of 3,600 in the voting population of ten thousand normally. The average saloonkeeper controls the vote of his bartender and of at least two bums who hang around his place, and they leave their voting papers in his saloon. Here you have political power for evil."[13]

Thompson promised that Ben Hooper would win the gubernatorial election and call out state troops if necessary to enforce Prohibition. He also wanted Hooper to create a state police force to supersede the Memphis police. Thompson was so determined to see Prohibition upheld that he was willing to see the termination of the city charter and direct rule by the state government to guarantee its enforcement.[14]

In 1912, Crump's Shelby County delegation joined the Fusionists, a political party made up of independent Democrats and Republicans, for control of the Tennessee General Assembly. The new allies reached some agreements, including defeating Malcolm Patterson in his bid for the US Senate and Frank Dibrell for state comptroller. More importantly, the Fusionists agreed not to introduce additional liquor legislation in return for Crump's support. Governor Hooper approved of the agreement until word spread that he had made a deal with the proliquor mayor. Crump kept his part of the bargain, but Hooper tried to save face among his Prohibitionist supporters and pushed for new liquor legislation. Crump accused the Fusionists and Hooper of deception and returned to the Democratic Party. A war of words broke out between Crump and Hooper that left the two bitter enemies.[15]

Hooper was determined to make Chattanooga, Nashville, and especially Memphis, abide by the four-mile laws. He even considered the use of the state militia until the state attorney general informed him he lacked legal authority to do so. Instead, Hooper proposed six new legislative measures in September 1913 to enforce Prohibition: a nuisance bill to shut down drinking and gambling establishments for causing inconvenience or damage to surrounding property; a bill to remove city and county officials for not performing their assigned duties; a requirement of municipalities to enforce laws; laws to prevent the transport of liquor into dry territories; replacement of noncompliant judges; and a law empowering the governor to intervene in cases of gross violations in cities.

Fig. 2.3. Edward Hull Crump, circa 1910. Courtesy of Memphis Room, Memphis Public Library and Information Center.

Hooper took aim at Crump during a political rally in Memphis on October 8, 1913. Crump helped facilitate a convention of factionalized Democrats to nominate Benton McMillin for candidacy for governor in 1912 in hopes of modifying the law to allow alcohol sales in Memphis, Nashville, and Chattanooga. The defiant Hooper declared, "When I am elected governor . . . I will with the help of an honest legislature and a good God, clean out every saloon and low-down dive in Memphis." Now Hooper intended to fulfill the promise.[16]

On October 17, 1913, the state legislature passed two laws to prevent the shipment of liquor into the state and a nuisance law aimed at drinking establishments after a chaotic session that included the threat of gun violence. Bedlam broke out when Democratic Speaker of the House William M. Stanton claimed that Hooper and Maj. Edward Bushrod Stahlman of the *Nashville Banner* sent "armed thugs" to threaten him for his opposition to the new liquor laws. Armed penitentiary guards and city detectives arrived with suitcases of firearms for the superintendent of the capitol because of the shouting and threats of violence.[17]

The federal courts also stepped in. Judge John E. McCall issued an injunction at the request of the Law Enforcement League and nonresident property owners who claimed drinking places depreciated the value of adjacent property. The nuisance law became a powerful weapon against any activity defined by the court as the unreasonable, unwarranted, or unlawful use of property that caused inconvenience or damage to others, whether to individuals or the general public. This included gambling, drinking, or any other bothersome activity. The court shut down the Memphis saloons October 23, 1913, and again on February 28, 1914.[18]

A revised nuisance law went into effect on March 1, 1914, and called for the confiscation of supplies and fixtures to saloons, brothels, and gambling houses. Proceeds from the sale of seized items would go to pay court fees, and anything left would go to the property owner. Violators of any injunction to close faced a workhouse sentence of thirty days, a fifty-dollar fine, and contempt of court charges. Hooper went so far to threaten to declare a state of emergency and call in the state militia if city officials refused to comply.[19]

Crump complied, and at first, the nuisance law brought the city's crime rate down. The city jail had only 46 prisoners, as compared to the 146 held a year earlier, the police station reported fewer arrests, and the grand jury saw fewer cases. The courts reported 178 crimes of personal violence, 526 crimes against personal property, and 191 miscellaneous indictments from March to August 1913. A year later the court logged 52 cases of personal violence, 238 cases of property crime, and 86 miscellaneous offenses excluding liquor violations.[20]

The murder rate dropped as well for a time since, as a long-time lawyer noted, almost every murder in Memphis involved liquor, gambling, and women. The court reported forty-six indictments for first-degree murder in 1913 between March and August, but only eleven indictments for first-degree murder during the same period in 1914. Despite the initial success, crime picked up again at the end of August, prompting a reporter to write, "Saturday [August 29] was a black day in the criminal annals of Shelby County, Sunday was not much better, and yesterday surpassed both put together. The saloons are re-opening."[21]

The Shelby Count Chancery Court in late September 1914 targeted Memphis businesses still selling alcohol, including dry goods and shoe stores. Deputies nailed the doors shut with five-foot-long and eight-inch-wide black painted boards with the words "This place is closed by order of the Chancery

Court" painted in white. Shelby County assistant attorney general William R. Harrison and detective Robert Wilroy made a follow-up inspection of Memphis businesses and asked for injunctions against two remaining violators: J. G. Duncan at Calhoun and Main Street and J. H. Bowers of Boon and Bowers Soft Drinks in the so-called Whiskey Chute off Main Street. Satisfied with the raids, Harrison declared that liquor enforcement was "proceeding merrily, and there is less liquor sold now than at any time since March 1."[22]

• • •

Reformers in the early twentieth century found it difficult to curb even the most blatant violations because no political organization with expectations of remaining in power dared challenge the powerful saloons. A Shelby County Grand Jury investigation in August 1894 found that liquor businesses defrauded the state and county governments of nearly $2 million in unpaid tax revenue over the previous eight years. Under public pressure, the reluctant jury finally indicted 736 before turning its sights on the derelict government officials.[23]

Social and political activity in urban America often centered in saloons. Saloonkeepers served as liaisons between the machine politicians and the barroom voters, provided mail service, employment information, newspapers, rooms for wedding receptions and union meetings, and a place to vote. They traded hospitality and favors in return for votes for sympathetic politicians. Politicians, once in office, depended on saloonkeepers to make campaign contributions and rally voters. Saloon customers depended on ward bosses to find jobs, secure business licenses, help with legal problems, and, of course, keep their favorite drinking places open.[24]

Crump and the mayors that preceded him appeased saloonkeepers because they held the balance in elections through their control of the registration books. A bill of complaint in 1916 stated that Crump allowed saloonkeepers to operate "so that through the influence of various saloons and their allied lawless elements, large numbers of registration certificates were collected and turned over to the Crump machine to corrupt elections."[25]

Crump's critics claimed his administration put into place a "quiet cafeteria system of paying fines" rather than a campaign to shut down underworld activities. Saloonkeepers, madams, and gamblers arrived at the city court every Monday to pay their fifty-dollar fines, the maximum required without jail time, before returning to their occupations. The city collected an enormous amount of revenue from the fines, which led many to conclude that Crump profited from vice. Crump never supported Prohibition, not because

Fig. 2.4. Rev. Thomas Gailor. Courtesy of Memphis Room,
Memphis Public Library and Information Center.

he drank or supported liquor interests like Jim Kinnane and Mike Haggerty,
but rather because the majority of his constituents, and more importantly
the majority of businessmen, did not support it, which in turn meant that
the police and courts could not enforce it.[26]

All but the most ardent Prohibitionists realized Prohibition caused more
problems than it solved. Prominent Memphis cotton merchant J. P. Norfleet saw that the effort to enforce Prohibition had resulted in "perjury and
contempt for the law." Wholesale liquor dealers and distillers continued to
operate by selling their merchandise from steamboats or through phony
shipping companies. Episcopal bishop of Tennessee Thomas Gailor complained, "Many people thought statewide prohibition would be the ideal
remedy for the drink evil, but instead of calling to their aid some experts
on legislation and having laws passed which could be enforced, they forced
through the legislature a measure which has led to civic degeneracy."[27]

Before Prohibition saloons closed at midnight, police arrested gamblers,
policemen rarely drank on duty, and the court never had more than sixty
untried murders on its docket. Afterward, saloons remained open all hours,
police did nothing to stop gambling, officers openly drank in saloons, and
the court had 116 murders on its docket, a "condition without precedent in

Fig. 2.5. Gov. Tom Rye. Courtesy of the Library of Congress.

Memphis." The city had 763 saloons before Prohibition. After the new laws, the city had 822 saloons and another 150 "beer joints."[28]

Crump's stance put him on a political collision course with Prohibitionists. Even worse, many Democrats moved into the Prohibition camp and no longer offered him support, including Gov. Tom Rye. Even Malcolm Patterson had a change of heart after he left office and returned to law practice in Memphis. Patterson joined the Presbyterian Church in 1914, converted to the cause of Prohibition, and ardently spoke out on the topic to audiences around the country.[29]

The proposed Elkins Ouster Law provided that any person holding public office in Tennessee "who shall neglect to perform any duty enjoined upon such officer by any of the laws of the state of Tennessee . . . shall forfeit his office and shall be ousted from such office." The measure passed the legislature on January 28, 1915, and Rye signed it into law the following day. The Elkins Ouster Law was the Prohibitionists' newest weapon and it stood ready for use against Crump.[30]

Crump, in a calculated move, had saloons close the day after Rye signed the Elkins Ouster Law. Local critics stayed content long enough for Crump forces to press the legislature to amend the city charter to allow an earlier municipal election so that officials could voice support for the purchase of a municipal light plant. The Crump slate easily won on April 8, 1915, and in the same election, Memphians voted ten to one to acquire or build a municipal light plant.[31]

Prohibitionists remained at bay until rumors reached Nashville about the saloons reopening in August. Prosecutors filed a petition to oust, charging nonenforcement of the law and graft against Crump and vice mayor R. Aleck Utley and dereliction of duty against police inspector Oliver Perry. The move fell short, however, when investigators could find no proof of graft.[32]

State attorney general Frank M. Thompson went to Memphis at the request of Rye and confirmed the liquor trade had resumed. On October 15, he filed a second suit for the ouster of Crump, Utley, Perry, Sheriff John Reichman, and Judge William M. Stanton. The defendants pled not guilty and demanded a trial by jury, but the judge denied the request. A group of businessmen traveled to Nashville to appeal to Rye, but the unsympathetic governor told them he could not stop the proceedings.[33]

Crump's attorney believed he could rush the case to the Tennessee Supreme Court for a sure reversal on the ruling, so he advised Crump and his codefendants to plead guilty and waive trial. Crump, Utley, Perry, and Stanton agreed, but Reichman decided to wait for a trial. The plan, however, backfired when Frank Fentress, chancellor of the Shelby County Chancery Court, ruled the defendants could no longer hold the office. The Tennessee Supreme Court agreed, ordered Crump out, and placed George C. Love as acting mayor. Crump was to begin his third term as mayor on January 1, 1916, but the court issued a stay order after it decided that prosecutors could use the same evidence to remove him from office again.[34]

Crump accepted his fate but left on terms of his choosing. The law required that he take office within ten days of the legal beginning of his term. He and Utley met at the residence of one of the city commissioners and took the oath of office on February 22, 1916. Crump received a check for $678.31 in back salary and resigned as mayor. Utley collected a check for $439.65 in back pay and resigned as well. The commissioners then elected Crump's recommended replacement, commissioner Thomas C. Ashcroft. The state filed more ouster suits against Reichman and fire and police commissioner W. Tyler McLain for telling police not to raid saloons owned by powerful urban boss Jim Kinnane.[35]

City attorney Charles M. Bryan also tendered his resignation. Crump and his long-time ally had met when he was in the buggy business and became close friends after they fought side-by-side during a brawl in court in 1908. Bryan returned later as county attorney and remained a troubleshooter for the Shelby County Organization for another thirty years.[36]

The Law Enforcement League won the day with the removal of Crump, but they soon found that the law could no more keep liquor out of Memphis than keep Crump out of politics. Prohibitionists closed the saloons, but they could not curb the demand for alcohol. The liquor trade never went away; instead, it evolved into something far more sinister and difficult to control.

3

ROGUES' GALLERY

For a long time, the saloon has been a stronghold of politics, and a
good deal of dirty, mean, despicable politics at that.
—George M. Hammell[1]

Tom O'Sullivan ran one of the most respectable saloons in Memphis. The
Irishman came to America around 1840, opened his business, and later
ran it with his son William. The old two-story building at 157 North Main
Street with its gas lights and big mirrors was a Mecca for politicians and
sports enthusiasts. O'Sullivan was a true gentleman and his saloon was an
institution in the old Irish neighborhood until statewide Prohibition came
in 1909. On that day, the law-abiding O'Sullivan gave away his whiskey and
closed his doors.[2]

Memphis had 513 saloons in 1908 that varied in character from harmless
to sinister. Many saloonkeepers, such as O'Sullivan, Joe Mancini, and Charlie
Seat ran genteel, orderly, and crime-free businesses. Nevertheless, other places
were nothing more than dives run by gangsters. These places gave Memphis
a reputation as a "resort town" that embarrassed reform-minded citizens.
Eventually, the gangsters' high-profile antics made them targets of resentment, and their illicit businesses, much of which they conducted through
their saloons, gave the local ASL and WCTU their most powerful incentives
to crusade against vice, corruption, and liquor.[3]

. . .

Jim Kinnane's parents left Ireland about 1855 and settled in Pinch District,
the tough North Memphis Irish neighborhood of the First Ward. Kinnane's
mother ran a boarding house after his father died of yellow fever in 1878.
Kinnane landed a job as a mail carrier in the late 1880s and served as the

Memphis secretary of the National Association of Letter Carriers in the 1890s. After about ten years, he followed the lead of his brother Thomas, a part-time fireman, and opened his first saloon.[4]

Kinnane became well connected and influential over the years and eventually became the most powerful political figure in North Memphis after he usurped control from the bellicose Ed Ryan. Kinnane's saloons became interwoven into society and the political establishment as people met, developed friendships, shared political views, built business relationships, and with a nod and wink, kept each other's secrets.

Kinnane also had saloons and businesses catering to African Americans. He operated the Rialto Theater at Jackson Avenue and Decatur Street in North Memphis, The Blue Goose at Third and Auction, the Monarch Saloon on Beale, and Jim Kinnane's on North Main. Many emerging blues musicians, including Willie Jackson, Louise Johnson, and Robert Wilkins, recorded songs about or at least with mention of these notorious establishments.[5]

Kinnane's ability to rally African American voters and pay their poll taxes made him one of the most important political allies to any politician. Kinnane spent over $5,000 every election on poll taxes to ensure black Memphians voted for the appropriate candidate. A reporter claimed Kinnane had more influence over African Americans than "any delta plantation owner."[6]

The Monarch Saloon on Beale Street had a reputation for whiskey, cocaine, prostitutes, raucous music, gambling, and violence. Kinnane opened the place in 1910 in open violation of state Prohibition at the cost of $20,000. It featured a mahogany bar, gleaming brass fixtures, plush velvet seating, and mirrors on the walls. It had an upstairs gambling room and dance hall that hosted many local and traveling musicians, as well as secret exits and trapdoors in the event of police raids.[7]

The African American men Kinnane hired to run the Monarch were as tough as his customers. Jake Redmond managed the saloon while men like Julius Green, Long Charlie, Cousin Hog, Jimmy Turpin, and Bad Sam acted as "strong-armed assistants." The saloon's reputation for bloodshed earned it the nickname Castle of Missing Men. The staff hauled knifing and shooting victims to Levi McCoy's mortuary conveniently located nearby, where the mortician would quietly dispose of the bodies.[8]

Kinnane, like many other saloon owners, converted his saloons into soft drink stands in the wake of Prohibition but quietly continued to sell liquor. Jim Kinnane's Place at the corner of North Front Street and Winchester Avenue operated ostensibly as a pool hall, but it was rumored to have secret

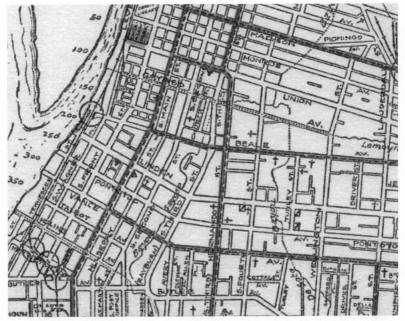

Fig. 3.1. Beale Street and surrounding neighborhoods. Courtesy of Memphis Room, Memphis Public Library and Information Center.

passages leading to six or more adjoining houses where Kinnane's men ran illegal gambling.[9]

Kinnane admitted during his testimony in the ouster of police chief William J. Hayes that he paid Hayes $22,500 a year for protection. Kinnane also escaped prosecution by working through loyal lieutenants who took the fall if caught and never implicated their boss. The men served sentences and Kinnane supplied money for any fines. Kinnane stayed in the background but made daily visits to his properties where gamblers and bootleggers operated to collect rent in the early morning hours. Each day he would deposit a large roll of cash in the bank at opening.[10]

Vice, however, served only as a means to an end. Kinnane utilized the money he made to invest in legitimate businesses, including a bottling plant, a fifty-ton ice plant, a towboat, and of course, real estate. Kinnane wielded great power and influence but largely stayed out of the headlines. His lieutenants, on the other hand, helped cement the city's reputation for lawlessness.[11]

. . .

Kinnane's associate Mike Shanley, another son of Irish immigrants, ran dives that became the scenes of sensational brawls. In January 1898, police arrested twenty-eight African American men for fighting and brought them before justice of the peace William Creagan. The irate Shanley stormed the chambers, leveled a handgun at the judge's head, and threatened to "send him to Hell" unless he released the men. Shanley's lawyer convinced the judge that the best and safest course of action was to appease the gangster.[12]

Shanley made national headlines when he started a gunfight at the crowded Montgomery Park Racetrack on April 4, 1899. Police officers broke up a fight between Shanley and Kinnane rival Ed Ryan. Officers let the two go free after they calmed down. Shanley changed his mind after a few minutes, pulled a revolver, and ran through the crowd in search of Ryan. Police chief Jerome Richards saw Shanley approach Ryan and tried to wrest the pistol away from him. Shanley managed to point his revolver over the shoulder of Richards and fire a shot that hit Ryan in the chest, killing him. Stray bullets wounded grocer Patrick Gleason in the foot and killed railroad employee Charles Clark.[13]

Attorneys Ralph Davis and William Fitzgerald claimed Shanley acted in self-defense, while prosecutor and future governor Malcolm Patterson painted a different picture. He claimed Shanley ducked behind bleachers and fired into the crowd at Ryan. Patterson, an accomplished orator, made an impassioned plea, but someone had tampered with the jury. On November 8, the jury found Shanley not guilty.[14]

Shanley still captured headlines even after contracting tuberculosis. In January 1908 during a balloon exhibition at Montgomery Park, one of the men running the show told Shanley to extinguish his cigar because it could ignite the balloon's hydrogen. The insulted Shanley left and returned with several henchmen, who then shot down the balloon with shotguns. Shanley, dying from disease, finally met his end when police gunned him down for resisting arrest on April 21, 1908.[15]

• • •

Mike Haggerty, another prominent Irish urban boss, rose to prominence through his network of business associates and allies. Haggerty married Mary Degg, the sister of notorious gangster George "Bud" Degg, and Haggerty's brother Daniel married Mike Shanley's sister Catherine. Haggerty and Degg ran the Old Turf at 122 South Second Street in the politically important Fourth Ward, which became a base of operations for many gangsters, including George Honan.[16]

Mayor J. J. Williams enlisted the help of the Haggerty Syndicate to win the 1904 election, but he came to regret that decision. The election was marked "by the use of torch and pistol in the hands of a lawless and riotous mob." The "crowning act of infamy" occurred when the gangsters entered the Ninth Ward polling place, ran everyone out, and stole the ballot box. The embarrassed Williams ordered brothel shutdowns, midnight closings of saloons, and a crackdown on gambling to try to appease the public outrage.[17]

Haggerty and the others got away with quietly ignoring the mayor's orders until July 11, 1904, when court squire Frank Davis ordered a gambling dive at 42 Desoto Street closed. Davis swore out warrants for owners Harry Hartley and Harry Keene and ordered magistrate deputy John Lawless to serve the writs. Lawless recruited three white deputies and one black deputy to accompany him. Along the way, deputy Frank Solly, an informer for Haggerty, made up an excuse to leave and went to the Memphi Theater at 372 Second Street where Haggerty's brother Daniel worked.[18]

Word of the raid made it to Haggerty, Honan, Degg, Hartley, and Keene, who rushed to the scene. They burst in brandishing pistols and demanded the release of the African American gamblers. The deputies refused, and the gangsters opened fire, killing two of the lawmen. Public outrage forced them to surrender, but defense lawyer Malcolm Patterson successfully argued that Honan acted accordingly because the African American deputy acted insolently. The jury, undoubtedly influenced by the Haggerty Syndicate, agreed and found Honan not guilty.[19]

Haggerty remained in jail until his lawyers successfully filed habeas corpus with Judge Jacob Galloway for his release under a $24,500 bond. The Tennessee Supreme Court overturned Galloway's ruling and upheld Young's decision to keep him in jail. Haggerty's lawyers then produced witnesses who claimed Haggerty had nothing to do with the shootings, forcing Galloway to release all five prisoners. The following day, Judge John T. Moss ordered Haggerty arrested again, and a deputy took him into custody on a train returning to Memphis. Lawyers argued habeas corpus and won Haggerty's release. Police arrested the gangsters again in January 1905, but defense lawyers successfully argued the court had denied their clients the right to a speedy trial. The judge released all five and shelved the case for good.[20]

Meanwhile, the corrupt Mayor Williams became so unpopular that even Haggerty and the regulars of the Old Turf turned against him. Haggerty swayed the opinions of voters in the Fourth Ward and helped James Malone win the 1905 mayoral election. This election also landed Ed Crump a position on the lower board of the legislative council. Haggerty only supported the anti-vice reform ticket because he expected the administration to return the favor by closing the saloons of their competitors who campaigned for Williams.[21]

Malone's crackdown on crime initially focused on prostitution, but it soon turned towards gambling. Police raided the Haggerty's Anchor Saloon on Front Street in March 1906. Mike and Daniel Haggerty and George Degg marched into the mayor's office before dawn and informed the vice mayor, John T. Walsh, that they would make public the surplus of three hundred premarked ballots prepared for the last election if police raided any more of their establishments.[22]

Ed Crump abhorred saloon politics, but as a realist, he realized that he needed the popular saloonkeepers as allies. The Irish gangsters and their followers became necessary assets, and much to Crump's chagrin, occasional embarrassments. Crump ran for Shelby County Trustee following his ouster, and the gangsters turned out to support him. Haggerty and sympathetic police officers drove supporters of Crump's opponent Harry Litty away from Beale Street polling places after Litty's men claimed to have discovered 265 fraudulent ballots. The driver of a wagon with an anti-Crump banner made the mistake of passing in front of the Monarch Saloon. Johnny Margerum ran out in front of a cheering crowd and pulled the sign off the wagon in a public show of support for Crump because of his anti-Prohibition stance.[23]

Haggerty took over the Monarch from Kinnane and ran it until about 1915 when he turned it over to his stepson Margerum, the nephew of George Degg. The hot-tempered Margerum and his former partner once traded shots one night at the intersection of Beale and Main Streets, and on another occasion, he fired shots at the Black Cat Restaurant in the Hotel Chisca. On the evening of December 15, 1918, Margerum came into the Monarch and found a black street thug named Ben Griffin beating up one of his African American waiters. Margerum demanded Griffin leave the man alone, but Griffin refused. The two reached for pistols and patrons rushed out the door as the shooting began. Margerum's friend O. P. Stroud rushed in from the cigar stand at the front of the building and found Griffin dead and Margerum bleeding badly from two bullet wounds. Stroud rushed Margerum to the hospital, but his friend died before he reached the operating table.[24]

Haggerty never made the switch to bootlegging and faded from the underworld, leaving many to believe he died in the early years of Prohibition. He worked various jobs including as a machinist, in a position at the Main

Coal Company, and as a salesman before retiring. The one-time ward boss, nearly forgotten, died at his home on 875 North Manassas at the age of sixty-three on December 29, 1929.[25]

. . .

George Honan's criminal record almost rivaled that of Mike Shanley. A reporter noted, "Into the years he lived, had been crowded more action, more gun plays, narrow escapes and thrilling scenes than ordinarily come into the lives of a hundred men. . . He is said to have escaped death in gambling rooms and other places only by a display of cool courage and an ability to draw quickly." Honan's propensity for violence earned him the reputation as a very dangerous man and the resentment of reformers.[26]

Honan was born around 1872 to poor Irish immigrants and grew up in a small apartment in an alley near Main Street and Jackson Avenue. Honan fell in with Haggerty and Shanley and became a public figure after Ed Ryan shot him with a Winchester rifle during an argument. The shooting left Honan with a bullet that doctors could not remove and a partially paralyzed arm.[27]

Honan belonged to the old school of politics wherein the victor was the one who could corral the largest number of voters and herd them into the polls on election days. A reporter recalled, "With defeat staring the mayor in the face, and the result of the election hanging upon the Ninth Ward, where the opposition was winning at every count, and minions of the administration shoot and burn to prevent the continuance of count." Honan continued to stir public outrage with his part in the Desoto Street incident in 1904 when the Haggerty Syndicate killed two deputies during a gambling raid. More mass meetings followed with demands for the mayor to address the growing lawlessness, but Honan once again escaped justice.[28]

Honan had a long police record, and in his mid-forties, he showed no signs of slowing down. Honan ran a saloon at 340 Beale in 1906 previously owned by African American saloon proprietor Alfred "Tick" Houston, and in 1914 Honan managed one of Kinnane's pool halls. In January 1915, Honan shot an African American man and faced an indictment on a charge of carrying a pistol.[29]

At 3:00 a.m. on January 11, 1915, Honan called Grace Frazier, a twenty-one-year-old prostitute. She refused to meet him at the Majestic Theater, so Honan stormed into Mabel Harris's brothel at 140 South Third Street looking for her. He found her room and tried to kick in the door. Frazier rose from the bed without turning on the light and opened the door. Honan shot her twice in the abdomen without saying a word and then took aim at Robert

Embleton, who was in bed with her. Embleton scrambled behind a wardrobe and began firing at Honan with a small semiautomatic pistol. Honan's shots missed Embleton by inches, but Embleton's bullets found their mark and brought down the gangster.[30]

A small number gathered inside his sister's modest little house to hear the services conducted by Father Leo of St. Mary's Catholic Church. A thousand other friends gathered outside and shared stories as moving vans delivered flower arrangements. The crowd grew so large that it spilled over into neighbors' lawns and completely blocked traffic until the family removed Honan's body to Calvary Cemetery.[31]

Grace Frazier remained in critical condition at St. Joseph's Hospital only a few blocks from Honan's home. Her doctors did not expect her to live, so they asked if she wanted a priest or minister while police asked for a dying statement. The young woman only laughed and told everyone that she would recover. The doctors doubted her chances to pull through but honored her wishes. To the amazement of her doctors, she survived, making her the last of Honan's victims, and one of the few to survive the gangster's wrath.[32]

• • •

Gennaro "John" Persica was born in May 1861 in Italy and came to New Orleans with his family in the 1870s. He sold coffee in the French Market before he moved to Memphis, and he opened his first saloon at 117 Beale with the help of his brother Salvador about 1891. Persica lived frugally and over time invested in real estate. He opened more saloons on and around Beale Street before he realized his dream of opening a combination saloon, boarding house, and theater at 67 Hernando.[33]

In 1905, Persica took the idea one step further when he bought the old car barn at 121 Hernando and turned it into the Garden Theater, a variety theater, dancehall, saloon, and restaurant. He operated without regard for mayors, the courts, or reformers and had a reputation for violating up to thirty penal codes a day. He had dancing in his place despite a city ordinance banning music in drinking establishments, served alcohol, and ran prize fights without paying municipal taxes.[34]

Persica also acted as the bouncer. Criminals knew not to push the limits of Persica's tolerance. Prostitutes could pick up men but had to take them elsewhere for anything more. Steerers who got customers drunk to rob them had to take their victims elsewhere. More than anything else, Persica would not stand for fighting in his saloons. He took anyone caught fighting in his saloon outside, where he beat them into bloody submission.[35]

Persica and druggist George Battier worked together as ward heelers among the city's Italian immigrants. No matter where they lived, the Italians came back to the Market House to vote where Persica acted as guardian of their registration papers. Their turnout always met the expectations of favored local politicians, and as one reporter observed, "Returns on election day were marvels of all forms of arithmetic except subtraction and division."[36]

Persica maintained close friendships in the police department. He once gave a banquet in honor of police chief William Hayes at his saloon where he made a speech to the officials in attendance and presented Hayes with a diamond-studded medal in honor of his service. Hayes had to return the award after Mayor Crump took office and inserted a provision into the charter forbidding city employees from accepting gifts under threat of fines and imprisonment.[37]

On November 9, 1913, Persica took some friends out to visit saloons in the suburbs. His party included three young actresses appearing at the Garden Theater—Marie Wood, May Waters, and Trene Nichols—as well as police sergeant Jack McAuliffe and an unnamed businessman from Vicksburg. They spent a long night of carousing before heading back into the city around four thirty in the morning in Persica's top-of-the-line six-cylinder Thomas Flyer.[38]

The chauffeur was driving along Madison Avenue when he saw a slow-moving ice wagon in his lane. When he pulled around to pass, the car's fender struck an oncoming car. The chauffer lost control, hit the ice wagon, and flipped the car. The car landed upside down and pinned Persica's head under the rear seat, fracturing his skull. The other passengers, also suffering from injuries, pulled the unconscious Persica from under the car and called for an ambulance, but he never regained consciousness and died shortly after arriving at the hospital.[39]

Persica's underworld influence did not end with his death, but rather, his legacy continued with his adopted family. Persica had married Anne Belluomini, the widow of the late John Belluomini, in 1891 and adopted her son Joseph, who became active in the underworld. He also hosted other members of the Belluomini family who had come to Memphis from Italy, including Luigi "Louis" Belluomini, whose sons Frank and John would one day dominate bootlegging in Memphis.[40]

· · ·

White Memphians worried about liquor among African Americans. Ward bosses drew the ire of whites by giving whiskey to African Americans in exchange for their votes, and Prohibition propaganda of the early twentieth century played on fears of drunken black men committing outrages against white women. Police targeted African Americans in liquor and gambling campaigns in the 1920s and 1930s because of pressure from whites concerned about immorality and violence.

Black bootleggers and gangsters drew attention in the press, but they often used aliases when arrested, so there is very little to use to piece together information about them. Nevertheless, some of these outlaws, such as gangster Charlie Pearce ("Two-Gun Charlie") and narcotics dealer Jimmy Price ("Ten-Dollar Jimmy"), received attention. John Floyd played an important part in the Taylor Liquor Ring led by US marshal Tyree Taylor and continued to bootleg through the 1920s. In 1923, Roosevelt "Black Hawk" Martin shot his customer John Castelvecci three times with a .45-caliber pistol during a fight over tainted whiskey. In the early 1930s, police referred to Robert Burrell ("Laughing Robert") as the Whiskey King of North Memphis because of his extensive bootlegging network.[41]

. . .

William Latura probably did more to cement Memphis's reputation for lawlessness than any other person. Police arrested Latura thirty-five times for liquor and gambling violations, the record for Memphis at the time. Latura stubbornly refused to abide by the law and had an almost mythical propensity for violence that made him the most feared man in the city.

Latura was the son of Italian saloonkeeper John J. Latura and cousin to Frank Monteverde, the successful grocer who became mayor from 1918 to 1919. His brother John became president of Latura-Whitten Coal Company, his cousin Joseph worked for Metropolitan Insurance Company, and ironically, his mother worked as a matron for the Juvenile Court. Latura, however, chose a different path. He had a long list of violent criminal activities, including trying to kill a saloonkeeper in 1903, nearly disemboweling a man with a knife, shooting a woman in 1905, shooting a man in 1907 over a gambling debt, and shooting another man during a bar brawl in 1908.[42]

According to Memphis historian, soldier, executive, and political leader George W. Lee, Latura held a grudge against the African American saloonkeeper Hammit Ashford. Latura's girlfriend and some friends said something offensive to Ashford as he rode his horse past them near Mike Shanley's dive in Raleigh. Ashford became angry and whipped the woman with a riding crop.[43]

One night in December 1908, Latura decided to even the score. He wandered into Ashford's Saloon on Beale with ex-boxer Punch Wilson. He did

Fig. 3.2. Memphis Police Department's Black Maria, 1910. Courtesy of Memphis Police Department Archives.

not see Ashford, so he asked barkeep George Harris to use the washroom. He walked back where six African American men were playing pool, pulled out a .38-caliber pistol, and announced that he was about to "turn the place into a morgue." He shot Speck Carter, Charley Miller, Clarence Allen, proprietor of the Bon Ton Saloon, and Leslie Williams as he tried to hide behind an icebox. Latura walked over to finish Williams but hit Birdie Hines as she shielded him. Latura wounded two more men and threatened to shoot doorman George Fitzhugh as he left.[44]

Latura threw his pistol away and walked back to the Rosebud Café to continue drinking with Wilson. Latura, knowing witnesses would report his crimes, nonchalantly drank at the bar, waiting for police to come for him. His bravado disappeared when he saw patrolman Powell Covey walk in with sergeant Mike Kehoe. The big Irish sergeant was the toughest man on the police force, and even Latura knew not to cross his path. Latura saw Kehoe and begged, "Don't kill me. I'm unarmed, and I'll give up."[45]

Latura's trial made a mockery of the justice system in Memphis. The jury did not consider the killing of black men by a white man a serious crime, so they let Latura go. By this point, Latura had no concerns about the police or courts. Latura killed two more men by 1912, each time claiming self-defense.[46]

Latura's mental illness became more apparent over the next few years. Dr. William B. Sanford described Latura's "progressive paranoia" as the cause of his degeneracy. Latura threatened to kill newspaper editor C. P. J. Mooney and his staff if they continued to refer to him as Wild Bill. Latura then began telephoning threats to police officers and even went so far as to threaten to kill sheriff Oliver Perry.[47]

Police chief Joseph Burney ordered officers Sandy Lyons and Charles Davis to arrest Latura. The two drove by Latura's blind tiger, an illegal saloon, at Poplar and Dunlap and found Latura standing near his car. Latura saw them and said, "Looks like you fellows are getting pretty hard on me." He accused Burney of lying to him and threatened to kill Lyons and Davis. As he reached into his coat for a pistol, Lyons shot him in the chest. Lyons shot him another three times as Latura tried to get a Winchester rifle from his car.[48]

Bystanders were so afraid of Latura that they would not touch him even as he lay dying, and the drivers of two vehicles sped away without offering to carry Latura to the hospital. Latura's twelve-year-old daughter heard the shots and ran to her father, but the crowd stopped her from throwing herself on his blood-soaked body. L. S. Akers, who lived nearby, was the only one to help the dying man. Latura lay on the sidewalk for an hour before patrolmen arrived with the Black Maria, the vehicle used to transport prisoners. By then it was too late; Latura died before reaching the hospital.[49]

The ASL and WCTU saw Latura as another example of the degeneracy of liquor interests. When Memphis Prohibitionists spoke out against liquor interests, they spoke out against gangsters like Latura. When they won their victory, they won it against these men. The faithful, in their naïveté, imagined a panacea in the wake of Prohibition. They had no idea that eliminating the saloons would give rise to a far more dangerous type of criminal. The next generation of outlaws would not only unleash an uncontrollable crime wave but set in motion the demise of Prohibition.

4

CONSPIRACY

Now that all liquor traffic is illegal, liquor is to be had by anyone who
wants it badly enough, but at enormous prices and with dealers paying
enormous sums for protection.
—*News Scimitar*, March 28, 1919

apt. John Couch needed to smash down a door. He paused outside the
blind tiger and sent one of his officers back to the police station for an
ax. The young man went to an old locker and discovered the hatchet the
late Carrie Nation had presented to Couch at a temperance rally ten years
earlier in Memphis. Couch took the forgotten gift and used it to force his
way in and destroy the dive's barrels of liquor and beer. From that point on,
it became part of his arsenal. A reporter noted, "Memphis is dry legally and
is being made dry in reality by the aid of Carrie's hatchet."[1]

The new city administrators embraced Prohibition and stepped up enforcement following Crump's 1916 ouster. Newton Baker, US secretary of
war, asked US mayors to "continue the war on lewdness (prostitution) and
sale of liquor to soldiers" following the world war. Mayor Frank Monteverde
promised in November 1918, "There shall be no let-up in the war on vice
in Memphis now that the armistice for peace has been signed." Three days
later, police rounded up ninety-six "gamesters, loafers, and violators of the
liquor law."[2]

The arrests over the next six months read like a who's who of the underground liquor business. Those arrested included: Loftis E. Wilkes at a
poolroom on McCall; Joe Barretta at his residence on Pidgeon Roost Road;
Emilio Devoto for selling liquor from his business in Orange Mound; notorious gunman and Haggerty associate William McVey while on bond for a

Fig. 4.1. Chief Joseph Burney. Courtesy of Memphis Police Department Archives.

murder charge; Joe Raffanti for selling twelve cases of liquor at his soft drink stand at Fourth and Beale; Velton Green and Joe Wilson for transporting six cases of whiskey; Harry "Silk Hat" Langley for selling liquor to a stool pigeon; and Joe Vaccaro for selling liquor from his soft drink stand at Main and Washington Avenue. Police also arrested Herbert Green, chauffer for attorney Ralph Davis; Bennie Bryan, café owner; J. H. Colbert, soft drink seller; ex-policeman Cliff Luke; Richard Carl "Dick" Rather; Nora Harvey; Jimmy Jones and his wife; and Beale Street police character John "The Pig" Cuneo.[3]

Liquor seized by police made a tempting target for bootleggers. Chief Burney locked confiscated liquor in a room on the second floor of the police station, but even there, he could not keep the contraband secure. Two break-ins by people familiar with the building accounted for several missing cases. Doctors of the early twentieth century still believed liquor had medicinal properties, so Burney sent the entire stockpile, worth $25,000, to local hospitals for use during the 1918 Spanish influenza epidemic.[4]

The war in Europe stopped imports, so George P. Woollen, postal collector of customs, allowed chief US marshal Stanley Trezevant to use the storage room at the US Customs House to hold evidence. The war ended, and Woollen needed the space again. While he waited for instructions to deal with the evidence, he had to fend off bribes, burglars, and many creative requests for liquor, including keeping car radiators from freezing, saving sick grandmothers, helping Spanish flu sufferers, and one request for whiskey to cure a dying dog.[5]

Police stepped up arrests of small-time bootleggers and their customers, but their efforts did nothing to stop the overall liquor trade. Minuscule fines for petty liquor violations did little to discourage recidivism. The city simply had far too many "hip-pocket" bootleggers and "half-pint" customers. Officials shifted focus to trafficking, believing that once smuggling ended, the liquor trade would finally dry up.

Bootleggers created a secret language to avoid detection. The code word *villa* got the customer whiskey, and *carranza* got him gin. Sam "Beale Street" Jones, the African American partner of white bootlegger Bennie Bryan, invented the dialect used by black bootleggers who distributed smuggled liquor. *Tweety-twa* and other terms, sung out or whistled in a dozen different ways, indicated the amounts and destinations of whiskey hidden in caches along the Gayoso Bayou, a waterway that ran through downtown Memphis. Jones also coined the term *shorty* for a half-pint of liquor.[6]

Thousands of cases arrived every month from northern distillers trying to dispose of inventories before national Prohibition went into effect. Liquor became so plentiful that prices decreased significantly. Old Taylor, Old Prentice, and Old Lancaster dropped to $6.60 per quart, while higher-end brands like Old Antidote, Old Grand-Dad, and Apple Orchard sold at $7.50 a quart.[7]

Police and marshals targeted liquor shipments coming in by boat. In February 1919, police took into custody Capt. Milt Harry of the *Liberty* while he was delivering whiskey to bootlegger E. A. "Pete" Vaccaro. They arrested Capt. J. A. Couch the following day after the discovery of ten cases of whiskey on his ferry *Minnie*. Chief US marshal Stanley Trezevant and his men seized fourteen unregistered vessels at the mouth of the Wolf River and surprised a group of bootleggers unloading a delivery in March. They arrested and later convicted four, including well-known gangsters Henry Laughter and E. G. "Smoky" Robinson. Two others sped away in a car into the night, barely escaping gunfire from the marshals.[8]

Random searches of passengers' luggage at the train station between November 1918 and February 1919 yielded forty-eight half-pints of whiskey in the trunk of Harry Ellington, a nineteen-year-old soldier, and eight cases of liquor aboard the segregated black section of the train from Illinois. Police also found a suitcase full of whiskey carried by an African American man named Jacob McFall and a dozen quarts of whiskey belonging to E. S. "Big Six" Fisk, a former patrolman.[9]

Businessman R. A. Barger of Mounds, Illinois, saw Nellie Brown struggling to carry two heavy suitcases, so he offered to help. Brown gladly accepted the offer and handed the burdensome luggage to the gentleman. Suddenly, police officers converged on Barger and demanded to search the baggage. Barger handed the suitcases over to the officers, who found they contained liquor. Barger tried to explain that he did not know the contents of the suitcases and that he had only offered to help the woman. He pointed to Brown, who promptly denied ownership of the suitcases and said she had never seen Barger before. Police arrested both of them and took them before Judge Fitzhugh. Fitzhugh fined Brown fifty dollars but released Barger after he brought in character witnesses.[10]

The same fate fell on another Good Samaritan a few weeks later. Police arrested Rev. A. J. Jackson, African American pastor of the Pilgrim Rest Baptist Church on Texas Avenue, after he helped a young black woman, Isabella Robinson, with her baggage at the train station. Police saw them struggling with the suspiciously heavy bags and demanded to search them. When they did, they found liquor and arrested both of them.[11]

Police also intercepted whiskey runners as they crossed the Harahan Bridge from Arkansas. Officers arrested three black men working for Jim Mulcahy as they transported thirty cases of whiskey across the bridge in November 1918. They arrested Mulcahy for his part, but Judge Fitzhugh released the gangster after the three whiskey runners refused to identify Mulcahy as the car's owner. Marshals had better luck when they intercepted hoodlums R. L. "Pug" Rodgers, Joe Conway, and Jim Conners as they drove a car loaded with whiskey over the bridge. Trezevant then found evidence connecting gangsters George Herman Tamble and R. E. "Happy" Lee to the liquor, resulting in their arrests.[12]

Sheriff Oliver Perry asked the county government for two more patrol cars and promised, "I'm going to break up the liquor business if it takes everything I make in the Sheriff's office." One night in December 1918, Perry received a tip that a shipment of whiskey had arrived near Covington, Tennessee,

Fig. 4.2. Mounted officer and patrolman using a police call box, 1909.
Courtesy of Memphis Police Department Archives.

from Caruthersville, and a caravan of cars would soon carry the contraband into Memphis. Perry, police captain Ed Pass, and the Rum Raiders set up a roadblock at the Hindman Ferry Road Bridge over the Wolf River.[13]

The lawmen saw the first big touring car speeding down the road around midnight. They pushed one of their smaller "flivvers" across the road and tried to flag down the approaching driver. The whiskey runner, however, had no intention of surrender. He gunned his engine and knocked the smaller vehicle off the road as the policemen jumped out of the way. As the second car approached, the officers climbed back on the road and brandished their weapons. The driver ignored their warning and roared past amid a hail of gunfire. The officers regrouped and stopped the decoy third car. After intense questioning, the drivers admitted to working for bootlegger Joe Robilio whose car, the fourth of the caravan, had broken down in Millington.[14]

Police in January 1919 intercepted a group of women driving a car loaded with liquor bound for a resort run by Bob Berryman. Birdie Mahoney, her daughter Nellie, and her sister Fannie Calvert stopped in Riverside Park for a brief rest after crossing the Harahan Bridge. Officers noticed the three and walked over to question them. The women panicked, ran for the car, and tried to drive away. Mahoney took the wheel, while Nellie and Fannie jumped on the fenders. Mahoney took a turn too sharply and threw the two off the car. Police stopped the car, arrested the women, and found a suitcase full of liquor in the car. The trio paid the meager court fines and returned to whiskey running and bootlegging.[15]

Berryman had been under investigation since the summer. Assistant chief Ed Pass and Trezevant sent civilian informers Rev. C. H. Williamson and George Morris to see Berryman's Riverside Boulevard place firsthand. Williamson found the place exceedingly busy with eighteen or twenty cars in the yard. He saw craps games being played on pool tables in one room and a piano in another room where women and girls as young as fifteen danced and drank. Williamson went into another room, where Berryman sold him a bottle of Sunnybrook that Williamson turned over to police.[16]

Berryman appeared before Judge Ed Richards and pled guilty to two charges, and was found guilty to three of twelve counts of gambling and liquor violations going back to 1911. Richards entered a *nolle prosequi* for the old charges upon payment of court costs, but he sentenced Berryman to sixty days on the new charges. Berryman paid his fine and served his time but soon returned to bootlegging and gambling and remained a leading vice figure until the 1940s.[17]

Violence was not limited to country roads and remote river landings. White bootleggers hired a team of African American men to unload 260 cases of liquor from a launch one night in March 1919. The roustabouts took advantage of the darkness, set aside twenty cases of the liquor, and came back for them later after the bootleggers left. It did not take long for the bootleggers to realize the men had stolen from them. A couple of days later, two of the bootleggers opened fire on the men as they were driving down Beale Street. Police arrived at the New York Café and found four wounded men and a touring car riddled with bullets. They questioned the dockworkers, but the men were too afraid to divulge the names of the gunmen. Memphians, outraged by the shooting on a public street, demanded the police go after the heads of the three big syndicates trafficking liquor.[18]

Bootleggers even had the audacity to strike at police. Sergeants John Brinkley and Joseph Hewitt found seven sacks of whiskey in a car in front of a garage at 352 Madison Avenue one night in May 1919. Officer Charles Brunner arrived to collect the evidence while the other two went in search of the bootleggers. Brunner left his flivver and drove the car with the whiskey back to the police station. After Brunner left, the bootleggers, who had been in hiding, stole his car, drove it to the foot of Vance Avenue, and pushed it over the bluff into the river. A group of longshoremen found the remains of the car strewn along the bank of the Mississippi River below the river bluff the next morning.[19]

Some bootleggers avoided roadblocks and raids by stealing from railcars. Because the federal government controlled interstate commerce, trains carried liquor to wet states through Memphis. Railroad hijackings cost businesses over $50,000 a month. A railcar could hold between 400 and 450 cases of liquor, valued at $10,000. Bootleggers would empty them and sell the stolen liquor at a rate of seven dollars per quart.

One morning before dawn in March, patrolmen Prince Albert Worley and D. E. McClannahan slipped into the North Carolina and St. Louis Railroad yard. They found a railcar with liquor, made a note of its location, and met up with men waiting in a car nearby on Calhoun Avenue. Soon after, a dozen men entered the yard, broke into the boxcar, and began unloading the cargo into their automobiles.

Unknown to Worley and McClannahan, special railroad agents Max Swindle and Ray Stansbury watched the events unfold. The two stepped out of the shadows and ordered the bandits to surrender. The men refused and opened fire. The agents fled and returned with the police, but by then the thieves had escaped with the liquor. The agents reported what they saw to commissioner C. W. Miller, who suspended the two officers, who had clearly helped the thieves, only to reinstate them, saying he could find no evidence to connect them to the robbery.[20]

The public complained that police still seemed only to arrest half-pint dealers whose cases rarely made it past the grand jury, while the big, protected members of the liquor rings never faced arrest. They demanded the police go after the heads of the bootlegging rings rather than waste time with the "small fry." Many took the lack of progress as evidence that a well-organized liquor ring operated with the protection from members of law enforcement.[21]

The Shelby County Grand Jury reached the same conclusion and demanded a cleanup of corruption. On October 28, 1918, Commissioner Miller took office with the promise to stop patrolmen from drinking on the job and "winking at the enforcement of liquor laws." A month later, the grand jury called on Miller, Chief Burney, Asst. Chief Pass, and Hulet Smith, chief of detectives, to know why liquor sales rose, while arrests seemed to drop.[22]

To make matters worse, the Memphis *News Scimitar* published the pay scales for bribes from bootleggers. Patrolmen and sergeants in residential wards with only four or five bootleggers earned between five and ten dollars a week in bribes. Those working in the heavier trafficking areas of the First,

Fig. 4.3. Commissioner C. W. Miller on the left. Courtesy of Memphis Room, Memphis Public Library and Information Center.

Second, and Third wards made twenty-five dollars a week, while those in the Fourth, Fifth, and Sixth Wards made as much as thirty to fifty dollars a week.[23]

Miller recognized that some of his officers took bribes from bootleggers, but he defended the others by saying they were as good as any policeman in the country. He said he would only terminate those corrupt officers once he "had the goods on them." Perry, on the other hand, demanded the names of deputies on the take so that he could fire them.[24]

Grand jury chairman Jacob Evans and secretary June Rudisill lost patience. They concluded an organized body or bodies operating the liquor traffic directed by men of means. They accused the police of taking bribes and placing the well-being of the liquor organization above public safety.[25]

Mayor Monteverde made a show of ordering the city attorney to charge anyone who violated the old injunctions related to the nuisance law of 1915 with contempt of court. The city attorney filed forty charges against soft drink stand operators William McVey, Harry Kiersky, Ezio Biondi, and Nello Grandi. The judges dismissed the flimsy charges and the bootleggers simply returned to their businesses, both legal and illegal.[26]

Miller suspected a conspiracy, but he needed more time to get to the heart of it. Desperate to appease the public in the short-term, he ordered his men to round up suspected bootleggers using the most meager charges of vagrancy and loitering. Hulet Smith told his officers that he hired "out-of-town men" to observe and report on their conduct. He threatened, "After this date whenever any officer is seen in conversation with any of these men, or pass by where they can see them, or their cars, and fail to make arrests, this officer will stand suspended from the city payroll."[27]

Frustration weighed heavily on the courts. Judge Tom Harsh refused to sentence Henry Mitchell because he had grown tired of dealing with only "small fish." Mitchell once ran a dive on McLemore Avenue, had the neighborhood slot machine monopoly, and shot a man for not drinking with him. Harsh explained his leniency, "While I cannot prove it, I know there are plenty of others selling liquor in Memphis, far more than is being sold by this defendant, and I know if it was my business to catch them I could do it. The officials seem to have no trouble in catching the half-pint, hip-pocket men, but do not molest the others who are bringing liquor here in motor boatloads and in automobile loads." The judge concluded by saying that such inequalities of justice sometimes caused him to regret being in court.[28]

Will Moore faced Judge Fitzhugh on his fourth charge of public drunkenness in one week. Fitzhugh, amazed that one man could acquire and drink so much illegal liquor, asked him where he got his whiskey. Moore replied, "Oh, I can't tell you that judge, but I have spent two hundred dollars for whiskey in a week." Fitzhugh's eyebrows went straight up as he gasped, "What?! You tell me you have consumed two hundred dollars' worth of whiskey here in Memphis in a week's time?" Moore explained, "Well, you see, judge, I treated some friends and did not drink it all. But two hundred dollars doesn't buy so much whiskey, judge. You must not have bought any whiskey in Memphis, or you wouldn't think so much of drinking up two hundred dollars of the stuff in five or six days."[29]

In March 1919, the US Court of Appeals for the Sixth Circuit affirmed each of the sentences of Joe and Louis Robilio at six months and a five hundred dollar fine following the ambush of their liquor caravan in January. Federal judge John McCall also sentenced E. A. Laughter, Dutch Anderson, Joe Persica (aka Joe Belluomini), and several others to terms at the Atlanta Federal Penitentiary. The convictions of these leading bootleggers, while significant, did not slow the amount of liquor coming into the city. Investigators sensed a larger conspiracy but struggled to find a lead.[30]

Their break came in April 1919 when an anonymous call to the US Marshals Service resulted in the biggest liquor raid to date and the first solid leads on the conspiracy to violate statewide Prohibition. Trezevant, three deputy marshals, and Hulet Smith stormed the vacant Moerlein Brewery building next to Jim Kinnane's Place on Front and Winchester. They forced the two African American guards, Lorenzo Dow and John Rhodes, to unlock

Fig. 4.4. Shelby County Courthouse. Courtesy of the Library of Congress.

the building. Once inside, they found forty cases of Old Kentucky bourbon in gunny sacks and about a thousand empty bottles. They arrested the two watchmen, left a guard at the building, and went to another suspicious house on the southwest corner of the intersection, where they found another 155 cases of the same brand.[31]

Kinnane's partner Dick Rather heard about the raid and became worried about his whiskey. He dispatched a crew to go to his house at Front Street and Jackson Avenue and move the liquor to a safe location. The five African American men had just begun to move the 141 cases when deputy marshal Orville Webster arrived with two police officers and arrested them.[32]

One rumor had it that Kinnane, "the Celtic purveyor of acid to Africans," had not paid for his liquor, and an angry middleman had made the call. Another rumor had it that a faction within the city government, angry over pay raises and term limits, made the call to get back at Kinnane's allies at city hall. Regardless of the reasons, the proverbial cat was out of the bag. The grand jury indicted the two guards and Kinnane.[33]

Kinnane rode in his big touring car to the courthouse with his bondmen Frank Tucker and C. T. Cannon. They signed the five-hundred-dollar bond, stepped back into the car, and went their way. But Kinnane's casual attitude only masked a deeper realization that the liquor conspiracy would soon be exposed.[34]

• • •

Fig. 4.5. Will Smiddy and John Klinck in Memphis Police Detective Division, 1912.
Courtesy of Memphis Room, Memphis Public Library and Information Center.

The first ten years of Prohibition ended as it began—with a gunfight in the street in broad daylight. The regulars at the Rosebud Café at 115 Monroe near Main Street often jeered at marshals as they passed. Deputy marshal Orville Webster asked his superiors what to do about the constant taunting from the hooligans. They told Webster to ignore it. On September 19, 1919, about two o'clock in the afternoon, Webster and chief marshal John Carrigan drove by the Rosebud Café again, and once more the bootleggers heckled them. Only this time the marshals lost their tempers.

The Rosebud Café had long been a gathering place of bootleggers and other assorted lowlifes. The leader of the rabble and part owner, William Walsh "Will" Smiddy was one of the Irish gangsters employed by Kinnane. Smiddy worked as a city detective from 1910 until 1913 when he and his partner Jack Klinck quit to open the first of a series of dives, the Majestic Saloon at Third and Gayoso.[35]

Webster stopped the car, got out, and struck Smiddy with his .44-caliber revolver. Smiddy reeled back and pulled his pistol. The two opened fire, and stray bullets flew in every direction. One hit a porter in the thigh, and another stray struck a bystander in the finger. A round went through Carrigan's coat while another, one that would have surely killed him, bounced off a bankbook in his vest pocket.[36]

The remaining bullets hit their intended targets with deadly consequences. Webster fell to the ground with four bullets in the face. Detective Walter Hoyle ran to the scene when the shooting started, and made it in time to hold Webster as he died. Only one round hit Smiddy, but the wound was serious. Friends rushed him to the General Hospital, but the gangster died on the operating table.[37]

The public outrage over the incident highlighted Memphians' concerns about the rising crime rate. Police blamed the Shelby County Grand Jury's lack of convictions for crime. Jurymen recommended the formation of a vigilance committee to track down bootleggers, murderers, robbers, and "pistol toters" because they believed Memphis had entirely too much crime for law enforcement to handle. Memphians were losing faith in law enforcement, and the events of the next year would do little to renew their confidence.[38]

5

TYREE TAYLOR

Conditions in Memphis will have a vital bearing upon the effort to
enforce the federal prohibition law.
—Wayne B. Wheeler, attorney and general counsel of the ASL, 1919

Tyree Taylor could not reach his pistol in time. The gunmen stormed into
the house and had weapons trained on him before he could react. His
wife and stepson cowered as the men waved their guns and shouted at
them. Taylor wanted to fight back, but all he could do was curse his captors.
The years of running had come to an end on that hot day in July 1921, and the
time had come for Taylor to pay for his crimes. Now, the man at the center
of the organization that supplied Memphis with bootleg liquor reflected on
his mistakes and where he went wrong.

The story began on a cold night in January 1918 when chief deputy marshal Lemuel Tyree Taylor walked into Jim Kinnane's Place in the Pinch District. Kinnane called the dingy pool hall a soft-drink stand, but that did not
fool anyone. His staff still sold liquor, only no longer from the bar. They sent
customers outside where they could buy bootleg liquor in the back alley out
of sight of police or informers. Taylor, however, was not interested in making
arrests. The thirty-year-old marshal needed money, and a man waiting inside
had an offer to make.[1]

The United States Marshals Service in Memphis had the burden of enforcing the Reed Amendment, the 1913 amendment to the Webb-Kenyon
Act that imposed a $1,000 fine for transporting liquor into a dry state. The
undermanned organization, consisting of Stanley Trezevant and his deputies John Carrigan, John Jopling, Charles King, and Taylor, could do little
to stem the flow of thousands of cases of liquor into the city. The harder
the marshals tried, the harder the bootleggers fought back. Marshals began

carrying heavier weapons, including rifles, semiautomatic shotguns, and large caliber handguns following a vicious shootout near the Nonconnah Creek. The United Press reported, "Booze smugglers and whiskey runners in the Memphis vicinity have become real bad men. They have been furnishing the United States Marshals with many thrills and the odds are that a quantity of hot lead will be spilled in the very near future."[2]

Taylor also had problems at home. He moved to Memphis when he received the appointment to the Marshals Service in November 1916, but his wife, Myrtie, remained in their home in Trenton, Tennessee. On June 1, 1917, Taylor's workload increased when he received a promotion to chief deputy. At first, he saw his wife on his occasional days off, but the demands of the new job made the visits increasingly infrequent.[3]

The turning point in Taylor's life came when he met and began an affair with May Harris. The two fell in love and wanted to start a life together, but neither had much money. Harris's husband left her and their son after learning of the affair, and she needed Taylor for support. Taylor, frustrated by his meager salary, decided to cash in on the business he had been hired to stop.

Taylor sat across from Kinnane lieutenant Will Smiddy. The two had no love for one another, but both had something to offer each other. Taylor had information that would allow whiskey runners to avoid river patrols, and Kinnane had money to pay for it. Smiddy offered Taylor cash to help him direct a liquor shipment from Caruthersville safely past the marshals. Taylor, disillusioned and facing an impending divorce, accepted the offer. The two stepped outside and Taylor took his first bribe.[4]

One bribe led to another, and before long, Taylor had a regular arrangement with the Irish gangsters. Taylor charged two dollars per case to distract law enforcement so whiskey runners could safely bring their contraband into the city. He arranged searches of uninhabited river islands or pointless meetings to occupy marshals to coincide with scheduled liquor deliveries.[5]

The Taylor Liquor Ring grew from about twenty bootleggers to include nearly everyone who moved illegal liquor into the city. This exclusive organization of criminals and corrupt law enforcement acted together with the intention of violating statewide Prohibition, the Webb-Kenyon Act, and the Reed Amendment. Taylor, who controlled the smuggling routes into Memphis, was the most important member of the conspiracy.

Ring members eagerly sought out Taylor and gladly paid his fees. Bootlegger Loftis Wilkes on April 28, 1918, paid Taylor with a $1,000 bill in front of Nabor's and McCall's Billiard Parlor on Monroe Avenue for safe passage of a shipment from Caruthersville. Joe Robilio became a customer and introduced Taylor to bootlegger Walter Boyles in February 1919. Boyles, so thankful for the help, gave Taylor several bottles of champagne in addition to his fee and after the delivery of twenty-five cases of whiskey from Paducah. Calls at his home and work at all times of the day and night made keeping his dealings secret difficult, so Taylor had May Harris handle his transactions from an apartment at 283 Union Avenue.[6]

Taylor had no qualms about strong-arming bootleggers to keep them in line. Jake Tuckerman paid up to $600 per instance for information until the rotund sporting promoter made the mistake of making sexual overtures to Harris. Taylor beat him up, threw him out of the liquor ring, and cut him off from his liquor suppliers.[7]

Taylor's creation of a liquor ring was only the beginning of his rapid descent into crime. He broke into the evidence room at the US Customs House and stole liquor seized from Loftis Wilkes. Wilkes thought Taylor would return shipment, but instead, the marshal sold it for himself. Taylor bought a boat, hired a crew, and began hijacking bootleggers who refused to pay him. He even kept liquor seized in raids. Walter Boyles once offered to let Taylor use his farm to store stolen liquor. Taylor replied, "Why store any whiskey when I can sell it in five minutes?"[8]

The debonair ex–World War I soldier Anderson "Andy" Wallace paid Taylor fifty dollars on three occasions in May 1919 to bring whiskey into the city. The two had a good relationship, so Taylor asked Wallace to borrow his car. Wallace agreed, not realizing that Taylor needed the car to transport stolen liquor. Taylor's plan went awry and led to a shootout with police in Covington, Tennessee. When Wallace got the car back, it had a damaged roof, a patched tire, and bullet holes in the body.[9]

• • •

Charles "Doc" Hottum was a worried man. He called his friend John Reichman, president of Reichman-Crosby Machinery Supply, to speak with him. The former sheriff still had contacts within the legal community, so Hottum hoped his friend could help him out of a bad situation. Hottum, in his rumbling voice, nervously rubbed his hand over his bald head and characteristically popped his lips as he told his story. Reichman listened as Hottum told how he had made an enemy of Taylor.

Hottum earned the nickname "Doc" from his time working as a pharmacist, but Memphians knew him best as a sports promoter who organized boxing matches and swimming events. Hottum once ran a popular saloon and liked rubbing elbows with outlaws. He became intrigued by Taylor's

Fig. 5.1. William Kyser. Courtesy of Memphis Room, Memphis
Public Library and Information Center.

liquor ring and pestered the marshal about working with him as a middleman. Taylor reluctantly agreed and let him collect a $400 fee from H. B. Wolfe
in May 1919. Hottum tried again but failed after Missouri bootleggers Carl
Bond and William Dunnavant refused to pay him $2,600 owed to Taylor.[10]

Their relationship became further strained when Hottum refused to pay
money owed to Taylor. May Harris provided information for safe passage of
the *Molly*, a launch purchased from bootlegger Allen McNamara. Hottum
only paid part of his fee, so Taylor took possession of the *Molly*. The two
met to discuss payment at a neutral place on Madison Avenue, where they
began to argue and then fight. Taylor reached for his pistol and Hottum
threatened to choke him. The two backed down, but Hottum knew Taylor
would eventually come after him again.[11]

Reichman urged Hottum to talk to Stanley Trezevant. Hottum agreed and
Reichman called the marshal, who came to the South Front Street office with
special agent William McElveen. Trezevant, McElveen, and district attorney
William Kyser became suspicious of Taylor in March but never imagined the

extent of his activities. Shocked by Hottum's account, Trezevant exclaimed, "Taylor has gone hog-wild on grafting!"[12]

Hottum explained how Taylor's business revolved around transactions with "Main 5922," the telephone at the Union apartment. Agent William Farrell used a wiretap from a switchboard at the Customs House to overhear Harris give instructions to bootleggers and haggle over costs of bribes. Before long, Farrell learned nearly every detail of Taylor's liquor ring and the names of those involved.[13]

• • •

In the Spring of 1919, Taylor brought May Harris and her son to their new home near Imboden, Arkansas. After a year of dealing with bootleggers, Taylor finally had enough money to settle down. West Tennessee chancellor John William Ross granted Myrtie Taylor a divorce, finding Taylor guilty of adultery and citing May as a corespondent on May 12, 1919. Two days later, Taylor married the former Mrs. William Harris in St. Francis, Arkansas. In July, he purchased a 465-acre farm and fifteen head of cattle.[14]

No one can say whether Tyree Taylor intended to give up bootlegging, but it is safe to say that May and Tyree finally had what they wanted all along—a quiet home where they could live as a husband and wife and raise their son. Their happiness, however, was short-lived. A telegram from Tyree Taylor's attorney Charles Bryan arrived notifying the couple that a federal grand jury had indicted both of them.

Tyree Taylor made a crucial error just before he left Memphis. He accepted $375 and a $350 checks for bribes on behalf of bootleggers Allen McNamara and G. C. Jernigan from their middleman Benjamin Crockett. Taylor took the two checks to the Security Bank and Trust Company but forgot to sign them. The teller would not complete the transaction without the signatures, so Crockett went to the bank and retrieved the unsigned checks. Taylor had already left for Arkansas, so Crockett tried to return them after forging Taylor's signatures. The suspicious teller refused to take the checks and turned them over to her supervisor, who called the police.[15]

News that police had evidence linking Taylor to bootleggers leaked to the public. Trezevant removed Taylor from his duties and suspended him without pay on May 22, 1919, by order of the Department of Justice. Three days later, the *Commercial Appeal* ran an article exposing the undercover investigation by Department of Justice agent C. H. Oldfield into the local US marshal's office, the Memphis Police Department, and the Shelby County Sheriff's Department.[16]

US district attorney William Kyser moved quickly to secure affidavits for a grand jury indictment against Taylor. He offered deals in exchange for testimony to Crockett, who faced a sentence for bootlegging, and Jim Mulcahy, who admitting paying Taylor $120 for the protection of a whiskey shipment. The grand jury issued the indictment and prosecutors brought Mulcahy to Memphis from the Atlanta Federal Penitentiary to testify.[17]

Allen McNamara and Jesse "Sport" Hillman also offered to testify. The two paid for safe passage of whiskey from Caruthersville; however, either through a double cross or oversight by Taylor, marshals caught the young men red-handed. Judge John McCall prepared to pass sentence when attorney Ralph Davis sprang to his feet and promised the judge that his clients would testify against the man they bribed in return for suspended sentences. McCall demanded the name and Davis replied, "Well, a man named Taylor is the one who received the $250 to let the whiskey come in."[18]

Tyree Taylor returned alone on August 11 to Memphis to place a $6,000 bond co-signed by his brother Mercer and a friend. The judge demanded to know the whereabouts of May Taylor. Tyree lied about May having to stay behind because she was pregnant, and he promised to bring her back to appear in court. The Taylors, however, had other plans. May was busy preparing their escape as Tyree set aside money for his bondsmen to cover the broken bond.[19]

Tyree Taylor believed the Department of Justice would make him take the fall for everyone involved in the liquor ring. He told a reporter he had been unfairly singled out, and there were "other sheep at the shambles." He had no intention of being punished alone and promised, "If I do come back, I'm going to make it hot for somebody." On August 15, Taylor's real estate agent James McKamey drove the Taylors to the Iron Mountain Depot in Hoxie, Arkansas. Taylor told McKamey that he hoped to find someone in St. Louis and Caruthersville to corroborate his testimony. The Taylors, however, left on the noon train and never returned.[20]

• • •

The United States Department of Justice sent special agent Frank Garbarino to head the Taylor investigation. The veteran investigator ran the Philadelphia office and helped establish the Mann Act, the legislation that made it a felony to transport any woman or girl across state lines for the purpose of "prostitution or debauchery, or for any other immoral purpose." He also led investigations into German espionage, a nationwide blackmailing organization, and white slavery rings. The smooth-talking, immaculately dressed agent replaced his predecessor C. H. Oldfield, retraced research, reinterviewed witnesses, and tried to make sense of the botched investigation.[21]

Oldfield, an agent with experience investigating suspected communists, had posed as a bootlegger to gather information months earlier. He infiltrated some of the gangs with the help of Memphis police officer Leroy Linson and brought in for questioning bootleggers including E. A. Laughter, Will Smiddy, and Allen McNamara. His reports painted a picture of large-scale corruption in Memphis at every level of government and law enforcement.[22]

Oldfield, who many considered "erratic if not crazy," did not understand that Kyser, McElveen, and Trezevant allowed Tyree Taylor to continue to operate to gather evidence against him. Instead, he accused them of protecting Taylor. Kyser scoffed at the accusations and told US attorney general Mitchell Palmer that Oldfield needed "help of the best character."[23]

Oldfield's conspiracy-laden report did not sit well with department heads. Congress had not raised sufficient money to fund the war efforts, so the government put a policy of retrenchment into place to redirect money from less important functions to the military. The department conveniently labeled Oldfield nonessential and terminated him.[24]

They rid themselves of Oldfield, but his report continued to fuel conspiracy theories. The author of an editorial suggested that Kyser and Trezevant "should be relieved of the unpleasant task of handling the investigation." Stephen S. Preston, secretary of the Memphis chapter of the ASL, and Edward T. Leech, editor of the Memphis *Press-Scimitar*, went so far as to accuse local officials of conspiring with bootleggers. On June 2, Mayor Monteverde and city commissioners sent a telegram to Attorney General Palmer requesting he investigate the accusations.[25]

Wayne Wheeler, general counsel of the ASL, believed the case had a "vital bearing upon the effort to enforce the federal prohibition law." Wheeler hoped Tyree Taylor's prosecution would quiet naysayers who doubted the viability of the proposed Eighteenth Amendment to the US Constitution. An assassination attempt by anarchists delayed Palmer's response, but on June 6, 1919, he assured Wheeler that the Department of Justice would look into the situation in Memphis.[26]

Wheeler's plan to make an example of Tyree Taylor fell through a few weeks later when Garbarino's investigation turned into a manhunt. Taylor returned to Imboden just long enough to get his wife and stepson as well as some cash and jewelry before fleeing. The special agent spent the next two years heading the nationwide search for them.

· · ·

Taylor moved his wife and stepson to a bungalow at the corner of Iberville and Pierce Street in New Orleans in February 1921. It was another in a long line of temporary homes. Traveling under the alias Louis Taylor, he first took his family to Canada. They spent a few days in Edmonton before purchasing a 160-acre farm 350 miles away in the Northwest Territories. The cold proved too much for the southerners to handle, so they gave up the farm and relocated to Vancouver in October where Taylor started a life insurance company.[27]

The Taylors soon tired of Canada and headed for the warmer climate of Cuba. They could not apply for passports because of the required background check, so they pawned some diamonds to cover the five-hundred-dollar fee to the captain of a small boat to smuggle them in. Unfortunately, the weather took a turn for the worse the day they planned to leave. The waters of the Straits of Florida became so dangerous that the captain and his passengers had to abandon the trip.[28]

Unable to escape the country, the Taylors moved from city to city, staying only one step ahead of Garbarino's agents. In December they left Florida for Akron, Ohio, where Tyree worked for the Goodyear Tire Company and the Baltimore and Ohio Railroad until they saved enough money for a new car. They lived in Los Angeles for about a month until friends in Memphis let them know that Garbarino's men received a tip about their location. They fled to San Diego, where Tyree took a job as a mechanic.[29]

Life on the run drained them of their savings, so Tyree Taylor decided in December of 1920 to risk going back to Tennessee to collect money he had loaned his brother Mercer. He traveled by train to a cousin's home in New Orleans after Christmas, continued to Bemis, a suburb of Jackson, Tennessee, and drove to Trenton. His family warned him that he risked capture if he stayed, so he waited in Henderson County, where his brother promised to meet him with the money. Mercer, however, never showed up, so Taylor returned to San Diego for his wife and son and moved to New Orleans. Desperately short on cash, Tyree sent a letter to a friend in Jackson to help get the money from Mercer.[30]

Trezevant had been on the lookout in Jackson because of rumors that Taylor was in hiding in the area. A postal worker notified him about the letter, and with it, Trezevant discovered Taylor's address in New Orleans. He passed the information to Garbarino, who informed Dr. J. M. Toliver, head of the New Orleans branch of the Department of Justice.[31]

On July 11, 1921, an agent named Joseph Condon and local police gathered up the street from the Taylors' home on Iberville Street near Carrollton

Avenue. Tyree had just returned home from work at a local garage when Condon made his move. He rode into the front yard on the running board of the squad car as the police rushed the house. The furious Tyree told Condon, "I had every intention of killing you. I would have, and I'd have escaped too, but I knew you had my wife covered, and I couldn't see her suffer because of me."[32]

. . .

Kyser asked for a $50,000 bail against the Taylors. He mailed the indictments to US commissioner A. H. Browne to obtain warrants and have them returned to Memphis as soon as possible. Tyree Taylor raised suspicions when he asked about the travel plans. Toliver decided to keep them secret until the time came to leave for the train station so Taylor could not contact cohorts and arrange an escape.[33]

Reporters, eager for details of the liquor ring, tried to coax an interview from Taylor. He replied, "You must think I am some kind of fool to make a statement or give an interview. I ain't a fish. I won't squeal. [The Department of Justice] can go ahead and pop their whip. Tell them you saw me and I refused to talk. I suppose they thought I was going to talk my head off. Well, I ain't and they ain't gonna find out anything from me, no matter what happens."[34]

Reporters continued to hound Taylor, to which he replied with more verbal abuse and guarantees that he would never "squeal." He told reporters, "No, I have nothing to say. . . . You newspaper men are too goddamned inquisitive and pry too much into people's affairs!" When asked about cooperating with the Department of Justice, he responded, "If those Guineas in Memphis think they are going to learn anything from me, they have a grim awakening coming to them because my lips are sealed, and I'm not going to talk at any time."[35]

Tyree remained unrepentant and confrontational, but his wife could not handle confinement. May became visibly frail and remained under constant observation by a female deputy. Taylor, willing to accept his punishment, pleaded to agent Condon, "Take me back to Memphis so my wife can furnish bail and get out of jail. I'm willing to stay in the lockup, but I don't want her to be held. She has done nothing."[36]

Federal agents transported the prisoners to Memphis where they met with Garbarino and Kyser on July 17. Tyree denied that he ever said that he would expose his "higher-ups" as reported in the press, remained uncooperative, and even refused to eat. At two thirty in the afternoon, two of Garbarino's

Fig. 5.2. Tyree Taylor after his capture. Courtesy of the Library of Congress.

men picked Tyree up from the county jail and brought him downtown for a second meeting.[37]

A newspaper photographer tried to take a picture of Taylor as agents escorted him up the front steps of the courthouse. Taylor covered his face until he got close enough to kick the camera out of the photographer's hands. He told the man, "Nothing doing on that photograph stuff. Nobody has got one of me since I left Memphis and nobody is going to get one now—that is, not while I have my health."[38]

Garbarino finally had enough of Taylor's antics. A "sharp verbal clash" changed Taylor's attitude. Taylor put on the act of contrariness mostly for show; he knew he faced a lengthy prison sentence but wanted to gain any small piece of leverage to save his wife. On the evening before he left New Orleans, Taylor told Commissioner Poole that he would not post bond and would accept his punishment.[39]

Tyree Taylor gave a full confession in exchange for all charges being dropped against his wife. The federal court met in special session and convicted Taylor on eight counts, two for each transaction: one for directly accepting a bribe, and one for failing to inform the government of the bribe. Judge John Ross fined Taylor $6,895, three times the amount of the bribes. He sentenced Taylor to three years for each bribery charge and one year for each of the other counts but made all but three concurrent so that Taylor faced two three-year sentences and one one-year sentence. A reporter called his sentence "the longest in recent memory."[40]

May Taylor moved to Atlanta with her son and took a job in a ladies' hat shop so she could visit her husband at the federal prison. Tyree Taylor told a reporter, "But for the fact that I'm separated from my wife and child, my way of living isn't so bad." The guards assigned him to oil the sewing machines Monday through Friday until 4:00 p.m., and he spent his free time watching the other prisoners play baseball. Taylor's days of running had come to an end, but that did not mean that life would be easy; the former fugitive would in two months become the government's key witness in the most anticipated trial since Prohibition came to Memphis.[41]

6

BIG FISH, LITTLE FISH

Just above the lowest element of society that I can imagine is a bootlegger.
—Judge J. W. Ross, May 1923

The Lawyers' Club and Memphis Bar held a dinner at the Hotel Gayoso to welcome John William Ross, the new federal judge for the District Court for the Western District of Tennessee on December 3, 1921. The event did not go well, and the legal establishment took a calm dislike for him. Unlike his predecessor John McCall, he had few friends and despised the press. He had an abrasive personality, took offense as easily as he gave it, and believed that Memphis was nothing more than a "hotbed of lawlessness." He told dinner guests, "In the discharge of my duties, I close my eyes to all except two things—right and the law as I see them."[1]

Ross's inconsistency and practice of subtly prejudicing juries subverted legal proceedings and infuriated lawyers. Ross had the "delightful little custom" of telling the jury he believed the defendant guilty and then telling them they should not be influenced by his opinion. He issued the city's first dismissal of a liquor case due to a lack of search warrant in December 1921, but in May 1922, he convicted Joe Murphy of bootlegging though the search warrant had neither Murphy's correct name nor his correct address. In January 1925, Ross explained in court that while evidence procured by city or state authorities without a search warrant was competent, the same evidence obtained by federal agents in like manner was not.[2]

Ross also rushed the legal process. Faced with 230 criminal cases in May 1922, Ross announced that he would hear cases within a week of indictment. Defendants had never had so little time to prepare for court appearances.

When lawyers asked for more time, Ross accused them of deliberately delaying proceedings in hopes of acquittal.[3]

Judge Ross's admirers liked his dedication to conservative rural values, his "impartial and speedy methods," and "his strict enforcement of the laws," but the legal community resented his dictatorial approach. Ross's conduct not only created a toxic atmosphere at the federal courthouse, but it would play a crucial role in the outcomes of the Taylor Liquor Ring trials—cases that the Department of Justice needed to win to prove the viability of Prohibition in Memphis.

• • •

The time came for Tyree Taylor to honor his part of the bargain he made in exchange for his wife's freedom—to serve as a witness against his former liquor ring coconspirators. The Department of Justice transferred Taylor from the Atlanta federal penitentiary to Memphis on September 16, 1922. Special agent Frank Garbarino also brought May Taylor back to testify and secured a payment of eight dollars per day, far more than the typical $1.50 per day for witnesses. At night, Tyree and May shared meals brought in from restaurants and discussed their plans.[4]

The United States Customs House sat at the corner of Front Street and Court Avenue, with the rear of the building overlooking Riverside Drive and the Mississippi River. The 169,000-square-foot building, built in the Italian Renaissance Revival style, opened in 1885 and housed the post office, customs office, United States marshal's office, and district federal court located on the third floor. The old building had for decades represented the power and orderliness of the federal government.

Tyree Taylor's return shook that sense of stability. The building became "steeped in mystery" as rumors of conspiracies, frame-ups, and double crosses circulated among investigators, attorneys, police, reporters, and curious onlookers who filled the halls. US district attorney William Kyser, worried about intrigue, asked reporters not to print the names of witnesses out of fear they "might get knocked off." A story even circulated that former investigator C. H. Oldfield refused to testify out of fear for his life.[5]

Memphians believed Oldfield's report held the key to the conspiracy, so investigators could not discard the document without drawing suspicion from the public. It also presented a problem because prosecutors considered it unreliable overall but truthful enough to provide evidence against Taylor. Kyser promised a federal grand jury would view the report but said, "If that pack of lies was so [true], I ought to be in Atlanta."[6]

Garbarino claimed to know the identities of every conspirator but delayed making any arrests because he could not get a conviction solely on Taylor's unsupported statements. An arrest at that time and a hearing before the US commissioner to fix a bond would have put the accused in possession of the primary evidence. Instead, the government gathered proof and waited until September to proceed.[7]

Most of the fifteen indicted on September 20 avoided the deputy marshals who came to bring them to the courthouse. It was too late to arrange bail by the time the marshals got started, so most stayed away from their homes to avoid having to spend the night in jail. Instead, Bob Berryman, Charles Auferoth, Joe Robertson, and Cyril Oursler arrived the next morning and Judge Ross set bail at $3,000 each.[8]

Jim Kinnane, jointly indicted with Dick Rather and Herbert Green, did not arrive until nine o'clock in the evening. The veteran political boss, now bent over and suffering from rheumatoid arthritis, struggled through the Customs House on two canes. His attorneys, Charles Bryan and Arthur Brode, arrived with several nephews and cousins as well as sisters Josephine Brennan and Annie Riley, who signed his bond. Kinnane, worried the court might find him guilty, transferred property including valuable lots in the Pinch District and Beale Street valued at $165,000 on September 26 to his sister Josephine, widow of former police captain J. J. Brennan.[9]

. . .

On November 28, 1921, the federal court opened with over 215 cases. Most dealt with the Taylor Liquor Ring, so Ross postponed all other civil cases until January. He intended to speed through the proceedings and threatened to replace any tardy lawyer with another appointed by the court. US attorney general William J. Burns intended to come to Memphis to take charge of the proceedings but changed his mind when Ross set a record by hearing sixteen cases and had a seventeenth on the floor by noon.[10]

The jury found Jake Tuckerman and Loftis Wilkes guilty of one count of bribing Taylor on November 29. Judge Ross sentenced Tuckerman to two years and fined him $1,500. Wilkes received a three-year sentence and a fine three times the amount of his bribes. The next day, Ross sentenced Anderson Wallace two years and fined him $350 after the jury found him guilty, in only six minutes, on three counts of bribery.[11]

Meanwhile, bootleggers waiting to face Ross took time away from prying eyes and fortified themselves with the very product that got them into trouble in the first place. A reporter discovered half a dozen empty pint bottles on a windowsill and the smell of corn liquor in an anteroom of the courtroom. Apparently, even a federal trial could not curb the appetite of the accused for bootleg whiskey.[12]

Tyree Taylor's testimony was destroying the bootleggers' defenses. Defense attorney Charles Bryan, who once represented Taylor, knew Taylor might slip up if he lost his temper and discredit himself, so he tried to provoke Tyree by suggesting that he and May were not legally married. While defending bootlegger Walter Boyles, Bryan pointed out that Myrtie Taylor had named May Harris corespondent in the divorce proceedings and that Tennessee law at the time stated that a man and woman cannot marry if one appears as a corespondent in the other's divorce trial. Bryan accused May of corroborating Tyree Taylor's testimony only to secure her freedom. Bootlegger Walter Hindman's attorney also tried to rattle Tyree by questioning him about his relationship with May Harris before his divorce.[13]

The attorneys fought dirty, so Tyree Taylor decided to fight back. He searched through unattended case files in the federal offices during the holiday recess and used the information to make it appear that he had leverage with prosecutors. He met nightclub owner and bootlegger Bob Berryman on the front steps of the Customs House and produced a witness's affidavit. Taylor apologized to Berryman for implicating him and offered to "kill the case" in exchange for $500 and his cooperation. Taylor also promised Roy McCutcheon that he would remove his name from an indictment in exchange for testimony against bootlegger Dick Rather.[14]

The trials resumed in January 1922 with some colorful defenses. Ross dismissed the case against Charles Auferoth for bribing Taylor after the defendant's lawyer produced a doctor's note stating Auferoth was in bed sick at the time of the alleged bribes. Accused briber James L. Howard, also known as William Estes "Big G" Gee, claimed that he was with his sick baby; however, he could neither produce medical documentation nor proof of having a child. US district attorney S. Eugene Murray presented cancelled checks as evidence that bootlegger H. B. Wolfe had paid off Taylor. Wolfe examined the checks as Murray spoke to the jury. When Murray retrieved the checks, he saw that the dates had been smeared. Murray angrily accused Wolfe of defacing the evidence. Wolfe denied the accusation and said the idea that anyone would do such a thing left him "the most surprised man in the world."[15]

The prosecution's biggest victory came when the jury found Jim Kinnane guilty of bribery and violation of the Reed Amendment. Ross, in a rare exhibition of mercy, told him, "The court has some sympathy for your age and physical condition, but it has understood that you have been guilty of many violations of the federal law. See that you never come into this court again on charges." With that warning, Kinnane wrote a check to cover his $7,500 fine, returned home, and left the underworld for good.[16]

Dick Rather admitted to transporting liquor once from Caruthersville in 1918, but he denied paying Taylor bribes. The jury found him guilty anyway and fined him $900 and sentenced him to eighteen months. Sentencing stalled for eight months because Rather's codefendants Luke Kyle and Ellithorpe remained at large. Agents eventually arrested Kyle but never found Ellithorpe. Ross fined Kyle $175 and Rather $200 on additional charges of conspiracy on November 29, 1922, ending the last of the thirty-seven indictments. Even so, the legal battles were far from over.[17]

Ross, angered by the hung jury during the Boyles trial, demanded to know the identity of the single dissenter. Upon learning that a bookkeeper named Joseph Clare Mahannah held out, Ross told him, "You are excused from further service. You may go to the clerk any money that may be due to you." To make matters worse, Ross intentionally influenced the jury by having C. W. Patton, a childhood friend of Tyree Taylor, testify to Taylor's good character. Ross influenced the jury not because of any fondness for Taylor, but rather because he wanted to maintain the integrity of Taylor as a government witness.[18]

Attorneys for W. F. Mackey, Wilkes, Tuckerman, Wallace, Hindman, Wolfe, Oursler, Berryman, and Joe Robilio appeared before the US Court of Appeals for the Sixth Circuit in Cincinnati in April 1923, accusing Ross of prejudice and directed verdicts. They won new trials, but each appeared before Ross and the same jury members who tried them the first time. Not surprisingly, they were found guilty again. Sentences ranged from eighteen months to three years and a day, while fines ranged from $900 to over $2,000. Their lawyers fought on and won early paroles for their clients. All were free by January 1925, and all returned to the lucrative business of bootlegging.[19]

Doc Hottum's lawyers R. Gratton "Gratz" Brown and Abe Waldauer paid careful attention to the proceedings and planned a strategy to tarnish Tyree Taylor and exploit Ross's weaknesses. They filed a motion requesting Ross's removal because of "prejudice shown in charges shown to the jury." The move put Ross in a bad light even though he quickly overruled the motion. Brown and Waldauer then paraded character witnesses to counter Taylor's testimony. Statements from John Reichman; Stanley Trezevant; Roane Waring, member of the Memphis Chamber of Commerce and the American Legion; C. P. J. Mooney, newspaper editor; and Judges A. B. Pittman and H. W. Laughlin

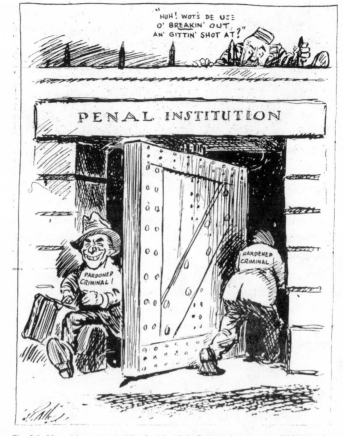

Fig. 6.1. Memphians resented the fact that light fines and sentences did little to de-
ter gangsters from returning to crime, as seen in this editorial cartoon by J. P. Alley.
Caption: REVOLVING DOORS MIGHT EXPEDITE MATTERS! Courtesy of Memphis
Room, Memphis Public Library and Information Center.

did not completely convince the juries of Hottum's innocence, but they cast
enough doubt on the prosecution's case to cause the juries not to agree on a
verdict, resulting in mistrials in December and January.[20]

In March 1922, Hottum's lawyer Gratz Brown filed another affidavit charging Ross with prejudice and conspiracy because of his dismissal of juror J. C.
Mahannah. Ross responded by filing a charge of contempt against the two.
Hottum apologized, but Brown refused and had to pay a $300 fine. Even so,
the gamble paid off and Ross was replaced.[21]

Hottum appeared in court again on April 20 with a different judge. This
time his lawyers worked a deal with prosecutors that allowed Hottum to

plead guilty and pay fines without serving time. He secured the money, wrote a check to the court clerk for two thousand dollars, and walked out a free man.[22]

Ross not only damaged the government's cases by trying to sway juries, he also became known around the country for firing a juror and publicly rebuking him for failing to convict a defendant. The embarrassment would have caused most judges to resign, but Ross, as obstinate as ever, continued on. Ross started a pointless confrontation with attorney C. H. Williams during the litigation between Clarence Saunders and Piggly Wiggly over the trademarked name and the patent for the self-serving merchandising system. Ross then made a blunder in court that allowed gangster John Belluomini to go free on narcotics charges in 1925.[23]

The final blow to his prestige came when the Madison County (Tennessee) Grand Jury indicted Ross for fraudulent breach of trust and accessory to embezzlement in his part in the mismanagement of the People's Savings Bank of Jackson. After receiving the news, Ross left a farewell note on his secretary's desk and drove his Studebaker over an embankment and into a canal off the Forked Deer River. The lack of skid marks indicated suicide, but investigators took pity on his widow and declared it an accident so she could collect the life insurance.[24]

. . .

The trials also marked the end of Stanley Trezevant's career in the US Marshals Service. On July 12, 1921, the day after Taylor's arrest, he submitted his resignation to Rep. Lon Scott, who then notified US assistant attorney general Guy Goff. The new head of the Department of Justice, William J. Burns, planned to ask for the resignations of both Garbarino and Trezevant, not as punishment, but only to replace Democratic appointees from the previous administrations. Burns, a Republican, replaced Garbarino with William Farrell and replaced Trezevant with William F. Appleby, brother of New England Prohibition director John Appleby.[25]

Trezevant traveled to Washington, DC, in December to transport Homer Simmons, a local teenager, to the National Reform School for Boys. While in the capital, he was accompanied by Sen. Kenneth McKellar and Rep. Hubert Fisher to an interview with assistant attorney general Rush Holland. Holland assured Trezevant that his office did not consider the Taylor scandal a reflection on his service and he never thought the marshal played a part in the ring. Trezevant stayed in his position until January, at the recommendation of Judge Ross, to assist the prosecution.[26]

Fig. 6.2. Mabel Walker Willebrandt. Courtesy of the Library of Congress.

Trezevant left for the private sector to form a real estate business with the most unlikely of partners—Ed Crump. His partnership proved successful, but Crump's reputation led to some undue attention. In response to complaints about bootlegging in Memphis in 1925, Mabel Walker Willebrandt accused Crump, Trezevant, and their associates of acting as "dryers and cleaners" for bootleggers. Fortunately, no one in Memphis took the unfounded accusation against Trezevant seriously.[27]

• • •

Tyree Taylor typed and mailed dozens of letters requesting support for a full pardon during downtime. Appleby, as chief marshal, allowed Taylor to make calls and drove him around town to make pleas in person. Taylor secured letters, but the Department of Justice refused pardons in cases like that of Taylor "except under unusual circumstances or where further imprisonment might cause the death of the prisoner."[28]

Taylor then reported finding threatening letters left under his pillow on his bunk in his cell at the Atlanta Federal Penitentiary. Fearing for his life, Taylor asked the prison officials for a transfer on June 3, 1922. Judge Ross sent the request to the attorney general, who approved Taylor's transfer to McNeil Island Penitentiary near Tacoma, Washington.[29]

Appleby and J. L. Ettlinger, deputy marshal, escorted Tyree Taylor, now prisoner 4212, from the Shelby County Workhouse to the train station on June 6. May Taylor kissed him goodbye as he boarded the Frisco train with the marshals. The train traveled by way of Kansas City and Omaha to the island in Puget Sound where he spent his first night at McNeil on June 11.[30]

May Taylor exhausted every avenue for early release. Eugene Murray, the district attorney, felt that Tyree Taylor should serve his full term, since, in his opinion, he had gotten off with a relatively light sentence. Pres. Warren G. Harding turned down her appeal as well, so the couple could only wait until Tyree's eligibility for parole.[31]

The parole finally came through on Thanksgiving Day, 1923. Taylor took advantage of a government transportation allowance, left for Memphis, and checked in with marshals at the Customs House on December 5. After four years of life on the run, incarceration, threats, and public disgrace, Taylor finally got what he wanted—a new life with his wife and son.[32]

• • •

The Taylor scandal should have served as a warning about the unenforceability of Prohibition and the corruptibility of law enforcement. Tyree Taylor warned reporters in May 1919, "Washington ought to know that four deputy United States marshals, all have been at work most the time in Memphis, are not enough to fight a traffic which, according to the newspapers, is bringing thousands of cases of whiskey into Memphis every month." Taylor only made $1,500 per year as chief deputy marshal, but he made over $75,000 dollars in bribes.[33]

In 1924, Prohibition agents arrested Seattle police officer Roy Olmstead after the discovery of his bootleg operation. The case was similar to Taylor's case. Both lawmen ran lucrative liquor rings, both involved leading community figures, and the government resorted to wiretaps to collect evidence.

Memphis, as a test case, showed how easily the enormous profits of bootlegging could corrupt law enforcement. Unfortunately, advocates of national Prohibition, blinded by fanaticism, ignored what happened in Memphis. They pressed on in their campaign and indirectly brought the corruption and violence that plagued city to the rest of the country.

7

NO CAMPAIGNS

Enforcement of the prohibition amendment will not come at once,
but several years will be required to run down and put out of business
those who will still persist in dealing in the beverage.
—Malcolm Patterson, January 17, 1919[1]

Former Tennessee governor Malcolm Patterson believed most would "readily submit" and "quickly readjust" to the national Prohibition, but admitted that it might take several years to bring the last diehards into the fold. Patterson, whose political career lay in ruins because of his association with Duncan and Robin Cooper, returned to Memphis in 1911, took up law practice, and converted to the cause of Prohibition. While Patterson spouted predictions of an alcohol-free panacea, law enforcement officials had to deal with the reality of Prohibition. They faced problems with manpower shortages, recidivism, geographic barriers, legal challenges, and corruption. They may not have shared Patterson's optimism, but they were determined to overcome the challenges they faced.

"Take this and forget about it," said Ettore Bertasi as he slid a fifty-dollar bill across the counter to police inspector William D. Bee. Just minutes earlier, Bee sent a paid informer to come in the grocery at 245 South Fourth Street to buy a half-pint of liquor. The informant made the purchase, walked outside, and turned the evidence over to officers. Bee and two other raiders entered the store, found more liquor, and arrested the proprietors. Bee took the fifty-dollar bill as evidence and charged Bertasi and his brother-in-law Pete Tonoli with attempted bribery. It looked bad for the two Italian-born merchants, but their problems had only begun. Newly arrived federal Prohibition agents found out about the raid and rearrested Bertasi, Tonoli, and

Fig. 7.1. Chairman of the House Judiciary Committee Andrew Volstead.
Courtesy of the Library of Congress.

an African American man named Henry Yerger, who Bee arrested on an
unrelated liquor charge, making them the first Memphians charged with
violation of the Eighteenth Amendment to the US Constitution.[2]

The Eighteenth Amendment, effective after midnight January 16, 1920,
prohibited the production, sale, and transport of intoxicating liquors. Andrew Volstead, chairman of the House Judiciary Committee, followed up by
introducing the National Prohibition Act, drafted by Wayne Wheeler of the
ASL, to provide definitions of "intoxicating liquor" and penalties for violations. The act, commonly called the Volstead Act, put the Department of the
Treasury in charge of enforcement, over the protests of the commissioner
of the Bureau of Internal Revenue and of the secretary of the treasury, who
argued that they lacked the money and manpower to carry out the duties.
Forced to comply, the secretary created the Prohibition Unit to enforce liquor
and narcotics laws.[3]

Fig. 7.2. Memphis Police Department Emergency Squad. Courtesy of Memphis Police Department Archives.

Prohibition agents arrived in Memphis to find local law enforcement in a decade-old losing battle with bootleggers. The city and county had too many bootleggers, too many places for them to hide, and too few lawmen. Agents quickly realized that if they were to make any headway, they and their partner agencies would have to come up with some new tactics.

Chief agent A. L. Story had only six agents spread out through West Tennessee, so his agents in Memphis, Travis L. Comer and Bond Harmon, teamed up with police, sheriff's deputies, and marshals to conduct undercover stings. Two agents would act as customers and enter a restaurant or soft-drink stand and look for anyone drinking. If they saw customers drinking, two more agents posing as customers would come in and ask to buy liquor. If the business owner or staff member sold the agents liquor, the agents would leave with the evidence and return with police and raid the establishment. Administrators in Washington, DC, complimented them for their efforts but wanted more headline-grabbing arrests and prosecutions.[4]

The Prohibition Unit organized agents from across the region and local police into "flying squadrons" to stage raids to impress the public. In May 1922, state administrator W. H. Tyler sent one of these groups on a four-day campaign to raid stills and dives and set up road blocks. Tyler responded to complaints of searches without warrants by saying, "Instead of jackleg lawyers, we have for our authority, the law of the land as interpreted by the United States Attorney General and the high courts." Tyler claimed victory, and as he left, he called Memphis the cleanest city in the state.[5]

Tyler spoke too soon. Twelve days later, Prohibition agents and deputies found a six-hundred-gallon still and a thousand gallons of fermenting mash in Frayser, just north of Memphis. Another flying squadron, made up of five agents, twenty police officers, and six deputy marshals rounded up thirty-three suspected bootleggers in September following a thirty-day investigation. Afterward, chief agent G. S. Griffin concluded, "Memphis has the worst liquor traffic of any city we have visited."[6]

Bootleggers had stills, whiskey, and beer hidden in attics, sheds, garages, and houses throughout the city. In April 1925, Prohibition agents raided a home at 590 East Trigg Avenue and discovered a thousand-gallon still in the attic. John Ellis and James Reino had been turning out about three hundred gallons of home brew beer a day. In September 1927, Prohibition agents and police discovered a moonshine operation in a beautiful two-story brick residence at 1133 North Parkway. The couple who lived there made mash, ran the still, and bottled liquor in the two upstairs rooms, connecting hoses to the plumbing to dispose of waste and vent fumes from the still so their neighbors would not notice the smell. In March 1932, police discovered a still, four hundred gallons of whiskey, and three thousand gallons of mash in a raid on a home on 1116 Madison Avenue previously owned by Mayor Thomas Ashcroft.[7]

Bootleggers began recognizing undercover agents, so the Prohibition Unit recruited civilians as informants. Cousins Hadley Strange and Otis Mather began accompanying Otis's father, Prohibition agent Frank Mather, on liquor raids in Kentucky at the age of fifteen and worked as informants during their breaks from college. Agents arrested Harry "Silk Hat" Langley and J. Elmer Robb after the teens bought whiskey from them at the Hotel Gayoso. Following the trial in September 1929, Harry Anderson, the federal judge, expressed concern about the safety and reliability of the young men. Strange replied, "I like the excitement and activity connected with the life, and I'll probably keep on working for the government during my summer vacations. I've been testifying in cases for the past two years, and the question of my youth was never brought up by any judge. And I've convicted bootleggers on my testimony alone in Kentucky."[8]

The cycle of raids, arrests, and fines did little to deter bootlegging, so the Department of Justice began using "padlock" court orders to close businesses where bootleggers had operated for up to a year and seize and sell vehicles that had been used to transport liquor. Memphis agents placed their first padlock on the LaBella Heights Barbecue Stand on Pidgeon Roost Road in May 1925 after the owner Lunzo Turins sold a half-pint of liquor to an

Fig. 7.3. Memphians felt that law enforcement focused on petty bootleggers rather than more important leaders of criminal gangs as seen in this editorial cartoon by J. P. Alley. Caption: "THE DADDY OF 'EM ALL!" Courtesy of Memphis Room, Memphis Public Library and Information Center.

informant. The federal court issued padlocks on lunch stands, grocery stores, taxi stands, pressing shops, and soft drink stands as well as roadhouses and pool halls. Local law enforcement even went so far as to adopt the same tactic against gambling establishments and brothels.[9]

Even so, the new measures had limited effect. In 1924, Mabel Walker Willebrandt, the US assistant attorney general, realized she could make better use of her limited manpower by having agents focus on liquor suppliers rather than small-time bootleggers and their customers. Agents in Memphis focused on the heads of bootlegging syndicates, the so-called Liquor Barons. They continued their raids, but now with an eye on gathering evidence for a larger investigation, leaving the hip-pocket cases to the Shelby County Sheriff's Department and Memphis Police Department.[10]

• • •

On evening of May 23, 1924, Shelby County sheriff Will Knight received a call that bootleggers were delivering liquor to the Chelsea Inn. Knight quickly formed a posse and sped off towards the roadhouse. He arrived expecting to find trucks with liquor and rowdy partiers but instead found the popular gathering place completely dark. Knight ordered his deputies to surround the building and cover the exits.

The sheriff drew his revolver and quietly climbed the front steps. He took a deep breath and kicked in the front door. He found the main room completely dark. He called out, but the only response was muffled snickering. Something was not right. Lights suddenly flashed on. Instead of bootleggers, the sheriff found sixteen judges, lawyers, constables, and other friends waiting for him a long table lined with American Beauty roses and broiled chicken dinners. The surprise party had caught Knight completely off-guard. The lawman, amid a roar of laughter, drawled, "I'll be eternally horn-swaggled!"[11]

Knight was the most loved man to hold the sheriff's office, and no other law enforcement officer during the time of Prohibition came so close to shutting down moonshining in Shelby County. The county court elected Knight in January 1924 to finish the term of the late sheriff Oliver Perry. At the urging of Ed Crump, Knight ran for office two more terms and served until 1931. When asked about his spectacular drives on bootlegging or vice, Knight humbly insisted, "We don't have campaigns, just steady work."[12]

The majority of local liquor came from moonshining, unlike in the North and on the East Coast, where bootleggers relied on international smuggling or the risky process of trying to remove poisonous chemicals from denatured industrial alcohol. Newer equipment and refined techniques increased the quality and quantity of liquor and turned the quaint backwoods pastime into large-scale manufacturing that rivaled bootlegging anywhere else in the country. Most stills ranged in capacity from twenty-five to three-hundred gallons with copper cisterns and pipes to remove the taste of sulfur. Moonshiners soaked cornmeal and sugar in hot water, added malt to convert the corn starch into sugar, and used yeast to start the fermentation process. They poured the resulting mash into the still, where they heated it to about 172 degrees. The evaporated alcohol rose to the top of the still, where it collected and flowed through a cap arm into an adjacent thump keg. The vapor then moved through the "worm," a copper coil immersed in water that caused the alcohol to cool and return to liquid form. The purified alcohol passed through the worm and dripped into bottles, jugs, or cans.[13]

Larger operations used stills with capacities of thousands of gallons and incorporated gasoline-powered generators and pumps. In December of 1924, agents and deputies found the "grand-pappy of all stills," with a capacity of 5,250 gallons, near Collierville. Built on a permanent brick foundation, and capable of producing a thousand gallons of whiskey per day, it was the largest found in West Tennessee to date. Deputies used dynamite to destroy the still because they could not carry the equipment that would be necessary to dismantle it.[14]

The geography of Shelby County proved ideal for liquor production and transportation. Waterways nearly surround Memphis, with the Nonconnah Creek in the south, the Wolf River and Loosahatchie River in the north, and the Mississippi River to the west. In addition, each had tributaries running throughout the county into the city. Boggy areas unfit for land development in the county, including islands in the Mississippi River, provided a nearly perfect cover for moonshining.

Raids often took deputies deep into the wilderness. Working on a tip, deputies C. E. "Brill" Willis, William Goswick, McCorley Wyatt Palmer, Joe Hendricks, and Abe Beatty took a muddy road northeast of White Station, where they located an unattended still on the opposite bank of the Wolf River. They hid and waited until bootlegger Carl Queen and his helper returned on a skiff and made it back to the still. Willis stripped off his clothes, swam across the river, and returned with the bootlegger's boat. The deputies then used it to get across the river and surprise the bootleggers. As they approached the camp, Queen jumped in the water and tried to swim away. Willis dove in after him. The two fought until the deputy subdued Queen and dragged him ashore.[15]

Most bootleggers either employed lookouts or paid locals to cooperate. Deputies Phil Armour, George Becker, and William Key heard church bells while on patrol one day in May 1929. As they wondered aloud about the bells, an elderly African American woman came up and chastised them, "White folks, don't you know the deps are after your still? Didn't you all hear that bell?" Realizing that the woman had mistaken them for bootleggers, the deputies rushed into the nearby woods to catch the real bootleggers, only to find their abandoned five-hundred-gallon still and seventy-five hundred gallons of mash.[16]

Knight and his deputies often spent days at a time in woods and swamps tracking down bootleggers and destroying their operations. They set a record when they seized eight stills in one week in the Benjestown area north of the city along the bluffs in February 1924. They broke that record the next month when they captured ten stills in a week along with forty-two hundred gallons of mash and arrested five men.[17]

Fig. 7.5. Sheriff Will Knight standing by a car with deputies, a trustee, and a seized still. Courtesy of Shelby County Archives.

Even so, some questioned the effectiveness of Knight's efforts. In May of 1926, he answered critics by allowing reporters to inspect more than seven hundred captured stills and thousands of gallons of confiscated liquor and home brewed beer. He astonished his visitors when he told them deputies had to pour the contraband into the sewer regularly to make space for more evidence. The reporters learned that deputies donated confiscated sugar and cornmeal to the county workhouse and local orphanages and routinely sold bottles and copper from the stills, making Knight the only sheriff in Tennessee to give the money back to his county.[18]

Knight declared, "I'm going to continue to enforce all laws, particularly the prohibition law. And the whole United States seems to be agreeing that's one hard law to enforce, but we seem to be doing pretty well here." Knight hounded bootleggers from Normal, Orange Mound, White Station, Raleigh, Collierville, Germantown, and Cordova to the outskirts of the county and beyond, and by 1930, he seized over two thousand stills.[19]

• • •

The exposure of the Tyree Taylor Liquor Ring brought to light the extent of corruption in the Memphis Police Department. In February 1920, city commissioner John B. Edgar set out to clean up the 240-member department from the top down. He reappointed Joseph Brown Burney as chief, appointed C. Jake Gwaltney as chief of detectives, and promoted William D. Bee to inspector. Edgar then turned his attention to the captain positions. He needed trustworthy men who could motivate and lead officers, so he chose Sgt. William D. Lee, from the mounted division of the Barksdale Precinct, and Sgt. Mike Kehoe, a thirty-year veteran and living legend of the police department.[20]

Kehoe had a well-earned reputation as the toughest and most honest cop on the force. A gunman, "crazed on booze or dope," once barricaded himself in a second story boarding house room. Patrolmen demanded that he open up, but the man refused and threatened to kill the first cop to try to come in the door. An officer sent for Sergeant Kehoe, who came on the run to find his men held at bay. Kehoe walked up to the door with his sidearm still holstered, pounded on it with his fist, and bellowed, "This is Mike Kehoe and I'm asking ye to open up and surrender. If ye don't, I'm comin' in!" A few moments of silence passed while the gunman considered the probable outcome of a confrontation with big Irishman. The door slowly opened and the gunman, earlier so eager to shoot it out with police, handed over his weapon and sheepishly surrendered.[21]

Michael Christopher Kehoe, born April 1, 1865, left his home in County Clare, Ireland, to join his two brothers in Memphis at the age of eighteen. He worked at a cotton compress and grain elevator before joining the police department, where he "pounded a beat" for fifteen years before earning a series of promotions. He made hundreds of arrests, but only fired his pistol once, and then it was only to wound a fleeing suspect who fired on him first. His stern expression, powerful voice, and six-foot-two-inch and two-hundred-and-forty-pound frame had a way of convincing most criminals to give up peacefully. Those who resisted did not do so for long. Kehoe readily took down tough guys with nothing more than a hickory nightstick or, in some cases, his bare fists.[22]

Few cops were as honest as Kehoe. Overworked and underpaid policemen frequently took small bribes to turn a blind eye to restaurants, grocery stores, and pool halls where people bought liquor. The proprietors grew overconfident after a time and carelessly conducted transactions in the open. The mayor would receive complaints and would in turn order periodic campaigns on businesses that sold liquor.

Kehoe, on September 17, 1924, chastised his patrolmen at roll call, "You don't have to arrest the whole town to put the fear of the law in the hearts of bootleggers and vagrants. Use a little horse sense and occasionally you'll find your shillelaghs are for [something] other than ornamental purposes." That night, Kehoe walked alone into a dive in the Greasy Plank section of the Fort Pickering neighborhood in South Memphis. Silence fell in the room when the customers saw the sergeant standing in the door with a cigar clenched in his teeth and a billy club in his right hand. After a moment of hesitation, the crowd bolted for the rear exit, knocking the door off its hinges. They hoped to escape but instead found a contingent of police officers waiting to capture them in the alley. Over the next four days, Kehoe and his men arrested over a hundred people and smashed to pieces every place they raided.[23]

Despite the best efforts, weekend raids had little effect. Most bootleggers simply appeared en masse in court Monday morning and paid fines at what Judge Clifford Davis called the "club rate." Once released, they resumed bootlegging. They saw fines more as a minor business expense than a deterrent.

· · ·

Improperly worded or executed search warrants became the bane of law enforcement following United States Supreme Court rulings in *Amos v. the United States* and *Gouled v. the United States*. Search warrants stood up in about one out of every ten cases, and judges, regardless of personal opinions, had to rule out any evidence obtained without proper documentation. "Spectacular raids do not mean anything in these days of legal technicalities when nobody but the proverbial Philadelphia lawyer can draw up a flawless search warrant," complained a reporter. "A lot of whiskey may be seized and destroyed, but in most cases the bootlegger only loses his liquor and not his liberty."[24]

Lawyers routinely attacked the validity of search warrants after Judge Ross dismissed a case against bootlegger Caesar Cattaneo in December 1921. Attorney Thomas J. Walsh seized upon the opportunity and placed five more cases before the judge with the suggestion that he enter *nolle prosequi*. Police caught John Vaccaro and his son with seven fifty-gallon barrels of liquor in July 1928, but once again made a mess of the paperwork. The frustrated Judge Lewis Fitzhugh complained, "This warrant is clearly invalid. . . . I refuse to hold such cases for the state, only to have my decisions overridden." Fitzhugh declared more than fifty search warrants invalid in his first seven months on the bench.[25]

Fig. 7.6. Cartoonist J. P. Alley portrays justice fainting from shock when the court finally convicts a bootlegger. Caption: THE SHOCK WOULD BE TOO MUCH FOR THE LADY! Courtesy Memphis Room, Memphis Public Library and Information Center.

Sheriff Knight was determined to get around the problem. Deputies raided the largest moonshine operation since the beginning of Prohibition near Pidgeon Roost Road in August 1922 and arrested gangsters Herbert Green and Charles Walter Costello. Knight knew he could not hold them without a warrant, so he added the charge of "threatening a breach of the peace." The charge, first used by county sheriff Mike Tate, resulted after the Tennessee Supreme Court, in *State v. Reichman* (1916), interpreted "breach of peace" to include the violation of any law enacted to preserve peace and good order. The court in 1913 deemed the sale of liquor a nuisance and, by definition, a breach of the peace. These decisions allowed the sheriff to arrest without a warrant anyone taking part in the unlawful sale, actual or threatened, of liquor and hold the person in custody without bond until he determined that the threat to the peace passed.[26]

Frustrated by the search warrant problem, police found other ways to mete out punishment. In February 1927, Judge Clifford Davis, after releasing five liquor and gambling violators because police did not have search warrants, told the arresting patrolmen, "If you officers were to go back to their place, break up things, slam bottles around, and accidentally hit them over the head, I wouldn't say a word." Inspector Kehoe said after raids on the Memphitenn Club and Bob Berryman's Idle Social Club that if police could not stop the violations, his men would destroy everything in the places. The damage officers caused far exceeded any fines, as they routinely smashed liquor containers and gambling apparatuses as well as furniture, windows, and fixtures.[27]

Prohibition agents also had difficulties with search warrants. On February 8, 1933, W. R. Wright led a raid on the Walnut Grove Road farm of twenty-six-year-old Pete Lenti, searched the property, and followed the smell of whiskey to a secret entrance behind a feed bin in the barn. He opened it and followed a stairwell fifteen feet down into a ninety square-foot underground room. There he found two vaults filled with 4,150 gallons of liquor worth $50,000. It was the biggest cache of liquor seized in the county.[28]

Lenti faced a possible ten-year sentence and a $10,000 fine, but his lawyer, Clarence Friedman, argued that the agents' tip and observations were not enough to justify a search. The case came before United States commissioner Lester Brenner. For much of the history of the federal courts until the Federal Magistrates Act of 1968, commissioners assisted federal judges and provided the federal government with local officers to support the enforcement of specific laws. Citing a recent and similar US Supreme Court case, Brenner agreed with Friedman and dismissed the case against Lenti. One simple error cost the Prohibition Bureau its biggest catch.[29]

· · ·

Corruption and lack of enthusiasm for Prohibition plagued the lower ranks of law enforcement. With the incredible profits from bootlegging, criminals found they could corrupt deputies and police to an extent never before considered possible. Low-paid officers sometimes allowed suspects to escape or simply ignored moonshine operations in exchange for money.

In September 1921, H. P. Childress complained to Sheriff Perry about moonshiners "running full blast" near his home by the Nonconnah Creek.

Perry ordered Deputies Palmer and Goswick to raid the operation. The two delivered the captured still to the courthouse, but their lack of prisoners raised suspicions. Rumors circulated that Anderson Wallace and Joe Robilio had paid Palmer, Goswick, and Perry's nephew Stratton Barboro to "look the other way" from their $6,000 operation that produced a 140-proof "double-distilled, triple-kick variety of white mule."[30]

Childress had Mose Jones, an African American man who worked on his farm, appear before the Public Safety Committee, a group of Memphis Chamber of Commerce members investigating corruption, and a federal grand jury. According to Jones, who acted as a paid guide for the raiders, Wallace and Robilio seemed to know the deputies. One bootlegger turned to leave but stopped and asked to retrieve some clothes left behind. The deputy replied, "Come on get your clothes and beat it."[31]

The grand jury indicted Wallace along with Goswick, Palmer, and Barboro. Perry suspended the deputies pending the conclusion of the investigation, though he believed them innocent. Meanwhile, Jones mysteriously disappeared before the trial, leading to rumors of foul play and the dismissal of the indictment in June 1922.[32]

Dissatisfied with the outcome, Col. Roane Waring and the Public Safety Committee, also known as the Vigilantes, launched an independent investigation. Waring claimed to have hired investigators posing as bootleggers to bribe deputies and police. US district attorney Eugene Murray called the investigation "bunk." He turned the report over to Shelby County attorney general Sam Bates, but the Shelby County Grand Jury threw it out. Undercover Prohibition agent Joe Phillips also posed as a bootlegger and claimed to have bribed the same men. Phillips presented his findings, including an affidavit from bootlegger Velton Green, but again, nothing came of his investigation.[33]

Bribery continued in the Memphis Police Department as well. One night in March 1925, Sgt. C. F. Skillman received an anonymous telephone call from a bootlegger who offered money in exchange for protection. Skillman, unlike his predecessor Claude Duvall, turned down the offer. A few days later, patrolman W. O. McGaha approached Skillman on behalf of the bootlegger. Skillman again refused the bribe and reported the incident to his superiors. Two police board trials reviewed the charges but acquitted McGaha due to the lack of evidence.[34]

The Beale Street beat was a plum for police officers on the take. Prohibition ended the neighborhood's "free-swinging, big-money, wide-open days," but it did not stop drinking and other vices. Places like the Grey Mule, Red

Front, Midway, Pee Wee's, and the Hole in the Ground offered half-pints of moonshine for twenty-five cents. Both white and black bootleggers operated surreptitiously from soft drink stands, grocery stores, garages, and on the street. They paid "regular and ample" bribes to patrolmen to allow them to conduct their business.[35]

Internal investigators found a payoff book found during a raid on a Fourth Street joint in the fall of 1923. The book went to the police identification bureau for photographic duplication, but according to Sgt. Mario Chiozza, officials did not pursue the case. Police again quietly filed away another payoff book found in July 1926. Investigators had no way to prove who wrote the entries or that the payoffs occurred. Officials knew the public would not understand that they could never substantiate the authenticity of the books and use them as evidence, so they made it a point to keep the books secret.[36]

Corruption, legalities, and the sheer scope of Prohibition wore heavily on law enforcement. Bootlegging flourished and public confidence began to fade despite the best efforts of its most respected members. Few believed Prohibition would succeed after bootlegging peaked in the mid-1920s. Malcolm Patterson said, "The illicit distiller and dispenser must be followed to their lair." Like most Prohibition supporters, he had no idea how many lairs existed or what it would cost to find them.[37]

8

EQUALITY BEFORE THE LAW

Equality before the law is probably forever unattainable. It is a noble
ideal, but it can never be realized, for what men value in this world is
not rights but privileges.

—H. L. Mencken

The doctrine of equality before the law, as enshrined in the Fourteenth
Amendment to the US Constitution, states that all persons, regardless of
wealth, social status, or political power, are to be treated the same before
the law. The Eighteenth Amendment explicitly applied to all citizens of the
United States, but in practice, law enforcement often allowed those with
power and influence to skirt the law. Case after case of favoritism towards the
wealthy fed into growing resentment and led many to not only lose respect
for Prohibition but to question its validity.[1]

Wealthy Memphians often bought their alcohol from exclusive liquor
rings. Clerks in downtown offices took orders by telephone, from numbers
that changed every few weeks, and sent couriers from secret warehouses
to make deliveries. Well-dressed, well-mannered young men or women arrived discreetly at designated times with bonded liquor or wines of choice,
smuggled into the country through New Orleans or ports on the East Coast.[2]

Society bootleggers typically avoided the attention of law enforcement, but
on March 28, 1928, police raiders stumbled onto one such operation in the
Caradine Building in the heart of the business district. The third floor, listed
as vacant in the city directory, had over ten offices devoted to taking liquor
orders. Officers arrested Dave Walsh, the office manager, and confiscated over
150 sales slips with dates, names, and addresses of customers including bank-
ers, physicians, club men, society women, and one dry-crusading evangelist.[3]

Fig. 8.1. Memphians resented that law enforcement seemed to allow the wealthy access to alcohol as seen in this cartoon by J. P. Alley. Caption: THE POOR FISH! Courtesy Memphis Room, Memphis Public Library and Information Center.

Memphis police chief Will Lee promised to arrest the ringleader and his customers. Lee received a barrage of phone calls that night from people begging him to "have a heart" and keep their names out of the press. One club woman pleaded, "Please don't let anyone have my name or learn about it being on the list. If my husband finds out, he will leave me!"[4]

Lee intended to pursue the case despite the pleas, but commissioner Clifford Davis and city attorney Tyler McLain had second thoughts. McLain, who initially supported Lee, changed his mind during the night. McLain said, "In the opinion of the grand jury, the alleged evidence that a bootlegger had been catering to a superior class of Memphians with superior booze was not even established from the body of all of the proof."[5]

Davis and McLain ordered police to stop the investigation after their raid on the ring's warehouse and their arrest of delivery drivers Miles Mason and Joe Alderson. The Memphis Protestant Pastors' Association "earnestly requested" that McLain question the bootlegger's customers. The pastors also pointed out the hypocrisy of keeping the names secret while readily publicizing the names of policemen from the 1927 Belluomini bribery scandal. Davis and McLain ignored complaints, closed ranks with the upper crust, and dropped the case. Memphians could hardly miss the blatant favoritism in the handling of what the newspapers facetiously called the "Booze-Who List."[6]

• • •

In October 1929, police arrested William Taylor "Billy" Overton after the car he drove collided with another vehicle, killing fifty-four-year-old salesman Joseph Harris Martin. The seventeen-year-old cousin of Mayor Watkins Overton and scion of a wealthy founding family had a history of arrests for reckless driving but never faced any serious charges until now. Detective Sgt. Milbourn A. Hinds interviewed thirty-four witnesses, some of whom stated Overton and companions were racing another car at a speed in excess of fifty miles per hour. Others claimed they smelled whiskey in the car, and one witness saw a broken bottle and another smaller bottle filled with liquor.[7]

"His report speaks for itself. The blame is placed squarely on Overton," said Clifford Davis, who praised the detective's "thorough, complete, and conscientious investigation." Overton's case had a preliminary hearing in Judge Lewis Fitzhugh's court before it went to the Shelby County Grand Jury. The grand jury reviewed the evidence and returned a bill charging Overton with reckless driving, driving while intoxicated, and second-degree murder, which carried a sentence of twenty to thirty years in the state penitentiary.[8]

Overton's defense attorney Charles Bryan said the boy was innocent and claimed Martin caused the accident because he ran the stop sign. Witnesses at the trial, including the mayor, said Overton had not been drinking or speeding. A porter told of mixing highballs for Overton and his friends, and Overton admitted to having a "teaspoon" of liquor in a soft drink to be social. He was quoted as saying, "Mother, I had one little drink at three o'clock, and that's all."[9]

Judge Lewis Fitzhugh called the proceedings a "mock trial." The mayor, the attorney general, and the assistant attorney general, Will Gerber, pressured Fitzhugh to dismiss Overton's case during the preliminary hearings, but Fitzhugh refused and sent the case to the Shelby County Grand Jury. Even so, the case disintegrated charge by charge as McLain and Gerber deliberately threw the trial. Gerber told the jury after the opening statements, "The state has failed to prove the boy was intoxicated when the crash occurred. It will not be necessary for you to consider this angle of the case." McLain and Gerber then excluded relevant witnesses, and at the end of testimony, McLain reduced the second-degree murder charge to involuntary manslaughter. McLain secretly asked Judge Tom Harsh to drop the remaining charge of reckless driving, while publicly blaming the jury for not convicting Overton.[10]

The jury deliberated for over sixteen hours before reaching a unanimous decision as required by state law. They took seven ballots before the holdout jurors relented and voted to acquit Overton of manslaughter. His joyous supporters escorted the teenager out of the courthouse to the family's chauffeur, who whisked him away from reporters. Bryan said, "The verdict will set at rest a lot of misconceptions concerning the accident, particularly the popular misconception that Billy was drunk." The jury foreman, clearly prejudiced, said, "I would have stayed in that box until Christmas before I'd convicted that boy."[11]

• • •

"I did make home brew. There's no denying it. What else was I to do? Starve?" said Emma Knoll. The seventy-eight-year-old woman worked for a harness maker for fourteen years until her manager fired her after her eyesight began to fail. She made home brew beer, based on an old family recipe, to supplement the meager income her infirm husband made from his Mississippi Boulevard shoe shop. One day in the summer of 1929, a customer, impressed by the quality of her beer, asked if she would start brewing for him. Knoll gladly took up the offer, and the man paid her two dollars a day—one dollar for every twenty-six bottles she made.[12]

Knoll's friends raised the fifty dollars to pay her fine following her first arrest in July 1929, but they could not help her when police arrested her again. She admitted her crime and told the judge that she did it because she was too old to work and too proud to beg. The judge ignored Knoll's offer to work off the fine by cleaning or washing windows and sentenced her to 140 days in the county jail. From her cell, Knoll pulled her threadbare shawl around her shoulders and told a reporter in October, "Rich folks make all the beer or wine they want, but the police have to go pestering and jailing an old woman who isn't bootlegging and who was only trying to help her old man."[13]

• • •

Fig. 8.2. Cartoonist J. P. Alley portrayed the attitude of many of the wealthy towards prohibition. Caption: DENIAL OF DEMOCRACY. Courtesy of Memphis Room, Memphis Public Library and Information Center.

Officers Pat Cox and S. J. Newman pulled over a car driven by a fifty-three-year-old man in the company of two young women at the corner of Summer Avenue and East Parkway at 3:40 a.m. on May 13, 1936. The officers, after a brief struggle, took the trio to the police station and charged them with drunk driving, disorderly conduct, and profanity. The man gave the desk sergeant the phony name of "John Smith" to protect his identity. One woman, who was married, "almost went into hysterics" when the police matron asked her name. She calmed down once she realized she could give an alias. "John Smith" put up a bond for both women, but neither appeared on the appointed court date.[14]

A reporter found that "John Smith" was the prominent Leonard Palmer Janes Sr., president of the Memphis Furniture Manufacturing Company. The reporter asked why officers allowed Janes to use an alias. Commissioner Davis explained that police had to take any name given by an arrestee, but the desk sergeant could insert a prisoner's real name as an alias if he knew it.[15]

A jury made up of leading businessmen took pity on Janes and voted to ignore the charges. A reporter called the blatant show of favoritism a "blot on justice." Dissention broke out among the jury, and foreman J. Thomas Wellford called the action "the most palpably flagrant miscarriage of justice which has come under my observation in my service of seven years as foreman of the Shelby County Grand Jury."[16]

Jury member Ike Gronauer, vice president of the Memphis Paper Company, disagreed and believed Wellford's comments out of order. Wellford relented after some closed-door meetings. Gronauer told reporters, "We replied to this criticism, but everything had been patched up, and now we are just one big peaceful family." Wellford, perhaps not quite so peaceful or patched up, declined to comment further.[17]

• • •

Memphians typically abided by the Jim Crow laws that kept the races separate; however, their attitude changed when it came to liquor. They did not care who made their liquor. Blacks sold liquor to whites, and whites sold liquor to blacks. Considering this outlook, it would appear that race had less of an impact on bootlegging than bootlegging had on race. Bootleggers and their customers disregarded social conventions regarding race whenever it was expedient. Simply put, among drinkers in Memphis, Jim Crow was less important than John Barleycorn.

This attitude, however, did not extend to the enforcement of Prohibition. Here, the treatment of African Americans epitomized inequity in the legal system. They faced discrimination, abuse, and a lack of effective legal representation. Humiliation, extortion, and disregard for due process made the enforcement of the Volstead Act no more than a thinly veiled attempt to victimize those already suffering under institutionalized racism.

Judge Clifford Davis felt "compelled to step outside the law" to vent his frustration after he had to release six African American bootleggers because the arresting officers did not have search warrants. He decided to pick on a young man whose only crime was sitting in the bootleggers' car. Davis ordered John Williams, a light-complexioned young man with a pompadour, to rake his fingers through his hair in front of the court or pay a fifty-dollar vagrancy fine. Williams reluctantly complied, ripping through the enamel finish and making a mess of his carefully coiffed hair. Williams left the courtroom humiliated with "hopelessly mussed hair," to the amusement of Davis and the others. "That nigger would rather have paid fifty dollars!" laughed Davis.[18]

"Fee-grabbing," in the guise of Prohibition and antigambling enforcement, allowed sheriff's deputies and constables to extort money from the poor, especially African Americans. Deputies made Saturday night raids of large gatherings to arrest as many people as possible. Justices of the peace rendered guilty verdicts for the weakest offenses, charged exorbitant fees instead of jail terms, and funneled the money to the arresting deputies.[19]

Former Memphis mayor Harry Litty complained to the City Club in 1924, "More damnable Bolshevism is practiced in Memphis today in the form of raids by deputy sheriffs and constables on innocent Negroes for the sake of fees than any other place of which I know." He pointed out that during a recent raid, deputies arrested 120 black people at dance, but allowed the only one with whiskey to escape. Each arrestee had to pay the deputies $5.90, the same amount they would have paid in court costs.[20]

Sheriff Knight promised to "put a stop to the wholesale raids of Negroes and ignorant whites on flimsy charges." He threatened to fire deputies working in the courts if they did not leave all "criminal business" to his staff and police. Three months later, Knight fired five deputies working for squire Rudy Strehl, including the squire's son C. J. Strehl, after they forced roadhouse owner Harry Kiersky to give them money in exchange for the release of over thirty African American men detained after a raid. A year later, Knight fired deputies John Wortham and Roy Land after a black man complained about being beaten during a fee grab.[21]

Knight reigned in fee grabbing among deputies, but the practice persisted among constables. In 1929, Judge Clarence Friedman, Clifford Davis's former opponent, attacked the practice after Jesse Coleman, an African American man arrested in a fee-grabbing raid, died after he jumped from a truck carrying prisoners. Friedman called the constables "leeches preying on working Negroes" and said, "Ninety percent of the arrests made by constables are illegal and are made for the sole purpose of wresting fees from working men."[22]

African Americans were often deprived of due process and faced punishments greater than white counterparts. Wilson Polk waited in the county jail twenty-one days for his court date following his arrest by patrolman H. S. Vincent. Judge Tom Harsh, shocked at the man's treatment, ordered a verdict of not guilty and scolded Vincent in court, "There ought to be some means of redress for this Negro. . . . You had no excuse for holding [him]."[23]

Harry Anderson, a federal judge, showed unusual leniency on a black doctor found guilty of selling morphine without a prescription to addicts. In a move supported by Bishop Thomas Gailor, he placed Dr. Anderson Ross on probation, explaining, "I would not even consider probation for this man if it were not for a case of gross miscarriage of justice during the same term of court in which Ross was convicted. A white physician with a much less plausible story was acquitted by the same jury which convicted Ross."[24]

Anderson expressed thorough disgust with Prohibition agents' efforts. He criticized them for "fooling away time with half-pint cases" and imposing on the juror's time. In a rebuke following the acquittal of Richard Harris (also known as Pete Flemon) charged with selling whiskey to Prohibition agent Ralph Kitts, Anderson ordered, "Hereafter, when a poor, hardworking Negro is brought in on charges of selling a half-pint of whiskey, and the evidence against him is so thin you can see through it, acquit him without deliberation."[25]

Actions taken by Judges Harsh and Anderson were rare; most African Americans involved in Prohibition cases did not fare so well. Judge Fitzhugh fined Floyd Goodman, umpire for the Memphis Red Sox, the Negro leagues team in Memphis, thirty-five dollars simply for watching a liquor raid through a peephole in a fence in September 1934. He then took out his wrath on another defendant, Henry McDaniel, who Fitzhugh said looked "sleek and well-fed." The judge told McDaniel, "You look like a bootlegger. Bet you have a Lincoln and a Cadillac." When McDaniel hesitated, Fitzhugh ordered the clerk to fine him twenty-five dollars.[26]

Most Prohibition cases involved only a small amount of liquor, a half-pint or maybe a pint, but fines of twenty-five or fifty dollars were heavy burdens for working-class people who only earned a few dollars a day. Every case like this further exposed the hypocrisy of the law. Stories of the rich and influential avoiding punishment while the working class and poor paid dearly for the smallest infractions added fuel to the growing resentment for Prohibition.

9

LOOPHOLES

So Memphis is to have a new brand of harmless grape juice, unless
some careless individuals forget to keep it cool and it ferments.
—*Press-Scimitar*, August 17, 1931

Prohibitionists had the straightforward goal of ridding the country, and
eventually the world, of alcohol; however, the Volstead Act left enough
loopholes that it opened the door to various schemes to evade the law.
Lawmakers allowed certain exceptions to the law to settle medical, religious,
and property concerns, but these exceptions, in the end, only complicated
and confused enforcement. They resulted in continued alcohol production,
disregard for the law, and a health crisis.

The Prohibition law allowed pharmacists to dispense whiskey by prescription for any number of ailments, ranging from anxiety to influenza. Medicinal alcohol, once scoffed at by the American Medical Association, became big
business because of Prohibition. Patients could buy a prescription for three
dollars, take it to a local pharmacy, and go home with a pint of liquor every
ten days. Some pharmacists did not even bother with prescriptions and sold
alcohol surreptitiously. Memphis pharmacist S. F. Levy sold whiskey, Jamaica
Ginger, and other alcoholic "medicines" without a permit for months before
his arrest in July 1924.[1]

Another loophole allowed for personal winemaking, as long as the maker
did not sell any. Although not as popular as moonshine or home brew, wine
played a significant part in the illegal alcohol trade in Memphis. Police confiscated 200 gallons of elderberry wine in raids in October 1926. The following
year, police arrested Angelo Carono for possession of 44 bottles of raisin wine
in March, and they arrested Frank Belluomini in July for possession of over

20 gallons of wine. Police raided Annie Colucci's house in April 1928 and seized 150 gallons of wine after a man complained that he had been robbed of $300 after he passed out during a party.[2]

The general public, however, found wine difficult to make. Grocers began offering canned grape juice concentrate in 1922, but as one grocer explained, "The trouble was, no one got good results. I couldn't tell them how to make wine; it was against the law." P. Leon Goodwin, a sales representative for a grape juice company, faced liquor charges for selling wine in August 1926. The charge stemmed from a neighbor who complained, not of Goodwin making wine, but rather, that Goodwin swindled him by selling him wine so weak that it was little more than grape juice.[3]

The popularity of winemaking spiked in the summer of 1930 because of newly available ingredients and information on fermentation. Merchants, forbidden to sell materials for use in the manufacture of alcohol, found they could skirt the law by simply posting signs that warned buyers not to use supplies for illegal alcoholic beverage production. Even more laughable were the US Department of Agriculture brochures circulated explaining how to avoid fermentation in making grape juice. A reporter noted, "The bulletin, which is being circulated downtown, shows most of the operations used in making wines and is filled pictures of operations that might as well apply to home brew manufacture as to innocent grape juice making."[4]

US district attorney Lindsay Phillips and deputy Prohibition administrator Finis Wilson tried to reign in home brew beer and wine by cracking down on the sales of kegs, corks, bottles, malt, and other supplies. Phillips hoped the US Supreme Court ruling in May 1930 would allow the prosecution of these merchants, but as attorney Charles Bryan pointed out, it was not illegal for a person to make beer or wine for home consumption. Wilson realized the futility of controlling home wine-making after the ruling in June 1930 reaffirmed the rights of merchants to sell the supplies. He shrugged off the disappointing news and said that his men had too much work anyway "damming up the sources of the moonshine liquor supply to spend much time on the malt shops."[5]

• • •

Prohibition laws allowed for the sacramental use of alcohol, but requests often met with confusion and suspicion. Rabbi Joseph Reich, a Hungarian immigrant and grocer, appealed to Elwood Hamilton, collector of internal revenue, to release a barrel of brandy for use among his Memphis congregation in November 1919. The rabbi claimed that he intended to distribute enough to each male member of his congregation to perform the required sacraments at home. It was the first request for alcohol from the government bonded warehouse following the Wartime Prohibition Act of 1918, which, along with the Lever Act of August 1917, banned distilled spirits production for the remainder of the war to reserve supplies of grain for food production. Hamilton, unsure of how to proceed, wrote to the commissioner of the Internal Revenue Service Daniel Roper for a ruling.[6]

Brandy, specifically plum brandy or slivovitz, became popular among European Jews out of religious necessity. For poor eighteenth- and nineteenth-century Jews, wine was an expensive import in the non-wine-growing regions of Central and Eastern Europe and thus not always available. Rabbis addressed this problem with the *chamar medina*, or "drink of the land." This law allows observant Jews to use local beverages for sacramental purposes in the absence of wine.[7]

It was a legitimate request from the rabbi, but Roper refused to help even though the Wartime Prohibition Act allowed him to make modifications to meet the needs of a particular case. The suspicious Roper maintained the law only permitted wine for sacramental purposes. In February 1922, the Prohibition commissioner reaffirmed the stand on brandy, but in April, a District of Columbia justice ruled that rabbis could use brandy.[8]

Section 6 of the Volstead Act allowed Jews free exercise of religion and aligned the law with religious custom, but by the first Passover, it had already gone terribly wrong. Instead of enhancing Jewish life, it facilitated illegal activities both by Jews and in the name of Jews. The law allowed ten gallons for every adult per year, so as a result, congregations grew as a much as ten times. More problems in enforcement arose because there was no official way to determine who was a rabbi, so people who claimed to be rabbis would get licenses to distribute to nonexistent congregations.[9]

Prohibition agents in Memphis arrested members of three Jewish merchant families in July 1925 for illegally selling wine. They took into custody members of the Rosen, Cohen, and Minor families after agent M. R. Wimmer posed as a buyer and bought wine at ten dollars a gallon from their North Main Street markets. The agents raided the stores and seized 1,375 gallons of wine and fortified wine from the stores.[10]

Attorneys argued about the fate of the wine over the next several months. Attorney Dave Puryear asked John J. Gore, a federal judge, to return confiscated wine. He maintained that Rabbi George Bacarai authorized the merchants' purchases and had the legal right to give it to his congregation.

Gore knew nothing of the allowance for sacramental wine and wanted it destroyed.[11]

Meanwhile, the Baron Hirsch Congregation notified district attorney Eugene Murray that they had no part in the dealings and did not claim ownership of the wine. Judge Harry Anderson fined the merchants for their violations in the following term and ordered the return of wine to the John G. Dorn bonded warehouse in Sandusky, Ohio, where the now former Rabbi Bacarai and the merchants originally purchased it.[12]

• • •

Emanuel Dreyfous made the mistake of telling his friends about his alcohol collection. He could keep it because of a loophole in the Volstead Act that allowed him to keep what he had purchased in the years preceding Prohibition. The thirty-seven-year-old New Orleans native worked at his father's store Dreyfous and Company in New Orleans, Maison Blanche in New Orleans, Cohens in Richmond, Virginia, and Kaufman's in Pittsburgh, before coming to Memphis. He came from a wealthy family, attended Tulane University, where he played football, and enjoyed deep-sea fishing and hunting. His expertise in his field made him popular among department stores, and his parties made him even more popular among employees.[13]

Earl P. Flood, a superintendent for the prominent Memphis department store Bry's, heard Dreyfous brag about his liquor collection. Flood knew he could make a small fortune selling it if he could only think of a way to steal it. Dreyfous, as treasurer at Lowenstein's department store in Memphis, occasionally traveled to New York City on business, but a maid stayed at his house at 1689 Overton Park. For added security, he also hired the store detective B. C. Carter to watch his place.

Unknown to Dreyfous and the management of Lowenstein's, the fifty-year-old store detective had a criminal record. Working as a private detective in New York, Carter tried to blackmail a New Jersey dentist and a woman with whom he had an affair. The plan backfired, resulting in Carter's arrest. A judge sentenced Carter to serve three months in jail and pay a $1,000 fine on June 5, 1918. Carter moved to Memphis after his release and became a department store detective.

Flood found out about Carter and began badgering the detective until Carter reluctantly agreed to help him steal the liquor. During the night of April 1, 1922, they entered the home through a lattice door to the rear porch, went down to the basement, and pried open the closet that held Dreyfous's

Fig. 9.1. Samuel O. Bates. Courtesy of Memphis Room,
Memphis Public Library and Information Center.

collection. They took three boxes and several bottles upstairs to Flood's car
and took them to Carter's apartment at 262 Madison.

Two days later, Clarence Turley, a superintendent at Lowenstein's department store, telephoned Carter on behalf of Dreyfous, who was still out of
town. The cook had reported that she noticed some suspicious characters
in the yard. She did not want the stay in the house alone out of fear that
someone would break in, so Dreyfous had Turley call Carter to watch the
place again. Carter returned to the house, and over the next two days, he and
Flood stole the remainder of Dreyfous's collection.

The greedy Flood now had over three hundred quarts of alcohol, valued
at $6,000. He realized that he needed to get the stolen goods out of his house
or risk discovery by the police. Desperate for hiding places, he moved most
of the liquor into the Bry's shipping room and moved the last two cases to
Carter's house several days later.

In the meantime, Dreyfous discovered the break-in and called the police.
Inspector Will Griffin suspected Carter and ordered detectives to watch his

apartment. The detectives found some empty liquor bottles in the garbage can, so they raided the apartment and found the two cases of stolen liquor. Carter confessed to the crime and implicated Flood. Distraught, he told the detectives that he was ruined. He reached for a handgun and tried to kill himself, but Griffin wrestled the pistol from Carter before he could pull the trigger. After pleading guilty, Flood received a sentence in the Shelby County Workhouse and Carter received a sentence in the state penitentiary.[14]

The fate of Dreyfous's coveted liquor left the courts in a quandary as lawyers argued over the nuances of overlapping liquor laws. Dreyfous believed he had the legal right to his liquor because the Volstead Act allowed him to transport it from his previous home in Pittsburgh, Pennsylvania, but Shelby County attorney general Sam Bates argued that, under the state Prohibition law, Dreyfous could not move liquor across the state line. Attorneys Auvergne Williams and Clarence Friedman filed a writ of replevin, and Dreyfous paid a $600 bond, but Bates ordered Sheriff Perry not to return the liquor. The case dragged on for months in chancery court until Dreyfous gave up in February 1923. He took a job in Salt Lake City, Utah, and left his liquor in the custody of the sheriff. Williams and Friedman dropped the case once their client left, and the court never reached a decision. The fate of the liquor remained in limbo, as well as the issue of legal rights of owners of pre-Volstead liquor.[15]

. . .

Writers of the Volstead Act made exemptions to accommodate the growing need for industrial alcohol. This included such products as colognes, cleaning supplies, and fuel. The Prohibition Unit provided manufacturers with instructions to add toxins to their alcohol to discourage people from drinking it. Even so, it was not enough to deter the most desperate alcoholics.

In September 1922, police arrested twenty-two-year-old Sam Wardell after calls from neighbors. Officers found a bottle of wood alcohol about two-thirds empty and Wardell nearly blind and in the throes of alcohol poisoning. They rushed the young man to the General Hospital, where doctors pumped his stomach. After four hours of intense treatment, Wardell spent the rest of the night in the jail, hoping to recover his eyesight. Doctors treated more cases of alcohol poisoning, including eighty-two-year-old Mattie O'Neal two weeks later and James Draggon in December after someone found him unconscious in a Sunday school room at Central Baptist Church.[16]

The Sterno Company created the alcohol-based jellied fuel Canned Heat as a means to heat food for cooking outside a traditional kitchen and advertised it as "The magic fuel that is solving the cooking problems of millions of people." Hobos and poor alcoholics sometimes resorted to straining the fuel through cheesecloth or a sock and mixing it with fruit juice to make what they called "jungle juice" or "sock wine." Police in April 1927 found two men and a woman lying unconscious in a vacant house on Huling after a "canned heat party." Later that month, police found seventy-three-year-old Harry McFeterich dead from drinking Canned Heat in his North Second Street boarding house.[17]

The down-and-out drunks who lived by the Mississippi River had a notorious reputation for drinking denatured alcohol, commonly called "derail." Police referred to them as the Willow Gang because of the trees that grew from the willow mats engineers used to minimize erosion along the riverfront. In 1934, police began to crack down on the gang after its leader, fifty-three-year-old Robert Malone, nearly died from knife wounds inflicted by a rival. Judge Lewis Fitzhugh ordered police to run several members out of town and the remainder of the gang began to disperse in the wake of drives to rid the city of vagrants, prostitutes, and other undesirables.[18]

Willow Gang member Clint Murray had the distinction of the city's most arrested man. Murray spent three-quarters of his life incarcerated because of charges relating to drinking denatured alcohol and vagrancy. Fitzhugh took pity on Murray in January 1930, took up a collection for the vagabond, and allowed him to leave town rather than serve more time in the workhouse. Murray promised to change his ways and headed for Nashville. He sold some chickens and eggs but spent most of his time panhandling. He soon tired of Nashville and returned to Memphis in April, where police arrested him again.[19]

Murray, who spent time in hospitals recovering from alcohol-related illness, complained to reporter Eldon Roark, "Now you take the 'Legacy Hospital' [Pellagra Hospital], once in a while they'll have a good meal when they kill a calf or something, but even then they'll cook turnips and spoil it. Besides, it's so full of broken-down sick people that a fellow can't enjoy himself." Murray found that the city hospital offered the best meals of red beans, fat meat, and cornbread, but complained that they chased him out after he recovered. He liked the doctors and nurses but recommended avoiding the "gouging" interns who insisted on conducting medical examinations. He found the city jail clean but crowded and in need of recreation like cards, dominoes, or pool tables, and he liked the new Shelby County Workhouse but complained about the staff's insistence that he take a bath.[20]

Police continued to arrest Murray on a regular basis for vagrancy, disorderly conduct, and drunkenness. He complained about his treatment by police but eventually ran out of excuses for not getting a job and promised to give up drinking. The man Eldon Roark called "wood alcohol connoisseur and institutions expert" died July 1, 1932. The coroner gave the cause of death as kidney failure, but noted under the heading of contributing causes "wood alcohol, bay rum, and anything he owned to drink."[21]

· · ·

Poisonings were not limited to drinking denatured alcohol. One of the worst cases occurred in 1928 when three people died from drinking moonshine laced with ammonia. Police arrested bootlegger P. F. Frazier and his accomplices Stella Stublefield and J. C. Carter after I. J. Burleson became violently ill after drinking their liquor. While on bond in April 1928, the unrepentant Frazier sold more tainted liquor to one man who became seriously ill and three others who died.[22]

Unskilled newcomers took advantage of the power vacuum and flooded the market with improperly made moonshine after the Prohibition Bureau brought down the Liquor Barons. Raids by Prohibition agents made it impossible for them to keep liquor stored for the usual three-month aging period, so they sold it as soon as they made it. An agent explained, "Bootleggers who last year sold aged whiskey and prided themselves on the fact that their product was pure, now are selling booze less than twenty-four hours old."[23]

Under-aged moonshine, commonly called "green hootch," became a source of many health problems. Moonshiners stopped making stills with copper and instead used cheap tin or galvanized iron that caused a toxic chemical reaction. The Prohibition Bureau warned Memphians about the increasingly poisonous liquor after nineteen-year-old Paul Edmiston died after drinking moonshine purchased near the Harahan Bridge in July 1929.[24]

Prohibition agent Finis Wilson discovered an operation near Lake View, Mississippi, that turned out 250 gallons of tainted whiskey per day. Wilson and his men chased down and arrested two twenty-two-year-old men, Earl Howard and Willie Badger, and destroyed their thousand-gallon galvanized metal still. The zinc acetate in the still had poisoned their thousand gallons of beer and seventy-five gallons of whiskey. The men not only faced liquor charges but attempted manslaughter charges for selling the poisonous alcohol.[25]

Bootleggers sometimes unknowingly used toxic agents when coloring liquor. Police raided the Cadillac Inn on Beale Street in February 1927 and found that not only was Frank Liberto filling bottles with liquor, but his assistant John Green was coloring whiskey with embalming fluid in the house behind the building. Officers arrested the two along with the owner George

Mazzetti, but Judge Clifford Davis had to dismiss the charges because the officers did not have a search warrant. It turned out to be an apparently fatal mistake. Floyd Sullivan, cousin of detective Sgt. Larry Fox, died after drinking liquor colored with embalming fluid on April 1, 1929. Police suspected the Beale Street bootleggers of selling him the whiskey but could never prove it.[26]

• • •

Jamaica Ginger extract, known by the slang name "Jake," was a patent medicine for headaches and digestive problems that contained between 70 and 80 percent ethanol by weight. The Prohibition Bureau would have banned Jamaica ginger like most patent medicines, but the makers agreed to add a component that made their product difficult to drink in great amounts. Inspectors insured compliance by periodically testing samples.

A pair of chemists and amateur bootleggers thought they found a way to make Jake drinkable and still pass the Prohibition Bureau's test. With advice from an unwitting Massachusetts Institute of Technology professor, Harry Gross and Max Reisman of Hub Products in Boston used a plasticizer called tricresyl phosphate, or TOCP. Believing the new ingredient nontoxic, they produced over six hundred thousand bottles of Jamaica Ginger with the new additive. The shipments passed inspection, and the company began distributing it throughout the South and Midwest.

The TOCP was in fact extremely hazardous. Medical authorities faced a health crisis after hospitals around the county began reporting cases of paralysis in February 1930. Doctors, unaware of the TOCP, knew Jake caused the illnesses, but they did not know why. The acting Prohibition director for Tennessee and Kentucky, Ernest Rowe, moved quickly to seize shipments of Jamaica Ginger that made it into the Mid-South. He traced the Jake to a distributer in Kentucky that supplied companies in Memphis, Dyersburg, and Halls, Tennessee.[27]

Dr. Andrew Richard Bliss Jr., dean of the University of Tennessee School of Pharmacy, worked with the US Department of Agriculture's Food, Drug, and Insecticide Organization to determine the cause of the paralysis. Bliss tested Jake seized in Corinth, Mississippi, where 150 people had fallen ill. Bliss and his counterparts in Washington found toxins such as isopropyl, creosote, and carbonic acid, but nothing that would cause paralysis.[28]

Five victims suffering from the effects of tainted Jamaica Ginger from West Tennessee and Mississippi arrived at Baptist Hospital in Memphis in late March complaining of weakness and paralysis in their extremities. More victims came in April, but fortunately, their symptoms cleared up within

Fig. 9.2. Jamaica Ginger advertisement. Courtesy of the Library of Congress.

a few weeks. Memphis Health Department food inspector S. L. Hollowell inspected drug companies' inventories and confirmed they had not sold tainted Jake; however, some made it into the city from nearby communities. Doctors treated the city's first victim, G. H. Watson, with glucose and released him soon after. The second victim, a twenty-six-year-old barber named B. P. Glimp, suffered paralysis in his hands and legs.[29]

Victims lost control over the muscles that enabled them to point their toes upward. The condition, known as Jake leg, caused them to raise their feet high with the toes flopping downward, which would touch the pavement first followed by their heels. The toe first, heel second pattern made a distinctive "tap-click, tap-click" known as the Jake walk.

The Prohibition Bureau seized most of the poisoned Jake within a few months, but by that time, it was too late. The contaminated Jake claimed between thirty and fifty thousand victims nationwide. Gross and Reisman went to jail, but the victims received little help and no compensation.[30]

Alcohol-related deaths brought increased criticism of Prohibition. About forty Americans per million died each year from drinking illegal and industrial alcohol. Prohibitionists like Wayne Wheeler had no sympathy. The president of Columbia University, Dr. Nicholas Murray Butler, on the other hand, called the use of denatured alcohol "legalized murder." Comedian Will Rogers commented, "Governments used to murder by the bullet. Now it's by the quart."[31]

That they took advantage of loopholes illustrated Americans' determination to continue drinking. When they could not buy alcohol, they tried to make it. If they could not make it, they used medical practices and religious institutions as ways to get it. When that did not work, they took their chances and drank toxic alcohol. In the end, one has to ask: How could anyone enforce a law that people were willing to risk not only their liberty but injury or death to break?

10

KU KLUX KLAN

> The policy of the Ku Klux Klan would tear down order and substitute
> mob law when there is no occasion for it. It is a menace to the principle
> of Americans and far more dangerous than Bolshevism.
> —Rabbi William Fineshriber[1]

A reporter called the inauguration of Judge Clifford Davis on New Year's
Day 1924 "dramatic and unusual in municipal history." The scents of
floral arrangements and lavish evergreens filled the police courtroom.
Gasper Pappalardo and his orchestra performed as guests arrived. The mayor,
the commissioners, and their wives occupied the front seats, while lawyers,
police, friends, and Davis's political opponents like anti-Klan lawyer Clarence
Friedman filled the seats behind them. Rev. William McDougall, one of the
Klan's official rabble-rousing "spellbinders," led in an audience that included
a "noticeable predominance of Ku Klux Klan leaders." These included county
coroner Needham Taylor Ingram, Clyde Koen, defeated mayoral candidate
W. Joe Wood, and Davis's campaign manager Homer Higgs, who acted as
master of ceremonies.

At 11:10 a.m., Lt. Joseph Cole lifted his hands to signal the audience for
quiet. The orchestra burst forth "Dixie" as city commissioner Thomas Allen led Davis through the crowd. Behind them followed the retiring Judge
Lewis Fitzhugh, Rev. A. U. Boone of First Baptist Church, and other judges
and clerks. Others stood outside to catch a glimpse of the Klan's candidate
taking office.[2]

The Ku Klux Klan, originally founded in Pulaski, Tennessee, in 1865,
laid dormant after Reconstruction until D. W. Griffith's *Birth of a Nation*
inspired William Simmons to revive the organization in 1915. Chapters,

Fig. 10.1. Ku Klux Klan march on Washington, DC, 1926. Courtesy of the
Library of Congress.

called klaverns, formed in every state after Texas dentist Hiram Evans took
control of the Klan in the 1920s and expanded its focus to include attacks
on Jews, Catholics, and immigrants. Casting themselves as defenders of
Anglo-American culture, Klan members enthusiastically supported religious
fundamentalism and Prohibition. Prohibition was so important that the first
official act of Atlanta's powerful Nathan Bedford Forrest Klan Number One
after its inauguration at the October 1919 Confederate reunion was to hold
a giant temperance bonfire celebrating the enactment of the Eighteenth
Amendment to the US Constitution.[3]

Klansmen established a klavern in Memphis in 1921 and by 1923 boasted
having over ten thousand members, mostly in South Memphis between
McLemore and South Parkway, west of the Memphis Fairgrounds to the
neighborhoods of Barksdale, Lenox, and the western part of the Binghamton.

Fig. 10.2. Cartoonist J. P. Alley's depiction of the Ku Klux Klan. Caption: MR. COOLIDGE "SEES" HIM CLEARLY ENOUGH! Courtesy of Memphis Room, Memphis Public Library and Information Center.

As their numbers grew, they set sights on taking over the city. The army of Klansmen stood ready under banners of race, religion, and Prohibition, but they faced determined opposition.[4]

Newspapers and established politicians waged a relentless attack on the Klan in 1923. *Commercial Appeal* editor Charles Patrick Joseph Mooney, a second-generation Irish Catholic, and cartoonist J. P. Alley made such a determined stand that the paper won a Pulitzer Prize. The *News Scimitar* warned that a Klan victory would leave the city "shackled in the chains of intolerance and sacrificed on the altar of un-American hate."[5]

Mayor Rowlett Paine and Ed Crump had little love for one another, but their mutual loathing of the Klan led to a temporary alliance. Election night came, and the Klan acted as predicted. Fist fights broke out, Klan members bullied election officers, and riot alarms went off in fifteen precincts.

A reporter called it "the worst situation with which the police ever had to combat." Even so, the slate of Crump-approved anti-Klan candidates defeated all the Invisible Empire's candidates but Clifford Davis.[6]

Internal strife hastened the Klan's eventual downfall in the city. The Memphis provisional klavern under E. E. Bolin applied for an official charter with the Atlanta headquarters on March 21, 1924, but officials claimed the klavern had not fully kept its contract. During the negotiations, a rift formed when a second klavern under R. H. Causey challenged Bolin.[7]

Four months later, R. D. Jones, a Birmingham deputy, and Rube Ozier, representing imperial wizard James Esdale of Birmingham, came to the Memphis headquarters in the Goodbar Building and demanded the klavern's records. Three Klan members, W. A. Blankenship, H. M. Folsom, and spellbinder Rev. Otis L. Spurgeon, refused, and a fight broke out. Jones pulled a pistol during the melee and fired a bullet that went through the floor and into the office of attorney Pat Lyons. Police arrived and found Jones with one hand around the throat of Blankenship and pistol at his head. Judge Davis, at the insistence of district attorney Sam Bates, held Jones to the grand jury on charges of shooting with the intent to kill.[8]

In May 1925, detective Sgt. Larry Fox and a group of officers broke up a Klan meeting after L. A. Jones and J. A. Goodwin tried to resolve a disagreement with a lead pipe and a knife in a back alley as fellow Klansmen cheered them on. In June, a car driven by Orton Grantham, brother of cyclops Matthew Grantham, broke down in front of the home of M. L. Saunders. Saunders, who had never met Grantham before that night, offered to help Grantham repair his flat tire. Grantham took offense and started a fight with the Good Samaritan. Deputies arrested Grantham for drunkenness and breach of peace, but not before Saunders hit Grantham in the head with a tire pump and "stopped all arguments." Three weeks later, police rescued Orton and a friend from angry gas station attendants who beat the pair as they tried to steal gasoline and a tire.[9]

The Klan, reeling from the election outcomes, launched new attacks on law enforcement in March 1925. Klan candidate Will Taylor filed suit charging voting fraud against county sheriff Will Knight. Cyclops Matthew Grantham, to tarnish Knight's reputation, claimed that deputies John Friddle and A. O. Clark took bribes from bootleggers on President's Island during a recent raid. Grantham and several other Klansmen traveled to Hulbert, Arkansas, in search of a group of African American loggers who were on the island at the time of the raid. The Klansmen posed as government agents to coerce statements to back up their charges.[10]

A woman who claimed to be a relative of the men called Knight's office and told what Grantham and his friends had done. Deputies Charles Garibaldi, James Wilson, and Albert Solari drove to Hulbert to interview the loggers. Meanwhile, Deputies Friddle, Clark, and Leake stormed into the klavern office in the Goodbar Building in search of Grantham. A fight broke out, and Grantham fired a pistol as deputies beat him with blackjacks. They arrested Grantham on charges of shooting with intent to kill, but Knight released him after doctors determined he was too injured to stay in custody. Grantham went home to recover under the watch of armed Klansmen.[11]

Knight tried to quiet rumors about a war between the Klan and the sheriff's department. He stood by his deputies but ordered them to treat all law-abiding citizens with respect regardless of their beliefs. Tensions escalated, however, after Knight dismissed Klan attorney Richard Busby when he found out Busby secretly held a commission as a deputy. The situation worsened when Clark beat up another Klansman, O. W. Rakestraw, in front of a South Memphis grocery.[12]

The Klan, meanwhile, reached out to the sympathizers in the Prohibition Bureau. Agents met with Grantham, Busby, Taylor, and policemen J. P. Crums and J. K. McDaniel at the Hotel Chisca on May 15. They conspired to offer immunity to bootleggers in return for testimony against the police and sheriff's departments. Knight, Commissioner Allen, Chief Burney, and Inspector Griffin learned of the plot in July, confronted the group, and forced them to abandon their plan.[13]

Knight cracked down harder on Klan activity after the meeting. He rounded up Klansmen after they harassed an African American man, Carl McKinney, brother of Cap McKinney, former Beale Street hotel owner, and Charlie McKinney, of the Waldorf Hotel. McKinney's pregnant wife received warnings that a "committee" would punish McKinney for an unnamed offense. Over forty masked Klansmen came to their house one night and demanded to speak to "Mr. McKinney." McKinney assumed the men meant his father and told them he had gone to the dairy where he worked. Once the posse left, McKinney contacted a deputy who lived nearby to ask for help. Knight learned the names of the Klansmen and the location of their Monday night meetings, and then he began making arrests.[14]

Matthew Grantham and fellow Klansman R. B. Thompson tried to block the confirmation of Harry Bennett Anderson as federal judge of the Western District of Tennessee. They filed affidavits claiming that Anderson got drunk at a press dinner and accepted a $10,000 bribe from the "King of the Bootleggers," Nello Grandi. The US Senate, however, dismissed the accusations and confirmed Anderson's nomination in 1926 after receiving recommendations from reputable members of the law enforcement community.[15]

Klansmen had a policy to "help, aid, and assist the duly constituted authorities of the law in the proper performance of their legal duties." Klansmen not only felt they had the right to participate in law enforcement, but they believed they had the right to remove members of law enforcement who did not execute their duties as the Klan saw fit. In June 1926, the "Raiding Parson," Rev. Robert E. Connely, who was pastor of McLemore Avenue Baptist Church, joined E. B. Henson, a Prohibition agent, and Earl Barnard, a vocal antimachine police officer and Klan supporter with political aspirations, in accusing W. R. Wright and M. R. Wimmer of corruption. The agents, frustrated by the lack of support from the bureau, resigned against the wishes of friends. Wright said, "My conscience is clear. I have done nothing wrong. Nothing else matters." US attorney general Eugene Murray, unsatisfied with the evidence presented by Connely, refused to submit the case to a federal grand jury and exonerated Wright.[16]

The Klan, however, was not ready to give up on Wimmer. That night, Grantham and four agents including E. B. Henson and C. J. Wallace arrested Wimmer on Benjestown Road, searched his car, and found a thirty-five-gallon keg of whiskey. Wimmer claimed Knight deputized him and the whiskey was evidence he intended to deliver to the Prohibition Bureau. The sheriff, however, denied the claim.[17]

Prosecutors made the mistake of basing their case against Wimmer on the testimony of A. J. Carroll. Carroll admitted to having taken fourteen sacks from Wimmer's office but claimed not to know what they contained. Anderson lost patience with Carroll, charged him with perjury, and ordered an injunction against every piece of property he owned or operated. Anderson then instructed the court to provide a directed verdict of acquittal for Wimmer on bootlegging charges.[18]

Rev. Connely had his first chance to appear in court as a witness in June 1926 after posing as a liquor buyer to obtain evidence against accused bootleggers Joe Attardi, Charles Bartolini, E. J. Kehoe, and Frank Moore. Once on the stand, the Raiding Parson had his moment to shine, but he could not identify the Italian merchant who had sold him liquor only a month earlier. Anderson promptly threw out the case and chastised Connely for wasting the court's time, wondering aloud about whether the Klan or the Prohibition Bureau was really in charge of liquor enforcement.[19]

Connely's crusade came to an abrupt end in March 1927 when he suddenly resigned his church position. A week later, a reporter discovered that

Fig. 10.3. As shown by cartoonist J. P. Alley, most Memphians did not believe the Klan represented American values. Caption: THE STRAGGLER FROM A ROUTED ARMY. Courtesy Memphis Room, Memphis Public Library and Information Center.

Connely owed reputed bootlegger Angelo Cattaneo $250. Connely took the "loan" during a raid but left town to avoid paying it back. Gus Romeo, bootlegger and owner of the Terminal Billiard Hall, bought the note from Cattaneo and filed a claim in squire Louis Morris's court to force Connely to repay the loan. Morris rendered a judgment in favor of Romeo but allowed Connely to collect some household goods before the remainder of his possessions, including three volumes of *The Story of the Bible*, went up for sale to cover the debt. Connely, disgraced after his discovered involvement with bootleggers, left Memphis for St. Louis.[20]

In May 1929, Frank Fischer, chairman of the Memphis Park Commission, refused to grant a permit to Rev. J. Frank Norris of Fort Worth, Texas, to use Peabody Park to address the Klan during the Baptist convention. From his Klan dominion that included the congressional district around Fort Worth, great titan Clarence Howell challenged Fischer. Howell, infuriated by Fischer's refusal, promised that Norris would discuss the "Roman question" anyway. Norris moved his gathering to Court Square, where he attacked modernism and Catholics and declared, "Liquor is being openly sold to high school boys and girls; young students are out on all night whoopee parties. Federal, county, and city officials sit idly by while the work of the devil goes on. Somebody is getting rake-offs on the vice conditions!"[21]

Hiram Evans led a rally at Ellis Auditorium to a small crowd of die-hard followers in October 1929. He railed about voting rights for African Americans, Catholicism, the League of Nations, the British prime minister, and Ed Crump, who he claimed led "the most corrupt political machine in the country." Those verbally attacked by Evans paid little heed since most Memphians had lost interest in the Klan. Crump, firmly in control of the city and county, did not even bother to comment. Even Prohibition, once a rallying cry that drew legions of supporters, was no longer enough to drum up support.[22]

11

FLAMING YOUTH AND POLICE CHARACTERS

Corn liquor and the automobile have conspired to undermine the morality of young people, going far toward destroying their respect for the law and weakening their resistance to evil influences.

—Sam Bates, Shelby County attorney general[1]

Robert Tanner blamed his downfall on girls, gasoline, and gin. "It certainly takes a lot of cash for the jelly bean of today to keep pace with the rest of the bunch, wear good clothes, buy red liquor at ten dollars per quart, hire automobiles, and play at the Marigold Gardens and roadhouses," lamented the twenty-four-year-old as he sat in his jail cell. Four years earlier, Tanner had left the farm where he was born near Alamo, Tennessee, for the big city. Memphis gave him what he wanted—an exciting nightlife and plenty of girlfriends. When asked about them, Tanner said, "Some of 'em were good girls, and some were the other kind." Unfortunately, his monthly salary of $145 as a fireman was not enough to keep them entertained, so he robbed his lieutenant of a $798 payroll. By the time police arrested him the next day, Tanner had spent all but $20 of it on liquor, clothes, a chauffeur, and the "general running expenses of going out and having a good time."[2]

Nothing illustrated the failure of Prohibition to win popular support better than the backlash against it by America's youth. Young "flappers" and "sheiks" rebelled against temperance in an attempt to redefine themselves in postwar America. Their love of liquor, automobiles, jazz, cigarettes, and sex shocked the older generation, who referred to them as "flaming youth," a term borrowed from the Coleen Moore movie of the same name. By 1923, nine out of ten white men appearing in the Shelby County Courthouse were between the ages of nineteen and twenty-five. Jimmy Jones, a bootlegger

Fig. 11.1. Cartoonist J. P. Alley portrays how the disregard for one law leads to the disregard for all laws. Caption: MY BOY AND I. Courtesy of Memphis Room, Memphis Public Library and Information Center.

and drunk who spent ten months out of the year in the workhouse in the 1920s, complained, "And the young people! You never caught them hanging around the saloons in the old days; the law wouldn't let 'em. Now they're riding around and drinking it [corn liquor] by the pint, or making whoopee in half a dozen places that are worse that the open saloon."[3]

In August 1924, Sheriff Knight promised to keep after flaming youth "until they stop riding up and down the roads of the country, drinking, yelling, and putting on debauches that outrage the decencies of society." Knight told his newly organized motorcycle unit to be hard on violators. Knight, appalled by their open sexuality, said, "Trips along the country roads at night are pointers to the immorality that a lonely road, an automobile, and a few drinks induce."[4]

The tragic shooting death of Robert McDonald and the wounding of fourteen-year-old Beth Seavers by young bootlegger John Wesley Turner at a party in Germantown in 1928 aroused concerns over the flaming youth lifestyle. Reporter Mary York asked Judge Alfred Pittman how to stop "the wild nightlife, racing automobiles, and drinking orgies." Pittman urged parents to accept the fact that social mores had changed and to better communicate the dangers of alcohol to their teenagers.[5]

Not all young Memphians were flappers or sheiks. The five-hundred-member Slow Club formed to "throw a wet blanket on the flaming youth." The nineteen-year-old club chair Helen Newsom said, "I'm simply tired of going out with fellows who expect a goodnight kiss. It ought to be possible to have a good time without petting and drinking."[6]

Judge Lewis Fitzhugh said, "It is the nature of youth to be adventurous, to want something that is forbidden. If they could get liquor legally, a large percentage would not want it." Most just spent their time dancing and drinking in roadhouses; however, for others, the lifestyle was a springboard into serious crime. Youthful rebellion gave way to disregard for authority as young scofflaws went from being flaming youth to becoming habitual criminals known as "police characters."[7]

· · ·

"What did he do to you?" asked the prosecutor. Seventeen-year-old Mary Thompson hung her head for a few moments. When she answered, it was the jury's turn to hang their heads. Court reporters had never before recorded anything so sexually explicit. The jury, shocked by his crime, found twenty-three-year-old Allen McNamara guilty of rape and sentenced him to die in the electric chair. The Taylor Liquor Ring member struggled to appear emotionless at the reading of the sentence, while his wife burst into tears as she clutched their two-year-old daughter.[8]

On the night of August 29, 1919, county sheriff Oliver Perry received a telephone call from a man who heard the screams of three teenaged girls. Perry rushed to the Raleigh Road Bridge where he saw McNamara, Jack Frey, and Fuller Langley struggling with the girls. He leaped from his car and tackled McNamara. Langley ran, but Frey joined in the fight. The hoodlums had almost taken Perry's weapon when the man who made the call jumped in and fought them off. Frey escaped, but Perry bound McNamara hand and foot with a rope and dragged him cursing to the car.[9]

McNamara's friends and family would not rest until the young man received a pardon. Someone who referred to himself as "The Silent One" sent a letter threatening to kill Sheriff Perry and Judge J. Ed Richards if McNamara went to the electric chair. Meanwhile, McNamara's brother Augustus McNamara coerced Thompson into marriage and had her sign an affidavit claiming prosecutors made her lie about the attack. McNamara's mother then presented Gov. Albert Roberts with a petition for a pardon with nearly fourteen thousand names. Roberts commuted McNamara's sentence to a life term, and in January 1922, the new governor, Alfred Taylor, issued a full pardon. McNamara, once free, returned to his old ways. In 1925, police arrested him for vagrancy, fighting, bootlegging, and molesting a twelve-year-old girl. More importantly, he began working for the city's most notorious gangster, John Belluomini, and rose from a street punk to an important underworld criminal.[10]

. . .

Herman "Butts" Werkhoven, son of respected police officer Edward "Babe" Werkhoven, never outgrew being a hellion. Neither serving in the US Navy nor getting married tamed the unruly teenager. He made headlines two months into his marriage when he gunned down a man he caught *in flagrante delicto* with his wife in November 1920. Butts fell in with various criminals and bootleggers afterward and faced arrests with "monotonous regularity."[11]

In December of 1923, Werkhoven and a partner led federal agents on a wild boat chase up the Wolf River. The agents spotted the two ferrying supplies to three stills set up on stilts above floodwaters. Werkhoven saw the two boats approaching and tried to flee. He outmaneuvered one and caused it to flip over and spill two agents into the icy water. He began to outrun the other boat until a volley of warning shots convinced him to surrender. Werkhoven, at the time of his arrest, had outstanding warrants for armed robbery, manslaughter, and Prohibition violations.[12]

In May 1924, a young woman visited Werkhoven at the workhouse, and the two quietly planned his escape. A couple of days later, the young woman drove her car along Hindman Ferry Road until she found Werkhoven's chain gang on the levee. Werkhoven, still in chains, saw her and made a break for the car. The gun bull on duty took aim but did not shoot because at the same moment a group of women and children drove through his line of fire.[13]

Deputies discovered Werkhoven's location after receiving a report about a shootout. Werkhoven, teamed up with a liquor hijacker named Joe Kilpatrick, had tried to hijack liquor from a band of African American bootleggers. The bootleggers opened fire on them and ran them into the woods. Deputies found Kilpatrick with a shotgun wound to the shoulder and a mud-caked Werkhoven hiding in a trench with a .30-30 rifle.[14]

Deputies brought Werkhoven to federal court, where he entered a guilty plea and received a $250 fine for each charge from his December arrest to be paid after his ninety-day workhouse sentence. Judge Ross warned, "Young man, you're going to keep on until you'll get in the penitentiary." Werkhoven only smiled in response.[15]

Werkhoven made another attempted escape days later as guards led him to the Black Maria to carry him to the workhouse. He broke for the Wolf River, pulling off his clothes as he ran. The guard held his fire as Deputies Solari and Wilson jumped into the river after him. The deputies dragged him back to the bank as he swore he would rather drown than return to the workhouse.[16]

A few weeks after his release, Werkhoven started another bootlegging operation with John "Flop" Burress. Knight soon found out about it and sent deputies to raid the outfit. Rather than surrender or flee, the two made the mistake of firing shotguns at Deputy Clark. A jury found the two guilty of assault to murder, and the judge sentenced them each to twenty-one years in the state penitentiary.[17]

Werkhoven, after an early release three years later, opened a roadhouse at 525 North High Street with his second wife. Police raided the place in May of 1928, but the two smashed most of the bottles of home brew before officers forced their way in the door. Police charged the Werkhovens with running a disorderly house and arrested their customers on charges of disorderly conduct. Unrepentant, Werkhoven continued his wild lifestyle until a stomach ailment in 1929 cut his life short.[18]

. . .

Collins-Sturla ambulance attendants received an emergency call a few hours before dawn on June 16, 1923. They rushed to the foot of Beale Street, where they found Dick Rather laying horribly burned and naked on the cobblestones. Rather's partner William Estes Gee explained that his burns were the result of a still explosion. The attendants carried the mortally wounded Rather to the hospital as Gee walked back to a waiting motorboat and vanished into the misty night with his fellow bootleggers.[19]

Richard Carl Rather was one of the city's most contemptuous recidivists. A plumber and automobile mechanic by trade, he came to Memphis around 1911 and soon became involved in larceny and bootlegging. Rather was sentenced to eighteen months in the Atlanta Federal Penitentiary and fined $900 after he tried to break into a Mississippi impound lot to take back one of his cars seized in a raid. While the court considered his appeal, police arrested Rather and his three accomplices after they robbed Levy's Toggeries of furs valued at $3,000. Rather received a sentence in the state penitentiary for three to ten years; however, an unexpected pardon led to rumors that Rather bribed the governor. He faced conspiracy charges seven months later for his part in the Taylor Liquor Ring.[20]

Rather's personal life proved as tumultuous as his criminal career. He divorced his first wife Nellie, the mother of his daughter and son, and married twenty-four-year-old Edna Bechtold on June 10, 1921. She died seven days later after Rather lost control of his car on Macon Road. Rather married Gladys Boatner in Dallas, Texas, six months later but soon abandoned her and moved in with his twenty-two-year-old girlfriend Edna Mitchell. On March 12, 1923, Boatner divorced him and named Mitchell as corespondent. Rather and Mitchell married in Marion, Arkansas, shortly after the divorce since Tennessee would not recognize a marriage between a divorcee and the person named as corespondent.[21]

Rather made the last in a long line of bad decisions three months later while tending a still he co-owned with Joe Robilio. The men working with Rather saw that the steam-powered unit was about to explode and took cover. Rather jumped on top of it and tried to open a pressure valve. He could not release the pressure soon enough, and the still exploded. Scalded over nearly his entire body, Rather died the next day.[22]

• • •

Of all the Memphis police characters to emerge during Prohibition, few won more notoriety than Neil Kerens Pumphrey. His brother gave him the nickname Popeye as a child because of the wild-eyed expression he gave following losing a game of marbles. The name stuck as he grew up because he continued to have the same look whenever he lost his temper.[23]

Popeye Pumphrey's lengthy arrest record, flagrant disregard for the law, and tendency to escape punishment frustrated police and prosecutors across the country. His well-publicized antics inspired writer William Faulkner to base a character on him in his novel *Sanctuary*. Pumphrey admitted to bootlegging, gambling, carrying a pistol, speeding, housebreaking, and larceny; however, he took offense when Judge Clifford Davis charged him with vagrancy. Davis asked, "Just what is your definition of a vagrant?" Pumphrey answered, "A person without visible means of support." Pumphrey then fell silent because he realized he could not admit the sources of his income. Davis, having made his point, replied, "I fine you twenty-five dollars."[24]

Pumphrey walked into Memphis police chief Will Lee's office one afternoon and informed him that he just shot two former friends. An argument over $160 from an apparent liquor deal prompted the shooting. The two men survived their wounds, although one lost an index finger from a bullet. Pumphrey's father put up his $5,000 bond, and Popeye was free again.[25]

The Shelby County Grand Jury returned an indictment, and two weeks later police found a pistol in his car. His lawyer appealed to the Tennessee Supreme Court, claiming the police had no right to search the vehicle, but the court upheld the ruling, and Popeye had to serve eleven months and twenty-nine days. Pumphrey's parents made an emotional appeal to Gov. Austin Peay for a pardon. Peay agreed, but his terms for Pumphrey included staying in at night, cleaning up his habits, getting a job, and going to work. Pumphrey's lawyer promised that Popeye would go to Earle, Arkansas, and open a soda fountain business. Three days after his release, Sgt. Martin Cleary arrested Pumphrey and thirteen other men in a raid on a craps game.[26]

On June 14, 1924, Pumphrey, Beverly Stegall, William "Splint" Manley, and a troubled war veteran named Joe Carter posed as Prohibition agents and demanded C. A. Lott, an elderly Raleigh farmer, turn over his still and whiskey. Lott, who was not a bootlegger, refused to let the young men search his property. An argument began, and Lott shot Carter with both barrels of his shotgun, killing him instantly. His companions took his body, wrapped it in a blanket, weighed it down with a tire jack, and dumped it the Wolf River. Fishermen discovered the body after it floated to the surface ten days later.[27]

Deputies arrested the trio, but prosecutors ran into problems. Pumphrey, while out on bail, quickly sold his car to someone in Chicago so prosecutors could not use it as evidence. Also, Lott's memory faded over the next few months, and he could not identify the men when the case went to court the following March. The state, without a witness, had no choice but to dismiss the cases.[28]

Pumphrey became involved with increasingly dangerous criminal endeavors. He received gunshot wounds to both arms in a shootout in front of a Kansas City hotel in 1929. He worked with notorious safecrackers B. B. Wright, Fred "Brick" Peeples, and Warren "Snappy" Chandler in well-publicized robberies, including the Arrow Food Store and the American-Woodlawn Bank in Birmingham, Alabama. Pumphrey hid out in New Orleans until the honeymooning Memphis police detective William Raney happened to see him. Pumphrey fought extradition but eventually returned to Memphis, where once again his father put up his bond. He escaped prosecution again after police failed to find reliable witnesses.[29]

In August 1930, police in Saratoga, New York, arrested Pumphrey, Adolph Wood, Fred Callahan, and Hubert Coates after they tried to rig a $1,000 gambling operation using an elaborate system of mirrors. After his release, Pumphrey returned to Hot Springs, where he had recently married. His notoriety made him so unpopular that a local judge threatened to put him on a chain gang if he did not leave town.[30]

Pumphrey faced similar treatment in Memphis. He accused the police of beating him up and trying to run him out of town because he won $10,000 from an officer's friend in a downtown hotel. He maintained he was the innocent victim of the vicious rumors spread by the press. He said, "I'm a gambler and a rambler, and I've seen some pretty tough things, but I have never robbed a bank. I have been in the liquor business, and I have been caught, and I took my medicine."[31]

Pumphrey, suffering from syphilis, returned to Hot Springs in hopes the spas would help him regain his health; however, the waters could not help his deteriorating condition. With his health failing, Pumphrey ended his life with a self-inflicted gunshot wound in October 1931. His widowed mother, devoted until the end, blamed herself for not raising her son properly. She said Popeye was simply a misunderstood boy who "sowed his oats in wild adventure."[32]

• • •

On July 22, 1933, George "Machine Gun" Kelly and Albert Bates abducted oil tycoon Charles Urschel and Walter Jarrett during a bridge game in Oklahoma City. The kidnappers checked their captives' wallets to determine which one was Urschel, stole fifty dollars, and set Urschel's friend Jarrett free. E. E. Kirkpatrick, another friend of Urschel, received a ransom note four days later demanding $200,000. He delivered the money, and the kidnappers released Urschel, who returned home on July 31.

FBI director J. Edgar Hoover made the capture of kidnappers his top priority. He saw the case as a way to restore public confidence in the FBI after the embarrassment of the agency's handling of the recent kidnapping and murder of Charles Lindbergh's baby and the escapades of John Dillinger, Ma Barker, Alvin Karpis, Bonnie Parker, and Clyde Barrow. Hoover pulled his best investigator Gus Jones off the Kansas City Massacre case to track down Kelly and his cohorts. Jones, with the help of Urschel, discovered the hideout in Paradise, Texas. The FBI arrested members of the gang, including

Fig. 11.2. Machine Gun Kelly, 1933. Courtesy of
Memphis Police Department Archives.

Kelly's in-laws, while Kelly obnoxiously mailed taunts and threats to prosecutors and agents, whom he referred to using the underworld vernacular
term "G-men."[33]

Kelly returned to Memphis and recruited the help of his former brother-
in-law Langford Ramsey, John Tichenor, an injured auto mechanic, and
Tichenor's brother-in-law Seymour Travis, a former Piggly Wiggly manager.
Police and agents stormed the little brick bungalow at 1408 Rayner at 6:45
a.m. on September 26, 1933, and arrested Tichenor and Travis in the front
bedroom. Sgt. Louis Crosby had his sawed-off shotgun leveled at Kelly as
he came out of his bedroom. Kelly dropped his weapon and surrendered
without a fight. Officers, somewhat disappointed that Kelly only had a pistol,
asked about his famous submachine gun. Kelly replied that he left it behind
because he did not think he would need it in Memphis.[34]

Police blocked the traffic on Second Street as Department of Justice agents
led the Kellys, Tichenor, and Travis from the police station to the county jail
past curious crowds. Seven police officers, flanked by ten agents, walked the
four down an alley to the back door where they met six deputies armed with
pump shotguns. Deputies locked the men in the bullpen while agents pulled
Kathryn Kelly away from her husband as she tried to speak to him. Newspaper cameramen tried to take pictures of the glamorous auburn-haired gun
moll as she stepped into the elevator, but she quickly covered her face with
a handkerchief as the cameras flashed.[35]

Harry Allen, a member of the crowd gathered outside the jail, recognized
Kelly as he passed despite his dyed blonde hair. Allen told Inspector Griffin

Fig. 11.3. Machine Gun Kelly escorted to the Shelby County Courthouse. Courtesy of the Library of Congress.

that Machine Gun Kelly was a former schoolmate named George Barnes, and word spread quickly through the building. Clifford Davis came downstairs, looked in the cell, and asked, "Kelly, do you remember me?" Barnes replied, "Why sure I do. I went to school with you in 1915 at Central High. You were our class orator. I knew you when you were the judge. You tried me one time." Lawyers Ben Kohn and Julian Cohen remembered him from high school, as did Capt. John Foppiano and J. W. Grisham. Lt. Lee Quianthy and Det. Larry Fox had grown up with Barnes in North Memphis. Other officers remember arresting Barnes numerous times as an "ordinary hip pocket bootlegger."[36]

George Barnes's father was an insurance salesman, and his mother, Elizabeth Kelly, was the daughter of Irish immigrants. The manager of the Porter Building in downtown Memphis remembered Barnes as a spoiled child who would storm into his father's insurance office and throw tantrums. Barnes often skipped class during his freshman year in 1915 to drive cars loaded with liquor down from Caruthersville. He would play hooky for days at a time and return to school and show off fifty- to seventy-five-dollar rolls of bills to impress the girls.[37]

Barnes briefly cleaned up his lifestyle and married Geneva Ramsey in the fall of 1919 in Clarksdale, Mississippi. He drifted back into a life of crime following the death of his father-in-law George Ramsey, a man he admired and who gave him a job in his levee business. Barnes made half-hearted attempts at running a garage and selling insurance, but he eventually returned to bootlegging and divorced his wife. On May 30, 1924, police again arrested Barnes, who used the alias Bonner, along with V. M. "Commodore" Stepp and Frank Stuhl, in possession of three cases of whiskey.[38]

Barnes left Memphis, changed his name to George Kelly, and married Kathryn Thorne, stepdaughter of R. G. Shannon, in Minneapolis in 1927. His new wife, enthralled by the escapades of gangsters, bought her husband a Thompson submachine gun and helped create his Machine Gun Kelly persona. Barnes, now Kelly, did not fare well and was arrested on March 14, 1927, for Prohibition violation in Santa Fe, on July 24, 1927, for vagrancy in Tulsa, on January 12, 1928, for Prohibition violation in Tulsa, and on February 11, 1928, for possession of liquor in Leavenworth. Bootlegging was not paying off, so Kathryn encouraged her husband to become a bank robber, and later a kidnapper.[39]

As captured members of the Kelly gang went on trial in Oklahoma City, Kathryn passed word through Fort Worth attorney Sam Sayers that in return for leniency for her and her mother, she would surrender her husband. US attorney Herbert Hyde passed the offer along to special assistant attorney general Joseph B. Keenan, who replied, "I am hoping that Judge Vaught could see his way clear to being very lenient to Mrs. Shannon and Mrs. Kelly, even to the point of absolute release." Luther Arnold, a hitchhiker the Kellys befriended in Texas, told the agents he heard George tell Kathryn he would go along with her plan. The deal that would free Kathryn and her mother appeared closer than ever, but time ran out.[40]

A break came to the FBI when they interviewed twelve-year-old Geraldine Arnold, the daughter of Luther Arnold. The girl posed as the Kellys' daughter during one of their trips and knew the details of the couple's plans, including the whereabouts of their hideout in Memphis. The FBI and the Memphis Police Department, with no help from Kathryn, arrested the fugitives and all deals were off. Agents questioned Kelly late into the night as he sat in his cell with an Oregon boot—a large, solid iron ring that fit just above the ankle—shackled to his cot. After extradition to Oklahoma City, the federal judge Edgar S. Vaught sentenced George and Kathryn to life under the recent Federal Kidnapping Act, commonly known as the Lindbergh Law. Their attorneys filed motions for new trials, but the judge overruled them. A total of twenty-one people received sentences for their connection with Kelly's gang, including six who received life sentences.[41]

Fig. 11.4. Machine Gun Kelly leaving Shelby County Courthouse. Courtesy of the Library of Congress.

It was Friday the thirteenth, October 1933, and the special train arrived on track thirteen at Kansas City, Kansas. Kelly wrote obscene wisecracks on autographed pieces of tissue paper and handed them out to officers and newspaper men as he waited for the train to take him to Leavenworth Prison. Kelly, as he boarded the armored car in shackles, bragged that he would escape within a week or by Christmas at the latest. The train carried him to prison, a switch engine pushed the car inside the gates, and Kelly remained there until he died from a heart attack July 17, 1954.[42]

Kathryn, her mother, and her stepfather were tried, convicted and sentenced by Vaught to life in prison. In 1958, W. R. Wallace, US district judge in Oklahoma City, ordered the government to turn over its files on the case to the new team of lawyers representing Kathryn and her mother, who claimed the FBI pressured their lawyers into putting on a less than vigorous defense. The government respectfully defied the judge's order, and Wallace responded by ordering a new trial and freeing the two women on $10,000 bond. Wallace was killed in a car accident in 1960, leaving the case in a virtual state of limbo, and Kathryn and her mother, still free on bond, received paroles with no further action by the government.[43]

Fig. 11.5. Bootleggers moved into more serious criminal pursuits as shown by cartoonist J. P. Alley. Caption: READY FOR BUSINESS AT THE SAME OLD HANG-OUT. Courtesy of Memphis Room, Memphis Public Library and Information Center.

A 1991 Cato Institute study found that, in thirty major US cities, the number of crimes increased 24 percent in just the first year of Prohibition. Time and again, flouting the liquor laws led to a breakdown in respect for all laws. Judge Alfred Pittman observed, "The more rigidly righteous persons undertake to regulate the morals of others, the worse things get. . . . Laws can't make people moral; only their conscience can."[44]

12

ROADHOUSES AND PIG STANDS

We are a wicked lot living in a wicked world, and the guy with a fat
pocketbook and a good expense account can find wickedness anywhere he wants to look for it.
                              —Ralph Millett, January 19, 1935

Hey buddy, where can a guy get a drink in this town? Any cab driver
worth his salt could answer this question, because Memphis had plenty
of places to drink. These were not fly-by-night speakeasies, but rather
known hotels and restaurants where proprietors sold liquor or beer to carefully screened customers. These places became not just surrogate saloons,
but new gathering places that reflected the changing times. They catered
to men and women, respectable citizen and outlaw, and provided the latest
entertainment. Their proprietors, once just restauranteurs and entertainers,
took on new roles as bootleggers. Business was good, but operating outside
the law could be dangerous. Yeah, I know a place you can get a drink, but
you'd better watch your back.

• • •

At about three o'clock in the morning on October 6, 1932, an ironing board
flew out a window of the Hotel Desoto. Frank Tamble, the manager and
bootlegger, began fighting with another man during a party. As the two
wrestled for control of Tamble's pistol, a stray shot went off and killed a
bystander named Everett Lackey. The man Tamble had fought escaped from
the room along with the other partygoers, who ran shouting and screaming
down the halls.

In a drunken rage, Tamble stumbled down the hall with the pistol in search of his adversary. He stopped at what he thought was the room of the man he chased, pounded on the door, and demanded to be let in. Inside, a dance instructor named Art Martin told Tamble he had the wrong room. Tamble ordered him to let him in, but Martin and his girlfriend Helen Phillips, frightened by the commotion and gunshots, refused to open the door. Tamble, angered by Martin's refusal, shot at the door. The bullet passed through and grazed Martin's head before it struck the wall.[1]

Once back at the party, Tamble realized he had to get rid of Lackey's body. He knew the police would arrive soon, so he quickly improvised a story to explain the hotel guest's death. Tamble had a black porter, Haywood Richardson, drag the body to the lobby to make it appear as if Lackey had tried to rob the hotel cashier. Tamble said, "The coppers ain't gonna find a pistol on me," and handed the gun to the porter to dispose of it before police arrived.[2]

Detectives found Lackey in the lobby with a cigar in one hand, but without a gun. Richardson, as Tamble instructed, told police that Lackey appeared to have a pistol in his pocket and had demanded the money. Richardson claimed he could not open the cash register, so he asked to call Tamble to open the drawer. Tamble said, "[Lackey] told me to hold them up. I wasn't taking any chances, so I fired." Detectives determined that Lackey died somewhere other than the lobby because of the lack of blood, but they had no way to refute Tamble's story. Without a murder weapon or witnesses, investigators had to drop the case.[3]

Hotels were frequent scenes of bedlam and police raids. Bellhops supplied liquor to guests and management allowed all-night parties involving drinking, gambling, and other vices. The city's "notoriously wide open" hotels received such notoriety that Mable Walker Willebrandt ordered E.C. Yellowley, the regional federal Prohibition director, to investigate the "flagrant disregard of prohibition in Memphis." Law enforcement led periodic raids, but that did not stop the parties. Without search warrants, police and agents could do little to stop drinking in a hotel room until the party got out of hand and someone called for help.[4]

Pig stands caused problems for law enforcement as well. These small drive-up barbecue shops specializing in sandwiches and soft drinks became popular in the Mid-South with the coming of the automobile. They were also "notorious retailers of bootleg liquor," and the scenes of "scandals and lurid parties at which liquor flows freely." On one such occasion, a police officer arrested prominent Memphian Thomas Semple, his wife, and their African American chauffeur on charges of drunkenness and disorderly conduct outside a pig stand on Summer Avenue in October 1920. Other incidents followed, including the tragic deaths of two young partygoers John Torino and Evelyn Roberts in an alcohol-related automobile accident after leaving a pig stand in January 1925.[5]

Mayor Rowlett Paine was driving along East Parkway in August 1925 when he noticed someone had converted an old garage into a garishly painted pig stand across from the Memphis Fairgrounds and named it "Joe's Place." The owner and former ward boss Dominick Zanone, who once operated a saloon and wine room in the same spot, had tables and chairs in the yard and brightly colored lights strung from the trees. Paine had city attorney E. B. Klewer file an injunction to close it. Zanone petitioned to keep it open but met fierce opposition from the city adjustment board and residents, who suspected the place would become a liquor joint. It probably did not help Zanone's case either that he had on the sides of his stand pictures of huge bottles painted in red and yellow.[6]

The Three-Way Inn was a well-known Italian restaurant on South Parkway where the antics of its owners and customers rivaled those of the old saloons. Police arrested two men in September 1923 when they sold liquor to an undercover officer. They raided the place again and found twenty-three half-pints of liquor hidden under a floorboard and a refrigerator full of home brew hidden under boards below a sand pile in the back yard in July 1925.[7]

Police arrested the owner, Attilio Grandi, also known as Little Grandi, after he shot and wounded Adolph Pierotti in October 1933. Grandi made Pierotti leave earlier in the evening after he became drunk and unruly. Pierotti went home, continued drinking, and decided to confront Grandi again. This time he came at Grandi with a knife, forcing Grandi to have to defend himself by shooting Pierotti in the legs.[8]

Another similar incident occurred at another place called the Three-Way Inn at Horn Lake and Whitehaven Roads in June 1929. This so-called "soft drink stand" owned by Louis Onetta was a favorite gathering place to buy and drink moonshine. Onetta's nephew Joe Belluomini and his girlfriend Virgie Russell hung around drinking until about four o'clock in the morning. Belluomini, the adopted son of saloon owner Joe Persica and cousin to gangsters John and Frank Belluomini, then got into an argument with Russell over who was sober enough to drive. The argument became physical and resulted in Russell shooting Belluomini. Deputies arrived and found Russell hysterical, Belluomini wounded, and Onetta too drunk to stand up. Russell claimed the gun accidentally discharged, Onetta claimed Russell assaulted Belluomini, and Belluomini claimed unknown assailants robbed him. Deputies dropped the charges since no one could agree on what happened.[9]

• • •

Reputable upscale restaurants featured dancefloors, orchestras, comedians, vaudeville acts, and plenty of liquor. The popular nightspots evolved from roadhouses into nightclubs and attracted patrons from the city's elite as well as its underworld. Law enforcement led frequent raids, but the popularity and profitability of these places led their owners to risk arrests and fines to keep them open.

J. H. "Spec" Horton came to Memphis when he was eighteen years old to study undertaking, but he left the funeral business to work at Luehrman Hotel, where he learned to tend bar. Horton ran the Eureka Club saloon in 1919, a billiard hall, the Incorporated Bible Distributing Company, the Sunset Inn in West Memphis, and he had the copyright on a manuscript entitled *The Newlyweds* by the late author Elbert Hubbard. He claimed that, despite public perceptions, he never gambled and his dancehalls were no more disreputable than the average hotel. "Yet people take it for granted that a nightclub owner's bad," said Horton. "He's got to resemble some dark character of the underworld."[10]

Horton ran the Rendezvous and purchased the Riverside Inn at 10 West Calhoun from Joe Kiersky in 1925, where police officer Harry Lee made headlines after getting drunk and firing his weapon in the place in March 1929. Horton also ran The Showboat near West Memphis until an arsonist destroyed it in 1928 and the Mid-South Kennel Club Track until Crittenden County officials shut it down.[11]

Horton believed he understood human nature, especially when it came to his customers. "They're all hypocrites," he once said. "They're all kidding themselves along." Horton found that Memphians paid lip service to liquor and gambling laws in polite company during the day, but at night they flocked to nightclubs and casinos.[12]

Harry and Joe Kiersky, sons of Jewish immigrant and merchant Adolph Kiersky, ran some of the most popular and most frequently raided nightclubs. Harry Kiersky ran five places including so-called soft-drink stands at Hindman Ferry Road and 151 West Georgia Avenue, as well as the Riverside Inn. Police arrested Kiersky numerous times in the early 1920s on liquor and gambling charges, and once in August 1923 for offering a railroad clerk $200 to leave a boxcar unlocked so bootleggers could steal over seven hundred bags of sugar to use to make moonshine.[13]

In August 1927, police raided a place on Plum Street Joe Kiersky operated with his wife's cousin Chloe Vannucci Morehead, wife of police officer Arthur Eugene Morehead. Capt. Hulet Smith and his officers stormed Kiersky's Dixie Night Club and arrested 230 guests on gambling, disorderly conduct, and liquor charges on April 6, 1930. The establishment, built on the site of the burned Crystal Gardens on Summer Avenue, had a large dance floor, bandstand, and restaurant area where officers found whiskey bottles under nearly every table. Kiersky had a pool table modified for craps in the attic and home brew on ice in the back yard.[14]

Chloe Morehead and her brother Rigo Vannucci opened a nightclub called The Barn on the northern limits of the city at Chelsea Avenue and Hyde Park Street in 1930. This upscale venue featured the best music acts, dancing, and food and attracted both the best and worst people in the city. Anybody who was anybody frequented the club, and most everybody there had a drink in one hand and dice in the other. The new nightlife hot spot naturally drew the attention of law enforcement, especially since Vannucci had a long criminal record that included bootlegging and bribing Prohibition agents.[15]

Sheriff's deputies discovered about forty liquor bottles after clearing over two hundred and fifty people out of The Barn in a Saturday night raid in April 1930. Sheriff Knight could not prove that Vannucci sold the liquor, but federal district attorney Lindsay Phillips charged Vannucci with violating the nuisance law and accused him of allowing teens to drink on the property. Vannucci and Morehead maintained that they had tried to stop the drinking, but their customers had ignored them. Judge Anderson found Vannucci not guilty but placed a federal padlock on the place and warned him not to open another nightclub.[16]

Reno Devaux took The Barn over in January 1932 and reopened it after the lifting of the padlock. The colorful Devaux acted as host, Art Minor was master of ceremonies, and Nate Evans led the fourteen-piece house orchestra. The debonair dark-eyed, dark-haired Devaux had run away from his home in Mobile, Alabama at seventeen. Both his mother and the parish priest thought he would attend seminary, but the roll of the dice lured him into the life of a gambler. Devaux ran a gambling place in Clarksdale, Mississippi, where he met William Faulkner through mutual acquaintances in 1918. The two became friends, and Devaux introduced Faulkner to Memphis's most colorful police characters.[17]

Devaux had a history of run-ins with the law. Sheriff Knight raided his place on Horn Lake Road for liquor in April 1924. Prohibition agents arrested

Devaux after they purchased liquor from one of his customers in June 1925, and Knight arrested him again in November when more liquor turned up in his place. Devaux moved just north of the city limits to avoid raids, but in 1928, Knight temporarily shut down roadhouses along Jackson Avenue after a young woman tried to kill herself after a night of drinking in Devaux's establishment.[18]

Devaux also got the attention of out-of-town gangsters trying to muscle in on the Memphis liquor trade in December 1929. A man made his way through the crowded dance floor of the New Crystal Gardens on Castalia Street and slipped into a dressing room. He came out of the room empty-handed and melted into the crowd. A few moments later, a fire erupted from the dressing room. Flames engulfed the building as the seven hundred guests rushed out the exits to safety. Across town, another fire destroyed the original Crystal Gardens on Summer Avenue.[19]

Two weeks earlier, Spec Horton's nightclub The Showboat burned down mysteriously, and the fire marshal and the sheriff began to suspect that the fires were connected to the ongoing bootlegger war. Stories circulated about rival factions in Chicago and St. Louis vying for control of liquor in Memphis, and his benefactors could no longer protect him. Devaux's refusal prompted a group of gangsters to retaliate by burning his clubs. He denied knowing who could be responsible, but he added, "If I knew who did it, I couldn't say anything."[20]

Devaux opened the New Crystal Gardens in Lake View, Mississippi, in the summer of 1931, but the Desoto County sheriff Sid Campbell proved as troublesome as Sheriff Knight. Devaux escaped through a side door during a raid and fled to Memphis to hide at the Hotel Chisca. He returned to Desoto County, appeared in court, and promised to keep his new club free of alcohol and gambling. He renamed the club The Seville, but constant harassment by the sheriff led Devaux to leave in frustration for his "old gulf coast home" in November with a promise to never return.[21]

Devaux had a change of heart and reopened The Barn in January 1932, but he found the new sheriff William Bacon less than welcoming. Bacon hounded Devaux and briefly shut the club down. In March 1933, Deputies Barboro and Campassi quietly entered and took a seat around one thirty one Sunday morning. To the dozen or more guests, they were just two late stragglers, but to Reno, they were a couple of headaches. The deputies shut the place down because couples were dancing after midnight, in violation of blue laws. Devaux had to spend eight hours in a jail cell before paying a ten dollar fine.[22]

Devaux gave up The Barn and sold it to Joe Kiersky in 1933. The new owner boasted of the club's "steam-heated orchestra and red-hot dance floor" and hosted holiday benefits for the Good Fellows to raise money for under-privileged children. Owen Payne White visited The Barn in October 1934 with his friend "Mike" while writing his exposé on vice. He was looking for sin, and his visit to Kiersky's place did not disappoint him. He paid his forty-cent cover, left his hat with the "hardest looking check girl" he had ever seen, and took a table near the center of the room. The waiter brought White and his friend each the standard order of two Coca-Cola set-ups and a bottle of corn whiskey. White wanted to see sin, but the crowd was a little too unruly for his tastes. He watched the bouncers break up several fights and prostitutes solicit johns and left before the scheduled floorshow featuring "some unclad girls doing a muscle dance."[23]

An accidental fire started by an employee destroyed The Barn a month later. The property owner Frank Garrison quickly rebuilt the club, and Kiersky was back in business. He continued to host holiday charity events and weathered the occasional raid, including one in March 1937 that yielded 256 half-pints of whiskey, thirty pints of gin, eight slot machines, dice equip-ment, and a pinball machine.[24]

The Tourist Inn at the corner of North Second and Benjestown Road, run by Frank Belluomini and Frank Tamble, was another thorn in the side of law enforcement. The federal district attorney and the Prohibition Bureau served the two Liquor Barons notice in June 1930 that any liquor violation would result in "double prosecution." Belluomini and Tamble took heed, kept their liquor off the property in a potato house owned by Joe Torti, and carefully screened potential customers. The closest the Sheriff's Department came to arresting them came when deputies discovered four cases of whiskey in a roadster owned by employee Frazier Bellora during a raid in April 1937.[25]

On the night of January 11, 1935, James Keenan, a reckless and inept Prohi-bition agent based in Forrest City, Arkansas, tried to raid the roadhouse. He needed a getaway car, so he stood outside and ordered a passing tow-truck to pull over. The driver, William Bullifin, saw Keenan in the road waving a gun and tried to speed away, but the chain between his tow truck and the car behind him snapped. Bullifin stopped in front of the Tourist Inn, and Keenan ordered him to unhitch the vehicle. Keenan harassed Joe Cannon, the owner of the car, and pistol-whipped Bullifin for not working fast enough.[26]

Keenan then stormed into the Tourist Inn and pulled a gun on barkeep Willie Cigalina. Everyone in the place thought he was trying to stage a holdup and panicked. Keenan looked away, and Cigalina bolted for the kitchen.

Keenan lowered his pistol and tried to follow, giving Cigalina's coworker James Cullen Baw the opportunity to reach for a shotgun. Baw leveled the weapon at Keenan and ordered him to halt. Baw kept Keenan at bay for a moment, but his arm, recently injured in an auto accident, weakened and he lowered the heavy weapon. Keenan, who still had his sidearm, quickly raised it and fatally shot Baw in the neck. Guests and staff jumped Keenan, disarmed him, and beat him with his pistol before sheriff's deputies arrived to arrest him for murder.[27]

Keenan's lawyers, led by C. P. J. Mooney Jr., the son of newspaper editor C. P. J. Mooney Sr., faced the prosecution led by Tyler McLain. Keenan and his supervisor claimed that the agent had pursued an Arkansas bootlegger named Jack Butler to the Tourist Inn and had entered to make an arrest. Eyewitnesses, including recently elected legislator Percy Walker, testified that Keenan never identified himself as a Prohibition agent, appeared drunk, and no one in the roadhouse saw or ever heard of Jack Butler. The jury, despite the preponderance of the evidence, sided with the defense and acquitted Keenan in December 1936.[28]

The violence at the Tourist Inn, as sensational as it was, paled in comparison to the events at the Golden Slipper. Charlie Cianciola started out in Memphis selling produce after arriving from Italy. He later ran liquor from Paducah and operated a major gambling house until a falling out with his partners and a police lid in 1935 forced him to relocate in Tipton County. With the help of his bouncer William "Red" Jennings, he opened the Golden Slipper, a sleazy dive and tourist camp with pool tables, slot machines, a small bandstand with a piano and bass, and a dancefloor with a sign saying, "Respect the ladis [sic]."

Red Jennings became greedy and decided to stage a robbery to rip off Cianciola. He recruited brothers John Thomas "Jack" Richardson and Leonard Richardson and a man named Augusta Wilkins. Together, they put together a plan to hold up Cianciola and make it appear as if Jennings was a victim.[29]

The Richardson brothers and Wilkins met up on the night of November 6, 1936, and waited for the club's customers to leave. Wilkins, a fair-skinned black man with slicked back hair and a pencil-thin mustache, became bored and decided to visit a nearby African American dancehall. He caroused with some friends for a while until he returned to the Richardsons' car.[30]

The trio drove by the Golden Slipper several times until they saw that all the customers had left. Wilkins came in, bought liquor, and asked about starting a craps game. Cianciola spread a blanket on a table and they began to play. Cianciola, distracted by the dice, did not notice the Richardson brothers come in. The brothers leveled their weapons at Cianciola and pulled money from the cash register. They also took three slot machines, a radio, and a watch.[31]

Something in Jennings's actions tipped off Cianciola that he was involved with the robbery. He also recognized Leonard Richardson from his days of selling produce. Cianciola realized Jennings had set him up and began to fight back. The robbers beat him into submission, bound and gagged him, and left him in his bedroom in the back of the roadhouse. Jennings convinced Jack Richardson that they had to kill Cianciola to keep him from calling the sheriff. Jack Richardson agreed, went into the back room, and shot Cianciola in the head with a rifle.[32]

Jennings, playing the part of the victim, walked up the road, found a telephone, and called the Tipton County Sheriff's Department. He told deputies that three unidentified men robbed the Golden Slipper and killed Cianciola. He claimed that the robbers had taken him outside to shoot him but ran away when some members of a nearby church congregation saw them.[33]

Sheriff Will Vaughn's investigation uncovered the truth within a few days. The bouncer claimed that he and Cianciola had been great friends; however, Cianciola's seventeen-year-old son said otherwise and suspected Jennings had something to do with the murder. The break in the case came when Wilkins confessed during questioning and implicated the Richardsons and Jennings. The jury found all four defendants guilty of first-degree murder and sentenced the Richardsons and Wilkins to ninety-nine-year terms and Jennings to a twenty-one-year term.[34]

. . .

The Cianciola murder was just another in a long line of crimes that occurred at roadhouses just over the county line. Constant harassment by deputies drove many roadhouse owners to relocate out of the jurisdiction of the Shelby County Sheriff's Department where they hoped to avoid law enforcement and attract customers from Memphis. They had a free hand to sell liquor as they pleased, but the lack of law enforcement made business very dangerous.

Sheriff Will Bacon and chief deputy Charles Garibaldi showed up at The Barn in an all too familiar raid on November 22, 1930. Rigo Vannucci and Chloe Morehead, like most other nightclub owners, ignored the blue law requiring their business to close at midnight on Saturdays. The early closing on their busiest night crippled their profits for the week, so nightclub owners took their chances and stayed open as long as possible. Bacon ordered the place closed. The orchestra played Taps as grumbling partygoers rose from their tables covered in glasses smelling of liquor and exited with the promise to take the party to Bob Berryman's Silver Slipper at the corner of Bristol Highway and Macon Road.[35]

The Silver Slipper also felt the wrath of the sheriff that night. Berryman had built up a long history of run-ins with law enforcement, including a term in the Atlanta Federal Penitentiary for his part in the Tyree Taylor Liquor Ring; an arrest with partner Ferdinand Folbe in April 1926 on liquor charges; a padlock on his roadhouse in May 1926 for selling liquor; raids on his Idle Social Club on North Second Street in October 1926; and raids on the Silver Slipper in July and December 1929. Berryman had weathered many run-ins with the law, but he had finally had enough.[36]

Berryman, like others targeted by raiders, moved just below the state line near the small community of Lake View, Mississippi. The area featured places like Berryman's The Paddock, Reno Devaux's New Crystal Gardens, Louis Barrasso's The Shanty, and John Phillips's the Mississippi Club. Law enforcement described the nightclubs as "worse than anything in New Orleans or Hot Springs," and The Paddock in particular as "a glittering pleasure palace where visitors can court Lady Luck on various devices."[37]

Lake View was close enough to attract business from Memphis. The Memphis and Lake View Railway ran hourly to a station in the city where passengers connected to the Lauderdale Streetcar Line. It ran during daylight hours and until 10:30 p.m. on Saturdays. After dark, Memphians took cabs or drove the Horn Lake Road out of the city to the nightclubs for all-night parties.[38]

The roadhouse owners bought liquor from bootleggers who delivered their wares by way of the Mississippi River or from moonshiners in the nearby woods. The surrounding woods and swamps were the favorite haunts of the Laughter brothers. Ed Laughter supplied liquor to the roadhouses, Lonnie Laughter ran a moonshine operation with partner Henry Johnson until Shelby County deputies found his three-thousand-gallon still just above the state line in November 1926, and Bob Berryman partnered with Lucian Laughter to supply The Paddock.[39]

The Marigold Gardens, the most popular of the nightclubs in Desoto County, Mississippi, had the reputation as a "rendezvous of the bootlegger, the gambler, and the gunman." It won notoriety in August 1923 when an Illinois Central Railroad conductor named A. M. "Dude" Mitchell died in a gunfight with the club's owners Charles Auferoth and John Kirkman and H. L. McGhee, a moonshiner who supplied their liquor. Neighbors of the nightclub, fed up with the all-night carousing, demanded Desoto County officials shut it down. Witnesses said that the place had been running "full sway amid the flow of corn liquor, the ragged music of a jazz band, shooting affrays, automobile wrecks, stabbing melees, drinking bouts, and other wild and Bacchanalian orgies." Shelby County sheriff Oliver Perry complained about having to arrest unruly partygoers on the Horn Lake Road returning to Memphis in the middle of the night. Deputy Charles Garibaldi reported that "young girls scantily clad, under the poisonous influence of corn whiskey have participated in the Marigold orgies." The roadhouse began operating again until Prohibition agents arrested Kirkman for moonshining as he delivered cornmeal, sugar, tin cans, and corks to McGhee's moonshine outfit in June 1925.[40]

An incident at the Mississippi Club signaled an end to the free-for-all in Desoto County. Gul Steed had to close his Highway 61 nightspot after guests sued his bouncer John Phillips for assault in August 1938. Phillips had a history of violence, including attacking attorney Ben Kohn. Phillips pleaded guilty and admitted that a pro-Crump Memphis police sergeant had paid him twenty-five dollars to attack Kohn for supporting Crump foe Gov. Gordon Browning. After the sympathetic judge let Phillips off with a light fine, Phillips faced arrest again for beating another man with battery cables. Stanley Puryear, later convicted of murdering his wife with an ax, tried to cut the throat of Phillips during a knife fight over money lent to Puryear's mistress.[41]

Ada Berding, a divorced beautician, and an unnamed married "prominent Memphis woman" met up with friends including the girlfriend of Phillips at the crowded club and stayed well past midnight. Phillips, who was working as a bouncer, had designs on Berding, an attractive young blonde, and became upset when he found that she planned to leave without him. Phillips grabbed Berding and her friend and beat them while the crowd watched. He ripped Berding's dress off, hit her in the face with a wooden rack from a dice table, and dragged her outside where he punched and kicked her. No one could stop the enraged Phillips, so an employee resorted to shooting Phillips in the legs with a shotgun in order keep him from killing Berding.[42]

The Desoto County Grand Jury ordered the closure of the roadhouses and Mississippi legislators drafted bills to keep gamblers away in December 1937, but officials were slow to act. After the incident at the Mississippi Club, residents demanded stronger actions. The governor responded by ordering the National Guard to raid remaining roadhouses throughout the state. In February 1939, guardsmen and local deputies raided The Paddock, The Palace, and The Tom Cat, made arrests, smashed furnishings, and destroyed gambling equipment. This crackdown, however, did not mean the end of nightlife. Changes just over the horizon in Tennessee meant that new nightclubs would soon open in Shelby County.[43]

13

LIQUOR AND OTHER VICES

I spent half my money on gambling, alcohol and wild women.
The other half I wasted.

—W. C. Fields

L ewis Pope's campaign sign hung in tatters. During a rally at the Memphis
Fairgrounds the day before, Pope had accused local police of allowing vice
to operate to fund Ed Crump's political machine. Pope had demanded
that the commissioner Clifford Davis shut down Dinty Moore's, C. D. "Suggs"
Peeple's Place, Poker Pete and Jake Tuckerman's Place, Cliff Moriarty's Place,
Louis Barrasso's Log Cabin, and the new Silver Slipper on Third Street.

Pope's campaign manager, J. C. Carruthers, hoped to send a message about
his candidate's stance on vice by placing the sign at Madison and Second Avenue halfway between Dinty Moore's and Peeple's Place. After police shut the
gambling houses down, angered gamblers responded to Pope's message with
one of their own. Vandals climbed the billboard and ruined the gubernatorial
candidate's advertisement with knives and clubs during the night of July 18,
1934. The battered sign hung as testimony to Memphians' defiance of vice laws.[1]

The ASL and WCTU promised Americans that Prohibition would end the
social evils associated with saloons; however, vice not only continued but also
kept the illegal liquor trade going. Much of the liquor trade that centered in
saloons shifted to gambling halls and houses of prostitution in the wake of
Prohibition. Supplying alcohol to customers effectively turned many of the
city's gamblers and prostitutes into bootleggers.

Police and sheriff's campaigns to shut down gambling often overlapped
with liquor campaigns. Well-known bootleggers including Bob Berryman,
Nello Grandi, Albert Barrasso, Reno Devaux, Rigo Vannucci, and Jim Mulcahy

ran poker games, craps, policy, and horse race betting. Gamblers also liked to drink, and their hosts made sure they had plenty of their favorite beverages on hand.

Memphians who gambled did so with a passion. Sheriff Knight raided a craps game at Axle and Lauderdale Streets one night in September 1924 and rounded up forty African American men. The gamblers were so rowdy and caught up in the game that they failed to hear the pistol shot fired as a warning by the lookout. Police and deputies regularly hauled in anywhere from twenty-five to a hundred African American men in Saturday night craps game raids in the 1920s.[2]

On Monday morning, Judge Clifford Davis would have them appear en masse and release them after each paid a two- to three-dollar fine Davis facetiously called the "club rate." Those who could not afford the fines called their employers to come to court with money. White businessmen complained in 1925 about the police pestering their workers "merely for indulging in the customary amusement" and argued that gambling kept them out of "more serious mischief." The homicide lieutenant Frank Glisson disagreed. He insisted on the necessity of enforcement because arguments resulting from gambling alone resulted in nearly one murder a month.[3]

• • •

W. F. Silvey came to town from Seymour, Missouri, and stopped in at Dinty Moore's café at Third and Madison Avenue. Silvey, a tall red-headed man with a matching mustache, wore a collared shirt without a necktie and a blue hand-me-down suit. The self-described mountaineer talked his way into the good graces of Joe Conley and asked if he might purchase a half-pint of corn liquor. Silvey seemed the furthest thing from a police officer or Prohibition agent, so Conley sold the stranger a bottle. Silvey thanked Conley, walked outside to a waiting car, and handed the evidence over to Police Inspector Will Griffin. Silvey had come to Memphis at Griffin's request to act as an informant for the police department. Officers returned later and arrested Conley and his whiskey runner Fred Werkhoven, cousin of Butts Werkhoven.[4]

Brothers Phil and Joe Conley, second generation Irish Catholics, opened their café and pool hall and named it after a character from the famous comic strip *Raising Father*. The Conleys loved betting on baseball games, horse racing, or anything else. Constables arrested Joe Conley in August 1926 after he bet Piggly Wiggly founder Clarence Saunders $1,000 that Austin Peay would receive the nomination to run for governor. Sheriff Knight made sure he did not follow through on the bet by holding Joe under the charge of threatening breach of the peace until the nomination passed.[5]

No amount of interference could stop the Conleys from gambling. Each time the city attorney put a padlock on Dinty Moore's, the Conleys would reopen at a new location. Police chief Will Lee, in frustration, posted an officer to stand watch over Dinty Moore's in 1928 to make sure the Conleys obeyed the law. Of course, once Lee removed the officer, gaming and drinking resumed.[6]

· · ·

Prohibition not only made gamblers into bootleggers, but it made the world's oldest professionals into liquor dealers as well. Those who frequented disorderly houses expected alcohol and their hosts made sure they got what they wanted. Journalist Owen Payne White, in his jocular search for sin in Memphis, wrote, "[prostitutes] were plentiful, beautiful, and, as I judged from the fact that they spoke to me on the street, smiled at me in the hotel lobbies, called me over the phone, waved to me out of their own front windows, and cooed at me from their cars, not at all discriminating or particular. It was the openest [sic] expression of friendly hospitality that I had seen anywhere in at least forty years, and I enjoyed it."[7]

In 1934, the police department allowed White to ride with two officers while they patrolled the city one night, and among the many strange and almost comical scenes, was a raid on a brothel. They arrived around a quarter after two in the morning at an "establishment conducted by some white girls for the two sinful purposes of selling booze and providing entertainment for blasé husbands." The officers parked a block away and snuck up to the house. One officer waited at the rear of the house under a high porch to catch anyone trying to escape while the other went to the front door. The other officer pounded on the front door and yelled, "Open up, it's the police!"[8]

A moment later, a partially dressed sixteen-year-old girl ran to the back porch, not to escape, but instead to push a ten-gallon crock of illegal home brew off its bench. She tipped it over and deluged the officer hiding under porch who let out a yell that woke the entire neighborhood. The girl laughed uncontrollably until the other officer told her to put on clothes and get in the police car. Her attitude changed with the prospect of arrest and medical examination, and she began to scratch, kick, and yell at the officers. They finally subdued the girl, tossing her in the back of the car with White.[9]

The driver took the police car, which by this point reeked of stale beer, by Beale Street on the way back to headquarters. There they saw a bloody brawl between two black men in the street. The officers got out of the car to disperse the crowd of onlookers and break up the fight. White also got out, but before walking away gave the girl, as he put it, "just six words of good, sound, fatherly, practical, wicked advice." He turned to her and whispered, "Beat it kid, run like hell." The officers cleared up the commotion, returned to the car, and saw that the girl had gone. One remarked, "Well I'll be damned. The kid's run away." White, in feigned surprise, replied, "So she has, so she has."[10]

The city's downtown red light district in the years before Prohibition had numerous houses of prostitution as well as many streetwalkers. One could find brothels along the so-called Tenderloin District that included Main Street south of Linden Avenue, Mulberry, Third, and Fourth Streets. Gayoso Avenue, a block north of Beale, featured higher-class establishments including those run by madams Grace Stanley and Anita Blanco. Mabel Harris ran the brothel on South Third for thirty years, Lillian Russell ran a place on Vance Avenue before Prohibition, and in 1928, Nell Miller still had a place "complete with pianos just like the days of old."[11]

Memphians typically referred to houses of prostitution with the more polite term "disorderly house." A disorderly house did not necessarily constitute a house of prostitution, but it happened that residents and guests at brothels tended to make a lot of commotion, typically in the middle of the night after drinking. This rowdiness led to the term "disorderly house" becoming synonymous with "houses of ill fame" or "bawdy house." Officers in May 1923 arrested Florence Smith for running a disorderly house at 989 Nelson and arrested her again a week later for possession of five gallons of liquor. A month later, neighbors' complaints brought police to a brothel run by an African American madam named Sarah House at 1222 Florida Street where three drunk white men from Widener, Arkansas, had caused a disturbance. Neighbors complained that "sleep was at a premium in the vicinity due to the noise."[12]

Not all brothels were as disorderly as Florence Smith's house; in fact, some quietly operated in upscale neighborhoods. The majestic Ida Simmons, who carried herself as a genteel southern lady, ran an operation out of a two-story mansion in an exclusive "silk stocking" neighborhood on East Parkway South, just north of Central Avenue. Mayor Rowlett Paine wanted to make a show of cleaning up vice and corruption in anticipation of the upcoming mayoral election and Simmons made for an easy target.

Paine hammered home the point that a vote for his opponent Watkins Overton was nothing more than a vote to return the city to the vice-funded Crump machine. Paine shook up the police department and promoted the

Fig. 13.1. Memphis Police Department's Black Maria, circa 1930. Courtesy of Memphis Room, Memphis Public Library and Information Center.

loyal John Plaxco to assistant chief. The crusading Plaxco, Capt. Tom Couch, and Capt. C. S. Rutland arrived at the mansion at eleven o'clock at night on July 21, 1927. Simmons had operated for years without interference from police, so the raid came as a complete surprise. The madam pulled the chief aside and said, "Why Mr. Plaxco, you know I've never been raided."

Plaxco replied, "Why Ida, you certainly know you've been raided this time." Officer Sandy Lyons brought the Black Maria around, and Plaxco and his men loaded up Simmons, three of her girls, and two gentlemen guests and took them to jail.[13]

Judge Clifford Davis dropped the charges of disorderly conduct, claiming the party had not disturbed the neighbors. Plaxco, however, was not prepared to give up so easily and had no qualms about embarrassing Davis. Officers met the women as they left the courthouse and arrested them for "being inmates of a house of ill-fame." Davis began to worry that having let the prostitutes go free would put him, and ultimately the Crump organization, in a bad light. Visibly disturbed, he explained he dismissed the cases and freed the women because he "was compelled to do so under the law and not because of any leniency toward undesirable characters."[14]

Miss Ida calmly stood before the court in the July heat, fanning herself with a palm leaf fan typically found among church congregations, as the prosecutor and arresting officers "assailed her with every uncompliment-ary term that could be couched in language fit to be heard in a courtroom in which ladies and gentlemen were present." Plaxco and his men told of arresting two couples *in flagrante delicto* and described the mansion as if it were part of "some risqué French novel." Miss Ida's attorney Ed Weinstein argued that the partygoers had not disturbed their neighbors and there was no evidence of a prostitution ring. The second round of charges fared no better than the first, and the judge freed Simmons and her girls. Simmons initially said she would leave town, but changed her mind and relocated her operation to a place on Rayburn where notorious madam Mae Goodwin once ran a brothel. In June 1939, Christian Brothers College, which had outgrown its Adams Street facility, bought the lot on East Parkway, where its administrators built the new Christian Brothers University.[15]

Bessie Howell's operation definitely fell into the category of disorderly house. She ran a brothel and sold alcohol at 356 Mulberry Street in the Tenderloin District south of Beale Street. Capt. Lee Boyles raided her place in November 1922 and discovered a fully stocked saloon complete with seventeen quarts of pre-Volstead Budweiser beer, ten quarts of Gordon's gin, three quarts of sloe gin, three bottles of Cedar Brook wine, twenty-eight bottles of home brew, and other assorted alcohol. Boyles took Howell into custody and arrested her assistant Edith Burch after he found Burch hiding in a closet. Police arrested Howell again in February 1930 after discovering thirty-one quarts of home brew in the shed behind her home.[16]

Howell's disorderly house came to an end after her activities drew the attention of the US Department of Justice. A federal investigation into a white slavery ring run by Jerry DeFrietas led to the arrest of Howell and another madam, Alice Batson, who ran a brothel out of a downtown hotel. DeFrietas, who operated prostitution rings in Atlanta, Georgia, Birmingham, Alabama, and Montgomery, Alabama, violated the Mann Act by transporting three underage prostitutes across state lines to work in Memphis. Howell faced charges for hosting the women and additional charges from Ruby McAlperin, a nineteen-year-old native of Jackson, Mississippi, who claimed she was held in the disorderly house against her will and beaten by Howell.[17]

The discovery of a sixteen-year-old runaway from a prominent family in a brothel on South Third Street spurred a campaign against prostitution in March 1928. Commissioner Clifford Davis promised to drive "immoral women" out of Memphis and shut down the red-light district.[18] Prostitutes, now mindful of unwanted publicity, no longer loitered on front porches or sat in front windows. They also reigned in much of the disorderliness and kept lower profiles in their neighborhoods. In 1935, police warned prostitutes not to wear "flaming red dresses" and to stay indoors after *Collier's* magazine published Owen White's article on sin in the city.[19]

Prostitution came under closer scrutiny in the 1930s as the FBI investigated violations of the Mann Act. Agents arrested Fayette Dexter Pierson for bringing a young prostitute named Vera Mae Lee from Birmingham to Memphis in 1932, and a madam named Mollie Fletcher for bringing a fifteen-year-old girl from Houston to work in her brothel in 1935. Other arrests followed as agents arrested pimps who brought girls in from other states.[20]

Health concerns about syphilis also moved law enforcement to take action. The Memphis Women's Protective Bureau, under Annie Jackson, had all white women arrested for prostitution tested for syphilis. Jackson found that, in the first six months of 1937, 69 of the 138 women arrested tested positive for the disease. The federal government provided funds to expand the syphilis clinic at John Gaston Hospital and the University of Tennessee pathology laboratory in 1938. With the allocation of federal funds through the La Follette-Bulwinkle Act of 1938, state health departments organized programs to combat venereal disease; however, medical workers in Memphis still struggled to deal with the nearly twenty thousand cases in the city. Memphis police, under pressure from Ed Crump, led a sweeping campaign on vice in 1938 and 1939 to end organized prostitution in the red-light district.[21]

Even those that did not become sick often met with tragic fates. The most infamous example occurred on October 8, 1916, when John Revinsky murdered Mae Goodwin, the city's best-known madam, when she discovered him in the act of stealing some of her jewelry. Gangster George Honan died trying to gun down Grace Frazier, a young prostitute working for Mabel Harris in January 1915. Harris ran the Third Street brothel for three decades until a streetcar struck her in 1925, leaving her crippled and bedridden. Dorothy McDowell came to Memphis from Alabama and worked for ten dollars a week as a waitress until she tired of the low wages. The lure of life as a flaming youth led her into prostitution and association with bootleggers and bandits. A wealthy family helped her through business school, but she fell back into her old ways. Despondent over her failures, she attempted suicide by swallowing a bottle of poison in May 1930.[22]

The effects of Prohibition were far from the promise of the ASL and WCTU of a richer, healthier, safer, more moral society with less crime and violence. The saloons had closed, but the demand for vice and liquor continued. Where once gambling and prostitution brought business to the saloon, in the wake of Prohibition, liquor brought business to gambling halls and houses of prostitution. As long as these vices continued, the ASL and WCTU could never deliver on their promise of a liquor- and crime-free country.

14

KING OF PRESIDENT'S ISLAND

If your honor, please, we fear that this defendant is dead.
—S. E. Murray, district attorney, June 22, 1923

President's Island seemed more like a setting from a Mark Twain novel than a real place. The ten-thousand-acre island sat in the Mississippi River just past the Harahan Bridge about three miles south of downtown Memphis. It had dense woods including several lakes, provided a home to local wildlife, and attracted hunters and fishermen beginning with American Indians before the arrival of European settlers.

The size of the island made it of interest to developers, but seasonal flooding limited the usefulness of the land. John Overton, one of the city's founders, left President's Island to his son John in his will. Over the years ownership changed hands, and most settlements only lasted a short time; the Freedmen's Bureau established a colony for recently freed slaves at the end of the Civil War, Nathan Bedford Forrest later opened a penal colony for prisoners, and city health officials set up quarantine camps for yellow fever victims in 1878. Absentee landlords maintained a few plantations and a small number of farming families formed communities, but most of the island remained a wilderness well into the twentieth century.[1]

The isolation of the island made it the destination of criminals on the run. Secluded places hidden in the woods and easy access to the river attracted desperadoes such as river pirates, runaway slaves, prison escapees, bandits, murderers, and of course, bootleggers. The most notable was Joe Sailors, a man law enforcement came to refer to as the "King of President's Island."

Joe Sailors came from a modest rural background but, over time, became a wealthy landowner and businessman. He and his brothers bought property

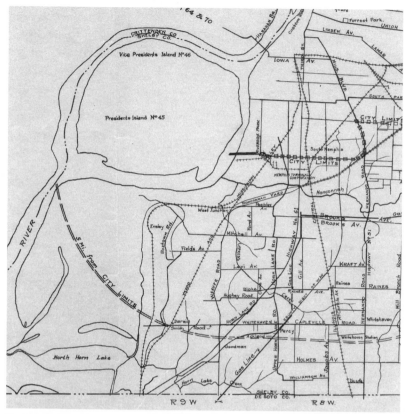

Fig. 14.1. President's Island and South Memphis. Courtesy of Memphis Room, Memphis Public Library and Information Center.

in Binghamton, a subdivision on the eastern boundary of the city that grew around a company that built railcars for the Raleigh Springs Railroad. Sailors also bought property in Fort Pickering, ran a boarding house on West Calhoun with his wife Beulah, and co-owned the Herrick and Sailors Saloon at 60 North Second Street before statewide Prohibition.[2]

Sailors, like many other liquor dealers, went into "soft drink" sales, which of course was just a cover for bootlegging. For a while, he had free reign in Binghamton because John Sailors, the town marshal, turned a blind eye to the whiskey his brother bootlegged with Tyree Taylor. This situation changed after Taylor's supervisor Stanley Trezevant and the Department of Justice discovered the Taylor Liquor Ring.

Trezevant arrested Joe Sailors and C. P. Powers in November 1918 after deputies found fifteen crates marked hardware loaded with smuggled liquor at the River and Rail Wharf. Taylor assumed Sailors tipped off investigators and threatened to get even with him. Sailors's attorney Charles Bryan requested the judge give a peremptory order to the jury for a not-guilty verdict because of Taylor's threat. The judge refused, but the grand jury acquitted Sailors anyway, even though they convicted Powers.[3]

• • •

Pete Sailors may not have been the most sophisticated outlaw, but he was loyal to his brother Joe. As a boy, Pete left home to live with his brother. He knew little of the world beyond his original Georgia home and the Alabama farm where the family relocated, but he managed to negotiate a train journey to Deverville, Arkansas. One day, Pete did something that he knew would anger his brother, so rather than take a beating, he decided to walk back home to Alabama.

Joe became concerned when he could not find Pete. He searched for the boy for several hours until he found him walking back and forth along the Mississippi River bank. Joe watched his brother's strange behavior for a few minutes before he called out. The boy refused to come near his brother, so the two negotiated an armistice from a distance of about a hundred yards. Joe finally walked over to Pete and asked, "What the deuce were you doing walking up and down the river bank?" Pete replied, "I was a-lookin' for a foot log, but this is the biggest durned creek I ever saw."[4]

In April 1919, Pete Sailors avoided a charge of violation of the Wartime Prohibition Act, the ban on distilled spirits production during World War I, when deputies failed to prove he owned liquor deliberately smashed by a courier. Sheriff Perry went after Pete Sailors in September 1919, but this time, he sent an informant to buy the liquor. The informant knocked on the door of Sailors's house and gave his name. Sailors told him to wait while he went into an adjacent field to retrieve a quart of whiskey. He came back and passed the bottle through a window. As the men made the transaction, Perry stepped out of the shadows and said, "I'll take that Pete, and you too."[5]

Sailors's predicament went from bad to worse when Deputy Goswick appeared with Sailors's dog and a case of whiskey. The overly friendly dog had led the deputy to the cache hidden in the field. Sailors, when he saw the deputy with the whiskey, threatened to kill the dog. Perry made the arrest, but because Sailors did not complete the transaction, Judge John McCall gave the jury a directed verdict of not guilty. Perry freed Sailors, and much to the relief of neighbors and those following the story in the newspaper, Sailors forgave the dog.[6]

• • •

In March 1919, three bandits posing as special officers searching for liquor raided Joe Sailors's home and stole $302. The robbery and the incidents with Pete Sailors convinced Joe to move his operations. He bought a 395-acre plantation on President's Island from Capt. J. A. Couch of the steamboat *Minnie* in October 1919. The island not only gave him access to the river for liquor transportation and plenty of places to hide whiskey stills, but it also gave him a profitable cotton farm.[7]

Over the next twenty years, Sailors's plantation remained frozen in time, a throwback to antebellum days. Life on the island, except for modern improvements at the "big house," remained as it had been a century earlier. The island was home to a community of about three hundred African Americans, and Sailors employed about a hundred as workers. The plantation typically had a hundred head of hogs and around sixty mules, as well as chickens and turkeys. Sailors directed the work from his home several miles from President's Island in Fort Pickering and left the day-to-day activities to his overseer Brick Woods.

Meanwhile, Sailors's gang turned the idyllic island into a major source of moonshine for Memphis bootleggers. Agent A. L. Story and his men arrested six men and found seven stills ranging in capacity from one hundred to three hundred gallons in December 1921. The *Commercial Appeal* announced, "President's Island yesterday was literally swept clean of illicit liquor stills when federal agents staged the greatest raid in the history of Shelby County." The victory, however, was short-lived.[8]

Prohibition agents tried to build cases against Joe Sailors, but the wily bootlegger proved difficult to prosecute because of his ability to tamper with juries and eliminate witnesses. In September 1921, Dist. Atty. William Kyser found out that Sailors told a grand juror, Frank Taylor, former saloon owner and friend of twenty years, what to say during testimony. Kyser cited Sailors with contempt. Judge Ross admitted that Sailors's behavior seemed suspicious, but the lack of evidence kept him from doing anything more than fining Sailors two dollars for the court fee.[9]

Police detective William Griffin, working with Prohibition agents, sent informants to gather information about liquor and gambling aboard Sailors's fifty-five-ton steamer *Whisper*. Griffin secured search warrants and led a raid on the boat in April 1922. As they stormed aboard, Metro Ward, a twenty-one-year-old farmer from Binghamton, reached for a .45-caliber pistol. Detective Quianthy ran after him, stuck his shotgun barrel in his side, and ordered, "Throw 'em up, or I'll blow you in half!" Pete Sailors surrendered without resistance as agents seized the vessel.[10]

Officers also arrested Joe Sailors and nineteen others in connection with liquor running and gambling in a seemingly airtight case in April 1922. The prosecution, confident in its arguments, eagerly prepared for its day in court. Sailors, however, would not go down so easily. The Shelby County Grand Jury met, but deputies could not locate the prosecution's key witness. The informant mysteriously disappeared, leading jurors to suspect Sailors of murdering him. Without the witness, the grand jury had no other choice but to return not true on the cases.[11]

Catching Sailors with a still would not be easy either. Prohibition agents T. L. Comer and Bond Harmon raided the island in September 1922 and found a three-still outfit with a 1,000-gallon capacity that produced 125 gallons of whiskey daily. The agents destroyed the still and 3,000 gallons of mash, but they could not tie it to Sailors because it sat just off his property.[12]

Agents discovered a barge carrying a pair of 2,000-gallon stills and another on the island in May 1923. The raiders wounded bootlegger W. B. Ward and captured his African American assistant Ben "Rock" Dawkins as they tried to escape. Neither implicated Sailors, and Dawkins was soon free on a $1,000 bond. Again, they sat far enough from Sailors's property for him to deny ownership.[13]

Prohibition agents thought they had a lucky break in June 1923. Five agents and sixteen police officers raided the island and captured two stills worth $10,000, ten thousand gallons of mash, and one hundred barrels of corn liquor. The agents, in a stroke of rare luck, captured Early Williams and Henry Bell as three other moonshiners escaped through the woods. Even better, the two African American men agreed to cooperate and testify against Sailors.[14]

A federal grand jury indicted Joe Sailors, Pete Sailors, C. D. Holland, Mrs. S. Foster, Clarence Whitt, Jessie Pierpaoli, and Julius Pierpaoli on charges of possession of whiskey, manufacturing whiskey, and possession of a still. Judge Ross arraigned Pete Sailors and released him on a $5,000 bond signed by his brother. Joe Sailors was arraigned and released a few days later on bonds signed by Pete Sailors and gangsters Nello Grandi and John "The Pig" Cuneo.[15]

Eugene Murray, US district attorney, had Williams, Bell, and a third witness, Jack Burns, scheduled to appear before Judge Ross the day Joe Sailors surrendered. Williams appeared in court as scheduled, but the other two did not show up. Burns had received several beatings and police suspected he either ran away or someone had murdered him. Ross delayed the trial while police searched for the two missing black men.

They found Bell dead in a vacant house in Binghamton with his throat cut, but they saw no sign of Burns. A week later, prosecutors surmised that Burns had met the same fate. Murray told Ross, "If your honor, please, we fear that this defendant is dead—that some of the people whom he aided government officers to catch have made away with him." Murray dropped the charges, and Ross released Sailors and his crew.[16]

After Sailors's release, a "steady stream of booze poured into the city" from President's Island, supplying gangsters Nello Grandi and Herman Tamble as well as various liquor dealers. President's Island played such an important part in Memphis bootlegging that in March 1924, gangster Eugene "Cockie" Oliver and three other men ambushed and tried to kill Sheriff Knight and Dpty. Vernon Brignardello at Riverside Drive to protect the supply line.[17]

Federal and local law enforcement led raid after raid on President's Island from 1923 to 1925, but bootleggers rebuilt their stills as quickly as lawmen could tear them down. Expensive stills with thousand-gallon capacities reappeared overnight. Prohibition agents destroyed dozens of outfits and thousands of gallons of mash, but investigators could never link them to Sailors.[18]

Prohibition agents caught a break when thirty-year-old Joe Hays offered to cooperate. Hays, fed up with tending a still for a local bootlegger, offered to act as an informer in the summer of 1926. The information Hays gave resulted in several raids, but when word leaked to the underworld about what he did, his days were numbered. A group of bootleggers caught up with him at a party one night on President's Island. They smashed his head, shot him in the chest, and dumped his body in the river. Police found his body washed up on the shore on another island downriver. Agent Jack Davis rounded up suspected bootleggers for questioning but never found out who killed Hays.[19]

On August 15, 1927, Prohibition agent O. H. Warren and US marshals J. O. Tuck and John Haggard raided President's Island and caught Joe Sailors and his African American assistant James Johnson red-handed making moonshine. It should have been an open and shut case, but Sailors's attorney claimed that his client was not making moonshine, but rather, he was trying to run the moonshiner off his property. Eleven voted for acquittal, but one juror, who was perhaps smart enough not to believe the obvious lie, held out, resulting in a hung jury and mistrial. After a second trial ended the same way, the Department of Justice gave up and ordered a dismissal of charges.[20]

The legalization of 3.2 percent beer and the influx of bonded liquor from outside the state after the 1933 repeal of the Eighteenth Amendment to the US Constitution did not entirely end the demand for moonshine as predicted by repeal advocates. President's Island continued to host moonshiners working for Sailors, or at least with his consent, through the 1930s. In June 1934, Judge Harry Anderson passed sentences on members of the McRae family, a leading bootleg gang on President's Island, ranging from probation and fines to terms in federal prison. Federal agents and deputies arrested Alex Ross, Billy Boyd, and a Mexican named Michael Cavosos after finding a large galvanized iron still, ten thousand gallons of mash, and a hundred gallons of whiskey in October 1934. Judge Fitzhugh gave.the three probation instead of fines and jail time because they were only "fifty-cent a day workers" with no records.[21]

In September 1935, E. M. Corbett, head of the Alcohol Tax Unit under the US Bureau of Internal Revenue, returned with other agents to President's Island. They arrested Sam Mascari, Mack Mascari, Loren Hudson, George Butler, Alfred Williams, and Junius Dean as they unloaded 235 gallons of liquor from President's Island into cars at the riverfront. The agents believed the men worked for Joe Sailors but needed solid proof.[22]

Agents J. H. Denny and J. G. Yates went to the island and followed the distinctive tracks of a mule with a lame rear right foot. They followed the tracks to a swaybacked house. They found a wagon that smelled of whiskey in the yard, as well as the lame mule in the barn. They continued along the trail until they found a still made of twenty- to twenty-two-gauge galvanized steel with copper condensers capable of producing two hundred and fifty gallons of liquor a day.

Denny made a careful inspection of the still and noted the makes of the equipment. He also inventoried the supplies, including ten one-hundred-pound bags of sugar, five pounds of yeast, one hundred pounds of rye meal, thirty-two empty ten-gallon cans, an eighth of a barrel of corks, and ten five-gallon cans of whiskey. The agents also found four full thousand-gallon mash vats, and one empty vat set in the ground.

With evidence in hand, it remained for the agents to connect the operation with the operators. Denny traced the pump to the A. Y. McDonald Company that made the device and as well as to its seller, the Orgill Brothers Company in Memphis. Denny searched the property of the men arrested by Corbett and found the bill of sale for the pump in the effects of Sailors's employee Loren Hudson.[23]

The Department of Justice needed more evidence, so Denny wiretapped Sailors's telephone. He climbed the telephone pole near Sailors's house, opened the box, and located the numbered wires. He followed the wires to a junction box at Third and Iowa where the cable went underground. He connected a line from his house on West Illinois Street to an unused wire leading to the nearby Marine Hospital where A. E. Hickey and J. H. Denny transcribed Joe Sailors's conversations. A federal grand jury indicted Sailors and his crew in April 1936 after reading the transcriptions of Sailors ordering supplies and directing the operations of his stills.[24]

Sailors's attorney Charles Bryan quoted arguments in *Olmstead v. United States* (1928) in his opposition to the admission of the evidence against Sailors. Justice Louis Brandeis had vehemently argued against the use of evidence obtained against Seattle liquor kingpin Roy Olmstead through wiretaps, claiming they constituted violations of both the Fourth and Fifth Amendments to the US Constitution. Judge John Martin denied Bryan's motion to suppress the evidence and reminded Bryan the US Supreme Court had allowed the use of evidence from wiretaps over the protests of Brandeis. Prosecutor C. P. J. Mooney Jr. argued that agents had not invaded Sailors's privacy because they tapped telephone lines off his property and listened from the government-owned Marine Hospital.[25]

Bryan continued to argue against the admission of the evidence from the wiretaps. He pointed out that the Alcohol Tax Unit ignored the Radio Act of 1927, which made it illegal to divulge private telephone conversations without the consent of the parties. Bryan also pointed out that the Federal Communications Act of 1935 and Tennessee state law did not allow unauthorized wiretapping. He quoted Justice Brandeis who said that wiretapping constituted an unreasonable search and seizure, in violation of the Fourth Amendment, and that the use as evidence of the conversations overheard compelled the defendants to be witnesses against themselves, in violation of the Fifth Amendment.[26]

Judge Martin allowed the evidence over Bryan's objections. Bryan and Blan R. Maxwell, who represented Sailors, and John J. Shea and Harry Pierotti, who represented the other defendants, had little defense in light of information from the wiretaps. Bryan argued that Mooney had not connected Sailors to the still, but he could not get around the fact that the evidence clearly proved otherwise.[27]

The outcome of the case seemed a foregone conclusion until insurance agent Albert Perry Pipkin, the jury foreman, had Denny demonstrate how he transcribed the telephone conversations. Denny listened to a telephone conversation, wrote down what he heard, and turned it over to Pipkin. The jury foreman carefully read Denny's transcription, then turned to the court reporter and asked the record show that Denny had made some mistakes.[28]

The jury came back to the courtroom after less than an hour of deliberation and stunned prosecutors by acquitting Sailors and his four codefendants.

Sailors remained calm during the proceeding, but the verdict read by Pipkin visibly moved him. The sixty-eight-year-old brushed a tear from his eye as he stood to put his arm around his wife and shake the hand of his nephew. Sailors, tired after the two-week trial, returned with his wife and nephew to his shrubbery-shrouded home at 309 West Illinois Street.[29]

Bootlegging eventually ended on President's Island, but not because of law enforcement. A tremendous flood, worse than the 1927 flood, swept through the Ohio and Mississippi River valleys six months later and submerged President's Island. Sailors evacuated the island just as floodwaters destroyed crops, homes, and any other man-made structure in their path. Sailors could have rebuilt his stills, but he knew the moonshine market was coming to an end. Two years later, the Tennessee legislature voted in favor of allowing voters to decide to keep or repeal Prohibition in their home counties. The people of Shelby County voted in favor of package sales of liquor, and the market for corn liquor all but vanished.

15

JOHN BELLUOMINI

Detroit and Buffalo have the Canadian border; the southwest states
have Mexico just across the line; and Memphis has Eastern Arkansas.
—Finis E. Wilson, Deputy Prohibition administrator, July 25, 1930

Some believe dreams of floods warn of misfortune and death. Had the 1927 flood only been a dream in the mind of John Belluomini, he may have seen it as a premonition of his demise. The torrential storms that came on Good Friday caused the Mississippi River and its tributaries to smash levees and wipe out entire communities, leaving thousands of survivors homeless. While Memphians sheltered refugees and fought off floodwater, Prohibition agents staged a routine raid. The search for liquor unexpectedly exposed a scandal that began the downfall of the city's most notorious gangster, shook public confidence in law enforcement, and changed the course of local politics.[1]

At the center of the storm was John Belluomini, a small-time hoodlum and drug-dealer who became a kingpin because of Prohibition. Belluomini saw liquor as the means to hit the big time. He focused on both manufacturing and distribution with the intent of controlling the lucrative Memphis liquor market. Belluomini would stop at nothing to accomplish his goal. He was quick to anger and often violent, especially toward those who turned against him. No other Liquor Baron invested himself so entirely in bootlegging, and consequently, no other had a fate so determined by the outcome of Prohibition.

• • •

In the morning of March 28, 1924, sheriff's deputies Abe Beatty, Phil Armour, and Oscar Lockman turned their boat back to Memphis after a long night of searching for moonshine stills on Island 40. As they made their way down the Mississippi River, they spotted a suspicious vessel speeding towards Island 37. The deputies caught up with the launch, brandished their weapons, and ordered its crew to stop and allow them to board. The men appeared willing to surrender, but the pilot, John Belluomini, had other ideas.

Belluomini gunned the engine and aimed the launch at the deputies' boat. Before the deputies could react, the bootleggers' launch had rammed their boat and nearly cut it in half. The shattered boat began to sink into the freezing water, but for a brief moment, the two vessels hung together. The deputies had just enough time to leap into the bootleggers' launch. The deputies, with weapons drawn, quickly took control of the launch as their boat splintered under its keel. They commandeered the vessel, which contained materials to build a still, and ordered Belluomini to head back to Memphis.[2]

Sheriff Will Knight took the deputies back in search of Belluomini's moonshine outfit. Island 37 was within the jurisdiction of Tipton County, but the sheriffs of neighboring counties had recently worked out agreements to coordinate raids and allowed limited authority for Knight in pursuit of bootleggers. Knight found that Belluomini's massive still, the largest captured in that county, had a capacity of 18,700 gallons and generated 360 gallons of liquor every twenty-four hours. Deputies demolished the equipment and supplies while Charles Volz, sheriff of Tipton County, took Belluomini into custody.[3]

Arrests and fines could not deter Belluomini. He paid a $150 fine for possession of materials for a still and paid another fine in Tipton County for running a still. The following year, Belluomini's lawyer took advantage of Judge John Ross's error and had narcotics charges dropped against his client. After each release, Belluomini became a little bolder, while law enforcement became a little more determined to bring him to justice.[4]

Frustrated police officials and Prohibition agents in Memphis turned their attention to Belluomini's grocery store located a block from Beale Street at the corner of Butler and Fourth Street. This grocery, and many others like it, acted as a community center like the old saloons. Gus Bocchini worked the counter and took in about twenty to thirty dollars a day selling sandwiches, soft drinks, and cigars. Italians gathered to socialize, speak in their native language, and help each other find jobs. Mario Chiozza, police sergeant and editor of the local Italian newspaper, regularly delivered letters from the old country to the store, where immigrants could pick them up.[5]

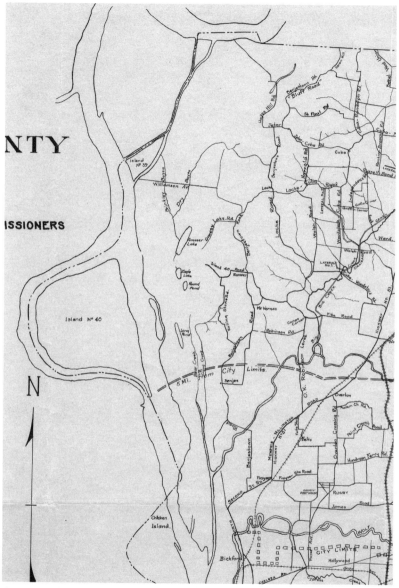

Fig. 15.1. North Shelby County and Mississippi Islands. Courtesy of Memphis Room, Memphis Public Library and Information Center.

Fig. 15.2. Police riot car driven by Sgt. Mario Chiozza. Courtesy of Memphis Police Department Archives.

This ordinary shop, however, was also a cover for one of the biggest boot-legging and gambling operations in the city. Belluomini moved there in 1925 after Capt. Will Lee's officers broke up two of his operations on Gayoso Avenue, a street just north of Beale mostly made up of boarding houses catering to African American laborers. He teamed up with Charles Donati, who along with his brothers Pete and Ernest "Skybo" Donati each had arrest records for liquor and gambling violations on and around Beale Street.

Captain Lee hoped to shut Belluomini down, but the gangster always seemed one step ahead of him. Belluomini avoided falling prey to police informers by having his African American employees sell liquor off the property. The store clerk Gus Alphonzo used a buzzer to warn the men running the policy game in the backroom if police were nearby. Most importantly, Belluomini secretly paid an informer in the police department to notify him of impending raids. Lee complained that he lacked the manpower to catch Belluomini, and said that he had done "everything to close the place except kill those Dagoes."[6]

The majority of the bootlegging activity, however, centered on a small house four doors down from the store that housed the liquor made at Belluo-mini's still at Blackfish Lake, Arkansas. Allen McNamara and Edgar Dorsey carried supplies by truck to the still and brought back whiskey in their weekly nighttime runs. Belluomini's partners Dino Chiochetti and Narciso Vannucci, a cousin of police sergeant Julio Vannucci, and other associates sorted the bottles for delivery. Drivers, typically young African American men, then took cars loaded with the liquor to various distribution points throughout Memphis during the night.[7]

Belluomini's operation ran smoothly until April 25, 1927, when Prohibition agents led by Alvin Howe raided the grocery. Typically, agents enlisted police officers to assist in raids; however, the city was in a state of emergency because of the flood and the refugee crisis. Mayor Paine ordered police and all other city employees to assist the Red Cross, so the agents conducted the raid alone. Because they did not inform the police, Belluomini's informant did not know of the raid and could not call in a warning.

The agents did not find any liquor, but Howe noticed a stack of green ledger books measuring eleven inches by five inches with gray canvas backs. Normally, Alphonzo would have kept the books hidden, but the raid caught him off guard. Howe found that most of the books simply listed business-related information, but two of them listed payoffs to law enforcement.[8]

The timing could not have been worse for the politically embattled Rowlett Paine. The discovery became such a scandal because the bitter struggle for the mayor's office guaranteed any hint of corruption would indeed become a political issue. Federal district attorney Lindsey Phillips took possession of the books and notified police commissioner Thomas Allen. Paine found out about the payoff books when he returned from the Chicago Flood Control Conference in June, but by then rumors about them had already become public.[9]

Paine wanted to keep the case out of the hands of Shelby County attorney general and Crump stalwart W. Tyler McLain because he knew that the Shelby County Organization would use the scandal against him in the upcoming election. Paine asked Judge Harry Anderson to call a special session of a federal grand jury before McLain returned from a vacation, but the judge was slow to respond. McLain called the ploy asinine and said it was all a "piece of faking and stalling" by Paine and Allen. He insisted the Shelby County Grand Jury take over the investigation and threatened to remove Paine and Allen if they did not cooperate.[10]

Paine defended his position by saying that federal agents found the books, federal authorities had possession of them, and federal courts had success in prosecuting similar cases in Terra Haute, Mobile, and Cincinnati. Paine accused McLain of trying to make the payoff books an election controversy. The mayor said McLain represented the people who "shake with fear and trembling at the thought of a thorough, searching, and far-reaching federal grand jury investigation."[11]

Frustrated by the lack of cooperation from Phillips and Anderson in pursuing the case, Paine traveled by automobile to Washington, DC, to make a personal plea to the Department of Justice to pursue the inquiry. While

Paine drove to the capitol, Phillips declared the evidence incompetent and advised Anderson against getting involved. Anderson and the Department of Justice turned down Paine's requests, leaving the investigation to the Shelby County Grand Jury.[12]

As Paine feared, Belluomini's payoff books suggested widespread corruption. They listed the names of fifty-one policemen, four deputies, a handful of constables, and periodic bribes paid to each of them ranging from five to twenty dollars. Assistant city attorneys John Exby and L. Estes Gwinn filed charges of conduct unbecoming of an officer, incompetency, and inefficiency. Thirteen officers either resigned or were fired, and Allen had Memphis police chief Joseph Burney suspend the remaining thirty-eight. Allen held off on charges of bribery in hopes a federal grand jury would investigate the matter when it met on October 3. The books listed so many names that one man close to the city administration said, "If these officers are crooks, we might as well close up shop."[13]

Ironically, the Shelby County Grand Jury could not hear the Belluomini case because Paine's new drive on vice, led by the new assistant chief John Plaxco, had bogged down the jury with eighty-three other cases. The grand jury delayed the investigation again because city attorney Tyler McLain went on vacation to Hot Springs, and his first assistant, Will Gerber, had just returned from vacation and was not prepared to pursue the case.[14]

Paine and Allen lost support from the City Club when they reneged on a promise to allow the watchdog group to view the payoff books. Club members including firebrand police officer Earl Barnard accused Allen of collusion. Allen, furious at the accusation, responded by hiring the law firm of Wilson, Gates, Armstrong, Kyser, Allen, Overton, and Gwinn to file a $100,000 libel suit. The City Club backed down, and Allen launched an investigation led by the detective Jack Ettlinger, a former Department of Justice agent who had worked on the Tyree Taylor case. A few weeks later, Allen released the names of the suspended officers once he was sure of the legal sufficiency of the evidence against them.[15]

Paine took advantage of the suspensions to clean house of political opponents. He had Allen place supporters in the major positions, while Burney hired thirteen new replacements and transferred seven patrolmen to the detective division. The next day, Burney suspended Capt. Will D. Lee for incompetency and inefficiency and replaced him with Capt. W. J. Herrington from the traffic division. Lee's name did not appear in the payoff books, but Burney claimed that Lee failed in his duty by allowing Belluomini to operate. Lee claimed Burney fired him because he refused to vote for Paine and blamed overbearing politicians and newspapermen and constant threats of termination for the lack of results in Prohibition enforcement.[16]

Prosecutors and defense attorneys prepared to appear before the police trial boards. Reviews by police trial boards were required for the suspensions to be permanent because the officers were civil servants. Charles Bryan replaced chief of detectives Will Griffin to defend the suspended officers. Allen named Plaxco, Herrington, and deputy inspector Edward Parker as the police trial board, and he appointed desk sergeant O. P. Caldwell to prosecute the cases but later replaced him with John Exby. Lee's attorneys Weinstein and Galloway demanded a separate public hearing for their client and a copy of the specific charges.[17]

Tensions within the police department came to a head in late September when Lt. Lee Quianthy and motorcycle officer Bob Turner confronted special investigator Frank Snedeker at the corner of Court Square in downtown Memphis. A shouting match between Quianthy and Snedeker turned into a fist fight. Quianthy took away Snedeker's pistol and beat him badly enough to send him to the hospital. Snedeker filed assault charges, but Judge Clifford Davis dismissed the case three weeks later after the embarrassed Snedeker failed to appear in court.[18]

Bryan used a two-pronged defense when the police trial board met on October 11, 1927. He first argued the payoff books, carried to court by Howe in a brown bag, were inadmissible because the mere appearance of a man's name in a book does not constitute guilt. Bryan then had each of the officers give essentially the same testimony: each knew of Belluomini but did not know Vannucci or Chiochetti; each went into his store but never saw anything suspicious; no one took a bribe, and no one knew of a payoff book. Each told about the homes they owned and how they paid for them to prove they had not received any large sum of money outside of regular work. Only Sgt. John Foppiano deviated slightly from the prepared defense when he said that he had personally known Belluomini since childhood.[19]

The board realized the payoff books were useless as evidence. Based on the testimonies, they could hardly find one officer guilty without finding all guilty. On October 15, Plaxco announced the police board found all but one of the officers not guilty of inefficiency and conduct unbecoming of an officer. Patrolman A. E. Rogers had to delay the presentation of his case because of illness, but the board found him not guilty as well. Allen delayed reinstating the suspended officers until November when Watkins Overton defeated Paine in the mayoral election by 19,548 to 6,948 votes.[20]

Fig. 15.3. Mayor Watkins Overton. Courtesy of Memphis Room, Memphis
Public Library and Information Center.

Prosecutors held out hope the payoff books would provide sufficient
evidence to convict Belluomini of bootlegging and bribery. Allen and Burney began cautiously and asked Belluomini to come to the commissioner's
office to answer questions. Belluomini agreed to come by on the evening
of July 7, and the three spoke in Allen's office for about an hour. Belluomini
denied any knowledge of the books or who put them in his store. Their
conversation had a "pleasant air," and they ended their meeting with talk
of Belluomini's recent trip to Florida.[21]

Bryan, the attorney of both the suspended officers and Belluomini, argued that the jury should not automatically assume the information in the
payoff books was genuine without supporting evidence. Agents sent the
payoff books to their regional headquarters in Louisville, where they made
photostatic copies, and handwriting experts analyzed the entries. Allen had

independent investigators study the books as well, but no one could prove their authenticity. Other store ledgers indicated unusually large monetary transactions, so prosecutors shifted away from the bribery charges against police officers and focused on the bootlegging charges.[22]

The pleasant air dissipated on August 16 when Ettlinger and Howe arrested Belluomini and his associates for conspiracy to violate the National Prohibition Act. Police and Prohibition agents grilled Belluomini for two hours about bootlegging and the payoff books but released him after he made a $10,000 bond. Belluomini was free again, but some of his associates worried they would not escape justice this time.[23]

Some of Belluomini's employees decided to cooperate with the government rather than face heavy fines and sentences. Joe Rinaldi agreed to work with prosecutors and was released on a $2,000 bond. Prohibition agents, worried someone would kill their star witness, announced that they had Rinaldi under protection to discourage any "underworld gentry" from "taking him for a long ride." Unable to raise $2,000 for bond, Jesse Rogers and Belluomini's other African American employees also agreed to cooperate with the government in exchange for lighter sentences.[24]

Other Belluomini cohorts proved harder to apprehend. Federal agents and Ettlinger tracked down Gus Bocchini in Chicago in late September and returned him to Memphis. Rumors circulated that Narciso Vannucci and Dino Chiochetti fled to Hot Springs and planned to escape back to Italy. The government put warrants out for their arrest and notified port authorities to keep watch for the fugitives; however, the pair evaded detection and left the Port of New York on the *Count Romeo* for Italy.[25]

Allen McNamara saw the case as a way out of prison. Gov. Austin Peay granted McNamara a pardon for the remainder of his sentence of eleven months and twenty-nine days for an unrelated liquor violation in exchange for his cooperation. In the rush to get McNamara to the federal court in Memphis, Peay neglected to pardon McNamara's fines. Commissioner Thomas Allen did not have time to contact the governor about pardoning the fines, so Allen had to pay them himself before he could take McNamara into custody.[26]

Deputies delivered the shackled McNamara to the Customs House at three o'clock in the morning to give his statement. There he saw Belluomini, who was waiting for release after his arrest the previous evening on charges of conspiring to violate Prohibition. After a heated confrontation, deputies took McNamara to District Attorney Phillips's office, where he began "squawking his head off" about Belluomini's store, his Arkansas still, and payoffs. Commissioner Allen later said, "I know more right this minute about what was going on at Belluomini's place than I ever expected to know." McNamara claimed to have seen more than twenty policemen take bribes at different times.[27]

The information seemed promising, but investigators soon realized that they had no way to corroborate McNamara's claims since the names he gave did not appear in the payoff books. McNamara faced an indictment for his part in running the still, but at the urging of Phillips, the grand jury dropped the charges in exchange for McNamara's cooperation. McNamara, in the end, cleverly dodged serving time without actually providing any useful information.[28]

The biggest surprise came in August 1928 when Narciso Vannucci unexpectedly returned from Italy, walked into the US marshal's office unannounced, and surrendered. The stunned marshal did not have an active warrant, so Phillips could only tell him to release Vannucci until Judge Anderson came back to Memphis. Anderson returned and fined Vannucci $1,000 for violating the National Prohibition Act. Vannucci gladly paid the fine and walked out of the courtroom a free man.[29]

Belluomini pled guilty to conspiracy charges and received a sentence of six months in the Dyer County jail. Belluomini began his sentence on October 24, 1927, as the federal grand jury at Helena, Arkansas, prepared to indict him on additional charges for operating the still at Blackfish Lake. Belluomini and McNamara appeared before federal court commissioner Lester Brenner to answer to the charges in November 1928, but Brenner had to drop the case because none of the government's witnesses appeared in court. In fact, Arkansas authorities could not locate any of them, leading many to suspect that Belluomini had had them killed.[30]

. . .

Tragedy wore heavily on Belluomini. His wife gave birth to a son in February 1928, so Judge John J. Gore allowed Belluomini to put up a $1,000 bond for a seven-day leave to visit his family. Louis Belluomini, John's father and brother-in-law to former saloon owner John Persica, drove to Dyer County to bring his son back to Memphis. On the return trip, the elder Belluomini lost control of his car and struck a telephone poll near Ripley. John crawled out of the wreckage and called an ambulance for his father. The crew carried his father to St. Joseph's Hospital in Memphis, where he lingered until February 15 before dying from his injuries. Belluomini remained free on bond just long enough to see his son and bury his father.[31]

Belluomini, though on an emotional downgrade, left jail determined to rebuild his business. Following his release, Belluomini and riverboat men Russell Warner and Frank Tamble pooled their resources and formed a syndicate. Belluomini operated from the islands in the Mississippi River and the swamps of eastern Arkansas, leaving Shelby County operations to his brother Frank Belluomini, Warner, and Tamble. Those not included in the syndicate became suspicious and jealous. Factions soon formed and the threat of violence grew. Suspicious bootleggers complained about "snitching, double-crossing, and general dissatisfaction," and police worried that even the smallest incident would lead to war among the bootleggers.[32]

Belluomini met his friend Joe Pacini just after Pacini's release from the workhouse one night in May 1928. The two walked along "bootleggers' row," the section of Fourth Street between Union and Beale, and stopped in front of Frank Marino's grocery. The store clerk, Louis Bargiacchi, noticed Pacini, a man he despised, standing outside talking with Belluomini. The enraged Bargiacchi reached into a drawer, pulled out a .32-20 revolver and stormed outside. Pacini saw him coming and pulled Belluomini in front of him as Bargiacchi began firing. One bullet struck Belluomini, who fell to the pavement. Bargiacchi continued firing and hit Pacini four times as he tried to run away.[33]

The shooting resulted from a feud that had begun weeks earlier after Pacini publicly humiliated Bargiacchi. Pacini, who had designs on Bargiacchi's wife, recruited Bargiacchi in St. Louis to come to Memphis to help with his bootlegging business and offered to let him live in his house. While Bargiacchi worked a still hidden in the woods just south of White Station, Pacini sent his wife Stella on errands and paid the maid to keep quiet so he could spend time alone with Bargiacchi's wife, Lexie. He swore to Lexie that he loved her and promised the young woman he would run away with her to South America once he made his final car payments. Lexie realized that Pacini was lying to her, so she told him she was finished with him. Pacini begged her to keep their secret and threatened to kill Bargiacchi if she exposed their relationship.[34]

Lexie broke down and admitted to having the affair. The infuriated Bargiacchi borrowed some money, moved his wife and infant son out, and took a job with Frank Marino. Once Bargiacchi left, Pacini began to brag about his relations with Lexie and went so far as to say the next Bargiacchi child would be his. Humiliated, Bargiacchi tried to take out his revenge on Pacini in front of Marino's store.[35]

The feud was far from over. Bargiacchi was released after he paid a twenty-five-dollar fine for carrying a pistol and a one-hundred-dollar fine for assault. Pacini, just after his release from the hospital, tried to kill Bargiacchi in a drive-by shooting. He fired three rounds from his car at Bargiacchi as he sat by a window in Nello Grandi's café at Fourth and Union. He shot out the window but missed Bargiacchi, who filed charges against him. Bargiacchi and Pacini continued to threaten each other over the following weeks. The fight only added to growing tensions among anxious bootleggers who took sides in the feud.[36]

Rather than resorting to open warfare, resentful bootleggers instead used the Prohibition Bureau against one another. They provided tips to agents about their rivals' activities that led to raids and arrests. Agents received so much information that they launched a city-wide campaign on bootlegging. Belluomini barely escaped to Arkansas as the Prohibition Bureau swept the city in June 1929. He evaded arrest, but his trusted lieutenant Harvey "Boxhead" Mitchell gave the locations of his stills following his arrest in September 1930. Agents systematically dynamited Belluomini's stills beginning with a massive still near Marion that produced fourteen hundred gallons of whiskey per day.[37]

Belluomini retaliated against the turncoat lieutenant in September 1933. He tipped off Mitchell's parole officer that Mitchell took part in a shootout in a local roadhouse. The recently released Mitchell had reconciled with his wife and planned to leave for Texas, but the sheriff's department found out about his violations before he could send his request to the parole board. Mitchell, whom one reporter called "Memphis's most notorious squealer," surrendered to deputies and returned to Atlanta to serve the remainder of his five-year term.[38]

The final blows to Belluomini's operation came with the legalization of 3.2 percent beer and the eventual repeal of the national Prohibition on December 5, 1933. Bootlegging continued because Tennessee still had statewide Prohibition in effect, but the nature of the business changed as bootleggers returned to smuggling bonded alcohol from wet states, as they had before 1920. The corn liquor market faded, as did Belluomini's importance. In the end, the Department of Justice lost interest in Belluomini and dropped its cases against him.

· · ·

Another super flood struck the Mississippi Valley in January 1937. Predictions of a fifty-five-foot flood crest struck terror into the hearts of residents in the Mid-South already struggling with torrential rains and overflowing tributaries. As before, the flood was a harbinger for the former Liquor Baron.

Belluomini, no longer a wanted man, returned to Memphis only a shadow of what he was in the 1920s. His unrealized quest for empire left him a bitter and broken man. He drank heavily and often became violent. He held a menial job at the Q. S. Café on Fourth near Vance and peddled half-pints on the side. His brother-in-law Joe Lenzi said, "John still bootlegs. That is all he has ever done and all he can do. He's just a small hip-pocket bootlegger now."[39]

On January 7, 1937, a drunken and belligerent Belluomini hit his coworker Louis Pagella in the mouth with a beer bottle. He left the café and went to the Lenzi grocery at 807 South Third Street around two o'clock in the afternoon looking for more trouble. Belluomini's nephew John Lenzi told him to leave the store, but Belluomini refused and challenged him and his cousin Rico to a fight outside. The Lenzis refused, and Belluomini stormed out to his car and drove away.

Belluomini returned an hour and a half later, confronted John Lenzi again, and chased the young man upstairs into the family's apartment. John's mother Rosa confronted Belluomini and ordered him to leave. Belluomini went outside but changed his mind about leaving. He pulled out his pistol and walked back toward the store.

Paul Lenzi happened to return home at the same time and walked in with Belluomini, unaware of what happened earlier. Belluomini punched him in the stomach and pushed him aside. Paul Lenzi backed away and asked why he hit him. Belluomini then pulled his pistol and shot him in the shin. Paul fell to the floor, and Belluomini shot him again in the arm.[40]

Joe Lenzi pulled a Luger pistol from behind the counter and shot once before the weapon jammed. Belluomini returned fire at Joe as Bastiano Lenzi opened fire with a Colt revolver kept in his office desk. In the chaos, two bullets struck Belluomini in the abdomen.[41]

Alex Marchesini, a baker working across the street, ran outside and found Belluomini as he stumbled out of the store. Belluomini ordered Marchesini to drive him to the hospital, but the baker refused. Belluomini pointed the pistol in his face and growled, "I ought to kill you too!" He pulled the trigger, but the hammer fell on an empty chamber.

Belluomini staggered to his car and tried to drive to the hospital alone. A patrolman rushed to the scene and tried to stop him as Rose Pike, the sister of Belluomini's landlady, reached in and took his gun. In the struggle, Belluomini nearly broke the wrist of the officer as he pulled the keys from the ignition.[42]

Police arrested Bastiano and Joe Lenzi on charges of shooting with intent to kill, but family and friends knew they were not to blame. A conciliatory Frank Belluomini arranged the $1,000 bonds for the two and drove Bastiano to the hospital to see his son. In February, patrolman Tommy Waterson testified to the good character of the Lenzis, while Sgt. Otis Caldwell explained that John Belluomini acted while "crazed by drink." Bastiano Lenzi said in his only statement, "He shot my boy twice."

Judge Carter thought for a while and said, "I'm going to dismiss these charges. [The Lenzis] seem to have been justified in protecting their home."[43]

Memphians, worried about the massive flood that inundated neighborhoods and brought over fifty-five thousand refugees to their city, hardly noticed the plight of the former gangster. Belluomini lingered in the hospital for weeks as the river bore down on straining levees. As the greatest flood stage in the history of the Mississippi River valley reached Memphis, Belluomini succumbed to his wounds and died at 12:30 p.m. on January 29, 1937. Days later, the flood, after wreaking havoc on the Mid-South, passed slowly downstream and faded into history.[44]

16

FALL OF THE LIQUOR BARONS

How can we make anything if some protected manufacturer comes in and sells for $1.25 and we have to sell for two dollars to make even a little profit? We are not violating any law when we dynamite stills—any citizen has the right.
　　　　—Unnamed syndicate bootlegger, August 17, 1928

The majority of liquor production in Memphis fell under the control of seven syndicates run by men known as the Liquor Barons. Business was good, and profits were high; however, as the expression goes—nothing good ever lasts. The absorption of the city administration into the Shelby County Organization triggered a series of events that threatened the reign of the Liquor Barons. By 1928, they faced a crisis so severe that its outcome would change bootlegging for the next decade.

The victory of Watkins Overton over Rowlett Paine in 1927 brought Crump back to power in Memphis. In the summer of 1928, the Shelby County Organization ran candidates in local elections and threw support behind Hill McAlister in his bid against Henry Horton for governor. To win the election, Crump's generalissimos E. W. Hale, W. Tyler McLain, and Frank Rice resorted to machine tactics of twenty-five years earlier to rally voters. Their efforts included encouraging the relaxation of the enforcement of recreational vices such as drinking and gambling to coax voter turnout. Though McAlister lost narrowly, Crump's candidates won every open position in the county.[1]

The *Commercial Appeal* bitterly opposed Crump and claimed that "bootleggers, gamblers, handbook operators, and distillers are the backbone of the machine." One reporter complained about the machine through a series of interviews with a fictitious person known as the Ex-Rounder, who said,

Fig. 16.1. Frank Rice. Courtesy of Memphis Room, Memphis Public Library and Information Center.

"Election time has rolled around again. With it come the old familiar things of yesteryear—a gradual loosening up of the bootleggers, a kindlier, more solicitous feeling for Negroes, a jollier gesture toward the ladies and greatly increased activity among the boys on the police force who do their bit in passing word down the line where poll tax receipts and registration certificates are garnered and bunched for the day."[2]

The Ex-Rounder claimed that police and sheriff's deputies canvassed neighborhoods while bootleggers like Jim Mulcahy and Ed Laughter packed polling places with African Americans. They paid poll taxes, held picnics, and rewarded voters with barbecue and liquor. According to historian Elizabeth Gritter, Black Memphians involved with the Shelby County Organization's voter manipulations sometimes worked the system to their benefit. They would change clothes and cast ballots in different wards up to four times a day to earn extra money.[3]

The Shelby County Organization's ward heelers canvassed African American neighborhoods on behalf of machine candidates. They solicited votes, payed poll taxes, and provided transportation en masse to polls on Election Day. Critics complained that the machine "herded" African Americans who would normally not participate in the electoral process to the polls to vote for its candidates in order to steal the election. The organization, for its part, had no qualms about its methods, but it did not want to advertise it because the sight of so many black people being "led" to polls appeared undemocratic and a threat to white supremacy.

Reporters who tried to photograph the machine in action met with violent resistance. Policemen, under orders from commissioner Clifford Davis, harassed journalists and seized their cameras. They arrested ten newspaper photographers and assaulted others. Two beat up Dickie Bolton and smashed his camera as he shot a newsreel of a voting place on Lauderdale Street. Police arrested eight Horton supporters and poll watchers and held them on trumped-up charges of breach of the peace. The worst offense occurred when Will Gerber, assistant to Dist. Atty. Tyler McLain, beat up photographer Billy Sisson. The Shelby County Grand Jury blatantly whitewashed Gerber's actions when it convened three weeks later. Reporters called it "the boldest, the rottenest, the most fraudulent, and by and large the most absurd election ever held in Memphis."[4]

The political machine's actions caused fallout in the underworld as well. Before the election, the Liquor Barons dominated the market and fixed prices. The independent bootleggers, who operated by paying bribes to sheriff's deputies, took advantage of the laxity in law enforcement during the election and flooded the market with cheap liquor. Their overproduction caused a drop in the price of white mule to as little as $1.25 per gallon, far below the rates set by the most powerful liquor barons Russell Warner and Frank Belluomini.[5]

The reduced market prices cut into the profits of the Liquor Barons to the point that their earnings did not cover production costs. A group of about thirty "unprotected" syndicate bootleggers "threw down the gauntlet" and began destroying stills owned by "protected" independent bootleggers. They dynamited over thirty stills between July and August 1928 to retaliate against the uncooperative independents and the deputies who protected them. They caused liquor prices to increase to over three dollars a gallon and deprived corrupt deputies of as much as $400 a month for every still they destroyed.[6]

The unprotected bootleggers also tipped off the Prohibition Bureau. They informed Alvin Howe, deputy Prohibition administrator for West Tennessee,

Fig. 16.2. J. P. Alley's depiction of the 1928 election in Memphis. Caption: THE "PRIMARY" TROUBLE IS BEALE STREET CARBON. Courtesy of Memphis Room, Memphis Public Library and Information Center.

about the location of a still run by the nephew of a high-ranking county official. Howe, who did not owe allegiance to the Shelby County Organization, raided the operation and discovered two sheriff's deputies standing guard. Howe destroyed the outfit and ordered the two deputies to leave when they tried to interfere. Soon after the raid, Howe received orders to return to the Louisville office. The official explanation stated Howe received a reassignment because he failed the civil service exam given two years earlier, though rumors circulated that some influential person affiliated with local machine pressured Washington officials to reassign him.[7]

Howe complied with the order, but he did not go quietly. Prohibition Commissioner James Doran ordered a campaign on bootleggers operating on river islands throughout the Mississippi River valley, so Howe, on his way back to Louisville, led one last raid on Centennial Island, an island in the Mississippi River north of Memphis near Tipton County, with agents Phil Armour and Arthur Ramsey. Howe found one of the elusive water-borne moonshine outfits that belonged to the Liquor Barons. The opera-tors had temporarily stopped production and hidden the 160-foot barge among willow trees in a chute on the island. The massive outfit included a four-thousand-gallon still, a three-thousand-gallon still, twenty-eight one thousand-gallon vats of mash, three gasoline engines, and a steam boiler. Howe, as his parting shot to the bootlegging community, had his agents load the barge with dynamite and blow it to pieces.[8]

Sheriff Knight caught up with the syndicate bombers and brought their campaign to a halt on the night of August 17, 1928. Knight and his deputies arrested Mack Thomas, Charlie Auferoth, Russell Warner, Charlie Vann, and Frank Belluomini as they drove out of Ensley Bottoms in Warner's Lincoln armed with twenty sticks of dynamite, fuses, rifles, and a sawed-off shotgun. The Shelby County Grand Jury indicted the five men for conspiring to de-stroy property, unlawful possession of explosives, and disturbing the peace by prowling, a charge commonly referred to as night riding. Knight also ques-tioned but then released gang members Alex Marrotti, Will Ledbetter, Velton Green, and George Herman Tamble in connection with the bombings.[9]

. . .

Jack Loague looked at the smoking wreckage of his still. The syndicate had targeted his operation first in its bombing campaign. Loague's partner intended to rebuild and start over, but Loague was "mad clean through." Loague told his partner he intended to go home, get his shotgun, and make someone pay back what he lost in that still. That night he hijacked his first liquor shipment.[10]

Jack Loague was the black sheep son of attorney Robert Emmett Loague and grandson of former mayor John T. Loague. He had run away from home after attending Christian Brothers College, joined the US Navy, and later enlisted in the US Army as a pilot during World War I. Afterward, he worked with a gambling clique in Minneapolis. He intended to return to Memphis with the money he saved to go into gambling, but insiders cautioned against the dangerous rackets and suggested he invest in bootlegging.[11]

During the rum war, the series of conflicts between competing bootleg-gers in the summer of 1928, Loague took out his wrath on the Liquor Barons by hijacking their liquor and cars. Loague, with no pretense of hiding his

Fig. 16.3. Jack Loague at a Chicago airport before Det. A. O. Clark
escorted him to Memphis to face charges of robbery in May 1935.
Author's Collection.

identity, telephoned the bootleggers and demanded payment for the return of
their property. The bootleggers time and again paid up, all the while looking
for a way to exact their revenge. Loague avoided five attempts on his life by
hired hit men, including an attempt by two out-of-town machine gunners.[12]

The bootleggers resorted to having one of their members "squeal" to the
Prohibition Bureau. Agents received information that led to a conviction of
Loague on liquor charges in 1929. Four months later, Loague was released
and resumed his war on the Liquor Barons. He had a change of heart when
his mother, on her deathbed, made him promise to give up his life of crime.[13]

Loague gave up hijacking, but he lived as a marked man. One night in July
1932, Loague noticed a car following him as he drove along Madison Avenue.
The driver followed Loague for several blocks until they reached Marshall
Avenue. He accelerated his car and tried to shoot Loague as he passed, but
lost control of his car and ran it into a curb. Loague looked back and saw
the shooter as he ran from the car. The would-be assassin was the informer

whose information had led to Loague's conviction. He told police, "I think the man who tried to put me on the spot is one I used to be associated with in the bootlegging racket. I'm out of the game now, but apparently, the man is reviving an old feud between us." That was enough for Loague. He knew the bootleggers would never forgive him, so shortly after the attempted hit, he intended to leave Memphis for good. He left town but broke his promise to his mother and returned to crime. Police arrested him for a string of robberies in 1935.[14]

• • •

Crump, once securely in power in Memphis, set about to improve the image his organization by purging it of "protected" liquor interests. Sheriff Knight promised to pay a hundred dollars to anyone who could prove his deputies extended protection to any liquor handler and promised to "prosecute that deputy to the limit of the law if the proof holds up." Overton and Davis eagerly began a drive on vice. Bootleggers and nightclub owners who considered themselves "paid-up" members of the organization complained about their treatment and demanded the removal of Davis, but Overton replied, "We would like to help our friends, but we can't let them violate the law."[15]

The Tennessee General Assembly Crime Committee launched an investigation in February 1929 into rumors of bootlegging, gambling rings, bandit gangs, and the complicity of law enforcement in Shelby County. The committee, headed by Lon C. Scott, included four state senators, seven state representatives, and Tennessee ASL superintendent Dr. James A. Tate, with funding provided by the state government and the ASL. They came to Memphis expecting the worst, but Davis and McLain impressed the committee with recently drafted legislation aimed at pool halls, providing harsher punishments for soft drink and hamburger stand operators who sold liquor, and punishing bondsmen when their clients failed to appear in court. The committee promised to look into improving state liquor laws to help and left satisfied that reports of corruption had been exaggerated. Tate concluded, "Memphis is looked upon by outsiders as a terribly bad place. The visit here has convinced me the city is well managed, and I appreciate the courtesy of the city officials."[16]

Meanwhile, the Prohibition Bureau prepared a new drive against the Liquor Barons following the violence of the rum war. Capt. Edmond A. Larkin gathered forty-two Prohibition agents along a road in Arlington, Tennessee, in the early morning of June 25, 1929. Larkin prepared to launch a "purification campaign" following a month-long undercover investigation by agents disguised as workmen, society men, and ordinary bar flies. Larkin divided his men into teams, handed out instructions received by coded telegram, and sent them after their targets with the instructions, "Bring them all in!" Larkin kept his plans secret, even from regional Prohibition chief William Mays, but despite his efforts, someone tipped off John Belluomini, who escaped to Arkansas just before the raiders arrived.[17]

Larkin's campaign probably would not have fared any better than previous efforts to eliminate bootlegging if it had not been for an anonymous letter received by Judge Edgar Webster of First Criminal Court in Memphis on September 22, 1929. The letter, signed by "a citizen in the jurisdiction of this court" detailed the activities of leading bootleggers, locations of stills, delivery lines, and details of bootlegging establishments. This anonymous letter, obviously from someone deeply involved with the underworld, was the "shot heard around Shelby County." Webster asked Prohibition chief James Doran to launch an investigation into the Liquor Barons' operations, as well as the allegations of police corruption mentioned in the letter.[18]

Prohibition agents raided operations run by Frank Belluomini and Frank Tamble in October. Prohibition administrator Finis Wilson and agents W. R. Wright, O. H. Warren, J. J. Richardson, and J. L. Molloy used a recently captured bootlegger boat to raid President's Island, where they smashed a five-thousand-gallon still and destroyed fourteen thousand gallons of mash. They destroyed a four-thousand-gallon still along with sixty gallons of whiskey on a raid on Centennial Island. They captured four more stills and made two arrests ten miles north of Memphis near the Benjestown Road the following day.[19]

Finis Elbert Wilson received his appointment as a Prohibition administrator in Memphis in 1928 and focused primarily on stopping the transportation of illegal liquor on the Mississippi River. Previously, Wilson had played four seasons as a minor league baseball player and one season in the major leagues before serving in the Kentucky General Assembly. He left his position with Green River Milling Company to take the job with the Prohibition Bureau and led the most damaging raids of any agent on the Liquor Barons' operations.[20]

Prohibition agents, police, and deputies struck hard at the liquor trade, beginning in November 1929 with the arrest of Henry Folbe and his wife in one of the biggest raids the year in Memphis. Folbe, who specialized in coloring, bottling, and making phony labels for corn whiskey, had seventy-five gallons of red whiskey, several quarts of gin, two gallons of grain alcohol, seven quarts of beer, an aging rectifier, foil seals, and labels. They raided Albert

Matrioni's grocery, the Golden Slipper nightclub, and Hermina B. Barrett's café at Chelsea and McLain. Deputies the next day captured a 750-gallon still on North Creek in southeast Shelby County.

The raids stunned bootleggers who could not understand why they could no longer "out-guess the cops." Wilson and his agents had already seized 1,783 gallons of whiskey, 48 gallons of beer, and 52 gallons of wine, valued at $3,075. They also destroyed twenty thousand gallons of mash, destroyed eleven stills, and made forty-one arrests in September before the mysterious letter arrived. The raiders, now armed with new inside information, crippled bootleggers at the most crucial time of the year as customers stocked up on holiday beer and liquor. Prices increased by two dollars per gallon. Bootleggers expected prices to rise from four to ten dollars unless they stopped the raids.[21]

The Liquor Barons made a fatal error by trying to fight back. A bootlegger crept down the riverbank before dawn on November 11 and placed dynamite with timed fuses in the Prohibition agents' two boats located behind the Customs House at Front Street and Madison Avenue. The blasts destroyed both vessels and left the agents without means to raid the islands. Bootleggers got away with dynamiting agents' boats in November 1927 and February 1928, but this attack set off a firestorm within the law enforcement community. The furious Wilson announced, "If it's war the moonshiners want, it's war they'll get." He immediately requested replacement boats, and police chief Will Lee, incensed by the audacity of the attack, asked for a boat as well. A reporter pointed out to Lee, "But Chief, you can't arrest people on the river, you know. The river belongs to Uncle Sam." Lee glared at him and yelled, "I can't, can't I? Well, if we get that boat we can run 'em into the bank on this side and arrest 'em, can't we?"[22]

Wilson found out about the next major syndicate liquor shipment from a rival gangster and sent seven veteran agents, including Frank Mather, E. J. Banet, and Johnson Walker, to intercept them. At one o'clock in the morning on November 12, 1929, agents swept down on the bootleggers as they unloaded a shipment on the banks of the Wolf River near the Second Street Bridge. George Herman Tamble, Frank Belluomini, and Frank Marino saw the approaching raiders and sounded special sirens in their cars to warn the crews. About half of the bootleggers escaped with much of the liquor, but agents captured Tamble, Belluomini, Marino, Kahn Baldridge, Bennie Atiolo, and James Walters and seized thirteen hundred gallons of liquor and five cars.[23]

The raid was only the beginning of a devastating campaign against the syndicate in late 1929. Larkin ordered police to "mop up the city" and directed

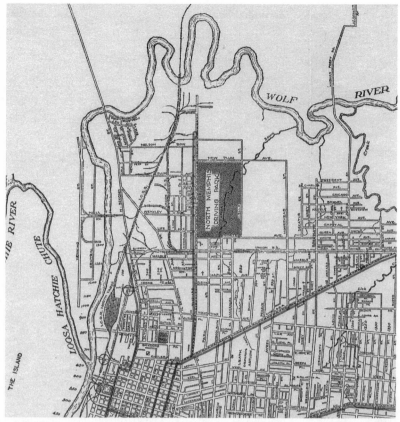

Fig. 16.4. Wolf River and North Memphis. Courtesy of Memphis Room, Memphis Public Library and
Information Center.

the sheriff's department to focus on destroying stills hidden in the woods
around the county. Larkin also received information from an anonymous
source that led him to the bomber's cache of fifty pounds of dynamite hidden in a house on North Second Street near the Wolf River. Wilson's agents
arrested six men and seized a barge loaded with several tons of sugar, meal,
and charcoal in the Wolf River. They lost the evidence when the overloaded
barge sunk as they tried to tow it downstream, but the seizure deprived the
syndicate of valuable supplies.[24]

Anonymous callers promised to kill Wilson and his agents if they did not
back down, but the defiant Wilson replied, "Those threats mean nothing. They
only spur us on!" He ordered new boats and placed a twenty-four-hour guard
with orders to shoot anyone who came too close to them. The following day,

police found the body of a would-be informer murdered by bootleggers in the Mississippi River. Wilson admitted, "Our office is watched, and whiskey runners may have got the idea the man was a stool pigeon." To Wilson's surprise, many Memphians who read the stories of bootlegger retaliations became outraged and called his office pledging support and offering information. Wilson's frontal attack hurt bootlegging, but the worst was yet to come.[25]

• • •

"Well Bill, the jig is up; I'm the law," said Ulric Berard.

Bill Forrest looked at his friend's stern expression and started laughing. He laughed even harder when he saw Berard's badge and gun. "Yeah, Berard, that's a great gag. Pull it on old Tom when he comes up!"

Berard replied, "No Bill, it's not a joke; you're under arrest. Here comes White now."

Bob White pulled the boat up to the dock and said, "Well Bill, has Berard broken you the bad news?"

Forrest continued to laugh as six more men emerged from the boat. At that point, the laughter stopped as Forrest realized his gang members were undercover agents. They not only caught him but knew the details of his syndicate's entire operation.[26]

The most devastating blow to the Liquor Barons came when members of the Prohibition Bureau's Silent 300, a secret undercover division, infiltrated their operations. Ulric H. Berard, Sylvan "Bob" White, Victor Armitage, and J. R. Fletcher posed as exiled Detroit bootleggers and joined a band of moonshiners operating out of the islands off Shelby and Tipton Counties in November 1929. The agents worked side-by-side with the outlaws for months, befriending them and gathering information in a mission so secret that the Memphis agents did not even know of their presence. The deeply imbedded agents, committed to maintaining their covers, once had to "run for their lives" with the bootleggers when Finis Wilson and his men nearly caught them during a raid on their island in June 1930.[27]

The operation ended prematurely in June 1930 as the Department of Justice took over the Prohibition Bureau from the Treasury Department. Even so, the new federal Prohibition administrators were no less determined to bring down the Liquor Barons. In late June, the Prohibition Bureau organized Tennessee, Kentucky, Ohio, and Michigan under W. N. Woodruff as an administrator based in Columbus, Ohio, allowing Wilson a greater pool of agents for periodic raiding campaigns and closer cooperation with federal district attorneys. Woodruff also increased the number of permanent agents

Fig. 16.5. Cartoonist J. P. Alley portrays the US government's use of falsi-
fied income tax returns as evidence against bootleggers. Caption: HE'LL
GO UP FOR THIS, SURE! Courtesy of Memphis Room, Memphis Public
Library and Information Center.

in Wilson's office from three to ten, giving local agents greater ability to work
independently of local police and deputies.[28]

Undercover Prohibition Bureau agents Ulric Berard and Paul Sullivan had
spent months identifying and tracking down the Liquor Barons. Now they
had their chance in court to bring Memphis's elusive bootlegger kingpins
to justice. They focused much of their attention on Frank Marino, the man
who had come to control the former Belluomini-Warner-Tamble syndicate
following the flight of John Belluomini in 1929. The gang, which included
veteran bootleggers Frank Tamble, George Herman Tamble, Russell Warner,
Frank Belluomini, Charlie Vann, E. W. Lane, and George Cook, trafficked
liquor and ran speakeasies off Benjestown Road in northern Shelby County,
on North Second Street in North Memphis, and on East Calhoun several
blocks south of Beale Street.[29]

Berard and Sullivan raided the New York Café at 358 East Calhoun on June 27, 1930. They did not find liquor, but they discovered records of liquor sales and payoff books recording bribes paid to law enforcement. The seized bank records indicated that Marino and his partner Albert Ricci owed $52,000 in taxes on unreported income. Excitement quickly spread through the law enforcement community as investigators vowed to uncover the biggest conspiracy and corruption case since the John Belluomini scandal of 1927.[30]

Prosecutors once again ran into problems with poorly worded and executed search warrants. Charles Bryan and Ralph Davis, attorneys for Marino and Ricci, soon found a fatal flaw in the government's case; the search warrant allowed Berard and Sullivan to search for liquor and stills, not business records. The attorneys filed formal motions for the return of confiscated bank records and payoff books in hopes the whole structure of the conspiracy case would collapse if they proved agents seized records illegally.[31]

On July 7, 1932, Judge Harry Anderson read the motions and called the seizure of the gangsters' documents "plainly and palpably unreasonable and illegal" and ordered their return to Marino and Ricci. Anderson said, "You can split hairs, bring in refinements, but the search was an ABC, elementary proposition, needing no Einstein for a solution. The Calhoun Avenue search violated every right guaranteed by the Constitution."[32] Assistant district attorney Carmack Murchison realized the hopelessness of pursuing the charges and recommended that Anderson dismiss the case against Marino and Ricci.[33]

Prohibition agents also arrested Marino's gang members, James Walton, Kahn Baldridge, Frank Tamble, Russell Warner, Frank Belluomini, Charlie Vann, E. W. Lane, and George Cook. The gangsters received fines totaling $1,200 and probated sentences of one year for conspiracy to violate the National Prohibition Act. The outcome proved disappointing to the agents and prosecutors, who hoped for lengthy prison sentences for Marino's gang. They knew that probated sentences and fines would not deter Marino's men, or any other bootleggers, from joining new gangs.[34]

Marino and Ricci avoided punishment for conspiring to violate Prohibition; however, the indictments cost the gangsters the opportunity to become US citizens. Merton A. Sturges, director of the naturalization office in St. Louis, appeared in Memphis to naturalize foreigners who applied for citizenship in local courts in November 1932. Sturges turned down the applications because of the indictments even though Judge Harry Anderson had dismissed the charges. Furthermore, he recommended that Anderson not allow the Italian-born Marino and Ricci to reapply for five years and made it clear that he would file deportation papers if the two broke the Prohibition law in the future.[35]

After the raid on the New York Café, the Prohibition Bureau turned its attention on Charles Walter Costello, whom agents considered the most important of the Liquor Barons after Frank Marino. Costello, the grandson of Irish immigrants, grew up in the South Main neighborhood of Memphis and frequently worked frequently with bootleggers Jim Mulcahy and Herbert Green. After a series of arrests and fines for bootlegging, Costello adopted a new business model to avoid detection by Prohibition agents. He gave carefully vetted customers an unlisted telephone number they would call to request liquor using a coded password. Drivers would then deliver to the caller's home or office and take payment. Acting on a tip, police raided Costello's operation in the Falls Building in February 1929, seized fifty gallons of liquor, and arrested Costello and his gang members Jimmy Wesson and Harry Haynes; however, the officers did not have a warrant, so they had to drop the charges.[36]

On April 16, 1931, Prohibition agents acting on information provided by Berard and Sullivan raided Costello's operations at the Chase Garage at 141 South Front Street. At the same time, deputy US marshal E. L. West raided the barbershop in the Sterick Building where Costello's gang sold liquor and kept payoff books that recorded bribes to patrolmen. The agents arrested Costello and the rest of his gang, including C. C. Cooper, Milton L. Chase, J. C. Richards (also known as J. C. Roberts), Fred Stinson, Steve Flauth, Jimmie Wesson, William "Red" Welborn, John Wells, and J. Tisdale.[37]

While they were free on bond and awaiting trial, Costello's gang grew suspicious of each other. They worried that one of the gang's members might turn over evidence to prosecutors against his comrades in return for a lighter sentence. On March 10, 1932, a fight broke out at the gang's headquarters. J. T. Hinton and Son ambulance attendants rushed to the Chase Garage to take an unconscious West Lynne "Cue-ball" Vaughn to the hospital. Vaughn, a former police officer fired for drinking, worked for Costello making as much as seventy-five dollars a trip transporting liquor. Costello's men reported that Vaughn fell and injured his head; however, Vaughn's injuries included a concussion, a broken jaw, and a fractured skull. Police commissioner Clifford Davis suspected foul play and ordered an investigation after Vaughn died at the hospital, but police investigators could not find enough evidence to make an arrest.[38]

On June 1, 1932, the Costello Gang appeared in federal court on charges of bootlegging. Memphians expected a lengthy trial, but Costello and his gang surprised jurors with a plea bargain. The gangsters pled guilty to charges of conspiracy to violate the National Prohibition Act, and in exchange, the judge gave the men suspended sentences of eleven months and twenty-nine days and a total of $1,250 in fines.[39]

The recently arrested members of the Dan Walsh and Sam O. Scott bootlegging gangs followed Costello's example and offered plea bargains on June 27, 1932. The Walsh Gang, including Minor Holland, Hall Thomas, Tom Nolan, M. Z. Edmonson, J. J. Walker, and C. H. McCauley received fines and probated sentences. Judge Harry Anderson also imposed fines and probated sentences on the Scott Gang, including Fred and Hans Kissling, Joe Robinson, Roscoe Berry, Tom Oliver, George Garner, Irvin Wise, John "Buster" Scott, Clarence Brown, and C. C. Culp, former constable of Crittenden County, Arkansas.[40]

In December 1931, Berard and Sullivan discovered the telephone number for another bootleg liquor delivery service. They posed as customers, called in an order for liquor, and captured the driver when he made the delivery. The driver gave information that led them to raid the Alex Atkins Gang in the Service Garage at 271 Court Avenue on New Year's Day 1932. Following Costello's example, Alex Atkins and his gang Lofton Rudy, Charles Rossi, C. H. McCauley, Edgar Jones, George Epps (also known as Joe Cleveland), Willie Donald, Frank White, Lewis Gregory, John Bradshaw, and R. T. Ferguson all pled guilty to conspiracy charges in exchange for paying $150 down on a collective fine of $1,250. The gang also included gang leader Dan Walsh and William Ledbetter, a former member of the Marino gang, as well as John Shanley, son of the notorious gangster Mike Shanley.[41]

The fines imposed by the court were hardly enough to deter the gangsters from pursuing their lucrative trade. The Atkins Gang left the courthouse on February 17, 1933, and immediately returned to bootlegging. Berard and Sullivan, perturbed by how easily the gangsters avoided prison sentences, used the same ploy from the first raid to arrest them again. The agents called and purchased more liquor from the same number. When the delivery driver arrived, they launched another raid on the Chase Garage. Within two hours of leaving the courthouse, the agents had the gang in custody for bootlegging again.[42]

Herbert Green, whom law enforcement had repeatedly arrested for bootlegging since the early days of statewide Prohibition, formed another liquor gang and built new stills with Swedish immigrant and master sheet-metal worker Oscar Moberg. The Moberg-Green Gang came to light on September 21, 1932, when Prohibition agents John Hammond, Ralph Kitts, and John

Phillips, followed a suspicious truck loaded with sugar as it left the Lipman Brothers Wholesalers at 1400 North Second Street in Memphis. They followed it to a moonshine operation with a 750-gallon still off a small road between Brunswick and Brownsville in northeast Shelby County.[43]

All but one of the moonshiners scattered into the woods when the agents raided the outfit. The agents captured an African American man named Gilly Leek before he could get away. The agents handcuffed Leek, took him to their car, and started back to Memphis when they noticed Leek's comrades following them. Fearing an ambush, the agents drove until they located a telephone and called the Prohibition agent in charge, Capt. Edmond Larkin, for help.[44]

Larkin left the Memphis office with fellow agent Paul Sullivan and immediately headed for Brunswick. As they approached the three agents and their prisoner, the moonshiners hiding in the woods opened fire, riddling the car with bullets and buckshot. Under a hail of gunfire, Larkin and Sullivan leaped from their car and ran for a clump of woods to join Hammond, Kitts, and Phillips. Larkin took a buckshot wound to the chest, and Sullivan took buckshot in the hands and arms. The agents returned fire, and the moonshiners turned and ran. Larkin wounded one of the retreating ambushers, Othar Edwards, and arrested him.[45]

News of the attack spread quickly, and law enforcement, incensed by the brazenness of it, rallied to track down the gunmen. Larkin met with US attorney general Dwayne Maddox and county sheriff Will Bacon the next morning to plan a "fight to the finish" to wipe out bootlegging in Shelby County.[46] Maddox questioned Othar Edwards from his hospital room and discovered that Oscar Moberg and Herbert Green owned the still. He suspected that gang members would try to kidnap Edwards, so he kept the prisoner under close guard. Deputies recaptured Gilly Leek, still in handcuffs and wounded, and held him in the county jail. Leek, after questioning, "spilled everything" about the shootout, the operation at Lipman Brothers Wholesalers, and Moberg and Green.[47]

Larkin and five agents returned to Lipman Brothers Wholesalers, raided the building, and seized sugar, cornmeal, rubber hoses, and thousands of five-gallon wooden kegs. The evidence would have played an important part in the case, but once again, lawyers discovered a flaw in the warrant. The Lipmans' attorney Sam Taubenblatt successfully argued that the seizure was illegal and Judge Harry Anderson ordered the Prohibition Bureau to turn over to the Lipmans the confiscated materials, altogether worth $25,000.[48]

US marshals arrested the twenty-one members of the Moberg-Green Gang in June 1933, including Charles Walter Costello, Charlie Richards, Joe

Robinson, Floyd Sturgeon, Clarence Baggett, and J. W. Johnson. A federal grand jury indicted the men on charges of manufacture and transportation of alcohol, and Maddox, at the recommendation of Berard and Sullivan, announced that he would not accept plea bargains, so the accused men would have to stand trial. The trial, set for July 1933, promised to be the largest of the liquor conspiracy trials.[49]

In May 1933, Berard and Sullivan arrested A. E. Marche and eleven of his cohorts for bootlegging. Marche worked in the city as a cotton merchant and general trader in the city and owned an estate in the country where he lived as a "gentleman farmer." Marche also headed a liquor ring that manufactured and sold liquor to the city's elite society members. The federal grand jury indicted Marche and the members of his ring, and the agents threatened to name the prominent Memphians who made up Marche's clientele. Marche initially denied the charges, but he and his ring members eventually relented, pled guilty, and paid $1,250 in fines.[50]

Berard and Sullivan broke up seven major liquor rings in just over two years. These cases proved the most successful in the effort to enforce Prohibition since its enactment; however, these victories came too late. In February 1933, Congress adopted a resolution proposing the Twenty-First Amendment to the US Constitution to repeal both the Eighteenth Amendment and the Volstead Act. Utah became the thirty-sixth state to ratify the amendment, achieving the necessary majority for ratification of the Twenty-First Amendment on December 5, 1933.[51]

Federal judges in Memphis concluded or dismissed any remaining cases involving violation of national Prohibition. Charles Walter Costello and Charlie Richards appeared in court again on December 21, 1933. Their attorney Clarence Friedman pointed out that two US courts of appeal recently held that cases pending could not draw sentences given repeal of the Eighteenth Amendment. At the recommendation of assistant district attorney Joe Bearman, Judge Anderson fined Richards and Costello twenty-five dollars each and an African American bootlegger Lawrence Hamler only one dollar. Anderson said the federal government was "probably lucky to get that much." In July 1935, Judge John D. Martin excused the last of the Liquor Barons, Alex Atkins and his gang Dan Walsh, Charles Rossi, C. M. McCauley, Edgar Jones, George Epps, Frank White, and R. T. Ferguson of the remaining $178 in fines.[52]

• • •

Pursuing corrupt law enforcement proved as frustrating as building cases against the Liquor Barons in the last years of Prohibition. Berard and Sullivan formed a team of thirteen Prohibition agents and twelve men from the Department of Justice to investigate allegations of collusion between bootleggers and local law enforcement. They did not receive much support from their superiors, and their efforts did little more than strain relations with local law enforcement.[53]

The investigation began clumsily in June 1930. Agents, acting on a tip, searched Sheriff Knight's property for a reported still. Knight, the bane of bootleggers in Shelby County, naturally did not have a bootlegging operation on his property, and the futile search only angered the sheriff's department. Two patrolmen discovered a suspicious man in a phony business front on Union Avenue, between Third and Fourth Streets, during a canvass of persons missed during the census. Officers saw that he had a wiretap operation and hidden cameras, so they assumed he was a blackmailer and arrested him, only to find out later that they had been the subjects of government surveillance.[54]

Payoff books recording bribes paid to police officers turned up in nearly every raid. In July 1930, Berard and Sullivan discovered payoff books at Frank Liberto's Holly Lunchroom at 139 Huling. In August 1930, they found payoff books in raids on wholesale companies G. W. Hurley Produce and Lipman Brothers in the conspiracy investigation of Curtis Duncan, a clerk with the Lee Line who used the steamer *Valley Queen* to transport liquor and supplies for bootleggers. Ledgers found in the raid on the Atkins Gang recorded locations of stills, the amount of liquor handled, and the amount paid for protection. One informant said, "Taking all in all, it may be a blow-off, taking the lid off local corruption and graft, if any. And again, it may be nothing at all."[55]

The informant was right; once again, payoff books proved insufficient evidence. Just as in the case of Belluomini's payoff books, the federal grand jury decided not to indict any of the fifty to seventy officers accused of taking bribes from bootleggers because the evidence from the payoff books would have been considered hearsay. And the US Department of Justice had no interest in bribery cases that did not involve administrators and government officials.[56]

Lawyers successfully argued against admitting payoff books as evidence; however, the books existed, and they existed for a reason. In March 1932, the recently retired deputy inspector Mike Kehoe told a reporter, "In my forty years of police work, I never heard of a payoff list that didn't mean something. Those bootleggers don't put an officer's name on a payoff list just as a joke."[57]

In May 1932, Berard and Sullivan continued to push for a corruption investigation though their superiors showed no interest in pursuing the matter. Chief Will Lee, angered by the probe by the agents, accused Sullivan of "trying to cut the throat" of the police department and claimed, "Payoff lists don't mean a damn!" Lee admitted that some officers occasionally took bribes but denied that corruption reached the administrative level. Police officials made announcements about cracking down on corruption when stories of bribery surfaced, but typically, they did little more than shift patrolmen around to different wards.[58]

An incident four days later illustrated the police department's stance on bribery. Traffic officer H. C. Clayton pulled over Charles Cianciola after a car chase for several blocks after noticing something wrong with his license plate. Cianciola, who had twenty-four quarts and sixty pints of liquor in his car, offered Clayton fifty dollars to let him go. Clayton refused the offer and arrested the bootlegger for transporting liquor and bribery. Even so, police commissioner Clifford Davis said he would not to pursue the charges because he had "never had any success in prosecuting a man for attempting to bribe an officer."[59]

The trials of the Liquor Barons fell far short of the expectations of the Prohibition Bureau. Prosecutors could not build effective cases against the gangs even after months of effort by undercover agents to gather evidence. Not one of the bootleggers went to prison for his crimes; instead, they received minimal fines and the proverbial "slap on the wrist." The campaign against corruption in law enforcement did not fare any better. The Prohibition Bureau did successfully disrupt the operations of the Liquor Barons, and its campaign did break up the large organized gangs. However, the influence it would have to end bootlegging in Memphis remained to be seen.

17

REPEAL OF THE EIGHTEENTH AMENDMENT

The word "prohibition" always has, and always will be, distasteful to Americans.
—Alfred Dalrymple, national Prohibition director, July 17, 1933

The world of Mike Haggerty and Jim Kinnane was gone. The saloons and politics that fueled the fires of reform in the late nineteenth century were all but forgotten. Haggerty had died in December 1929, and Kinnane, eleven months later. Haggerty had lost his saloons and political influence because of Prohibition, and Kinnane had bowed out of the liquor scene following the Tyree Taylor conspiracy trials.[1]

The new generation never experienced Kinnane and Haggerty's world; they came of age in a time of speakeasies, bootleg liquor, home brew beer, and jazz. They knew little of the old saloons, but they knew all too well about the hypocrisy of Prohibition and the lawlessness it created. The WCTU and the ASL successfully used patriotism and religion to shame Americans into acquiescing to their demands in 1919, but their tired old slogans lost effectiveness as the memories of the saloons faded.

Americans now openly challenged ASL dogma. The opponents of Prohibition became bolder and called for modification of the Volstead Act. Intransigence on the part of the Prohibitionists only made the rebels more determined and brought about demands for complete repeal of the Eighteenth Amendment to the US Constitution. The calls for repeal took on new fervor after with the start of the Great Depression in October 1929. With unemployment high and tax dollars down, many believed repeal would mean new jobs, business expansion, and increased tax revenues. The volatility of the debate split the country into two very polarized camps and made places like Memphis into battlegrounds over the fate of Prohibition.

Fig. 17.1. Kenneth Douglas McKellar. Courtesy of the Library of Congress.

Dry leaders dismissed reports of increased crime and liquor consumption as propaganda of the liquor interests. In December 1923, Wayne Wheeler said that Prohibition was the "nation's greatest Christmas gift." He falsely claimed that it had saved the lives of over five hundred thousand people, increased productivity, raised tax revenue, and reduced drunkenness.

The First Baptist Church in Memphis passed a resolution commending the US senator Kenneth Douglas McKellar for his stance on Prohibition. McKellar had come to the city after graduating from the University of Alabama School of Law in 1892 and served as US representative from Tennessee's Tenth Congressional District before becoming a senator. A favorite among temperance supporters, he ignored letters from constituents urging him to vote against Prohibition in 1919 and afterward dismissed reports of massive liquor seizures as "grossly overestimated." He told the congregation, "The beneficial workings of the prohibition laws cannot be better illustrated, perhaps, than in the case of my home city of Memphis." Congressman Hubert F. Fisher, also of the Tenth Congressional District, told the Westminster Presbyterian

Fig. 17.2. Rev. Billy Sunday, 1922. Courtesy of the Library of Congress.

congregation, "There is not a chance to change to Eighteenth Amendment as long as we live. If a change were made, there would be a revolution in this section of the country."[2]

Evangelist and antiliquor crusader William Ashley "Billy" Sunday visited Memphis five times during his career and never failed to stoke the fires of Prohibition. He spoke to a capacity crowd at a makeshift tabernacle built at Front and Jefferson Avenue in May 1924. He became so ill that his wife had to take him to the Mayo Clinic, but he returned in February 1925 to attack liquor traffic and the laxity of law enforcement. In March 1926, he told the crowd of ten thousand Memphians, "We are told that nothing was created in vain, but I doubt if God had anything to do with producing this breed of vultures who are known as bootleggers. Upon no other ground can I account for the brains of a buzzard, the heart of a hyena, and the odor of a polecat being found in a being called human. I think I would rather be in hell with Ivan the Terrible, Nero, Jezebel, Cleopatra, Guiteau, and Booth than live with such human lies!"[3]

Sunday returned in December 1928 and delivered another antiliquor tirade to nine thousand people at the City Auditorium. During his rant against anti-Prohibition presidential candidate Al Smith, someone in the east balcony hurled an egg at him. The egg splattered on the stage and Sunday halted his speech. Sunday snatched off his coat, tucked it under one arm, shook his fist at the balcony, and shouted, "Come down here, and I'll knock your damnable head off!" Sunday called out to police to bring the "dirty, yellow, sneaking coward" down to him as officers rushed to the balcony to break up a fight among hecklers and supporters. During the melee, Sunday turned to the audience and said, "Friends, there's a sample of the kind of hoodlums we're fighting."[4]

Sunday had many friends in Memphis and praised the city at every opportunity. He had a fondness for Clifford Davis and hugged his friend on stage during a sermon at First Methodist Church in December 1931. Later, Davis met him at the Hotel Claridge, where Sunday gave him a couple of neckties as gifts. Helen Sunday, ever vigilant of her husband's health, allowed him to speak to *Press-Scimitar* reporter Robert Dudley briefly before lunch. Sunday told Dudley that he never received "derogatory reports" of the moral life in Memphis and dismissed the crime wave and economic depression as effects of recovery from the world war. His supporters in the city followed his example by ignoring the increase in crime and loss of respect for law enforcement and refusing to give any ground to supporters of modification or repeal.[5]

The WCTU denounced its critics and refused to consider any compromise either. Belle McKnight Vernor, the wife of café owner Charles Vernor, led the "revival of the old crusade spirit" in the Memphis branch for most of the 1920s. She served as president for two terms, followed by Mrs. Albert P. Taylor, and served again in 1928. She matched the opposition move for move through newspapers, churches, rallies, and schools. The local chapter never had more than a few hundred active members, but its activities gave it the appearance of acting on behalf of the majority of Memphians.[6]

Refusal to acknowledge the failings of Prohibition dominated the WCTU rhetoric. WCTU evangelist Mamie Burnham Gilreath, in a sermon at Central Baptist Church in 1926, blamed the crime wave on the parents of youthful offenders, saying, "Youthful delinquency can only be laid at the door of the home." She called reports of increased crime "propaganda of the liquor interests."[7]

Tennessee WCTU president Minnie Allison Welch called the United States under Prohibition "a glory and a light to all humanity," and the secretary, Mrs. W. N. Newman, called the Eighteenth Amendment "the strongest and best enforced law in the Constitution." Delegate Lillian Childress, in an address to the WCTU convention at the Elks Hall in Memphis in November 1929, scoffed at reports of college drinking and the costs of Prohibition.

Furthermore, she applauded the fact that Prohibition agents were outshooting the bootleggers three to one, and that 142 had died to 56 law enforcement officers nationwide.[8]

The WCTU, secure in its position, prepared for a campaign for a constitutional ban on tobacco. The effort had a slow start, but by 1929, the WCTU organized a new campaign and Tennessee branches distributed propaganda literature and protested cigarette advertising. Memphis chapter president Belle Vernor expected to "take up the tobacco fight" before the end of the year. Their war on tobacco, however, came to an abrupt halt once they realized the seriousness of the repeal movement.[9]

The WCTU fell back on its old strategy of using children to influence voting parents. Since 1895, the Tennessee General Assembly had required teachers to instruct fifth and sixth graders in "Scientific Temperance," and teachers had to pass an examination on the subject to receive certification. Most children in Tennessee dropped out of school by that point, so the WCTU forced a law making every fourth Friday in October Frances Willard Day and October 4 Temperance Day for all public-school students.[10]

Vernor promoted new essay contests, awarded medals, and offered scholarships to keep Prohibition on the forefront of students' education and the minds of voting parents. Dr. Lilian Wyckoff Johnson, daughter of Elizabeth Fisher Johnson, founder of the state's first chapter of the WCTU, presided over the celebration of the sixth anniversary of national Prohibition at the Peabody Hotel, where members donated one penny for every year of their age for awards to a worthy teacher and student. They awarded fifty dollars to the public school teacher who wrote the best essay on "the principles on training young people to voluntary abstinence" and another fifty dollars to the fourth grader who wrote the best essay on "the value of total abstinence on a life." Johnson also awarded one hundred dollars to the University of Tennessee student who presented the best oration arguing "Prohibition is the best method of dealing with the liquor traffic."[11]

After attending the national WCTU conference in Houston, Texas, on November 13, 1930, Vernor pressured Memphis schools to increase temperance teaching and participation in essay contests. Over thirteen hundred students submitted essays in 1929, and Vernor hoped to have three times as many participate in 1930 on the new theme, "Eternal vigilance is the price of Prohibition." She also sponsored a poster contest and had WCTU members distribute literature to students.[12]

Over two hundred experts discussed rising adult and juvenile crime at the twenty-second annual National Prohibition Conference held in Memphis at

Fig. 17.3. Dr. Howard Hyde Russell, founder of the Anti-Saloon League. Courtesy of the Library of Congress.

the First Methodist Church in April 1928. Sixteen juvenile court judges from around the country attended, including Judge Camille Kelley, who presented at the opening. Dr. Sutton Griggs, African American activist and pastor of the Tabernacle Baptist Church, blamed crime on the lack of cohesion within the black community, and Judge H. G. Cochran of Norfolk, Virginia, claimed that prisons served only as "incubators of crime." All spoke of the problem of increased crime and liquor violations, but none would acknowledge Prohibition as a cause.[13]

The so-called drys believed Prohibition was the will of God and transcended due process and constitutional rights. ASL founder Dr. Howard Hyde Russell, general superintendent Francis Scott McBride, and legislative superintendent Thomas Jarvis visited First Methodist Church in June 1928 for a rally against Al Smith. Russell believed that, in his forty years with the league, the Prohibition movement was "the church in action against the saloon." Rev. F. B. Jones of Madison Heights Methodist Church in Memphis said, "I do not believe a sensible person considers the law [Prohibition] as a violation of his rights, but as a safeguard of his liberty." H. M. DuBose, the ASL president and a Methodist bishop, said, "Prohibition is here to stay, and all the clamoring of a boisterous minority to disrupt the machinery of government under a false banner of personal liberty will not change it."[14]

Minister H. D. Knickerbocker of First Methodist Church said that if he could sit as a criminal judge, he would consider every bootlegger an accessory before the fact of every crime and make life imprisonment the minimum penalty for third offense bootleggers even if the accused was a mother of seven. He opposed search warrants and called them "the greatest protector of the liquor law violators." The minister declared, "Why, search warrants are silly! Only criminals want them. No good man would object to police searching his home for liquor."[15]

• • •

The first local attempts to organize a movement in support of the modification of the Volstead Act met with stiff resistance. Police arrested five members of the Rational America League in November 1926 at the corner of Poplar Avenue and Dunlap Street. Norman Vollentihe of New York, H. D. and George Gillespie of Virginia, and E. W. Wilgus and C. V. Holland of Memphis faced vagrancy charges after collecting donations, recruiting members, and taking signatures on a petition.[16]

Two years later, Memphians were more open to the idea. Louise Gross, a native New Yorker and friend of presidential hopeful Al Smith, organized the Women's Committee for the Modification of the Eighteenth Amendment in 1926 and later headed the Women's Moderation Union until Pauline Sabin eclipsed her with the formation of the Women's Organization for National Prohibition Reform. Gross offered a voice to women who opposed Prohibition and countered the WCTU claim that it spoke for all women. During a visit to Memphis in 1929, Gross met with Mrs. M. F. Hudson and recruited her as the Tennessee representative to the Women's Moderation Union. Hudson, inspired by Gross, ardently supported repeal of the Eighteenth Amendment, calling it the "greatest evil in the history of the U.S." She attacked the drys, saying, "The American people whose forefathers fought for freedom are today in a worse state of slavery, simply because of a few fanatics, to gain notoriety, go preaching this curse upon the American people."[17]

Memphians, once reluctant to voice their opposition, began to speak openly about the failings of Prohibition in 1929. Sheriff Will Knight stated, "Ninety percent of all the people of Memphis, including church people, drink. They seem to believe in prohibition as a general thing, but they all want their own drink. I believe we are further away from the saloon than ever before, but there is more booze in the home than there used to be." Reverend A. B. Curry of Second Presbyterian Church complained about those church members who bought liquor, "And yet it is openly violated by many professing Christians and other reputable citizens. All laws are violated by some people; no law is kept by everybody, but this law is not only violated, but flouted, disdained, laughed at, and defied. And that not only by the vicious, but by many professing Christians."[18]

Dr. Eleanor Crosby Kemp, director of the Psychological Center of the New York League for Mental Hygiene in Children, told members of the Nineteenth Century Club, a historic philanthropic and cultural women's club based in Memphis, that intelligent people broke the liquor laws because they resented someone telling them what to eat or drink. Prohibition supporters scoffed at Kemp's ideas. Rev. Ben Cox of Central Baptist Church in Memphis said the desire for something forbidden may affect children, but not "civilized adults."[19]

Nevertheless, studies continued to bring to light the extent of disregard of the law. President Herbert Hoover appointed former attorney general George Wickersham in May 1929 to study the widespread crime and the growth of organized crime that plagued the United States. Wickersham's eleven-member commission's 1931 final report sent mixed messages. On the one hand, it supported Prohibition, but on the other hand, it concluded that Prohibition, as it existed, was unworkable and bred contempt for the law.[20]

The Association against the Prohibition Amendment studied official statistics regarding alcoholism and alcohol-related arrests and released a report in August 1929 showing that liquor consumption nationwide had increased since 1920. Bishop Thomas Gailor of the Episcopal Church in Tennessee observed, "Passage and attempted enforcement of the prohibition amendment has aroused nationwide indignation and resentment, not only from those who wish to drink whiskey, but from innumerable intelligent, thinking, high-minded persons. . . . We have become a nation of lawbreakers, in whose eyes the Constitution has been cheapened and stripped of much of the dignity in which it was formerly clothed."[21]

Beginning in 1930, newspapers and magazines conducted straw polls to measure where Americans stood on the issue of Prohibition. The *Pathfinder* took the first one of any size, with its predominantly rural readers leaning toward maintaining the existing laws. The *Yale Daily News* and *Harvard Crimson* conducted polls that showed its readers leaning heavily toward modification or repeal. Both sides of the issue found ways to generate numbers in support of their cause and flooded the media with their results. Reporter Rodney Dutcher commented, "Everybody is wallowing in analyses, poll figures, and past comparative statistics. . . . Anyone who hasn't had a chance to vote his or her convictions on prohibition in some kind of straw vote seems to be getting cheated."[22]

The staff of the *Literary Digest* announced a nationwide opinion survey in March 1930 to find out how Americans stood on the issue. The magazine had earned credibility when it predicted Hoover's election within four percentage points. The WCTU leadership, fearing the outcome, called the proposed survey unfair and discouraged members from participating. Memphis WCTU leaders said wets (Prohibition opponents) had probably rigged the questionnaire, but they encouraged its three hundred and twenty members to vote anyway. Campaign manager Lena Sparr called it a "propaganda stunt" and said the results would not have a bearing on the organization's stance on liquor.[23]

As the WCTU feared, the *Literary Digest* poll indicated that most Americans favored either repeal or modification of Prohibition. That poll reported by April 15 that Memphians were overwhelmingly wet; only 1,888 supported continued enforcement of Prohibition as it existed, while 1,675 favored modification, and 3,120 wanted repeal. Other Tennesseans who once supported Prohibition had changed their minds as well. The numbers for the state indicated a shift in support away from Prohibition, with 6,884 wet votes to 6,495 dry votes. Wets embraced the results, while drys claimed their lack of participation made the count inaccurate. Memphis broker Hardwig Peres said, "The Drys know that the prohibition amendment is safe, and they don't care much for the vote."[24]

In April 1930, the twenty-four newspapers owned by Scripps-Howard Newspapers conducted another nationwide survey to challenge the results of the poll. The local Scripps-Howard paper, the *Press-Scimitar*, printed ballots in every edition on April 16 and encouraged Memphians to complete them and mail them to the paper's Prohibition poll editor. The poll asked: Do you favor the continuance and strict enforcement of the Eighteenth Amendment and Volstead Act? Do you favor a modification of the Volstead Law to permit light wines and beers? Do you favor repeal of the Prohibition Amendment?[25]

The results surprised the editors of the *Press-Scimitar*. The poll not only confirmed the findings of the *Literary Digest*, but it indicated a greater repeal sentiment than even repealists expected. The paper took in 2,501 total votes including 300 for strict enforcement, 317 for modification, and 1,884 for repeal. Feelings ran strong, and many felt compelled to include with

Fig. 17.4. As shown in J. P. Alley's cartoon, most Memphis newspapers support-ed prohibition before the results of the opinion polls became known. Caption: ANYWAY, HE'S STILL HANGING ON! Courtesy of Memphis Room, Memphis Public Library and Information Center.

their ballots comments, jokes, pet theories, temperance literature, and the occasional beer bottle label.[26]

The battle of numbers continued through 1930. The *Christian Science Monitor* conducted a survey to challenge the results found by the *Literary Digest* and Scripps Howard Newspapers. The National Voluntary Commit-tee of the American Bar Association sent out a survey to lawyers across the country. Local attorneys participated, though Shelby County Bar Association president William D. Kyser opposed taking part in "prohibition controver-sies." The association's survey results in 1931 showed lawyers' support for repeal "unshakable as a petrified forest."[27]

The US government joined the straw poll craze when Prohibition director Amos Woodcock sent out questionnaires to over three thousand newspapers around the country. The Newspaper Enterprise Association, which took over the poll after Woodcock canceled at the last minute, confirmed what most people already knew: rural populations supported Prohibition more often than urban dwellers.[28]

Each poll encouraged more people to voice support for the repeal movement. Leading citizens joined up and gave the movement a sense of respectability. Fourteen of the city's elite met at the Parkview Hotel in May 1930 to form the Memphis chapter of Pauline Sabin's Women's Organization for National Prohibition Reform. They elected Mrs. Kenneth G. Duffield as chair and welcomed any Memphis woman willing to work to change the Prohibition law to combat crime and corruption. The members included: Mrs. R. H. Vance, Mrs. R. Brinkley Snowden, Mrs. Charles F. Blaisdell, Mrs. W. D. Stinson, Mrs. E. D. Mitchell, Mrs. Alex Austin, Mrs. J. P. Norfleet, Mrs. Hugh Humphreys, Mrs. J. T. Morgan, Mrs. M. M. Betts, Mrs. Fred Orgill, Mrs. Henry Hayley, and Ms. Celia Smith.[29]

Suburban white neighborhood organizations and the city's elite no longer saw Ed Crump's wet stance as a stigma. Crump, secure in his position, supported Al Smith over Tennessee's Democratic nominee Cordell Hull during the 1928 Democratic National Convention in Houston. Crump could pull this off in part because of the power of his machine and his large Republican following. Moreover, the various polls indicated that Memphis, the largest population center of the Tenth Congressional District, had a wet majority.

The public support for repeal or modification, in particular among the city's elite, gave Crump the opportunity to make a bid for the US Congress in June 1930. Crump wanted to replace the dry Hubert Fisher with Scott Fitzhugh two years earlier but met with resistance from Fisher supporters. Crump, annoyed that Fisher did not back down, decided to run in the next election. Crump waited until the final day to file his election papers so that any ardent dry or old-time enemy who may have challenged him would not have time to file. Fisher realized he could not defeat Crump and withdrew his bid.[30]

The Shelby County Organization urged over sixty-two thousand people to vote, the most in the history of the county at that time. The organization held rallies at the Memphis Fairgrounds and around the city in support of Crump and his ally Governor Horton. Crump weathered a corruption investigation by the Republican senator Gerald Nye and won in November against his Republican opponent Herbert Harper by fifteen to one.[31]

Congressman Crump proudly carried the repeal banner for Tennessee. He voted for the Beck-Linthicum amendment that would have repealed national Prohibition in 1932. Although the bill failed, it forced the wet and dry members to go on record as such, and once the dry members were identified, wet voters eventually voted these men out of office. Memphis lawyers Phil Canale and Bertrand Cohn of the Association against the Prohibition Amendment addressed an American Federation of Labor rally at Ryman Auditorium in Nashville and demanded the inclusion of a wet delegate at the Democratic National Convention. Crump gladly stepped in to fill the position and joined Senators McKellar and Hull, Secretary of State Ernest Haston, and Mayor Watkins Overton, who served as delegates at large.[32]

Overton came out on the side of the wets on June 17, 1932. He declined to make his views public until the convention, even after receiving twenty-five thousand petitions for repeal or modification. Overton derided the Republican plank as "one-third wet, one-third dry, and one-third ambiguity, well-stirred together and flavored with applesauce." Crump's shining moment came when Overton presented a resolution to legalize beer. The Tennessee Democratic delegation unanimously adopted the resolution, while Crump, who served as a floor manager for Roosevelt, took up the standard for Tennessee with a proud smile and led the state's delegates in procession.[33]

In June 1932, President Hoover conceded that the "noble experiment" had not worked. He blamed the states and municipalities that refused to help the federal government enforce the law. This breakdown in cooperation resulted in increased liquor traffic, spreading disrespect not only for Prohibition but for all laws, increased danger of practical nullification of the Constitution, and increased violence. Hoover would not give up on Prohibition but instead proposed its modification with a version of the local option. He believed people should have the opportunity to vote on a proposed amendment that would allow the "states to deal with the problem" so the "people themselves may determine whether they desire a change in the law."[34]

Regardless of who won the next presidential election, the Eighteenth Amendment was going to change. Even so, drys stubbornly refused to consider any compromise, while wets mobilized to overturn the law. The future of Prohibition in Tennessee depended primarily on winning support in the larger cities, especially Memphis. Each side understood this and tried to outdo the other by having bigger rallies and more petitions. Each sought to appear in the news to have the greater number of supporters and to speak for the majority of Memphians.

The Association against the Prohibition Amendment became a constant irritant to the WCTU and the ASL. The national organization formed in 1918 and gained momentum in 1928 following the polls. The Memphis branch organized in July 1930 under the leadership of Canale and Cohn and worked closely with Duffield's Memphis chapter of the Women's Organization for National Prohibition Reform. Its members gathered more than seven thousand signatures on petitions for modification allowing beers and light wines and sent them to Senators Hull and McKellar and Congressman Crump.[35]

The two sides took their battle to the city streets. They gave out stickers at first but later gave out 4½" x 11½" metal red, white, and blue plates based on the idea of New York City stenographer Herbert B. Sansom. The Association against the Prohibition Amendment sold over three hundred automobile license plates stamped with "Repeal the Eighteenth Amendment" in May 1932. By July, after the WCTU began making competing plates, each side began covering the cost of their plates so that they could distribute them for free.[36]

Annie Searles, the new president of the local WCTU, wanted to prove wrong the writer of an editorial who referred her organization as a "few pathetic country women." In July 1932, each of the 250 members promised to gather twenty names, circulate literature in a house-to-house canvass, and visit Sunday schools in a show of strength. They set up a booth for a week at New Bry's department store, where twenty-five girl volunteers collected names. They set up booths at Lowenstein's, Goldsmith's, and Gerber's department stores for a day to collect additional names, and after a week they had over fifteen hundred signatures of people pledging to support the Eighteenth Amendment.[37]

The most significant show of support came from the Allied Forces for Prohibition, a national organization of twenty-nine temperance groups formed in 1928 and led by Rev. Daniel Poling to combat the repeal movement. The Allied Forces for Prohibition, with the help of the WCTU, organized Memphis churches and staged a rally at the Auditorium South Hall at Main and Poplar Avenue on July 11, 1932. Dr. R. J. Bateman of the First Baptist Church led the local branch of the organization with Rev. C. A. Waterfield as secretary, Rev. Walter White of Linden Avenue Christian Church as program chairman, and Dr. Robert George of First Congregational Church as his assistant. The organization, under Dr. Casa Collier, led three rallies in October 1931 and hoped to follow up with an even greater show of unity.[38]

The Allied Forces for Prohibition delivered its message not only to a capacity crowd but to all of Memphis through a radio broadcast by WNBR. On July 10, 1932, speaker John Dean, of Dean, Paine, and Company, recalled

Memphis under the "saloon regime" and how liquor dealers dodged taxes and regulation, politicians won elections in the barroom, and statewide Prohibition meant nothing to saloon owners, who openly flouted it. Attorney John W. McCall's prediction of the failure of "dripping wet politicians" to overturn the Eighteenth Amendment and the verbal attack on the "wet press" by Rev. Robert G. Lee of Bellevue Baptist Church met with shouts, whistling, and stamping of feet by twenty-two hundred supporters.[39]

Even so, supporters quickly lost interest after the rallies. Rev. A. P. Moore, who replaced George J. Burnett as the ASL's West Tennessee assistant superintendent in August 1932, hoped to revive enthusiasm for the organization. Most businessmen found excuses to avoid him and sermons no longer brought in crowds, so Moore staged mock trials instead to attract a younger audience. Despite his efforts, membership fell, and the ASL headquarters on the third floor of the Goodwyn Building closed, forcing Moore to resort to running the operation from his house.[40]

The WCTU carried on in its desperate effort to save Prohibition. Its members reelected Annie Searles as president, formed two smaller chapters, and selected delegates for the state convention in Nashville in October 1932. On November 2, Prohibitionist and pioneer civil rights leader Dr. Lilian Wyckoff Johnson called Prohibition a "wonderful success in Memphis." Johnson, the daughter of WCTU leader Elizabeth Fisher Johnson, denied that Prohibition caused increases in crime and alcohol consumption and called anything to the contrary "wet propaganda."[41]

A week later, US congressional elections swept the so-called bone-drys out of office and guaranteed national Prohibition would either face modification or repeal in coming months. In March 1933, President Roosevelt signed the Cullen-Harrison Act, which amended the Volstead Act by permitting the manufacturing and sale of low-alcohol beer and wines up to 3.2 percent alcohol by volume. State legislatures then had to decide whether or not to modify state dry laws to fall in line with the revised national Prohibition laws.

The Memphis WCTU called the proposed Tennessee state convention to consider the modification of statewide Prohibition unfair and sent a formal protest to Senator McKellar. Johnson apparently forgot the political maneuvering the ASL and WCTU used to force the passage of Prohibition. She complained that only a direct popular vote for or against repeal would conform to the "principles of justice and the promises of the Democratic platform."[42]

Dyer County representative Ronald E. Little introduced to the Tennessee General Assembly a modification bill to allow the sale of 3.2 percent beer. The bill called for a forty-cent tax per gallon, one-hundred-dollar license to sell, and a fifty-dollar permit to allow consumption on premises. Revenue would go to the counties, to pensions, and to schools to pay for books for "indigent children." Speaker of the Tennessee House of Representatives Frank Moore and Tennessee Senate Speaker Albert Officer both announced support of the bill. The unexpected move sent many unprepared representatives hurrying home to check up on sentiment among constituents. In the meantime, legislators waited for the US Congress to vote before taking action.[43]

The WCTU held prayer vigils in the Tennessee General Assembly to protest the vote. Legislators huddled off in a corner by themselves or stood silently with hats removed as the WCTU knelt in prayer. On March 13, 1933, Roosevelt sent a seventy-two-word special message to the US Congress recommending modification of the Volstead Act. A few hours later, Senate majority leader Joe Robinson replied, "We have enough votes to pass the economy and beer bills." The US House of Representatives passed the bill legalizing 3.2 percent beer by 316 to 97 the next day. The Senate passed the bill on March 17, and Roosevelt signed it into law the following Monday.[44]

Hundreds of Tennesseans rushed to Kentucky and Missouri to buy beer. Many drove, several arrived by airplane, and others took advantage of the "Dry Throat Specials" offered by five Memphis railroads. Anheuser-Busch and Falstaff struggled to fill orders as store owners in Steele, Caruthersville, Poplar Bluff, Paducah, Mayfield, and Fulton remodeled their businesses to accommodate their new customers. Memphis nightclub owner Spec Horton saw an opportunity to sell beer legally and opened a new beer garden on the St. Louis Highway a mile from the state line.[45]

The *Commercial Appeal* reporter Hilton Butler, two more journalists, and a dry-voting member of the Tennessee legislature took a ride to Kentucky in search of beer. The representative said, "Come on boys, let's go to Bowling Green!"

Butler replied, "Oh yeah? Just last week you voted against beer for Tennessee, you know."

The representative said, "Well boys, that was just a vote. Now let's go up and see what that 3.2% stuff tastes like!" They traveled sixty miles to Scottsville, where there were only four bottles of beer left in the town. They made it to Bowling Green, where they found a corner drug store whose owner had sold all of his fifty cases in two hours. The owner directed them to a hotel where they found the last of the town's beer. The assemblyman thought about how much Kentucky was making from beer tax and said, "I guess that revenue idea is right. Boys, I think I'll speak to my senator about that beer bill."[46]

The New York Yankees arrived in Memphis on April 1, 1933, and reporters waiting at the train station assailed baseball legend Babe Ruth with questions on various topics including legalizing beer. Ruth told reporters, "It'll bring 'em back to the ball parks. And I think that the country will ride back to town on a wave of it." Ruth cut the interview short, saying, "I gotta be going. This sore throat has got me down and I need to sleep. Anyway, I want to watch Goofy Gomez [New York Yankee Vernon "Lefty" Gomez] playing with the ducks in the lobby of the Peabody!"[47]

Babe Ruth and his fellow Yankees traveled to Nashville, where they unintentionally caused a delay in the most controversial bill to come before Tennessee lawmakers since Reconstruction. On April 4, 1933, the Yankees played in Nashville at the Sulphur Dell stadium a few blocks from the Tennessee State Capitol. At the end of the session, Pete Haynes saw that the beer legislation only had forty-eight of the required fifty signatures. Haynes stood amazed that so many of his fellow legislators would abandon him at this momentous occasion. When he realized that most of them had left early to watch the game, Haynes declared, "Babe Ruth kept us from getting that bill into the hopper this afternoon!"[48]

On April 6, 1933, the Tennessee House of Representatives voted to legalize the manufacture and sale of 3.2 percent beer and wines, effective June 1. The bill passed exactly twenty minutes after the bill was brought up for consideration with fifty-two ayes, forty-two nays, two refusals to vote, and two absentees. The Tennessee Senate passed the beer bill with a surprising majority of twenty-two to eleven six days later. Senators amended the bill to make the law go into effect May 1 and to evenly distribute the revenue between the state, the municipalities, and the counties.[49]

The speaker threatened a half dozen times to clear the galleries because of disruptions from visitors and ousted anyone who snuck in. Repealists shouted support for their bill, while the WCTU hung banners from their wing that read, "We won't sell babies for beer!" Senator Brown from Shelby County moved to clear the chambers of visitors and begin consideration of the bill at 10:55 a.m. After the vote, the only thing left was the signature from McAlister.[50]

Meanwhile, Tennesseans prepared to take up the issue of repeal of the Eighteenth Amendment. The United States Constitution provides that an amendment may be proposed either by the Congress with a two-thirds majority vote in both the House of Representatives and the Senate or by a constitutional convention called for by two-thirds of the state legislatures. Although it provides two methods, Congress had only ever used the first method. The Roosevelt administration realized that many state lawmakers would not vote for repeal out of fear of the ASL and the WCTU, so A. Mitchell Palmer, a Roosevelt supporter and former United States attorney general, promoted the idea to use state conventions rather than the state legislatures. Congress formally proposed the repeal of Prohibition on February 20, 1933, and chose to follow Palmer's plan.

Crump and the Shelby County delegation to the state convention were eager to include a vote on statewide Prohibition in February 1933 but held off because the repeal movement did not yet have enough support in the rural-dominated legislature. In March, House leaders, ready to settle the matter of the Eighteenth Amendment, issued a special order for representatives to take up the Haynes-Moss bill, calling for a convention in July.[51]

The Memphis repeal movement mobilized in June and opened the West Tennessee repeal headquarters in the Peabody Hotel on July 8. The organization selected Mrs. Andrew Lawo, Mrs. A. R. Hudson, Roane Waring, C. D. Smith, Courtney Lewis, Joe Henkel, and R. G. Morrow as convention delegates. State chairman E. L. McNeilly announced that former congressman and president of the United Confederate Veterans Gen. Rice Pierce and Memphis cotton broker J. P. Norfleet would cochair the campaign in West Tennessee. Norfleet appointed as Shelby County committeemen Paul Dillard, Phil Canale, Bertrand Cohn, A. L. Parker, and E. M. Norment. Overton called on voters to register and vote for repeal, and attorney Thomas H. Keaton appealed to veterans for support.[52]

The pinnacle of the campaign came with the arrival of National Democratic Committee chairman James Farley. Roosevelt's right-hand man flew in from Atlanta, by way of Birmingham, and landed at the Memphis Municipal Airport on the afternoon of July 15, 1933. Following a ceremony that included a nineteen-gun salute from the 115th Field Artillery, county trustee Frank Gailor took Farley to a baseball game at Russwood Park. Overton and Norfleet hosted a banquet later at the Peabody for him that included several hundred guests and a prayer by Rev. Charles Blaisdell, rector of Calvary Episcopal Church. Farley thanked his hosts for their support of President Roosevelt and repeal of the Eighteenth Amendment and encouraged them to continue promoting the cause. The only break in the cheers and applause came when, amid a facetious round of boos, Prohibition chief Alfred Dalrymple rose to speak.[53]

Clouds moved in that afternoon and gave some relief from the heat to the more than ten thousand people waiting in Overton Park to hear Farley. The National Broadcasting Company crew prepared to broadcast the program to the nation, while the crowd received instructions to keep applause to a minimum in order not to interrupt Farley's thirty-minute speech. Cars parked in the grass between Rainbow Lake and the Doughboy Statue, the monument to Memphians who served in the world war. Police officers, dressed in their finest uniforms and white gloves, directed the 150 prominent visitors and repeal leaders to their seats, while the crowd of ordinary citizens stood behind them.[54]

The stage, set up by Rainbow Lake, had a large picture of Roosevelt hanging between two American flags to emphasize that Farley spoke on behalf of the president. The program began at nine o'clock in the evening, with Mayor Overton and Governor McAlister speaking briefly before state Democratic chairman Horace Frierson of Knoxville introduced the speaker. Farley explained the benefits of repeal and made a deliberate appeal to southern pride by telling listeners that allowing the conventions to decide the fate of Prohibition was the embodiment of states' rights. Farley told them that while the president and the Democratic Party supported repeal, the decision ultimately laid with the people. He emphasized that, the previous May, the US Supreme Court had determined that the Webb-Kenyon Act, the legislation forbidding the transportation of alcohol into a dry state, would remain in effect and the proposed Twenty-First Amendment included provisions to uphold any state dry law.[55]

Drys organized an antirepeal rally featuring war hero Alvin York at Rainbow Lake two days later. Unfortunately, York canceled, citing ill health, so organizers had nationally known dry leader Dr. A. J. Barton speak in his place. Barton tried to stir emotions by accusing Farley of using money from the US Treasury to finance his trip. He cast doubts on the federal government's ability to enforce the Webb-Kenyon Act and insisted that Farley violated states' rights by intimidating voters.[56]

The Shelby County Organization campaigned tirelessly by contacting voters through newspapers, the four local radio stations, telephone, and in person. Those at the headquarters in the Peabody Hotel understood the determination of the opposition and worried that overconfidence in repeal would lead to apathy. They needed a large turnout to not only win in Shelby County but to offset the high anti-repeal vote expecting in East Tennessee. Overton and County Commissioner Will Hale urged voters to "follow the leadership of the president," vote early and encourage others to do the same. Crump's most trusted "generalissimo" Frank Rice directed campaigners to distribute seventy-five thousand pamphlets, not by leaving them on doorsteps but rather by placing them directly in the hands of voters.[57]

The campaign paid off. Repealists in Shelby County won a landslide victory with 32,646 for repeal and 2,101 against. Victories in Memphis and Nashville helped offset the avalanche of antirepeal votes from East Tennessee and provided just enough ballots for the repeal movement to win the vote in Tennessee overall with 121,758 for repeal and 114,949 against it.[58]

Drys held a protest rally in Nashville at the Tennessee House of Representatives, where they called forth possible dry candidates to run for governor, including Ben Hooper, who graciously declined the offer. Pastor Dr. John F. Baggett, chairman of the local Allied Forces for Prohibition, claimed the referendum was in violation of the Tennessee Constitution because the repeal convention was elected before the submission of the proposed federal amendment. Tennessee assistant attorney general Nat Tipton countered by saying that the presentation of the repeal amendment outlined no particular method of electing delegates. Baggett then accused the repealists of rigging the election and claimed to have evidence of voter fraud in Memphis and Nashville.[59]

Bishop H. M. DuBose told Methodists in Memphis that he could not understand how the drys lost the vote. He said, "I stand as a lamb before the slaughter and a sheep before its shearer. I have been amazed. I can reach no further conclusion than that the people have acted under undue pressure from the administration, through constraint or party loyalty and hasty discounting of moral convictions. As it appears, license will come, and with it unspeakable demoralization of social, industrial, and ethical life."[60]

On August 11, 1933, the convention president took the podium in the House of Representatives in Nashville and announced, "I, E. L. McNeilly, president of this convention, do hereby officially declare that the State of Tennessee has duly ratified the Twenty-first Amendment to the Constitution, which repeals the Eighteenth Amendment." Applause and cheers, and a scattering of old-fashioned rebel yells, greeted the announcement. As the roar died down, six delegates demanded recognition, and the chair recognized J. E. Deford of Savannah, Tennessee. The independent Republican shouted, "I want to recommend that before we leave here, we lay plans to wipe out every prohibition law on the books of the State of Tennessee." It was the opening shot of the inevitable 1934 local option showdown—the new battle had begun.[61]

18

PROHIBITION AFTER REPEAL

You can't legislate morals into people and prohibition won't keep them
from drinking. Conditions are worse today than they were in the time
of the open saloon and more difficult to control.
—William J. Bacon, Shelby County sheriff, January 4, 1935

The repeal of the Eighteenth Amendment and the modification of state
alcohol laws created new challenges for officials in Memphis and Shelby
County who had less than a month to create a legal system to regulate
beer sales, production, and consumption. The rush to sell beer began with
Nathan Schatz, proprietor of the Fruit Store across from the Customs House,
who made the first application for a federal beer retailer's license on April
12, 1933. Schatz and the others who followed him eagerly waited to find out
how to sell beer in the city.

Mayor Overton had to move quickly, so he studied models used in Washington, DC, and other cities. After careful consideration, he decided to use the
best parts of the ordinance adopted by Minnesota municipalities as a basis
for the new Memphis law. Police commissioner Clifford Davis and assistant
city attorney Augustus Longstreet Heiskell then wrote up a beer ordinance
for the city and license fee schedule.[1]

The city beer ordinance passed on its first of three readings on April 18.
Tate Pease became the head of the committee that included police chief Will
Lee and drugstore owner Joe Hicks. Regulations included issuing licenses
only to US citizens and those without liquor convictions. It included rules
regarding gambling devices, sales to minors, and proximity to schools. The
committee did not allow sales between 1:00 a.m. and 7:00 a.m. Monday
through Friday and between midnight Saturday and 1:00 p.m. Sunday.[2]

Fig. 18.1. Many Memphians welcomed the return of legal beer. Caption:
THE TAXPAYER'S RUSH. Courtesy Memphis Room, Memphis Public
Library and Information Center.

On April 25, the city beer license board opened for business in room
17-A on the second floor of the police station in the office of the original
Prohibition agents, former Texas Ranger Capt. W. W. Pitts, Bond Harmon,
and Bert Bates. Carroll Seabrook, a cotton merchant and former member of
the city board of equalization, the agency charged with tax collection and fee
administration, became the licensing board secretary and took 225 applications, including 15 from women and 4 from African Americans. Seabrook
issued the first 37 permits two days later, beginning with the first to Miss
Hattie's Lunch Room at 10 West Calhoun.[3]

Squire Early E. Jeter, head of the Shelby County beer board, set a fee schedule that included a $15 fee to sell beer to be consumed at least two hundred
yards from the selling premises; a $100 fee to hotels, clubs, and lodges that

Fig. 18.2. The return of legal beer, 1933. Courtesy of the University of Memphis Special Collections.

served beer; and a $250 fee to brewers and distributors. Most county and city regulations agreed; however, Overton insisted the city not allow drugstores to serve beer with lunch. By April 30, Jeter issued 168 permits to sell beer beginning May 1.[4]

The first county license went to famed Memphis aviator Emma Harbin. The former champion swimmer earned her commercial pilot's license in 1929 and performed stunt shows at the Memphis Cotton Carnival and aerial exhibitions around the country in the early 1930s. A flight with Harbin cured Mrs. C. C. Bradbury of almost total deafness in 1932. Harbin became an overnight sensation and received numerous requests for flights from those suffering from hearing loss. Harbin also ran a tourist lodge with a swimming pool and lunch counter on Hernando Road, just outside the city limits. She paid a twenty-one-dollar state and county license fee and a one-dollar county clerk fee for "permit number one." On May 1, she and her husband turned on the lighted signs announcing "We Have Beer."[5]

Jacob and Valentine Schorr began hiring and planned to reopen the Tennessee Brewery by June 1933. The Memphis brewery in its heyday produced 110,000 barrels of beer a year, equaling 35 million bottles, and employed two hundred workers. Jacob Schorr expected Goldcrest beer to sell for fifteen cents a bottle. He promised, "We can't make it for a dime like in the old days with the new taxes, but we'll make the best beer you can get anywhere."[6]

Famous beer producers, in anticipation of the new beer law, signed up distributors in Memphis: A. S. Barboro carried Schlitz; Chase Bottling Company carried Cook's Goldblume; Davis-Mize Company carried Pabst's Blue Ribbon; D. Canale and Company carried Pitt City Pilsner; and Orange Crush Bottling Company carried Falls City Beer. Two days later, Blatz appointed the Eagle Malt Company as a distributor, and Atlas Special selected J. F. McCabe and Company.[7]

Crowds of Memphians eagerly waited for the first beer to arrive Monday morning, May 1, 1933. Walter Stewart wrote, "Old Jan Primus seemed to dance along before us in Falstaffian mirth, for beer was coming back." The reporter rode with driver Carl Williams as he steered the first beer truck out of St. Louis over the Harahan Bridge and into Memphis shortly after midnight. The truck groaned to a halt in front of the Anchor Malt Company where a crew appeared out of the darkness and quickly unloaded two hundred cases of Country Club Beer.[8]

Other trucks followed as well as another forty-four railroad freight cars carrying 845,000 bottles of beer. Traffic officer Tommy Waterson kept the curious and thirsty at bay while the crews worked. At H&H Distributing Company at the foot of Linden Avenue, shouting men clattered over the cobblestones with flashlights needling the darkness amid the roar of engines and the rhythmic rattle and clink of stacking cases of Prima beer. Well before the break of dawn, beer trucks for the city's distributors competed for space on the roads with the milk wagons as they delivered to highway restaurants and drink stands crowded with customers.[9]

Memphians consumed twelve thousand cases of beer on that first day. Hotels and clubs, like the Peabody and Silver Slipper, held parties that night featuring legal beer. Retailers soon ran short or ran out of beer but promised thirsty customers that they would soon have more. Wholesalers and retailers put two hundred men to work, and sales generated steady tax revenue. Memphis city government took in more than $23,000 by May 3 off the sales of fifteen- to twenty-cent bottles of beer, while the state received $5,460 in privilege taxes and $400 for bond recordings.[10]

Legal beer offered new opportunities for businesses. Abe Plough, local drug store pioneer, took advantage of the alteration in city beer law and ordered beer for his four drugstores. Peeple's Stag Cafeteria, once a saloon and the scene of numerous liquor and gambling raids, moved the pool tables to another location, bought more tables and chairs, and offered table service rather than cafeteria service to accommodate sales of beer. The Lipman

Brothers Wholesalers, only months earlier implicated in the Moberg-Green liquor conspiracy, became a major beer distributer.[11]

Advertisements and promotions signaled beer's return. Blatz began broadcasting radio commercials, with microphones picking up the sounds of bottles, one minute after midnight on April 6. In July, Memphis Distributing Company brought the Anheuser-Busch Clydesdales to Memphis for two parades that also featured the horses that had delivered the first cases of 3.2 percent beer to Al Smith in April. Kingsley's Beer jug band, made up of violin, ukulele, jug, and drum, paraded through the downtown loop daily, while Schlitz beer had a band play concerts in all the restaurants that sold beer.[12]

Wine and cider also returned to Memphis. The Anchor Malt Company received the first shipment of twenty-five cases of twenty-four ten-ounce bottles of 3.2 percent red wine on May 9. In September, National Fruit Products Company, which began in 1905 and went out of business with Prohibition, received a new charter, attracted investors, leased a new building, hired sixty-five employees, and began producing 3.2 percent apple cider once again.[13]

Methodist bishop H. M. DuBose proposed banishment of church members who sold beer and the boycott of any business that sold it as well. In Memphis, Methodist minister Rev. Horace Knickerbocker favored the idea, but most other Methodist churches did not see the point. Methodists met at the sixty-seventh Memphis District Conference at Epworth Church, where they decided that individual churches could make the call on any punitive actions if they so desired.[14]

Police and the courts made good on their promise to enforce the new laws. Sgt. Robert Almond arrested Ricco Gaia on the city's first beer violation on May 1. Gaia had twenty-four cases of beer to sell in his café, but he had no permit. Gaia received a fifty-dollar fine the next day and faced state charges. Judge Lewis Fitzhugh promised to show no mercy on drunk drivers and increased bonds from $250 to a $1,000. He went from seeing two or three drunk drivers a day to seeing only one in four days. Ironically, some pig stand operators, notorious for selling bootleg liquor and home brew, were not making very much money selling legal beer. Some asked whether, if they surrendered their permits, they could get their money back.[15]

Modification to allow beer not only created new jobs and tax revenue; it accomplished what thirteen years of Prohibition could not: it virtually eliminated home brewing of beer. Commissioner Davis reported a marked decline in the number of home brew and blind tiger cases due to greater enforcement and the availability of legal beer. In April 1933, dealers in crocks, malt, bottles, and siphons already predicted a decline for home brew because of increased prices of supplies and new taxes. In addition, drinkers liked the taste of the new beer better even though it had a much lower alcohol content. Beer smuggled in from Kentucky and Missouri became very popular in Memphis, and those who tried it declared, "No more home brew for me!"[16]

"What does repeal mean to you?" asked radio interviewers on the night of December 5, 1933. People interviewed rejoiced over the repeal of the Eighteenth Amendment, but those in dry states like Tennessee were still years away from drinking whiskey legally. Amidst the celebrations, Judge Harry Anderson warned, "For the past fourteen years, there has been a great deal of sympathy for the bootlegger because the general public did not favor the prohibition law. Prohibition died last night. There will be no more sympathy for the bootlegger. All illicit distillers who are brought into my court will get steep prison terms if found guilty."[17]

Bootleggers, however, had little to worry about as they shifted from dealing in moonshine to smuggling liquor from wet states like Illinois and Louisiana. Sheriff William J. Bacon told reporters that his department would be virtually powerless to stop them since deputies could not seize liquor without a search warrant. Police commissioner Clifford Davis and police chief Will Lee promised that they would treat sellers of contraband liquor the same as sellers of moonshine, but they acknowledged they would not have any officers specifically looking for cars with liquor.[18]

Prohibition agents could do little to help because of administrative confusion and lack of manpower. On July 1, 1930, the Prohibition Bureau was transferred from the Department of the Treasury to the Department of Justice. In 1933, as part of an omnibus crime bill, the FBI took over the Prohibition Bureau and renamed it the Alcohol Beverage Unit. Following Prohibition repeal in December 1933, the Alcohol Beverage Unit returned to the Department of the Treasury and became the Alcohol Tax Unit of the Bureau of Internal Revenue (later renamed the Internal Revenue Service). Once it resumed operations, agents could do little more than track people who made regular daily trips to wet states for large amounts of liquor while ignoring those who drove to wet states to purchase liquor for personal use.[19]

Hijacking became a problem as trucks carrying legal whiskey bound for wet states crossed through Tennessee. In August 1935, armed hijackers took control of a truck destined for West Memphis, Arkansas, near the Kentucky-Tennessee border. The gunmen threw the kidnapped driver on the side of the road near Brunswick and escaped with 215 cases of whiskey valued at $5,000. The same bandits held up Stewart Harris of Southern Forwarding

Company outside of Memphis as he drove a delivery truck loaded with 450 cases of liquor worth $6,750 across the Tennessee-Kentucky border in December 1936. Worse still, Memphian H. H. Jeter lost an arm because of a bullet wound following a gunfight with hijackers a year later.[20]

Police detectives arrested hijacker C. J. Wallace in a Turkish bath at the Hotel Devoy in Memphis in March 1936. Wallace had worked as a Prohibition agent from 1925 to 1928 but found more lucrative opportunities on the other side of the law. He and police characters Charles Porter Harlow, A. C. Davis, and Ed McKinley hijacked several liquor shipments from Kentucky bound for Louisiana by impersonating law enforcement officers.[21]

Repeal of the Eighteenth Amendment also meant that beer and wine producers in wet states could make beverages with more than 3.2 percent alcohol content. The popularity of stronger spirits tempted business owners to smuggle in and quietly sell the outlawed beverages. The sellers hoped to avoid federal tax penalties if caught, so in addition to their twenty-dollar federal 3.2 percent licenses, they paid the additional five dollars to the US government to sell stronger wines and beers. Seabrook became suspicious and promised strict enforcement of the state law, threatening to revoke licenses and make arrests of dealers who sold beverages with excessive alcohol contents.[22]

Sheriff Bacon reported bootleggers were eager to sell off their stocks of holiday liquor and equipment in anticipation of the flood of legal whiskey from Cairo, Illinois; however, the prediction proved premature. In a rush to meet demand, northern distillers sold a cheaply made whiskey that even drinkers of moonshine did not like. A local bootlegger said, "This so-called whiskey is just a lot of distilled water, colored with prune juice and spiked with alcohol." Some distillers resorted to using moonshine as a base for their cheaper whiskeys to cut costs and rush production. One local moonshiner boasted of producing a thousand gallons a day to ship to northern distilleries.[23]

Moonshiners tried to cash in on the initial interest in smuggled "legal" whiskey by manufacturing counterfeit name-brand whiskey and selling it as the genuine article. Shortly after repeal in December 1933, police raided a house in South Memphis, near Calvary Cemetery, where J. H. Spellberger and J. P. Lomax used equipment to age corn liquor artificially, color it, and then put it in bottles with phony labels, corks, and government seals. Inspector William Griffin's men confiscated over four hundred gallons in one of the largest liquor raids of the year.[24]

Police understood they could never wipe out liquor traffic in the city, so they put forth just enough effort to keep the city from appearing "wide-open."

Commissioner Davis announced he would put a "lid" on vice and began round-ups of bootleggers, gamblers, and prostitutes. According to Memphis historian, soldier, executive, and political leader George W. Lee, the 1933 lid that targeted Beale Street made the famous thoroughfare as "dry as the Sahara."[25]

Certain newspaper reporters grew more cynical towards the vice campaigns, and their attitudes began to shape the public perception of the Shelby County Organization as a partner in crime. A journalist in January 1934 wrote, "Cheating on the police lid started some time ago and has gained momentum daily until now the town is almost as wide open as before the sudden, unexplained, and long extended air-tight lid was clamped over the city." Liquor became plentiful again as "the good old days returned to gamblers' row." Davis defended the department's efforts and explained the difficulty in enforcing laws that no one respected. "Just when you think workhouse sentences and fines have broken a law violator," explained Davis, "you find him trying it all over again."[26]

Press-Scimitar reporters in June 1934 described a "tidal wave of legally manufactured and moonshine liquor" flowing through "wide-flung gates." Memphians bought higher-quality whiskeys for $4.50 a pint and spent as little as fifty cents a pint for "Beale Street" moonshine. The wealthiest bought their alcohol from rum-runners who brought their wares in from New Orleans or Cairo, while the average Memphian gave his business to a "certain and not at all mysterious party." This unnamed bootlegger freely gave the reporter his inventory and prices for whiskeys, gin, scotch, rum, wine, port, sherry, sauterne, champagne, and even absinthe. Customers no longer had to give a code phrase to make a purchase. They simply drove up to the business, and a clerk would take the order at the curb. Nightclubs and roadhouses just outside the city limits sold all types of liquor along with meals, with little or no interference from the sheriff's department.[27]

Journalists placed the blame for the lack of liquor enforcement squarely on "The Boys," which included Watkins Overton, E. W. Hale, Frank Rice, Clifford Davis, and other members of the Shelby County Organization. They promoted the idea of collusion and cynically suggested law enforcement only acted when it was necessary to force bootleggers to cooperate with the Shelby County Organization. One reporter claimed, "Last spring and winter, Memphis was afflicted with what is technically known as a 'police lid.' This was extremely tight while the 'Boys' were said to be wrangling over some unannounced dispute. These differences have apparently been patched up, however, and you can put your tonsils on the spot when, where, and how you please. Boy, another Manhattan."[28]

The police launched more raids in September 1934, beginning with the arrests of eighteen minor bootleggers including Splint Manley. Reporters issued the all-too-common complaint that larger operations continued their delivery services while police seemed only interested in the "small fry." Officials said they hoped to catch the small operators to get enough evidence to arrest the more prominent bootleggers. The raids ended in October and liquor prices returned to normal. Supplies remained ample, but sellers cautioned customers not to draw attention from police by drinking in public. Chief Lee pointed out the department's successes in bringing down burglary rates but admitted that police could not stop bootlegging.[29]

Crump and "The Boys" faced embarrassment and scrutiny after journalist Owen Payne White's article "Sinners in Dixie" appeared in Collier's magazine in January 1935. It painted a picture of widespread violations of statewide Prohibition and collusion between liquor interests and the Shelby County Organization. White claimed that men and women who ran gambling houses, dancehalls, blind pigs, policy rackets, and "houses of ill-fame" did so with the encouragement of the Crump machine, which in turn used tribute paid by these "professional sinners" to finance the organization. According to White, the political machine relied exclusively on money from vice so that it never had to ask for donations from legitimate businesses or citizens.[30]

Crump, of course, was furious with the accusations. Local newspapers that complained of the laxity of law enforcement even stepped up to defend the city. Ralph Millett of the Press-Scimitar claimed that White exaggerated his claims and that sin in Memphis was no different from what went on in other cities. Millet said that White could have just as easily heard a good sermon or had a good drink of Coca-Cola, but he chose instead to look for the kind of vice found in every city. Police responded to the criticism by launching another "lid" and made arrests of bootleggers and gamblers over the next month.[31]

Police continued the periodic "lids" through the late 1930s, but they focused on gambling and prostitution and paid less attention to liquor as time went on. Police launched another lid targeting white upper-class places in April 1937, following the flood crisis. Officers shut down bars in the Tennessee Club, University Club, Elks Club, Memphis Colonial Club, Chickasaw Club, Hunt and Polo Club, and Ridgeway Club. Commissioner Davis said the raids were only part of a continuing effort, but reporters speculated that they were an attempt to clean up the city in anticipation of the governor's investigation into local corruption. As usual, the liquor trade soon resumed, and prices returned to normal.[32]

Modification and repeal changed the liquor business in Memphis for better and for worse. Modification ended home brew bootlegging, but the successes of the campaigns against the Liquor Barons meant nothing after the return of liquor smuggling. The situation became so uncontrollable that law enforcement publicly admitted they could not stop it and advocated a repeal of the state dry laws. Editorial writer E. R. Turley wrote, "I am wondering whether Governor Browning honestly believes that we have prohibition in Tennessee. If he does, he is to be pitied. Tis true we have a prohibition law passed by the Legislature, mind you, in 1909, but we all know that the law does not prohibit, nor will it ever prohibit. Everybody knows that we have whiskey in great abundance, always have had it, further, always will have it."[33]

19

LAST BOOTLEGGERS

The whiskey business is about shot.
—Harvey "Boxhead" Mitchell, 1931

Memphians still wanted liquor, and as long as they were willing to pay for it, someone would be willing to supply it. The Prohibition Bureau's plan to bypass the "hip-pocket" bootlegger and focus efforts on organized liquor syndicates seemed like a logical solution to the problem of too many outlaws and not enough police. Agents brought down the Liquor Barons; however, the resulting vacuum allowed minor bootleggers and smugglers to take over the market. Most of the major bootleggers gave up, but some of the old-timers held out. Despite the best efforts of the law enforcement, these wily bootleggers operated almost unimpaired through three decades of Prohibition.

Waiting for transfer to the Atlanta Federal Penitentiary in May 1931, Harvey "Boxhead" Mitchell, John Belluomini's one-time lieutenant, explained, "Policy is the big racket in Memphis now. The whiskey business is about shot. Warfare among the liquor operators has caused their ruin. They fell out with each other, and now only one is really making money and that's Number One, the Big Shot. The others are broke, and they were made that way by Number One." Mitchell said of the so-called Big Shot, "He handles about 1,500 gallons of whiskey daily, at a profit of about a dollar per gallon, but his big money comes from policy. But as far as catching him, that just isn't being done. He never touches a pint of liquor himself, nor a policy ticket—that's one reason."[1]

Policy was a game of chance based on an intricate system of numbers, and it was popular among all Memphians regardless of race, gender, or class. The player gave the policy writer a dime and recited three numbers between one and seventy-eight. The policy writer made a note of the player's names and numbers. He gave a copy of the slip to the player and turned in another to the policy house. The policy boss made drawings at noon, and the policy writer would then deliver the prize of $11.50 to the day's winner.[2]

The "Big Shot" to whom Mitchell referred was the notorious racketeer Rizziere "Nello" Grandi, also known as Nollo Grandi, Big Grandi, or Big Grundy. The native of Voldattavo, Italy, ran gambling houses and policy games and, of course, sold liquor. He operated a dozen or more bootlegging establishments and employed men to care for the business and accept all responsibility including workhouse sentences. Grandi also used policy runners that police could never trace back to him. Everyone knew what Grandi was up to, but no one could collar him.[3]

Grandi had been on the wrong side of city officials since Rowlett Paine and his Citizens' League faced former mayor J. J. Williams in November 1919. According to the claims of the *Press-Scimitar*, police supplied falsified registrations to African Americans and transported them to various wards so they could vote more than once, while campaign manager Louis J. Moss ordered forty thousand cards listing the Williams ticket as the Citizens' League to fool voters into casting ballots for the wrong people. Sheriff Perry and his deputies raided places run by Jim Kinnane, Joe Raffanti, Attilio Grandi, and Nello Grandi, seized the cards and phony voter registrations, and arrested known gamblers, pickpockets, drug dealers, and prostitutes.[4]

Grandi was not deterred by arrests or fines. He ran a café at 236 Union Avenue at Fourth Street that served as a cover for policy, craps, and poker games. His customers expected liquor, and Grandi always had plenty on hand. Police raided the place repeatedly, finding over eighty half-pint bottles of corn liquor under some floorboards in April 1922, twenty-three half-pints in August 1924, and more whiskey along with gambling in March 1927.[5]

Grandi would post bond for his men after their arrest, and once released, Grandi would encourage the men to flee town. Grandi provided surety on bonds for two African American liquor runners, Bob Rolac and Allen Chambers, who failed to appear in court in January 1927. Judge Tom Harsh, furious that more of Grandi's men got away, ordered the minimum bond increased from $250 to $1,000 for manufacturing or transporting liquor. He also ordered that the court place liens on all property of sureties. Harsh declared, "I'm tired of having Grandi make bond for defendants who fail to appear."[6]

Grandi, like many other bootleggers, hid his liquor off his property. In the event that police discovered it, they could not prove he owned it. Inspector Mike Kehoe, during a series of downtown raids, went into a vacant store next to Grandi's place and found 270 gallons of liquor and several cases of home brew. Kehoe said, "We know whose it is, all right, but what can we do?" Not one to give up easily, Kehoe returned two days later and arrested Otto Lucchesi and Nello Grandi anyway, though a judge dropped the charges for lack of evidence.[7]

Grandi employed lookouts and occasionally paid bribes to avoid the attention of beat cops during their patrols. This practice kept the police from arresting him, but it also kept police from protecting his business. Early in the morning of January 6, 1929, Police received an anonymous call reporting a robbery at Grandi's café. Officers arrived and found about twenty-five men gathered around the restaurant. They told the officers that five armed men burst into the room and told the gamblers to "reach for the sky." Three kept their weapons trained and two collected between $7,000 and $10,000. As they left, one told the gamblers, "I hope to see you all in Miami!"[8]

Capt. Will Lee suspended Sgt. J. G. Kennedy, W. G. Smith, and R. P. Gipson for not breaking up the gambling game. This holdup was one of a string of such robberies and the second time someone had robbed Grandi. Lee suspected that Grandi and other gamblers had paid off police, but Inspector Kehoe argued that they kept lookouts who would turn out the lights whenever police passed by on routine patrols. The officers in question checked out Grandi's place three times that night before the robbery and believed it closed. The thieves had watched the patrols and timed the robbery to avoid the officers.[9]

Rival bootleggers struck at Grandi in February 1930 by burning two cars and a thousand gallons of corn liquor hidden in a house near the Hollywood neighborhood in Shelby County. Patrons of Joe Barsotta's nearby dancehall saw the fire consume the house, and several tried to pull liquor out before the cans exploded. Sheriff Knight questioned Grandi and well-known bootlegger Alex Baldi, but both denied any knowledge of the whiskey or the attack. Regardless, rumors circulated that the attack had been in retaliation for Grandi's cooperation with the Prohibition Bureau. Grandi told reporters, "The paper, he says I start the war by telling on some bootleggers. It's foolish. I tell on no one. I know nothing at all."[10]

Baldi raised suspicions when he could not explain why his burned cars, apparently used to run liquor, were in other people's names. Deputies raided a house near the fire and discovered seventy-five gallons of liquor two days later. Two drivers pulled up with a delivery of fifteen gallons of liquor, saw the deputies, and fled on foot. Deputies suspected that Baldi and Grandi owned the liquor but could not prove it.[11]

Grandi ran into more problems with his liquor runners in March 1931, when one of his drivers struck a man on a bicycle at East Butler and Avery Avenue. Wiley C. Goldman sued Grandi, and his partners John "The Pig" Cuneo and Dominick Aretta for $15,000 for a fractured skull. Goldman charged that Grandi operated a fleet of fourteen whiskey runners out of a bootleg operation at 238 South Fourth Street.[12]

Grandi, undeterred by robberies or attention from the police, continued his poker and craps games at his Fourth Street café. A salesman who gave the alias "J. H. James" accompanied a friend to Grandi's place after midnight. They met a lookout who stood watch at the bottom of the stairs on the Fourth Street side. The man knew James's friend, so he let the two go upstairs. James saw a poker game in one room and joined a craps game in the other. He lost thirty-nine dollars before he realized that the dealer had rigged the dice with two fives. The man in charge of the game refused to refund his lost money, so James reported them to the police. Night shift supervisor Capt. Phelan Thompson sent a five-man raiding party and made arrests. All eight arrested gave phony names as well as the man who posted their ten-dollar bonds.[13]

Commissioner Clifford Davis ordered an investigation into why police allowed the crooked dice game to operate, and once again did nothing more than shuffle officers to different precincts. At Davis's prompting, police raided Grandi's place the following day and found two hundred half-pints and ninety pints of liquor in the gaming area, but they made no arrests. Prohibition agents raided his business and found more liquor a few months later. However, James Wharton, sent by the Department of Justice to help prosecute liquor cases, dropped the case against Grandi because the agents did not have a search warrant.[14]

Local Prohibition agents tried to deport Grandi and other Italian-born gangsters as part of the campaign by the Department of Justice to rid the country of foreign-born bootleggers. Grandi applied for US citizenship in November 1930, but agents hoped to find fraudulent statements in his paperwork to use against him. Merton Sturges from the US Bureau of Immigration office in St. Louis and his assistant Walter Wolfe questioned Grandi, in the company of his lawyer Arthur Brode, about his property holdings, sources of income, and the nature of his occupation. After three hours, they found nothing to use against him and dropped the deportation plan.[15]

The fact that Grandi remained a thorn in the side of law enforcement was a glaring example of the ineffectiveness of Prohibition. In 1936, Grandi, after partaking of his wares, drove his car into a parked car, backed up, and drove into another parked car before police arrested him for drunk driving.

Later that year, dishwasher Herman Surrell filed a $5,000 suit against Grandi for beating him "without provocation." Grandi had kicked him, punched him in the face, and injured his eye after he caught the dishwasher stealing a half-pint of whiskey from his stock in the rear of the Club Lunch Room at 177 Beale.[16]

Grandi eventually left bootlegging behind once Prohibition ended. When he died in March 1968, Memphians remembered Grandi as a restauranteur, a merchant, and a real estate investor. He was active in his church, the Italian Society, and politics in his later years. Grandi achieved what few leading underworld figures could pull off—he weathered law enforcement, buried his shady past, and became a respected member of the community.[17]

· · ·

A police sergeant took newspaperman Westbrook Pegler on a tour of Beale Street one day in May 1934. The reporter had come to Memphis to see the Memphis Cotton Carnival at the invitation of the carnival officials and took some time to learn about the city. The carnival was a series of parties and festivities staged by the Carnival Memphis Association and its member krewes in the style of the New Orleans Mardi Gras. It included a secretly selected king, queen, and royal court, and it saluted the city's culture and industries. Pegler observed the crowds of African American farmhands in town for the weekend, swaggering sophisticates, and prostitutes with lips and cheeks "painted as red as a new trestle." The air was thick with the smell of barbecue and the sound of the blues.[18]

The sergeant directed Pegler to a corner place crowded with black patrons with the music of guitar and mouth harp radiating out the door. "This is Mulcahy's place," said the sergeant.

"A black Mulcahy?" responded the reporter.

"No, white man. Comes from a good family, too, I always heard, although I don't know much about that. They claim he was educated in college, and he talks like it might be so, but I never did know the exact straight about that. He has been down here more years than I know, running a pool hall and soft drinks. Peddles a little corn, too, I suppose."[19]

Mulcahy, a soft-voiced man of fifty, stood on the corner outside his club. "Everything's quiet, Sergeant," he said. "Negroes haven't got any money. Would you let me buy you a drink?"

"No, I'm on the wagon," replied the sergeant.

"That's good," said Mulcahy. "Yes, everything's quiet. No fights, no excitement. I wish these Negroes could get hold of a little money so they could spend a little. No better spender in the world than a country Negro with a ten-dollar bill."

"Well, good night, Mulcahy."

"Goodnight, Sergeant. Sorry I can't buy you a drink."[20]

James Joseph "Jim" Mulcahy had the longest career of any of the original Irish gangsters. Mulcahy maintained the image of a privileged upbringing, when in reality, his parents were poor Irish famine refugees. Mulcahy worked as a young man in the grocery store run by his brother William. The store also served as the residence for Mulcahy's widowed mother Alice and his siblings Lillian, William, and Thomas, who all died between 1905 and 1912 from either pneumonia or tuberculosis. After their deaths, Mulcahy worked briefly as an elevator operator and clothing cleaner.[21]

Mulcahy reportedly went to a local college and studied business. He had a remarkably quick mind, and he was widely known for his skill in mathematics. He could add long strings of figures at a glance, and his friends often gave him two sets of numbers in the thousands and checked him as he gave the product of the two almost before they had the last digit out of their mouths.[22]

Mulcahy ran some famous saloons and played a part in Crump's political machine as a ward heeler. He spent up to $1,000 per election paying poll taxes for African Americans so that they could vote for Crump and his handpicked candidates. One of Mulcahy's efforts to attract voters resulted in one of the most memorable songs about the city. During the 1909 mayoral campaign, Crump's opponents recruited the Eckford and Bynum bands to help with their campaigns, so Mulcahy approached W. C. Handy about writing and performing a song for Crump.[23]

Handy composed the instrumental tune on the cigar counter at Pee Wee's Saloon and had his band play it. Those that frequented saloons thought little of reformers, so audience members as well as band members would improvise lyrics mostly making fun of Crump. Handy wrote words to the song based on what the crowd's comments were. Handy and his band performed it at the corner of Main and Madison to an enthusiastic crowd who responded with whistles and dancing in the street. Fortunately, Crump did not hear the lyrics. Years later, Handy rewrote the song as "Memphis Blues" and took out any mention of Crump. He presented it to Crump to see if the mayor had any objections to the lyrics. Crump did not object, so Handy published it in 1913.[24]

Mulcahy served a term in the Atlanta Federal Penitentiary from May 31 through October 1, 1919, for his part in the Tyree Taylor liquor ring. Prison officials assigned him to balance and maintain the facility's account books,

Fig. 19.1. William Christopher Handy. Courtesy of Memphis Room, Memphis Public Library and Information Center.

but with his mathematical abilities, he quickly completed his daily duties and found plenty of free time to spend in the prison library. Here, Mulcahy met and became a friend of Eugene Debs, a founding member of the Industrial Workers of the World and the Socialist Party of America's candidate for the US presidency. He spent long hours in discussion with Debs, who was in prison for denouncing US involvement in World War I, and became a committed pacifist.[25]

Mulcahy returned to Memphis, where he bootlegged liquor out of his house on Polk Street. Police raided the home in August 1922 and seized liquor and coloring fluids. They arrested Mulcahy and thirteen others, including prize fighters Freddie Roth and Kid Duggan and gangsters Charles Walter Costello and Herbert Green. While out on bond, undercover Prohibition agents arrested Mulcahy after he sold them a bottle of whiskey. He pled guilty, paid a $250 fine, and served three months in jail. Police arrested him again for selling liquor to informants in April 1926 and again in April 1928.[26]

Mulcahy's fortunes changed as the ward heeler found his way back into the good graces of the Shelby County Organization during the 1928 elections. A shooting at Mulcahy's Cotton Club, a short distance from his house, exposed a gambling operation that resulted in his arrest in March 1932. Attorney general and Crump stalwart Tyler McLain saved Mulcahy by refusing to present the case and dismissing the warrant. Police arrested Mulcahy again during a 1933 police "lid," but the machine-influenced county grand jury returned a not-true verdict claiming a lack of evidence, even though police found seventy-five gallons of liquor in his home and three more in his car.[27]

At his peak in the 1930s, Mulcahy owned the Old Plantation on Polk, the Cotton Club on Main, the Reveille Billiard Hall on Main, and the Panama Café on Beale, and he ran a touring orchestra. Regardless of his success, Mulcahy never forgot where he made his money or his old-time customers. In 1931, Mulcahy set up soup kitchens on Beale Street for hundreds of African Americans forsaken by local welfare agencies. Someone asked him why he did it, and Mulcahy replied that his customers had spent money in his places when they had jobs, and he could not stand to see them hungry when they were out of work.[28]

His fortunes changed following downturns in his businesses and abandonment by the Shelby County Organization. The cash-strapped Mulcahy continued to run the Panama Café, where he stood out conspicuously in his loud silk shirts leisurely drinking three quarts of milk and eating three oranges every day. A suit had been filed against the sixty-one-year-old by the city for unpaid back taxes when he died on September 5, 1940, from heart failure. A writer from the *Commercial Appeal* noted his one-time importance and remembered that his name was once "a conjure word" among African Americans and politicians who wanted their votes.[29]

• • •

Edward A. Laughter and his pilot Theodore Robinson sailed the *Gypsy* down the Mississippi River past Memphis before dawn on July 18, 1917. They had 139 cases of whiskey from Caruthersville, Missouri, in the cargo hold as they headed for a rendezvous point just south of the city of Memphis near the Ensley Plantation. Robinson steered the launch up to a bank in the dark where W. Newton Fisher waited with a crew of seven men and six automobiles ready to carry the cargo to its destinations in the city.[30]

Laughter and Fisher had run a wholesale liquor business before the Webb-Kenyon Act had gone into effect in 1913. In January 1916, the two had argued that they ran a legitimate interstate business and filed a suit to halt the city

from shutting them down. Judge John McCall had issued a temporary re-
straining order on city officials but lifted it after he determined Laughter
and Fisher could no longer operate under the new law. The city officials had
closed the firm and left the two with the choice to either to give up their
business or become bootleggers.[31]

Suddenly, there was a noise in the woods. The men looked up and saw a
squad of deputies crash through the underbrush with weapons drawn. US
marshal Stanley Trezevant bordered the launch and disarmed Laughter. The
raiders hauled the prisoners to Memphis and charged them with conspiracy
to violate the Reed Amendment, the 1913 amendment to the Webb-Kenyon
Act that imposed a $1,000 fine for transporting liquor into a dry state, while
county sheriff Oliver Perry filed an additional charge of carrying a pistol
against Laughter.[32]

A jury found Laughter, Fisher, and A. L. "Dutch" Anderson guilty of conspiracy charges, but Laughter had no intention of surrendering. Laughter
appealed the ruling and was released on bonds signed by David Ostrich,
William Winter, and James Mulcahy. Laughter, scheduled to leave for Atlanta
on February 17, 1919, fled to Caruthersville before Sheriff Perry could reach
him. Laughter headed south for New Orleans and reportedly planned to
escape to Honduras.[33]

In the meantime, Laughter's attorney Frank Elgin filed a stay of mandate
with the US Court of Appeals for the Sixth Circuit in Cincinnati asking
for a ninety-day reprieve to prepare an appeal to the US Supreme Court.
Federal district attorney William Kyser protested, calling it a delaying tactic
to allow Laughter to escape. Trezevant wanted Laughter to serve his federal
sentence, and Perry wanted him to serve a sentence for carrying a pistol.
Both expected Laughter's appeal to fail, so each hurried to New Orleans to
try to capture him first.[34]

Laughter, while in New Orleans in March 1919, happened upon Shelby
County commissioner E. W. Hale during a visit to the city. Laughter complained to Hale about the high cost of protection. He named one man "on
the city payroll, very close to the top," and another related to city officials
that had received his bribes.[35]

Laughter returned, and Elgin presented the appeal to the US Supreme
Court in April 1919. He argued that Trezevant had arrested Laughter and
Fisher outside the four-mile limit of any school. The court, however, maintained that the two had violated the Reed Amendment and upheld the lower
court's decision. Fisher surrendered, but Laughter took flight and headed
for Arkansas.[36]

Police captured Laughter in Hot Springs, Arkansas, but the wily bootlegger had a plan for escape. Laughter, uncharacteristically cooperative, surrendered to Sheriff Perry and headed back to Memphis. Once the two left, friends of Laughter posed as the Hot Springs chief of police H. R. Wheeler and sent a telegram requesting that Sheriff James MacDougall at Forrest City intercept and arrest Perry on charges of kidnapping. They hoped that while Perry was in custody, the sheriff would release Laughter. The plan fell through after MacDougall, a friend of Perry, saw through the ruse. Laughter served the eleven-month and twenty-nine-day sentence on the pistol charge first, then two years in Atlanta, and another six-month sentence in the jail in Covington, Tennessee.[37]

Laughter and his siblings had long had ties to bootlegging and the underworld. Nicknamed "Coal-Oil Johnny," Laughter served as a police officer and patrolled Beale Street, where he had the reputation as a tough cop. He served from 1909 to 1915 before opening a saloon in Caruthersville, Missouri. Police arrested Henry Laughter and Tony Marino for transporting five gallons of liquor in March 1923. A year later, deputies in Hernando, Mississippi, arrested Henry Laughter, Eddie Campbell, and another man while they operated a fifty-gallon still hidden in the cellar of a house. Police arrested Lonnie Laughter after he crashed his car into a parked police car on Halloween night in 1924, and Sheriff Knight arrested him for running a three-thousand-gallon still near the Mississippi state line in 1926.[38]

Lucian Laughter, however, rivaled his brothers in notoriety. Police raided his home in May 1923 and discovered over a thousand gallons of liquor aging in charred barrels, the largest cache discovered in the city limits until that point. He received the first sentence under the nuisance law for continually possessing and concealing liquor in Memphis. Deputies arrested him in October 1924 in a raid on Ensley Plantation, where they found a fifteen-hundred-gallon still and six nine-hundred-gallon vats of mash. Laughter tried to appeal his fine and sentence, but the state supreme court upheld the decision in January 1926. Laughter fled to New Orleans, where police arrested him in April 1927. He jumped a two-thousand-dollar bond and remained on the run until police in Little Rock, Arkansas, arrested him in June 1931. Seven years after his conviction, he finally had to serve his original sentence in the Shelby County Workhouse.[39]

Ed Laughter returned to bootlegging following his release. Deputies arrested him with Herbert Green, R. A. Flowers, and Jack Harper in the act of assembling the pumping system for a still in a barn near the Felts community just north of the city in November 1923. In May 1926, Prohibition agents raided Laughter's roadhouse near Lake View, Mississippi, and confiscated eleven hundred quarts of home brew, twenty-five gallons of whiskey, and his car. Two years later, a federal grand jury indicted Laughter again on liquor charges.[40]

Laughter again made headlines following the municipal and gubernatorial elections of August 1928. He still had connections to the police department, and though he was anti-Crump, he became involved with the election because he was a political ally of Clifford Davis. Reporters were determined to capture the machine's tactics on film, while machine enforcers were determined to keep them away. This resulted in numerous assaults, including Laughter's attack on reporter James Seat during which he stole Seat's camera.[41]

Police arrested Laughter following the explosion of a moonshine outfit in a house at 217 West McLemore during the night of June 11, 1929. The rectifier, used to artificially age liquor, exploded, blowing part of the roof off and knocking down one wall. Fire engulfed and destroyed the remainder of the house and the one next door. Police and firefighters found the remains of a thousand-gallon still and five thousand gallons of mash in the wreckage. Laughter, who ran the Stockyard Hotel only a short distance away, immediately came under suspicion after police arrested his longtime associate Eddie Campbell in connection with the still.[42]

Douglas Darnell, the property owner, told police that he rented the two houses and two others on the street to Laughter. Capt. Will Lee planned to use Darnell as the key witness in a case against Laughter. He scheduled a second meeting, but Darnell did not show up. Laughter had convinced Darnell to recant his story before he could meet again with investigators. Police dropped the case after Darnell called Lee later and claimed he had made a mistake and that he rented to someone named George Moore.[43]

Laughter continued to bootleg even as the market dried up. Prohibition agents arrested Laughter again during a flying squadron sweep of the city in May 1930, but the charge was not enough to send Laughter to prison. Laughter continued to bootleg until prosecutors convicted him, not for liquor violations but for income tax evasion, in 1944.[44]

After serving three years at the federal prison at Seagoville, Texas, the sixty-seven-year-old received parole, returned to Memphis five days later, and found the police department waiting to arrest him. Crump took a personal interest and compiled extensive files on Laughter and his family to justify exiling him. Commissioner Joe Boyle kept Laughter incarcerated until Memphis probation officer Roy Nelms asked permission of Mississippi authorities to move Laughter across state lines. Boyle declared, "We're not going to al-low Laughter or his kind to hang around Memphis. I wrote Representative [Clifford] Davis about it today. We just don't intend to allow ex-convicts to congregate here. Laughter will never operate another place here."[45]

Law enforcement resorted to exile to get rid of Laughter, while Mulcahy and Grandi only quit bootlegging because Prohibition ended. Despite the best efforts of the law enforcement, the three operated through three decades of Prohibition. No punishment doled out by the courts could deter them from selling liquor. This glaring fact represented one of the fundamental causes of the failure of Prohibition—the profits outweighed the deterrents.

20

SIN AGAINST HIGH HEAVEN

What a joke, a sorry comedy—Tennessee, the ostrich prohibition state.
—Edward Hull Crump, June 28, 1937

The Twenty-First Amendment did not abolish Prohibition but instead turned the liquor problem over to the states. Most states voted to become wet, but some like Tennessee had a strong enough dry element to keep statewide Prohibition intact. This decision meant that the war over alcohol would continue in some states long after most Americans had laid the issue to rest. Tennessee's advocates for repeal continued the campaign to overturn state liquor laws with the help of a powerful ally in Memphis. Boss Crump's Shelby County Organization continued to grow in reach and strength all the way to the state capitol and beyond. The wets knew that if they could overcome legislative hurdles and get the people of Tennessee to vote on the liquor issue, the Shelby County voting bloc could help them win and finally overturn the state Prohibition laws.

Prohibition never became part of the Tennessee constitution, so a simple act of the state legislature could have easily wiped the dry laws from the law books. Prohibitionists still had influence in Nashville, especially among the senators and governor, so Rep. Walter M. "Pete" Haynes of Winchester, Tennessee, came up with a way to convince them the majority of their constituents wanted repeal. On January 1, 1935, he introduced a bill calling for a public referendum. Tennesseans voted against Prohibition in 1877 in a direct vote, and Haynes expected them to do the same again. The vote would not change the laws, but it would allow the people to voice their opinion, and that, Haynes hoped, would be enough to force politicians into action.[1]

The bill initially failed after its introduction by Rep. Robert P. Brown on January 15, but the idea would come around again. Brown quickly changed tactics and tried to gather support for a vote on repeal or at least a law to allow each county to decide whether to allow liquor within its boundaries. Brown felt that the Tennessee House of Representatives and much of the Tennessee Senate would vote wet, but he agreed to wait to introduce legislation until after a review of Gov. Hill McAlister's new revenue program.[2]

The Social Security Act of 1935 set up a national system of state pensions for people over the age of sixty-five, widows, and the disabled. Title I of the act established programs at the state level partially financed by federal contributions. The federal government meant the offer as an inducement for states to disburse pensions to the elderly on a matching basis; however, some states, like Tennessee, did not have old-age pension programs. To make matters worse, cash-strapped Tennesseans did not have a means at hand to raise the initial revenue to get the program started. McAlister knew his constituents would resent higher taxes, but with no other option, he drew up a bill for a 3 percent sales tax and a tax of one-fourth of one cent on wholesales. Crump and other urban leaders argued against the wholesale tax because most of the burden would fall on the cities and possibly drive away businesses.[3]

Wets immediately seized the opportunity to offer an alternative. For years, they had suggested that liquor sales would raise revenue for the state, only to have drys scoff at the idea. Wets argued that since law enforcement could not control the flood of untaxed contraband liquor, the state should legalize it and tax it to fund the pension program. Charles Bryan and Nashville attorney W. E. Norvell Jr. prepared a bill on behalf of the Shelby County delegation calling for the legalization of liquor sales with an accompanying tax scheme designed to generate a potential $2 million a year. The bill included a provision to accommodate drys by allowing voters the option to keep Prohibition in their counties. House Speaker Pete Haynes introduced the local option bill to an enthusiastic and noisy general assembly on February 13, 1935. Thirty representatives signed the alternative to the unpopular tax bill. The dry McAlister, however, believed he had enough support in the senate to push his tax bill through, so loyal legislators delayed Haynes's legislation.[4]

Drys attacked the legislation not only with their usual rhetoric but also with a new emphasis on drunk driving. Methodists at a conference in Jackson, Tennessee, cited liquor as the leading source of auto accidents in 1934 and maintained that its legalization had increased lawlessness. Bishop Urban Valentine Williams Darlington, head of Illinois, Kentucky, and Tennessee conferences, said, "Revenue at the price of human life to justify liquor legislation is a dear price to pay for life and character." Darlington called legalizing alcohol for revenue "a sin against high Heaven." Rev. J. Carl McCoy, of the Prescott Memorial Baptist Church in Memphis, said that regulation of drinking was impossible and that anyone who sold alcohol was as guilty of drunk driving as the drunk driver. Bishop Edwin H. Hughes of Washington declared, "Already enough blood has been shed from people hit by drunken or tipsy drivers of cars to bespatter into crimson the legislators who voted this legalized woe upon our lives."[5]

Drys in Memphis also took aim at women. Conference delegates at the St. Paul Methodist Church told women to "set the example of Christians and quit giving and attending cocktail parties." Dr. R. J. Bateman of the First Baptist Church said that women who drank or smoke were unfit for motherhood. He said crippled children were the result of "broken laws, indulgences, and willful acts" by mothers who "broke a plan with God."[6]

Prohibition supporters warned of the effects alcohol consumption would have on Americans. Rev. Peter Lunati, the inventor of the rotary lift, a hydraulic lift for automobiles, discussed the effects of alcohol on coming generations at the Strand Bible Class Theatre in Memphis. Lunati said, "Americans are drinking six million gallons of whiskey a week. How long can we expect to maintain our position as the greatest country on Earth at this rate?" Dr. L. R. Graham of Pentecostal Holiness Church in Memphis said, "Lawlessness will increase with the spread of drinking resulting from legalization of liquor. When the country has had its drinking spree, prohibition will return."[7]

Senator Blan R. Maxwell of the Shelby County delegation further annoyed drys when he sponsored a bill in the senate to raise state alcohol levels to 5 percent in April 1935. Senators, under pressure from dry constituents, rejected the bill. Maxwell argued that Tennessee brewers had a difficult time competing with out-of-state brewers who had increased their alcohol content from 3.2 percent to 5 percent following national repeal. Senators relented and passed the bill after Maxwell convinced them the state was losing revenue because of the loss in beer sales.[8]

Wets introduced another local option bill to finance the pension program in July 1935. It called for strict licensing, sales only by state residents, no sales to minors, no sales by foreigners or criminals, and no liquor sales at nightclubs and roadhouses "frequented by persons of both sexes under circumstances likely to promote immorality." Representatives introduced the bill along with an ill-fated second bill allowing the legalization of racing and pari-mutuel betting, a system in which the gambling house places all bets together in a pool and calculates payoff odds by sharing the pool among all winning bets. The state house defeated the liquor bill by forty-nine to forty-one, even after a rare appearance by Crump stalwart Frank Rice on the assembly floor. Instead, the house approved a bill that called for taking money from the general fund to pay for the state pension. The senate, under control of McAlister, refused to hear the bill, claiming that it would wreck the state budget.[9]

At the end of the day, legislators had done nothing to solve the pension problem. An editorial writer commented, "Tennessee has just as much liquor as Arkansas or Kentucky. The only difference is that it is sold by bootleggers and the state doesn't get any revenue from it." The writer pointed out that Tennesseans could no longer call the state dry when it was obviously "dripping wet." Arkansas legislators, facing the same problem, had voted for the local option in March 1935. A rush of customers, many from Memphis, depleted liquor stocks in West Memphis within days. Those who bought liquor returned to the city unmolested by police, while thousands of dollars of potential Tennessee revenue went to Arkansas.[10]

Wets, led by Haynes and Brown, argued that the majority of Tennesseans wanted to repeal and should have the opportunity to voice their opinion. In the event Tennesseans voted wet, they planned to request the governor call an extra session of the legislature to overturn the state dry laws and set up an old-age pension funded by tax from liquor sales. The house adopted the resolution forty-seven to thirty-four. Senators argued that the results of the proposed referendum would not be legally binding and therefore a waste of time and money, but they expected the bill to pass anyway.[11]

On August 3, with victory in sight, senate wets suddenly postponed the vote. Haynes announced his intention to run for governor and proposed to save the issue for the gubernatorial race in 1936. He hoped for the support of the powerful Shelby County delegation by campaigning on the platform of repeal and creation of a pension. The situation was chaotic. The house and senate barely had enough members for quorums because of the absence of so many lawmakers. Those who showed up were of little use. Nearly a dozen lawmakers in attendance were drunk, including one legislator who was escorted out by security.[12]

Gordon Browning won the 1936 gubernatorial race and inherited the pension problem. He knew liquor sales gave the state a way to raise the money without increasing taxes, but as a dry, he politically could not support legalizing liquor. He needed a way out, so he announced he would only support local option if a referendum showed that the majority of Tennesseans favored it.[13]

·

Fig. 20.1. Gordon Browning. Courtesy of the Library of Congress.

The wets, however, could not pull together a viable bill. Haynes and Senate Speaker Byron Pope worked on a plan supported by the Shelby County delegation that would have voters vote to retain Prohibition in their county rather than vote to abolish Prohibition for the state. Haynes once again derailed the effort when he tried to push legislation to allow hotels and clubs to sell liquor by the drink. Crump tried to salvage the effort by drafting an alternative local option bill. He had Watkins Overton deliver it, but drys voted to table it and later defeated it.[14]

A bill calling for a referendum finally passed the state house and senate in May 1937 despite the stalling tactics of Rep. Andrew Tanner, leader Allied Forces for Prohibition in Tennessee. Drys changed the referendum date from July 1 to August 12, and then a conference committee moved the vote to September 23. They also changed the wording of the ballot from the very simple "wet" or "dry" to the somewhat ambiguous "for repeal" or "against repeal."[15]

In another surprise move, wets, having passed the referendum, made a complete turnaround and began to oppose the measure they had fought so hard to pass. Crump withdrew his support for the referendum because he believed it would not bind legislators to overturn Prohibition even if the voters wanted to do away with the law. He feared that dry legislators would vote against repeal even though the majority of Tennesseans voted wet. Crump, still angry at the rejection of his local option bill, turned his back in disgust and left for his favorite health resort in Battle Creek, Michigan.[16]

The wets had reason to worry. The *Press-Scimitar* asked the 130 members of the legislature if they would abide by the results of the referendum. Twelve of the only fourteen legislators who responded said that they would vote for some kind of bill legalizing liquor if the referendum brought about a vote. Representative Lon Austin of Lexington, Tennessee, found most legislators would "abide by the will of their constituencies and not by a majority of the voters of the state should the wets win." To make matters worse, many in the legislature would not oppose Browning out of fear of losing patronage jobs.[17]

Tennessee ASL president and Methodist bishop H. M. DuBose saw the reversal as a political opportunity. He wanted the wets to appear as if they did not want Tennesseans to have the opportunity to voice their opinion on the liquor issue, and he pressured Tanner to withdraw the case to stop the referendum. Tanner initially promised to contest the act for a referendum in the courts after Tennessee attorney general Roy Beeler declared it "valid and constitutional." Drys changed tactics and began to urge their supporters to participate in the referendum. Allied Forces for Prohibition chairman Dr. John F. Baggett said the repealists forced the issue, so the Prohibitionists would go to the polls and "give them a spanking."[18]

Professor James A. Tate, president of the Allied Forces for Prohibition, announced at a meeting in Memphis that the organization would make a written request to have officers, judges, clerks, and watchers at the polls. Dry leaders in Shelby County claimed to have recruited over a thousand volunteers to work in the polls by late August. DuBose said, "If Shelby stays out, however, we will win by a majority of twenty-five thousand to forty thousand at least from the rest of the state."[19]

Browning's vagueness about his intentions only fueled wets' suspicions about the referendum to determine the opinion of Tennesseans on the issue of Prohibition. He could only say that if liquor sales became legal, he would prefer package sales over saloons. A committee of lawyers met in Chattanooga and argued that Browning had made the referendum meaningless by refusing to tell the state what sort of liquor control he would propose if the state voted wet. Nashville attorney Jay G. Stephenson called it a "waste of money" and presented the suit to stop the referendum, but Chancellor

R. B. C. Howell, a state-appointed judge of a chancery court, ruled the referendum constitutional. Abe Waldauer, president of the state election commission, had no other choice but to proceed with the referendum.[20]

Wet leaders turned their backs on the referendum. Justice W. L. Cook of the Tennessee Supreme Court, who refused to enjoin the referendum after another attempt to stop the vote, even said it could not have any political effect and called the election "no more than a political gesture." C. H. Witt, head of Memphis dry forces, believed the impending victory would settle the liquor question for years to come. The referendum produced the predictable dry victory on September 23, 1937, but it did not end the liquor question.[21]

The outcome of the referendum did nothing to slow down the momentum of repeal. In November, eleven state senators walked out of the general assembly in protest of a house-approved measure to make possession of a federal liquor license prima facie evidence of a violation of the liquor laws. Dissenting lawmakers prevented the passage of the bill by refusing to vote. The deserting senators barely escaped the sergeants at arms as they fled the building. The dry cause took another blow when Lem Motlow resumed production of Jack Daniel's Whiskey in Moore County after the state supreme court upheld a new law that allowed counties to manufacture whiskey for sale outside the state.[22]

Prentice Cooper defeated Gordon Browning in 1938 and became the third governor to face the pension crisis. Crump fell out with Browning over state appointments and launched a vindictive and devastating campaign against him that propelled Cooper into office; however, the dry Cooper would not openly support repeal. Tax commissioner Walter Stokes Jr. warned the new governor that the state must raise new revenue or delay pensions. Stokes suggested taxing liquor, but Cooper, like Browning before him, said the only way he would support a change in the liquor law was through a referendum.[23]

Representative Lon Austin introduced a new local option bill that would allow voters to decide the fate of Prohibition in their counties. He ignored Cooper's request for a referendum and suggestions to create a state-controlled monopoly of the wholesale liquor trade. The new bill worked differently from earlier bills by stating that if the state as a whole voted wet, then counties voting wet would stay wet and local control machinery would be set up under provisions of the bill. Cooper promised to veto any bill that did not include a referendum, so wets compromised and included a referendum in the revised Austin-Doak liquor bill. Attorney General Beeler, however, determined the referendum would be unconstitutional, so Austin removed it from the bill.[24]

The Austin-Doak bill went up for vote on March 1 and passed the house by fifty-two to forty-two votes. Legislators missed the morning vote in the senate but made the afternoon vote, where the bill narrowly passed by seventeen to sixteen. They rushed the bill to Cooper, who vetoed it as expected, and returned it to the house, where lawmakers overturned the veto by fifty-five to thirty-eight. The wets had finally cleared the legislative hurdle to allow the counties control of liquor regulation.[25]

State tax commissioner Estes Kefauver had his department order three million stamps in the shape of the state and announced he would confiscate any unstamped liquor, as well as any car used to transport it. The S. C. Toof Printing Company in Memphis won the contract for printing the stamps after Governor Cooper canceled the original contract with Consolidated Decal-comania Corporation of New York. Toof printers included serial numbers on the stamps to prevent counterfeiting.[26]

The law required that each county first complete a petition with signatures from at least ten percent of the population, followed by a vote within forty-five days. The Shelby County Organization began an intensive drive to get voters to pay poll taxes in anticipation of the petition. Commissioner Clifford Davis promised, "We are going to get rid of bootleggers if Memphis goes wet."[27]

Would-be liquor sellers, sensing a wet victory, began preparations to open their businesses. They rushed to real estate offices to secure locations for their stores and quickly drew up business charters. The first charter went to Gayoso Liquor Stores at 139 South Main Street, and Roy W. Hartwell, a former Dodge distributor, became the city's first liquor, wine, and champagne distributor.[28]

The Shelby County Organization worried that voter apathy would keep the county from going wet. Election officials predicted a turnout of only twenty-five to thirty thousand voters because most Memphians believed the wets would easily win. Organization members began an intensive drive to sell poll-taxes once the Shelby County Election Commission received the completed petition on April 11. Ward and precinct leaders held rallies and telephoned people to urge them to vote.[29]

Once again, the machine delivered the vote. On May 26, 1939, the people of Shelby County voted 22,249 to 974 for repeal, and Memphians voted 17,988 to 754 for repeal. The results caused a flurry of activity as would-be liquor sellers began the process to open their businesses. Shelby County assistant attorney general Will Gerber drew up a draft of city regulations, and the beer board expanded and became the Liquor Licensing Board. The state and county set taxes at $1,500 a year for wholesalers and $750 a year for retailers. Applicants filled out paperwork for licenses at the Shelby County Department of Finance and Taxation in the Sterick Building. Noted business leaders quickly jumped on the bandwagon. Barney Plough sold the White Way Pharmacy to Herman Lubin of Iowa and formed Consolidated Distributors, a wholesale liquor store, with Sam Plough, Leo Wurtzburger, and Milton M. Shurman. Two days later, Harry Kabakoff, John Shea, and Harry C. Pierotti incorporated Dixie Distilled Products, the first whiskey blending plant in Memphis. The wets had won the war, but the dry resistance was not ready to give up.[30]

CONCLUSION

I came home with a brand-new plan
I take the seed from Columbia and Mexico
I just plant it up the holler down Copperhead Road
—Steve Earle, "Copperhead Road"

A l Capone's men had driven all night to get to Memphis. The Chicago mob boss wanted to expand his operation, so he sent his men to muscle in on bootlegging in the Bluff City. As they crossed the Harahan Bridge over the Mississippi River, they saw a figure in the beams of the car's headlights. The driver slowed and stopped the car in front of the man blocking its path. The gangsters stepped out of the car to order the man to move out of their way. As they began to speak, the stranger cut them off. He told them in no uncertain terms that they were not welcome in his city and ordered them to turn back. The gunmen, amused by his audacity, asked the man his name. He told them he was Edward Hull Crump and it was time for them to leave. The gunmen, so confident moments before, now had second thoughts. After they considered the thinly veiled threat, they quietly stepped into the car, backed it up, and drove back to Chicago. They knew not to cross paths with Boss Crump.

This is a wonderful story, but it never happened; it is one of many urban myths passed around by Memphians. Nonetheless, stories like this often have a kernel of truth, and this one is no exception. Capone had an interest in new sources of liquor and sent men to Memphis to make overtures to local bootleggers in early 1928. Alphonse Capone's brothers Ralph and Albert and another gangster first went to New Orleans to make contacts with the underworld, but police forced them to leave on January 31. They boarded the train for Memphis and arrived to find a contingent of police waiting for

them at the station. The officers held the trio briefly before ordering them
to leave town.[1]

A month later, police arrested John Capone, another Capone brother, and
mob lieutenant Louis Rago at Linden Avenue and South Main. The two had
only just arrived when officers intercepted their car. They released Rago that
night and Capone the following morning with an order to leave town. Police
made it abundantly clear to the Capones and anyone else who happened to
come through the city that Memphis was off-limits to mobsters.[2]

Even so, one should not conclude that the treatment of Capone's men had
anything to do with protecting local bootleggers. Many historians assumed
Crump's political machine offered protection to gambling dens, houses of
prostitution, and bootleggers in the 1920s and 1930s in exchange for money.
The Shelby County Organization certainly took contributions from business
owners and municipal employees who owed their jobs to the machine, but
its reliance on money from the underworld is questionable. The 1928 election
and the Rum War exposed the existence of a small number of bootleggers
who operated with the consent of bribed deputies, but any money collected
from them was hardly enough to finance the organization.

No one can say to what degree the Shelby County Organization accepted
money from criminals; however, it is safe to say that Crump's reputation for
collusion with bootleggers was overstated. Crump's men did not, and could
not, corral every bootlegger and force him to pay tribute to the organization.
Furthermore, Crump could hardly collect sufficient money from bootleggers
when the sheriff's department, led by Crump supporters, ran the biggest
moneymakers out of the county after 1928.

The Shelby County Organization aided very few people involved with liquor. It occasionally helped old allies like Jim Mulcahy; however, the machine
had little protection to offer since it had hardly any influence on the federally controlled Prohibition Bureau. Mulcahy avoided punishment in local
courts, but the machine could do nothing to prevent him from serving time
in federal prison. In addition, the machine offered no help to Mulcahy when
he faced legal action because of unpaid city taxes shortly before his death.

Crump opposed Prohibition because he thought it a bad idea, not out of
loyalty to gangsters. He was a "teetotaler" who opposed the return of saloons
and cared little for so-called liquor interests like Jim Kinnane and Mike Haggerty. Ed Laughter had ties to members of the Shelby County Organization,
but he and Crump were certainly not friendly. In fact, the two despised each
other. Crump personally collected information to justify ordering the police
department to run Laughter out of town.

Fig. 21.1. Edward Hull Crump. Courtesy of Memphis Room, Memphis
Public Library and Information Center.

Crump became wealthy and powerful without the help of bootleggers.
In the years before his terms in Congress, Crump made money not through
liquor and gangsters, but rather soft drinks and insurance. He invested in
the Coca-Cola Company and started a real estate insurance company with
former chief US marshal Stanley Trezevant. Crump, despite his well-earned
reputation for despotism and vindictiveness, built political support by court-
ing suburban neighborhood organizations and focusing on improving an
image of the city soiled by bootlegging and other criminal activities. He built
relations with business elites and business-oriented progressives concerned
with upgrading the city's infrastructure with the goal of making Memphis
the most important commercial center in the South.

Crump helped lead the charge for repeal, but he was not responsible for
the failure of Prohibition in Memphis. Prohibition failed because of the lack

of public support and the ineffectiveness of law enforcement. Prohibition had a die-hard group of supporters in Memphis, but that group, no matter how vocal, never represented the majority of the population.

Many in law enforcement questioned the wisdom of Prohibition as well. Police commissioner Thomas Allen in 1923 pointed out, "It is hard to get the policemen to see the hard law on the subject when it is a conspicuous fact that the people are not in sympathy with the law." Nothing changed over the next decade. In 1935, county sheriff William Bacon conceded, "You can't legislate morals into people and prohibition won't keep them from drinking."[3]

The hypocrisy of Prohibition further eroded support for the law. The public became increasingly aware that the brunt of enforcement fell on African Americans, immigrants, the working class, and the poor, while the wealthiest used their influence to skirt the law. Police officers and sheriff's deputies made routine raids of gambling houses and small-time bootleggers and charged them with the slightest of offenses. As a result, cases dealing with petty infractions of low-income Memphians overloaded the courts and exposed African Americans to habitual abuse and humiliation at the hands of law enforcement.

The temperance societies directed much of their efforts against saloons and groceries run by the Irish, Italians, Germans, and Eastern Europeans. They not only wanted to purge Memphis of their alcohol but also wanted to disenfranchise these immigrants by destroying their political and social networks. Law enforcement specifically targeted Italians and even threatened them with deportation. Their stubborn refusal to abide by Prohibition was as much out of economic necessity as it was their refusal to conform to Anglo-Saxon mores.

The working class and poor, regardless of race or ethnicity, made up the majority of those arrested on liquor charges. Police, deputies, and Prohibition agents regularly raided their homes and gathering places, sometimes without provocation or legal authority. Working-class and poor people suffered more than wealthier Memphians because they did not have equal access to legal representation and faced economically crippling fines and jail sentences. In addition, the type of alcohol available to them exposed them to injury and sometimes death.

The wealthy, on the other hand, used their political influence and social connections with the Shelby County Organization to avoid punishment. They bought better alcohol through legal loopholes or from discreet liquor rings that catered to high-society customers. Cases involving the "Booze-Who List," Billy Overton, and L. P. Janes brought to light the blatant favoritism shown by the courts. Even within a community defined by racial and class boundaries, these cases made Memphians question the legitimacy of a law so heavily weighted towards those of privilege.

Repeal sentiment grew as Memphians became increasingly disillusioned with Prohibition and those who advocated it. The Ku Klux Klan embraced Prohibition as a means to make political gains and recruit law enforcement to help them intimidate African Americans and Catholics. The Klan's excesses in the mid-1920s turned public opinion against them as well as Prohibition. The old tired arguments of the ASL and the WCTU lost their appeal on Memphians exhausted by the increased crime, corruption, and hypocrisy that resulted from Prohibition. The younger generation rebelled against the conservatism of rural Protestantism by flouting the liquor laws and some-times delving into worse crimes.

Prohibition was one of the most important issues in politics and society in Memphis in the early twentieth century and a problem too big for any law enforcement agency or political machine to handle. It led to increased crime, corruption, health problems, and disrespect for all laws for three decades. Frustration over the liquor laws resulted in a repeal movement led by Memphians that overturned statewide Prohibition and helped overturn the Eighteenth Amendment.

Legal liquor returned to Memphis, but in a much different way than in the days before 1909. Mayor Watkins Overton wanted to follow the New York model and allow sales by specialized retailers and liquor by the drink sold only in places that served food. Crump, of course, had the final say. Contrary to what his critics said about his desire to bring back the saloons, Crump only wanted to see the return of package sales for off-premises consumption, and he got his way for decades.[4]

The city government restricted sales only to liquor stores and placed a limit on the number of liquor permits issued. The law excluded owners of restaurants and roadhouses, so their employees would sometimes offer to make purchases at nearby liquor stores for their patrons. Later, some res-taurants turned into clubs where, for a small fee, patrons could keep a bottle with their name on it and purchase drinks from the bar.[5]

Moonshining picked up again in the 1940s because of high taxes on legal liquor. Some drinkers preferred to buy a half-pint of corn liquor for twenty-five cents than spend sixty cents for the same amount from a liquor store. Tensions rose as police chief Carroll Seabrook directed police once again to seek out bootleggers hiding in woods and along railroad tracks, while federal "revenooers" used telescopes and movie cameras to gather evidence

Fig. 21.2. Deputies with captured moonshiners, circa 1960. Courtesy of Shelby County Archives.

for cases against moonshiners. In April 1952, game warden Carl Plant told reporters the greatest hazard in performing his duties was stumbling across trigger-happy moonshiners who mistook him for a federal agent.[6]

The Shelby County Sheriff's Department set up a display at the annual Mid-South Fair in 1965 to educate the public about the dangers of drinking moonshine. The deputy on duty had stills seized in recent raids on display under a sign reading "Don't Drink Moonshine." A woman from the nearby WCTU booth chastised the deputy for his display. The confused deputy tried to assure her of his good intentions, "There's really no problem. We're working for the same thing." She called the display ridiculous and said the sign should read "Don't Drink Any Whiskey." She complained about the sheriff's department display, "I still say they're just showing people how to make moonshine." The deputy, taken aback, thought about it for a moment and admitted that he was getting questions from fair visitors about the moonshine process.[7]

One of the last vestiges of statewide Prohibition came under attack in the late 1960s. On May 3, 1967, the Tennessee Senate approved a bill to allow the citizens of Memphis, Nashville, Knoxville, and Chattanooga to vote to bring back Prohibition, retain the current liquor laws, or include a provision permitting the sale of liquor by the drink. The chamber of commerce

Fig. 21.3. Deputies examine a moonshine outfit, circa 1960. Courtesy of Shelby County Archives.

campaigned for the provision while church forces claimed it would result in in open bars, traffic deaths, broken families, and higher taxes. Dry forces rallied and defeated the liquor-by-the-drink measure 61,827 to 52,240 in August. Shelby County attorney Phil Canale Jr. consoled disappointed nightclub and restaurant customers by reminding them that they could still "brown bag it," that is, they could bring liquor purchased elsewhere into establishments.[8]

It was not until 1968 that city legislators gave in to demands from restaurant and hotel owners to allow liquor by the drink. The issue came to a vote again in a special referendum and passed on November 25, 1969. Sixty years after the enactment of state dry laws, Memphians could finally go into a bar and order a drink again.[9]

Fig. 21.4. Vat of fermenting mash found during raid by deputies, circa 1960. Courtesy of Shelby County Archives.

Moonshining all but disappeared by the mid-1970s. Federal agents had seized over a thousand stills per year between 1960 and 1968 in Tennessee, but in 1976, they only broke up eight. The soaring price of sugar and a decrease in demand for moonshine had brought about its end. Bootleggers, however, saw opportunity in another market.[10]

Marijuana came to the Mid-South in the 1930s, and its popularity grew in the 1960s. Farmers who once made moonshine easily adapted to growing marijuana. Agents from the Alcohol, Tobacco, and Firearms Division of the IRS, the agency that had evolved from the Prohibition Bureau, began arresting an increasing number of ex-bootleggers in Tennessee for growing and transporting marijuana in the 1960s and 1970s. In April 1977, agents arrested a one-time whiskey-runner after he landed a plane at Memphis International Airport loaded with marijuana from Mexico. "There are a lot of examples, I can assure you, that ex-bootleggers are getting into narcotics," said agent Riley Oxley. "It's a big thing today, you understand, and the illegal liquor business is a declining occupation. Moonshiners and marijuana people want to make some easy money, a fast, easy buck. So, as the moonshine business disappears, they've got to come up with another gimmick."[11]

Lawmakers once again had to come to terms with an unpopular and unenforceable law. The so-called War on Drugs, like Prohibition, left the country with more problems than the one it meant to solve, including billions of dollars wasted, bloodshed on the streets of our cities, and millions of lives ruined by draconian punishment. In 2016, with no chance of success, the Drug Enforcement Administration conceded that drugs continue to become cheaper and more easily available.[12]

Public pressure on legislators in Colorado and Washington led to the legalization and regulation of marijuana in 2012. They hoped that a legal alternative to illicit drugs would curb the narcotics black market. In Tennessee, the Memphis and Nashville city councils passed ordinances to allow police discretion to hand out lighter civil citations for possession of small amounts of marijuana in 2016. Conservative lawmakers promised to fight the measures. In March 2017, the Tennessee House of Representatives approved a bill to nullify the partial marijuana decriminalization laws, and Gov. Bill Haslam signed it into law a month later.[13]

Americans are slow to learn from their mistakes. The United States Constitution exists to guarantee personal liberty, not to limit it. Nevertheless, the forces behind the Eighteenth Amendment did just that. They created the only amendment that contradicted the intent of the Constitution. The purpose of the Prohibition movement on the surface was reform, but the crusaders' underlying mission was to force their values on the rest of America. The fallout from their "noble experiment" resulted in years of social and legal disarray. As modern legislators wrestle with issues that infringe on personal liberty, they should take a careful look at their motives and remember an important lesson from the past—you can't legislate morality.

NOTES

INTRODUCTION

1. Iain Gately, *Drink: A Cultural History of Alcohol* (New York: Penguin, 2008), 375.

2. Sharon D. Wright, *Race, Power, and Political Emergence in Memphis* (New York: Garland Publishing, 2000), 30.

3. Roger Biles, *Memphis in the Great Depression* (Knoxville: University of Tennessee Press, 1986), 33.

4. Honey, Michael K. *Going Down Jericho Road: The Memphis Strike, Martin Luther King's Last Campaign* (New York: W. W. Norton and Company, 2007), 10.

5. Britton Haden and Henry Robinson Luce, "Tennessee: City and Country Crowd," *Time* 28, August 17, 1936, 14.

6. David M. Tucker, *Lieutenant Lee of Beale Street* (Nashville: Vanderbilt University Press, 1971), 98.

7. William S. Worley and Ernest Withers, *Beale Street: Crossroads of America's Music* (Lenexa: Addax Publishing, 1997), 21.

CHAPTER 1. RISE OF THE WHITE RIBBONS

1. Paul Coppock, *Memphis Memoirs* (Memphis: Memphis State University Press, 1980), 50. The *Columbia Herald* began in the 1850s in Columbia, Tennessee. The *Nashville American* began publication in 1851 in Nashville, Tennessee, and lasted until 1911. The *Memphis Daily Commercial* was a short-lived newspaper in Memphis, Tennessee, that ran from 1881 until 1891. Library of Congress, "Chronicling America: Historic American Newspapers," Library of Congress, last modified 2017, https://chroniclingamerica.loc.gov/.

2. "Defendant Sharp was Acquitted but Jury Cannot Agree upon Cooper Cases," *Eugene (OR) Daily Guard*, March 19, 1909.

3. "Tennesseans in Frenzy Over Bloody Crime," *Pittsburgh (PA) Press*, November 10, 1908.

4. "Carmack, Former Senator Slain," *Spokesman Review* (Spokane, WA), November 10, 1908; "Ex-Senator Carmack Killed," *Meridian (CT) Morning Record*, November 10, 1908.

5. "Murder of Mr. Carmack," *Gazette* (Montreal, Canada), November 12, 1908.

6. "Defendant Sharp was Acquitted but Jury Cannot Agree upon Cooper Cases," *Eugene (OR) Daily Guard*, March 19, 1909; "Pardons Cooper," *Daily Star* (Fredericksburg, VA), April 14, 1910; "Acquitted of Carmack Murder," *Evening Independent* (St. Petersburg, FL), November 15, 1910.

7. Coppock, *Memphis Memoirs*, 54.

8. Charles D. Johns, *Tennessee's Pond of Liquor and Pool of Blood: A Complete and Detailed Account of Our Shameless Condition in Tennessee* (Nashville: C. D. Johns, 1912), 134–35.

9. Ken Burns, "Roots of Prohibition," *Prohibition* (PBS: 2011), http://www.pbs.org/kenburns/Prohibition/roots-of-Prohibition/.

10. Mattie Duncan Beard, *The WCTU in the Volunteer State* (Kingsport: Kingsport Press, 1962), 1.

11. *Public Opinion* 20, April 1896, 559.

12. Burns, "Roots of Prohibition."

13. Paul E. Isaac, *Prohibition and Politics: Turbulent Decades in Tennessee, 1885–1920* (Knoxville: University of Tennessee Press, 1965), 1–12.

14. Helen M. Coppock and Charles W. Crawford, eds., *Paul R. Coppock's Midsouth* (Memphis: West Tennessee Historical Society, 1985), 75–80.

15. Preston Lauterbach, *Beale Street Dynasty: Sex, Song, and the Struggle for the Soul of Memphis* (New York: W. W. Norton, 2015).

16. Joe L. Coker, *Liquor in the Land of the Lost Cause: Southern White Evangelicals and the Prohibition Movement* (Lexington: University Press of Kentucky, 2007), 13.

17. Beard, *WCTU*, 5, 18, 31, 117.

18. Beard, 36–37.

19. *Toronto Daily Mail*, April 16, 1887; Miller, *Memphis during the Progressive Era, 1900–1917* (Memphis: Memphis State University Press, 1957), 123.

20. Miller, *Memphis during the Progressive Era*, 123; "The Future of Whiskey," *Boston Evening Transcript*, November 12, 1902.

21. Norman Farrell and J.S. Laurent, *An Annotated Index to the Public and General Statutes of Tennessee from 1897 to 1911 Inclusive* (Nashville: Marshall and Bruce Co. Law Publishers, 1912), 50–51.

22. Isaac, *Prohibition and Politics*, 116–17.

23. Miller, *Memphis during the Progressive Era*, 124.

24. Miller, 124.

25. Isaac, *Prohibition and Politics*, 147–49.

26. Coker, *Liquor in the Land*, 209.

27. Isaac, *Prohibition and Politics*, 136–37.

28. "Twice Told Tales," *NS*, January 8, 1919; "More Sentiment for Prohibition," *Turtle Mountain Star* (Rolla, ND), September 30, 1909; Miller, *Memphis during the Progressive Era*, 125.

29. Farrell and Laurent, *Statutes of Tennessee*, 50–51.

30. "Prohibition in Tennessee to Become Law Tomorrow," *Evening News* (San Jose, CA), June 30, 1909.

31. Coppock, *Memphis Memoirs*, 54.

CHAPTER 2. FALL OF THE SALOONS

1. "Statewide Prohibition Law is Now in Effect," *Freelance* (Fredericksburg, VA), July 3, 1909; William D. Miller, *Memphis during the Progressive Era, 1900–1917*, 126; Silas Bent, "Prohibition in the City of Memphis," *Mixer and Server: Official Journal of the Hotel and Restaurant Employees' International Alliance and Bartenders' Alliance League of America* 19 (January 15, 1910).

2. "Dry City Moist," *Toledo Blade* (Toledo, OH), July 8, 1909; John Preston Young, *Standard History of Memphis, Tennessee: A Study of the Original Sources* (Knoxville: H. W. Crew, 1912), 282; Bent, "Prohibition in the City."

3. Young, *Standard History of Memphis*, 282; Bent, "Prohibition in the City."

4. Bent, "Prohibition in the City."

5. Bent.

6. Bent.

7. Bent.

8. Bent.

9. Bent.

10. Bent.

11. Bent.

12. Bent.

13. Bent.

14. Bent.

15. Paul E. Isaac, *Prohibition and Politics: Turbulent Decades in Tennessee, 1885–1920* (Knoxville: University of Tennessee Press, 1965), 206–19.

16. Isaac, 200; William D. Miller, *Mr. Crump of Memphis* (Baton Rouge: Louisiana State University Press, 1964), 110.

17. "Speaker Stanton Says Paid Thugs Threatened Life," *Carroll Herald* (Carroll, IA), October 1, 1913.

18. "Memphis Went Dry Yesterday," *Evening Independent* (St. Petersburg, FL), October 25, 1910; "Eight Hundred Saloons Close Doors for Keeps," *Evening Independent* (St. Petersburg, FL), February 28, 1914.

19. "Memphis Goes Dry at Last; Enforce Law," *Miami (FL) News*, March 5, 1914.

20. "Liquor's Tribute to Crime," *Times Daily* (Florence, AL), August 28, 1914.

21. Ibid.

22. "Nail Up Bars in Memphis," *Kentucky New Era* (Hopkinsville, KY), October 1, 1914.

23. Miller, *Memphis during the Progressive Era*, 89; "Fraud in Memphis," *Sunday Herald* (Baltimore, MD), August 21, 1894.

24. Raymond A. Mohl, *The Making of Urban America* (Lanham, MD: Rowman and Littlefield, 2006), 158; Howard Abadinsky, *Organized Crime* (Belmont, CA: Wadsworth, 2007), 29–30.

25. Miller, *Mr. Crump of Memphis*, 104, 118–19.

26. Paul R. Coppock, *Memphis Memoirs* (Memphis: Memphis State University Press, 1980), 242.

27. "After Two Years' Trial Prohibition Declared a Failure in Two out of Five Southern States," *Reading (PA) Eagle*, April 16, 1911.

28. "What Prohibition Amounted to in Two Large Cities," *Arizona Journal-Miner* (Prescott, AZ), July 19, 1911.

29. Miller, *Mr. Crump of Memphis*, 108; "National Leaders in Dry Campaign to Be Heard Here," *Berkeley (CA) Daily Gazette*, March 28, 1914.

30. Miller, *Mr. Crump of Memphis*, 111.

31. Miller, 111.

32. G. Wayne Dowdy, *Mayor Crump Don't Like It: Machine Politics in Memphis* (Jackson: University Press of Mississippi, 2006), 23.

33. Miller, *Mr. Crump of Memphis*, 112.

34. Dowdy, *Mayor Crump Don't Like It*, 23; Coppock, *Memphis Memoirs*, 241.

35. Miller, *Mr. Crump of Memphis*, 113, 118–19.

36. "Charles Bryan," *CA*, December 8, 1936.

CHAPTER 3. ROGUES' GALLERY

1. George M. Hammell, *The Passing of the Saloon: An Official and Authentic and Official Presentation of the Anti-Liquor Crusade in America* (Cincinnati: Tower Press, 1908), 208.

2. "Old Saloon Here Bows to Progress," *PS*, July 21, 1934; "United States Census, 1900," database with images, FamilySearch.org, accessed May 18, 2016, https://familysearch.org/ark:/61903/1:1:MSZC-1GL; Thomas O'Sullivan, Civil District 15 Memphis city Ward 21, Shelby, Tennessee, United States; citing sheet 3B, family 59, NARA microfilm publication T623 (Washington, DC: National Archives and Records Administration, n.d.), FHL microfilm 1241599.

3. William D. Miller, *Memphis during the Progressive Era, 1900–1917* (Memphis: Memphis State University Press, 1957), 89.

4. *Postal Record: A Journal for Postal Employees* 5, no. 2 (February 1892), 171; R. L. Polk, *Memphis City Directory* (Memphis: R. L. Polk and Company, 1900), 570; David Evans, *Ramblin' on My Mind: New Perspectives on the Blues* (Urbana: University of Illinois Press, 2008), 73.

5. Evans, *Ramblin' on My Mind*, 73.

6. "Jim Kinnane Escapes Pen; Fined $7,500," *CA*, February 20, 1922; "Jim Kinnane, Bootleg Boss, in Law Toils," *NS*, April 23, 1919.

7. Giles Oakley, *The Devil's Music: History of the Blues* (London: Da Capo Press, 1997), 131; William Patton, *A Guide to Historic Downtown Memphis* (Charleston: History Press, 2010), 23.

8. George W. Lee, Beale Street: Where the Blues Began (College Park: McGrath Publishing Company, 1934), 81–85; Richard M. Raichelson, Beale Street Talks: A Walking Tour of the Blues (Memphis: Richard M. Raichelson, 1999), 65–66.

9. "Jim Kinnane, Bootleg Boss, in Law Toils," NS, April 23, 1919.

10. Ibid.

11. National Provisioner Trade Magazine 31, no. 27 (December 15, 1904); Industrial Refrigeration 27, nos. 1–6 (July–December 1904); American Marine Engineer 13, no. 1 (January 1918); "Jim Kinnane is Dead after Colorful Life," CA, November 12, 1930; "Services Today for Political Chieftain," CA, November 13, 1930.

12. Miller, Memphis during the Progressive Era, 95.

13. "A Sensation at Memphis," Daily Mail and Empire (Toronto), April 10, 1899.

14. G. Wayne Dowdy, On This Day in Memphis History (Charleston: History Press, 2014), 335.

15. Miller, Memphis during the Progressive Era, 96; Dowdy, On This Day, 225.

16. Shelby County, Tennessee, death certificate no. 4132 (1929), Michael J. Haggarty, Shelby County Archives, Shelby County, Tennessee; Shelby County, Tennessee, death certificate no. 2349 (1917), Mary Degg Margerum Haggerty, Shelby County Archives, Shelby County, Tennessee; Shelby County, Tennessee, marriage certificate page 341 (October 29, 1889), Daniel Haggerty and Catherine Shanley, Shelby County Archives, Shelby County, Tennessee; Polk, Memphis City Directory (1905–6); Miller, Memphis during the Progressive Era, 95.

17. Miller, Memphis during the Progressive Era, 132; G. Wayne Dowdy, A Brief History of Memphis (Charleston: History Press, 2011), 68.

18. Dowdy, Brief History, 69–70.

19. Dowdy, 69–70.

20. Paul R. Coppock, Memphis Memoirs (Memphis: Memphis State University, 1980), 68–69.

21. Miller, Memphis during the Progressive Era, 141–42, 159.

22. Miller, 144–45; Helen Coppock and Charles W. Crawford, eds., Paul Coppock's Midsouth (Memphis: West Tennessee Historical Society, 1985), 266–67.

23. William D. Miller, Mr. Crump of Memphis (Baton Rouge: Louisiana State University Press, 1964), 121; G. Wayne Dowdy, Mayor Crump Don't Like It: Machine Politics in Memphis (Jackson: University Press of Mississippi, 2006), 27.

24. Shelby County, Tennessee, death certificate no. 3508 (December 15, 1918), John Margerum, Tennessee State Library and Archives, Nashville; "Johnny Margerum is Killed in Gunfight," CA, December 16, 1918.

25. Polk, Memphis City Directory (1919–25); Shelby County, Tennessee, death certificate 4132 (December 29, 1929), Michael J. Haggarty.

26. "Honan a Leading Figure in Many Political Fights," ES, January 11, 1915; "Slayer of Honan Released on Bond," CA, January 13, 1915.

27. Edwards, Directory of the City of Memphis (New Orleans: Southern Publishing Company, 1874); Sholes, Directory of the City of Memphis (Memphis: Boyle, Chapman and Company, 1876; Memphis: Southern Baptist Publication Society, 1877; Memphis: S. C. Toof and Company, 1878–79); "Honan a Leading Figure in Many Political Fights," ES, January 11, 1915.

28. Ibid.

29. Polk, *Memphis City Directory* (1906), p. 669; David Evans, ed., *Ramblin' On My Mind: New Perspectives on the Blues* (Urbana: University of Illinois Press, 2007), 74; Polk, *Memphis City Directory* (1914), 690.

30. "Honan's Girl Victim Laughing at Death Expects to Recover," *ES*, January 12, 1915.

31. "Honan's Funeral Marked by Huge Crowd and Big Lot of Costly Flowers," *ES*, January 13, 1915.

32. "Shooting Victim May Yet Recover," *ES*, January 14, 1915.

33. "United States Census, 1880," index and images, FamilySearch.org, accessed Sept. 18, 2014, https://familysearch.org/pal:/MM9.1.1/MDX3-GPS; Angelo Persika, New Orleans, Orleans, Louisiana, United States, citing sheet 357A, NARA microfilm publication T9; "John Persica Meets Death in Joy Ride," *CA*, November 11, 1913; Polk, *Memphis City Directory* (1890–95).

34. "John Persica Meets Death in Joy Ride," *CA*, November 11, 1913.

35. Ibid.

36. Ibid.

37. Silas Bent, "Prohibition in the City of Memphis," *Mixer and Server: Official Journal of the Hotel and Restaurant Employees' International Alliance and Bartenders' Alliance League of America* 19 (January 15, 1910).

38. "John Persica Meets Death in Joy Ride," *CA*, November 11, 1913.

39. Ibid.

40. Shelby County, Tennessee, marriage certificate page 415 (July 30, 1891), Jno. Persica and Annie Bellomona [sic]; Shelby County Archives, Shelby County, Tennessee.

41. Lee, 55, 69; "Bad Booze Quarrel May End in Death," *CA*, June 25, 1923; "Liquor Raiders Still on Alert," *PS*, September 29, 1934.

42. Shelby County, Tennessee, death certificate no. 1903 (August 23, 1916), Will A. Latura, Shelby County Archives; Memphis, Tennessee, burial permit no. 23308 (July 6, 1911), John J. Latura, Shelby County Archives; "United States Census, 1870," database with images, FamilySearch.org, accessed Oct. 17, 2014, https://familysearch.org/ark:/61903/1:1:MD8S-DQ2, John Latura in household of Monto Verde [sic], Tennessee, United States, citing p. 33, family 250, NARA microfilm publication M593 (Washington, DC: National Archives and Records Administration, n.d.), FHL microfilm 553059; Shelby County, Tennessee, marriage certificate Book 3, page 254 (January 26, 1865), Antonio Monteverde and Mary Latura, Shelby County Archives; Polk, *Memphis City Directory* (1920); Allen R. Coggins, *Tennessee Tragedies: Natural, Technological, and Societal Disasters in the Volunteer State* (Knoxville: University of Tennessee Press, 2012), 236.

43. George W. Lee, *Beale Street: Where the Blues Began* (College Park, MD: McGrath Publishing Company, 1934), 92.

44. "Latura Kills Three Men," *The Freeman* (Indianapolis), December 19, 1908.

45. Ibid.

46. Coggins, *Tennessee Tragedies*, 236.

47. "Wild Bill Latura Killed by Officer; a Jekyll and Hyde," *ES*, August 23, 1916.

48. Ibid.

49. Ibid.

CHAPTER 4. CONSPIRACY

1. "Carries Old Hatchet Flies in Liquor Raid," *Victoria Advocate* (Victoria, TX), December 21, 1918.

2. "Soldiers Must Have Continued Protection," *NS*, November 15, 1918; "Police Round Up 96 Alleged Law Violators," *NS*, November 18, 1918.

3. "Wilkes Under Arrest," *NS*, November 1, 1918; "Hold Barretto on Larceny Charges," *NS*, November 2, 1918; "Held on Liquor Charge," *NS*, November 8, 1918; "McVey Indicted on Liquor Charge," *NS*, November 8, 1918; "Jimmie Jones is in Toils of the Law," *NS*, November 14, 1918; "Liquor Squad Gets 12 Cases of Whisky," *NS*, November 25, 1918; "Two Bound Over on Liquor Charge," *NS*, November 27, 1918; "Two Fined $100 on Liquor Law Charge," *NS*, November 29, 1918; "Joe Faccaro Closes Place of Business," *NS*, December 3, 1918; "Slayer of Cap Wooten Fined on Liquor Charge," *NS*, January 24, 1919; "Ex-Policeman Guilty," *NS*, March 28, 1919; "Two Raids Productive," *NS*, January 28, 1919.

4. "Capture $12,000 Worth of Shorty Here in Ten Days," *NS*, November 19, 1918.

5. "There's Plenty of It in Memphis, but It's Under Guard," *NS*, January 8, 1919.

6. "Carranza Means Gin and Villa Means Whiskey," *The Freelance* (Fredericksburg, VA), August 22, 1916; "Decks Clear for Big Bribe Inquiry," *NS*, July 29, 1919.

7. "Liquor Prices Firm and Trading Brisk," *NS*, April 3, 1919; "Liquor So Plentiful, Prices Are Falling, *NS*, April 2, 1919.

8. "Boat's Master Will Face Liquor Charges," *NS*, February 26, 1919; "Whisky Boxes Make Trouble for Capt. Couch," *NS*, February 27, 1919; "River Whisky Trade Dealt Severe Blow," *NS*, February 26, 1919; "Laughter and Three Others Arrested in Raid on Liquor Lair," *NS*, March 24, 1919; "Boatload of Booze Caught," *NS*, March 25, 1919.

9. "Draft Calls Him Up; He Stocks Up with Liquor," *NS*, November 4, 1918; "12 Suitcases and 8 Cases of Booze Seized," *NS*, January 8, 1919; "Faces Liquor Charge," *NS*, January 15, 1919; "Big Six Has Two Serious Charges," *NS*, February 27, 1919.

10. "Hooligan Role is Claimed by Barger," *NS*, January 6, 1919; "Hooligan Plan Works; Woman Stuck," *NS*, January 7, 1919.

11. "Whisky and Bible are Found in Pastor's Grips," *NS*, February 1, 1919.

12. "Mulcahy to Face Liquor Charges," *NS*, November 20, 1918; "Mulcahy Released on Liquor Charge," *NS*, November 21, 1918; "Marshals Get Thirty Cases of Poor Liquor," *NS*, April 30, 1919; "Seven Involved in U.S. Liquor Charges," *NS*, May 1, 1919.

13. "Sheriff Perry Going After Bootleggers," *NS*, November 13, 1918.

14. "Rum Car Leaps Barrier; Escapes," *NS*, December 4, 1918; "Whisky Car Ran Right Over Police," *NS*, January 13, 1919.

15. "Mrs. Mahoney Gets Time," *NS*, January 22, 1919; "Mahoneys Bound Over on Liquor Charge," *NS*, January 31, 1919.

16. "Berryman Found Guilty by Court," *NS*, January 23, 1919.

17. "Bootlegger Gets Light Sentence," *NS*, February 1, 1919.

18. "Deeper Mystery around Shooting," *NS*, March 15, 1919; "Solve This Mystery," *NS*, March 17, 1919.

19. "Leggers Run Police Car over Bluff into Mississippi River," *NS*, May 19, 1919.

20. "Grand Jury May Uncover More Whisky Sales," *NS*, April 16, 1919; "Big Whisky Ring Steals Car Lots for Local Sale," *NS*, March 27, 1919.

21. "Bootleg Agents Openly Solicit," *NS*, March 29, 1919.

22. "Miller on Job; Police Shakeup May Be at Hand," *NS*, October 29, 1918; "Law Enforcers Quizzed by Jury," *NS*, November 22, 1918.

23. "Booze Combine is Operated on Fixed Ward Rate," *NS*, April 8, 1919.

24. "Whisky Men Get High Protection," *NS*, January 17, 1919; "Will Judge Men on Their Records," *NS*, January 1, 1919; "Grand Jury's Report Will Be Passed Up," *NS*, January 18, 1919.

25. "Law Enforcement," *NS*, January 20, 1919.

26. "Injunction Used Again on Liquor," *NS*, February 7, 1919; "Forty Citations for Contempt are Filed," *NS*, February 8, 1919.

27. "Liquor Thefts Slow Down for Weekend Sale," *NS*, March 28, 1919.

28. "Judge Weary of Minnows While Big Fish Go Free," *NS*, May 10, 1919.

29. "Tells Court $200 Will Not Buy Much Liquor in Memphis," *NS*, May 8, 1919.

30. Robilio v. United States, 3224 and 3225 (6th Cir. Mar. 5, 1919); "Prison Gates Yawn for Seven Bootleggers," *NS*, March 5, 1919; "Persica and Mayer Guests of Uncle Sam," *NS*, March 6, 1919.

31. "Biggest Booze Raid in Local History Made," *NS*, April 10, 1919.

32. Ibid.

33. "Expose of Booze Barons by Tyree Taylor Promised," *NS*, May 31, 1919; "Citizens Must Fight If They Become Active," *NS*, April 17, 1919; "Indicts Negroes Taken in Seizure of Liquor," *NS*, April 18, 1919.

34. "Jim Kinnane, Bootleg Boss, in Law Toils," *NS*, April 23, 1919.

35. "United States Census, 1900," index and images, FamilySearch.org, accessed September 3, 2014, https://familysearch.org/pal:/MM9.1.1/MSZ4-TKD, Pierce Smiddy, Civil District 15 Memphis city Ward 9, Shelby, Tennessee, United States, citing sheet 11A, family 263, NARA microfilm publication T623, FHL microfilm 1241598; "United States World War I Draft Registration Cards, 1917–1918," index and images, FamilySearch.org, accessed September 3, 2014, https://familysearch.org/pal:/MM9.1.1/KZ6F-14N, William Walsh Smiddy, 1917–1918; R. L. Polk, *Memphis City Directory* (Memphis: R. L. Polk and Company, 1909–16).

36. Paul R. Coppock, "Shootout at the Rosebud Café," *CA*, April 9, 1972; "Deputy Marshal and Bootlegger Shot to Death," *NS*, September 19, 1919.

37. Ibid.

38. "No Wholesalers Indicted by Jury," *NS*, May 16, 1919.

CHAPTER 5. TYREE TAYLOR

1. "Jim Kinnane, Bootleg Boss, in Law Toils," *NS*, April 23, 1919.

2. "Bootleggers in Memphis Create State of War," *Pittsburg (PA) Press*, March 26, 1918; "Bootleggers Have War All Their Own," *Evening News* (San Jose, CA), May 7, 1918.

3. United States Department of Justice, *Department of Justice and the Courts of the United States* (Washington: Government Printing Office, 1918), 53, 182–83.

4. "Two Bribed Taylor Federal Juries Say," *CA*, November 30, 1921.

5. "Taylor Is Held in New Orleans," *CA*, July 12, 1921.

6. "Two Bribed Taylor Federal Juries Say," *CA*, November 30, 1921; "Hottum Asks for Special Judge in Bribe Trial," *CA*, December 1, 1921; "Second Drag of Bribe Seine Catches Boyles," *CA*, January 4, 1922.

7. "Two Bribed Taylor Federal Juries Say," *CA*, November 30, 1921; "Single Juror Says Hottum Gave Bribe," *CA*, December 2, 1921.

8. Ibid.

9. "Hottum Asks for Special Judge in Bribe Trial," *CA*, December 1, 1921; "Single Juror Says Hottum Gave Bribe," *CA*, December 2, 1921.

10. "Hottum's Tip in 1919 Brought Taylor Fall," *CA*, December 2, 1921; "Sportsman Awaits Fate," *EA*, January 6, 1922.

11. Ibid.

12. Personnel file for US marshal Stanley Trezevant, National Archives and Records Administration (NARA), Washington, DC; "Hottum's Tip in 1919 Brought Taylor Fall," *CA*, December 2, 1921.

13. Penn, "Bootlegging US Marshal," *New York Times*, February 26, 1922; "Hottum's Tip in 1919 Brought Taylor Fall," *CA*, December 2, 1921.

14. Shelby County, Tennessee, marriage certificate page 149 (August 18, 1914), Willie Harris and May Gotner, Shelby County Archives, Shelby County, Tennessee; "Hottum Asks for Special Judge in Bribe Trial," *CA*, December 1, 1921; "Garbarino Comes to Back Bribery Charges," *CA*, December 6, 1921; "Brown in Contempt; Apologizes in Court," *CA*, May 25, 1922: "Tyree Taylor Gets Choice of Prisons," *CA*, June 7, 1922; "Tennessee, State Marriage Index, 1780–2002," index, FamilySearch.org, accessed August 25, 2014, https://familysearch.org/pal:/MM9.1.1/VNH5-MLH, Tyree Taylor and Myrtie Willis, December 7, 1911, citing "Tennessee State Marriages, 1780–2002," Ancestry.com, p. 520, Gibson, Tennessee, United States, State Library and Archives, Nashville; Penn, "Bootlegging US Marshal," *New York Times*, February 26, 1922; "Arkansas Marriages, 1837–1944," index, FamilySearch.org, accessed June 19, 2014, https://familysearch.org/pal:/MM9.1.1/FQB4-48W, L. T. Taylor and May Harris, May 14, 1919, citing St. Francis, Arkansas, FHL microfilm 1022684.

15. "Guilty Plea Draws Seven Years for Taylor," *CA*, July 19, 1921.

16. Personnel file for US marshal Stanley Trezevant, NARA, Washington, DC; Penn, "Bootlegging US Marshal" New York Times, February 26, 1922; "Trezevant Suspends His Chief Deputy," *CA*, May 25, 1919.

17. Personnel file for US marshal Stanley Trezevant, NARA, Washington, DC; "Taylor is Held in New Orleans," *CA*, July 12, 1921; "I Won't Squeal, Says Tyree Taylor," *CA*, July 13, 1921.

18. "Expose of Booze Barons by Tyree Taylor Promised," *NS*, May 31, 1919.

19. "Guilty Plea Draws Seven Years for Taylor," *CA*, July 19, 1921; Penn, "Bootlegging US Marshal," *New York Times*, February 26, 1922; "Taylor is Held in New Orleans," *CA*, July 12, 1921.

20. "Trezevant Suspends His Chief Deputy," *CA*, May 25, 1919; "Guilty Plea Draws Seven Years for Taylor," *CA*, July 19, 1921; Penn, "Bootlegging US Marshal" *New York Times*, February 26, 1922; "Taylor is Held in New Orleans," *CA*, July 12, 1921; "Hottum Asks for Special Judge in Bribe Trial," *CA*, December 1, 1921; "Tyree Taylor Has Disappeared," *Covington Leader* (Covington, TN), October 6, 1919.

21. "Smuggled Explosives," *Herald Democrat* (Leadville, CO), March 13, 1917; "Blackmail Rich Men by White Slave Act," *New York Times*, January 13, 1916; "Taylor is Held in New Orleans," *CA*, July 12, 1921; "Taylor Due to Arrive Here Tonight," *CA*, September 16, 1922; "U.S. Grand Jury Will View Oldfield Report," *CA*, September 20, 1921; "Federal Net Bags 3 Former Officers," *CA*, September 23, 1921.

22. Personnel file for US marshal Stanley Trezevant, NARA, Washington, DC; "Tyree Taylor Is Held in New Orleans," *CA*, July 12, 1921; "I Won't Squeal, Says Tyree Taylor," *CA*, July 13, 1921.

23. "U.S. Grand Jury Will View Oldfield Report," *CA*, September 20, 1921; "Federal Net Bags 3 Former Officers," *CA*, September 23, 1921.

24. "Taylor Is Held in New Orleans," *CA*, July 12, 1921.

25. Personnel file for US marshal Stanley Trezevant, NARA, Washington, DC.

26. Personnel file for US marshal Stanley Trezevant, NARA, Washington, DC.

27. "Guilty Plea Draws Seven Years for Taylor," *CA*, July 19, 1921.

28. Ibid.

29. "Taylor Is Held in New Orleans," *CA*, July 12, 1921; "Guilty Plea Draws Seven Years for Taylor," *CA*, July 19, 1921; "I Won't Squeal, Says Tyree Taylor," *CA*, July 13, 1921.

30. "Guilty Plea Draws Seven Years for Taylor," *CA*, July 19, 1921; "I Won't Squeal, Says Tyree Taylor," *CA*, July 13, 1921.

31. "I Won't Squeal, Says Tyree Taylor," *CA*, July 13, 1921.

32. "Taylor Pleads to Be Returned to Memphis," *CA*, July 14, 1921.

33. "I Won't Squeal, Says Tyree Taylor," *CA*, July 13, 1921; "Taylor Pleads to Be Returned to Memphis," *CA*, July 14, 1921.

34. "I Won't Squeal, Says Tyree Taylor," *CA*, July 13, 1921.

35. "Bring Tyree Taylor to Memphis Sunday," *CA*, July 16, 1921.

36. "I Won't Squeal, Says Tyree Taylor," *CA*, July 13, 1921; "Bring Tyree Taylor to Memphis Sunday," *CA*, July 16, 1921.

37. "Denies All Threats to Get Higherups," *CA*, July 18, 1921; "Guilty Plea Draws Seven Years for Taylor," *CA*, July 19, 1921.

38. Ibid.

39. Ibid.

40. "Guilty Plea Draws Seven Years for Taylor," *CA*, July 19, 1921.

41. Ibid.; "Bribe Trials Open Again in U.S. Court," *CA*, December 5, 1921; "Federal Building Steeped in Mystery," *CA*, September 18, 1921.

CHAPTER 6. BIG FISH, LITTLE FISH

1. "Ross Born in Hardin," *CA*, July 10, 1925; "Ross Had Stormy Career on Bench," *CA*, July 10, 1925; "Judge Ross Honored by Members of the Bar," *CA*, December 3, 1921.

2. "Judge Made Wrong Guess in This Case," *CA*, February 13, 1925; "Murphy Is Convicted," *CA*, May 24, 1922; "Seized Evidence Is Valid, Ross Holds," *CA*, January 7, 1925.

3. "Judge Ross Honored by Members of the Bar," *CA*, December 3, 1921; "All Criminal Cases Set for Trial Today," *CA*, May 24, 1922; "Judge Ross Praised," *CA*, December 15, 1923.

4. "Tyree Taylor to Arrive Here Tonight," *CA*, September 16, 1922; "U.S. Paid $1,000 to Mrs. Tyree Taylor," *CA*, July 9, 1922.

5. "Federal Building Steeped in Mystery," *CA*, September 18, 1921.

6. "U.S. Grand Jury Will View Oldfield Report," *CA*, September 20, 1921.

7. "Guilty Plea Draws Seven Years for Taylor," *CA*, July 19, 1921.

8. "Five Arrests Follow Booze Probe," *CA*, September 21, 1921.

9. "Federal Net Bags 3 Former Officers," *CA*, September 23, 1921; "Dull Aftermath to Grand Jury Probe," *CA*, September 24, 1921; "Five Arrests Follow Booze Probe," *CA*, September 21, 1921; "Kinnane Transfers Much Real Estate," *CA*, September 27, 1921.

10. "U.S. Court Will Open Here Today," *CA*, November 28, 1921; "Burns Not Coming Now for Booze Graft Probe," *EA*, January 8, 1922; "U.S. Court Sets Record for Trials," *EA*, January 11, 1922.

11. "Two Bribed Taylor Federal Juries Say," *CA*, November 30, 1921; "Single Juror Says Hottum Gave Bribe," *CA*, December 2, 1921; "Hottum Asks for Special Judge in Bribe Trial," *CA*, December 1, 1921.

12. "Single Juror Says Hottum Gave Bribe," *CA*, December 2, 1921.

13. "Hottum Asks for Special Judge in Bribe Trial," *CA*, December 1, 1921; "Booze Trial Nearing End in U.S. Court," *EA*, January 12, 1922.

14. "Hung Jury in Berryman's Case Likely," *EA*, February 15, 1922; "Says Tyree Made Immunity Offer," *EA*, February 16, 1922.

15. "Auferoth Is Given Draw in Bribe Case," *EA*, February 22, 1922; "Pass Buck in Bribery Case Money Alibi," *EA*, January 8, 1922.

16. "Jim Kinnane Escapes Pen; Fined $7,500," *EA*, February 20, 1922.

17. "Says Tyree Made Immunity Offer," *EA*, February 16, 1922; "Near Scandal Blows Up on Smeared Ink," *EA*, February 18, 1922; "Scalds Prove Fatal to R.C. (Dick) Rather," *CA*, June 17, 1923; "Four Cases Left on Booze Docket," *EA*, March 29, 1922; "Close Tyree Taylor Case," *CA*, November 30, 1922.

18. "Ask Rehearings in Tyree Taylor Cases," *CA*, November 3, 1923; "Wolfe and Hindman Cases Before Ross," *CA*, December 4, 1923; "Boyle's Case Reversed by Court of Appeals," *CA*, January 15, 1924.

19. "Tyree Taylor Cases Up at Cincinnati," *CA*, April 13, 1923; "Ross Sentences Trio in Taylor Bribe Case," *CA*, January 31, 1924; "Bob Berryman Is Paroled by U.S.," *CA*, December 9, 1924.

20. Personnel file for US marshal Stanley Trezevant, NARA, Washington, DC; "Hottum Asks for Special Judge in Bribe Trial," *CA*, December 1, 1921; "Single Juror Says Hottum Gave Bribe," *CA*, December 2, 1921; "Sportsman Awaits Fate," *EA*, January 6, 1922; "Pass Buck in Bribery Case Money Alibi," *EA*, January 8, 1922.

21. "Hottum-Brown Contempt Case Continued," *EA*, March 28, 1922; "Brown in Contempt; Apologizes in Court," *CA*, May 25, 1922.

22. "Doc Hottum Pays $2,000 for Freedom," *CA*, April 21, 1922.

23. "Judge Ross Accused of Bias by Saunders," *CA*, September 4, 1924; "Ross Had Stormy Career on Bench," *CA*, July 10, 1925.

24. "Judge J. Will Ross Meets Death As He Drives into Canal," *CA*, July 10, 1925.

25. Personnel file for US marshal Stanley Trezevant, NARA, Washington, DC; "Stanley Trezevant's Resignation Is Asked," *CA*, November 29, 1921; "W.F. Appleby, U.S. Marshal, Succumbs," *CA*, February 29, 1924.

26. "Trezevant Record Is Clean Says Holland," *CA*, December 13, 1921; "Stanley Trezevant's Resignation Is Asked," *CA*, November 29, 1921; "Trezevant Stays in Office until Jan. 1," *CA*, December 6, 1921; "U.S. Court Opens Today," *CA*, December 3, 1922.

27. Mrs. R. R. Ash to M. W. Willebrandt, US attorney general, April 13, 1925, File no. 23-72, Sub. 55, Department of Justice, Mail and Files Division, National Archives Building, Washington, DC.

28. "Tyree Taylor Seeks Pardon for His Sins," *CA*, May 11, 1922; "Shelby County Jail Now Tyree's Office," *CA*, June 4, 1922; "Tyree Taylor Pardon Put Up to Murray," *CA*, June 10, 1922.

29. "Tyree Taylor Freed by Federal Parole," *CA*, December 6, 1923; "Taylor Enters Island Prison near Tacoma," *CA*, June 12, 1922.

30. "Taylor Enters Island Prison near Tacoma," *CA*, June 12, 1922; "Tyree Taylor Gets Choice of Prisons," *CA*, June 7, 1922.

31. "Harding Denies Taylor Pardon," *NS*, October 12, 1922; "Harding Denies Taylor Pardon," *NS*, October 12, 1922; "Mrs. Taylor Hopeful," *CA*, September 12, 1923.

32. "Tyree Taylor May Draw Parole Today," *CA*, November 29, 1923; Personnel file for US marshal Stanley Trezevant, NARA, Washington, DC; "Paroled Prisoner Gone," *Spokesman Review* (Spokane, WA), December 9, 1923; "Tyree Taylor Freed by Federal Parole," *CA*, December 6, 1923.

33. "Expose of Booze Barons by Tyree Taylor Promised," *NS*, May 31, 1919; "Seven Years for Tyree Taylor," *Covington Leader* (Covington, TN), July 21, 1921; "Mrs. Taylor Again Asks Tyree's Parole," *CA*, June 23, 1923.

CHAPTER 7. NO CAMPAIGNS

1. "Says Entire World Will Soon Be Dry," *NS*, January 18, 1919.

2. "18th Amendment Broken, Charge," *NS*, January 19, 1920.

3. Laurence Schmeckebier, *The Bureau of Prohibition: Its History, Activities, and Organization* (Washington, DC: Brookings Institution, 1929), 7.

4. "21 Agents Open War Here," *NS*, October 30, 1922; "New Whisky Officer Nabs Man, Two Stills," *CA*, December 13, 1921.

5. "Liquor Squad Gone; Praises Enforcement," *CA*, May 19, 1922.

6. "Find 600-Gallon Still," *CA*, May 31, 1922; "Federal Raids Net 33 Liquor Arrests," *CA*, September 17, 1922.

7. "Residence Raided; Big Still Uncovered," *CA*, April 8, 1925; "Parkway Raid Nets Huge Still, Whisky," *CA*, September 8, 1927; "Contractor Tries Moonshining to Feed Wife and Children," *CA*, March 24, 1932.

8. "Boys Veteran Liquor Spies Trial Reveals," *PS*, September 12, 1929.

9. J. Ann Funderburg, *Bootleggers and Beer Barons of the Prohibition Era* (Jefferson, NC: McFarland, 2014), 79; "Padlocking of Stands Is Next Liquor Move," *CA*, May 15, 1925.

10. "Woman Member of Cabinet Probable If Hoover Wins," *Evening Independent* (St. Petersburg, FL), July 6, 1928.

11. "Lights Turned Out as Sheriff Stages Raid," *CA*, May 24, 1924.

12. Frank and Gennie Meyers, *Shelby County Sheriff's Department Annual Report* (Marceline, MO: Walsworth Publishing, 1976), 22.

13. Iain Gately, *Drink: A Cultural History of Alcohol* (New York: Gotham Books, 2008), 374–75.

14. "Giant Still Is Seized by Prohibition agents," *CA*, December 11, 1924.

15. "Shiner Is Captured by Swimming Deputy," *CA*, July 18, 1923.

16. "Bell Heard by Wrong Party," *PS*, May 23, 1929.

17. "Eight Stills Week's Record for Sheriff," *CA*, February 10, 1924; "Sheriff Raids House on Old Cut-Off Road," *CA*, February 14, 1924; "Ten Stills and 4,200 Gallons of Mash, Five Men in Week," *CA*, March 2, 1924; "Seizes Six Still and Arrests Twelve in One Week," *CA*, March 10, 1924.

18. "Sheriff Makes Huge Exhibition of Stills," *CA*, May 16, 1926.

19. "Sheriff's 1927 Liquor Raids Cost Moonshiners $500,000," *CA*, December 29, 1929; "Knight Reduces Shelby's Stills," *PS*, May 8, 1930.

20. Bob Hildebrand, "The New Deal at Memphis, Tennessee," *National Police Journal 5* (February 1920):18–21.

21. "Dean of Police on Job for 40 Years," *PS*, April 21, 1930.

22. "The Town Policeman," *PS*, April 6, 1931.

23. "Kehoe as Crusader, Clamps Lid on Tight," *CA*, September 18, 1924.

24. "Get Warrant Before Searching Any House," *CA*, April 27, 1922; "In Police Court," *CA*, September 1, 1925; "Police Sponge Squad Bares Whisky Cache," *CA*, January 30, 1926.

25. "Liquor Raiders Must Hold Search Warrant," *CA*, December 6, 1921; "Vaccaros Freed of Liquor Charge," *CA*, July 12, 1928.

26. "Davis Tightens Up on Booze Law Offenders," *CA*, June 21, 1924; "500 Gallons Found," *CA*, August 1, 1922; Lewis L. Laska, *The Tennessee State Constitution: A Reference Guide* (New York: Greenwood Press, 1990), 73; Frank M. Thompson, *Reports of Cases, Argued and Determined in the Supreme Court of Tennessee, Western Division*, vol. 8, (Columbia, MO: E. W. Stephens Publishing Co., 1916), 686, 809; State v. Reichman, 135 Tenn. at 705 (Tennessee Supreme Court, 1916); "Injunction Used Again on Liquor," *NS*, February 7, 1919; "Sheriff Says He Will Not Let Up," *NS*, November 24, 1919.

27. "Lack of Search Warrant Frees Two on Charge," *CA*, February 25, 1927; "Raid," *CA*, October 6, 1926.

28. "4,150 Gallons of Whisky Seized in Raid by Agents," *CA*, February 9, 1933; "Pete Lenti Charged with Dry Violations," *CA*, February 10, 1933; "Lenti Contends Dry Agents' Act Illegal," *CA*, February 17, 1933; "Pete Lenti Freed on Illegal Search Grounds," *CA*, February 18, 1933.

29. Ibid.

30. "Shake-Up Follows Big Still Gossip," *CA*, September 21, 1921.

31. Ibid.

32. "Mose Jones Missing; Deputies Freed," *CA*, June 13, 1922; "Federal Net Bags 3 Former Officers," *CA*, September 23, 1921; "Dull Aftermath to Grand Jury Probe," *CA*, September 24, 1921.

33. "Vigilantes Now Ready to Start Police Expose by Experts, Says Waring," *CA*, December 12, 1922; "Alleged Liquor Graft 'All Bunk'—Murray," *CA*, January 21, 1923; "Dry Agents Will Tell Booze Scandal Facts," *CA*, February 9, 1923.

34. "Police Board Spurns Liquor Scandal Case," *CA*, March 22, 1925.

35. Margaret McKee and Fred Chisenhall, *Beale Black and Blue: Life and Music on Black America's Main Street* (Baton Rouge: Louisiana State University Press, 1981), 25.

36. "Officers Get Clean Bill by Board," *CA*, October 16, 1927; "Payoffs," *CA*, July 21, 1926.

37. "World-Wide Victory for Prohibition," *Covington Leader* (Covington, TN), January 23, 1919.

CHAPTER 8. EQUALITY BEFORE THE LAW

1. Michael A. Lerner, *Dry Manhattan: Prohibition in New York City* (Cambridge: Harvard University Press, 2007), 96.

2. "Hunt Legger King in Whisky Expose," *NS*, March 29, 1928.

3. Ibid.

4. Ibid.

5. "Probe of Wet Ring by Grand Jury Is Seen," *NS*, March 30, 1928; "Booze Buyers Won't Be Questioned," *NS*, March 31, 1928.

6. "Grand Jury to Weigh Pastors' Resolution," *CA*, April 3, 1928; "Booze List Echoes," *CA*, April 6, 1928; "Bootlegger Fine $250," *CA*, April 10, 1928.

7. "Davis Blames Overton Boy for Crash," *PS*, September 24, 1929; Shelby County, Tennessee, death certificate no. 2961 (September 16, 1929), Joseph Harris Martin, Shelby County Archives.

8. "Driver Faces Murder Trial in Auto Death," *PS*, October 4, 1929.

9. "Overton Not Drunk Pals Say on Stand," *PS*, April 1, 1930.

10. "Did Our Best, M'Lain Writes," *PS*, April 2, 1930; "Fitzhugh's Statement," *PS*, March 29, 1935.

11. "Overton Boy Not Guilty Jury Decides," *PS*, April 2, 1930.

12. "Woman, 78, Defies Liquor Law Rather Than Ask for Charity," *PS*, July 3, 1929; "Forgotten," *PS*, October 25, 1929.

13. Ibid.

14. "Police Conceal Names of Trio," *PS*, May 13, 1936.

15. "Police Accept Bogus Name from Traffic Violator," *PS*, May 14, 1936.

16. "Grand Jury Drops John Smith Case," *PS*, May 29, 1936.

17. "Freeing Janes Blot on Justice," *PS*, May 30, 1936; "Jury Patches Up Janes Differences," *PS*, June 1, 1936.

18. "Six Nabbed in Police Liquor Drive Freed," *EA*, March 11, 1927.

19. Roger Biles, *Memphis in the Great Depression* (Knoxville: University of Tennessee Press, 1986), 27.

20. "Deputies in Raids for Sake of Fees, Charge," *CA*, May 4, 1924.

21. Sheriff Stops Raids by Deps and Squires," *CA*, October 24, 1925; "Knight Fires Five of Squire's Deps," *CA*, January 14, 1926; "Raids," *CA*, May 13, 1927.

22. "Jurists Calls Fee Grabbers Sly and Cruel," *PS*, May 2, 1929.

23. "Whisky Arrest Brings Rebuke," *PS*, May 31, 1929.

24. "Negro Physician Put on Probation," *CA*, March 20, 1928.

25. "Half-Pint Cases Disgust Judge," *PS*, May 31, 1932.

26. "Negro Umpire in Liquor Net," *PS*, September 20, 1934.

CHAPTER 9. LOOPHOLES

1. Daniel Okrent, "Prohibition Life: Politics, Loopholes and Bathtub Gin," Interview by Terry Gross, *Fresh Air*, National Public Radio, May 10, 2010, accessed April 12, 2017, http://www.npr.org/2010/05/10/126613316/Prohibition-life-politics-loopholes-and-bathtub-gin; "Druggist is Arrested," *CA*, July 17, 1924.

2. "Home Searched; Liquor Seized; Man Arrested," *EA*, March 16, 1927; "Paine, Allen Tighten Lines to Rout Forces of City's Underworld," *CA*, July 13, 1927; "150 Gallons of Wine Seized; Women Held by Police," *CA*, April 27, 1928.

3. "Wine Bricks? Sure, You Can Buy Plenty of 'Em Here," *PS*, August 17, 1931; "In City Court," *CA*, August 11, 1926.

4. "No Brew Shop Raids Planned," *PS*, June 19, 1930.

5. "Enforcement of Dry Ruling Planned Here," *PS*, May 9, 1930; "No Brew Shop Raids Planned," *PS*, June 19, 1930.

6. "Brandy Asked to Be Given for Sacraments," *NS*, November 10, 1919.

7. Josh Tapper, "Slivovitz: A Plum (Brandy) Choice," *Moment* 39, no. 2 (March–April 2014), http://www.momentmag.com/slivovitz-plum-brandy-choice/.

8. Daniel C. Roper, "Ruling of Internal Revenue Commissioner Roper on Manufacture, Sale and Distribution of Distilled Spirits," *Commercial and Financial Chronicle* 109 (July 1–September 30, 1919): 33; "Brandy Cannot Be Used in a Sacrament," *NS*, November 17, 1919; H. S. Linfield, "A Survey of the Year 5682," *American Jewish Yearbook* 24 (September 23, 1922–September 10, 1923): 24.

9. Okrent, "Prohibition Life"; Marni Davis, *Booze and Jews: Becoming American in the Age of Prohibition* (New York: New York University Press, 2012), 175.

10. "1,375 Gallons of Wine Seized by Dry Agents," *CA*, July 24, 1925.

11. "Wants Wine Returned," *CA*, August 8, 1925.

12. "Will Arraign 115 on Prohibition Charges," *CA*, November 8, 1925; "Sacramental Wine Will Go Back to Warehouse," *CA*, December 5, 1925.

13. Eugene Middleton, "Personality Portraits of Prominent Utahns," *Deseret News* (Salt Lake City, UT), December 3, 1934.

14. "Solve Second Man in Liquor Burglary," *CA*, May 3, 1922; "Eight Memphians Are Freed by Uncle Alf," *CA*, January 16, 1923.

15. "Sheriff Still Clings to Dreyfous Liquor," *CA*, May 20, 1922; "Dreyfous Dismisses His Liquor Replevin," *CA*, February 24, 1923.

16. "Drinks Wood Alcohol," *CA*, September 12, 1922; "Poisoned by Alcohol," *CA*, September 30, 1922; "Blame Wood Alcohol for Man's Illness," *NS*, December 23, 1922.

17. "A Sterno Gift," *Good Housekeeping* 71, December 1920, 188; "Canned Heat Leads Trio to Jail," *EA*, April 6, 1927; "Man's Death Laid to Canned Heat," *EA*, April 29, 1927.

18. "Willow Gang Plot Ends with Knifing," *PS*, March 15, 1934; "Willow Gang Has Reunion in Court," *PS*, October 12, 1934; "Police Raiding Undesirables," *PS*, May 25, 1937.

19. "City's Most Arrested Man Home from Exile," *PS*, April 19, 1930.

20. "None 'o Them's Perfect, Says Clint of Our Institutions," *PS*, April 22, 1930.

21. Shelby County, Tennessee, death certificate no. 35 (1932), Clint Murray, Tennessee Department of Health, Division of Vital Statistics.

22. "Bootleg Booze Full of Deadly Ammonia," *CA*, February 22, 1928; "Poisoned Booze Puts Victim in Hospital," *CA*, April 15, 1928; "Third Death Occurs from Poison Booze," *CA*, April 18, 1928.

23. "Beware Booze; It's Poisonous!" *PS*, June 2, 1931.

24. "Trace Source of Poisoned Liquor," *PS*, July 1, 1929.

25. "Poison Whisky Still Is Taken," *PS*, December 31, 1929; "Raiders Seize Iron Still," *CA*, January 1, 1930.

26. "Lack of Search Warrant Frees Two on Charge," *CA*, February 25, 1927; "Drinker's Death Causes Search for Murder Bar," *PS*, April 1, 1929.

27. "Prohi Forces Move to Stem Jake Supply," *PS*, March 20, 1930.

28. "Jake Is Given to Guinea Pigs," *PS*, March 21, 1930.

29. "Three Mississippi Jake Victims Treated Here," *PS*, March 31, 1930; "Health Chiefs Seek Poison Jake Brands," *PS*, April 1, 1930; "Prohi Forces Move to Stem Jake Supply," *PS*, March 20, 1930; "Local Barber is Jake Victim," *PS*, April 7, 1930; "Local Jake Victim in Serious Condition," *PS*, April 8, 1930; "Jake Victim Very Ill," *PS*, April 11, 1930.

30. John Timbrell, *The Poison Paradox: Chemicals as Friends and Foes* (New York: Oxford University Press, 2005), 259–60; Robert F. Moss, *Southern Spirits: Four Hundred Years of Drinking in the South, with Recipes* (Berkeley: Ten Speed Press, 2016), 246.

31. Thomas Stephen Szasz, *Ceremonial Chemistry: The Ritual Persecution of Drugs, Addicts, and Pushers* (New York: Syracuse University Press, 2003), 212; Gerald Weinland, *1927: High Tide of the Twenties* (New York: Four Walls Eight Windows, 2001), 83.

CHAPTER 10. KU KLUX KLAN

1. Mark K. Bauman and Berkley Kalin, *The Quiet Voices: Southern Rabbis and Civil Rights, 1880s to 1990s* (Tuscaloosa: University of Alabama Press, 1995), 59.

2. "Judge Clifford Davis Takes Oath of Office," *CA*, January 2, 1924.

3. Juan O. Sanchez, *Religions and the Ku Klux Klan: Biblical Appropriation in Their Literature and Songs* (Jefferson, NC: MacFarland, 2016), 5; Kenneth Jackson, *The Ku Klux Klan in the City, 1915–1930* (New York: Oxford University Press, 1967), 31.

4. Jackson, *Ku Klux Klan*, 48–49.

5. G. Wayne Dowdy, *Mayor Crump Don't Like It: Machine Politics in Memphis* (Jackson: University of Mississippi Press, 2006), 38–39.

6. Jackson, *Ku Klux Klan*, 52–54; Jennifer Ann Trost, *Gateway to Justice: The Juvenile Court and Progressive Child Welfare in a Southern City* (Athens: University of Georgia Press, 2005), 27.

7. "Klan Meetings Conflict," *CA*, April 15, 1924.

8. "Klan Deputy Ordered Held for Grand Jury," *CA*, August 20, 1924.

9. "Klan Argument Ends with Ambulance Ride," *CA*, May 30, 1925; "Grantham in Fight," *CA*, June 24, 1925; "Grantham in Bad," *CA*, July 10, 1925.

10. "Cyclops Worsted in Fight with Deputies," *CA*, March 3, 1925.

11. Ibid.

12. "Sheriff's Firm Stand on Law Enforcement," *CA*, March 5, 1925; "Sheriff Discharges Adversary Counsel," *CA*, March 25, 1925.

13. "Klan Story Is Denied by Busby and Taylor," *CA*, July 3, 1925.

14. "Arrests Promised in Hollywood Mob Case," *CA*, July 3, 1925.

15. Affidavits of R. B. Thompson, December 28, 1925, and Matt C. Grantham, December 29, 1925; Harry B. Anderson File, Papers re: Nominations [SEN 18B-A3], 69th Congress.

16. "Roadhouses Ordered Padlocked by Judge," *CA*, May 6, 1926; "Prohi Office Probe in Murray's Hands," *CA*, June 11, 1926; "Wright Exonerated in Dry Office Probe," *CA*, June 30, 1926.

17. "Wimmer Up Next Month," *CA*, December 3, 1926; "Sheriff Offers No Solace to Wimmer," *CA*, August 1, 1927.

18. "Bootlegger to Face Contempt, Perjury Trial," *EA*, April 18, 1927; "Federal Grand Jury Will Be Quite Active," *CA*, September 14, 1927.

19. Leonard J. Moore, *Citizen Klansmen: The Ku Klux Klan in Indiana, 1921–1928* (Chapel Hill: University of North Carolina Press, 1991), 32, 102; "Six Arrested in Raid, Dismissed in Hearing," *CA*, May 8, 1926; "Connely's Case Fails When It Goes to Trial," *CA*, June 5, 1926.

20. "Raiding Parson Raids No More; To Leave City," *EA*, March 26, 1927; "Cattaneo, 18 Others Indicted by Probers," *EA*, April 8, 1927; "Postpone Connely Sale," *CA*, July 26, 1927.

21. "Park Won't Be Used for Klan Address," *PS*, May 4, 1929; "Order Banning Park Meeting to Be Ignored," *PS*, May 8, 1929; "Norris Moves Fireworks to Court Square," *PS*, May 10, 1929.

22. "Klan Boss Raps British Visitor," *PS*, October 9, 1929.

CHAPTER 11. FLAMING YOUTH AND POLICE CHARACTERS

1. "Youthful Criminals Crowding the Courts," *CA*, January 20, 1923.

2. "Farm Boy Squanders Loot in One Debauch," *CA*, December 7, 1923.

3. John M. Reisman, *History of Clinical Psychology* (New York: Brunner-Routledge, 1991), 121; "Liquor is on Decided Decrease," *CA*, August 4, 1922; "Youthful Criminals Crowding the Courts," *CA*, January 20, 1923; "It's Funny But Booze Expert Is Prison's Champ Water Boy Now," *PS*, April 14, 1932.

4. "War Just Begun on Roadside Petters," *CA*, August 24, 1924; "County Motor Police Organized by Sheriff," *CA*, June 11, 1925.

5. "You Can't Make Flaming Youth Be Good, Says Judge," *CA*, November 23, 1928.

6. "Flaming Youth Gets Wet Blanket as 500 Girls Join Slow Club," *CA*, March 11, 1927.

7. "Liquor—Forbidden Fruit—Lures Youth, Says Judge," *PS*, December 31, 1930.

8. James G. Watson, *William Faulkner: Self-Presentation and Performance* (Austin: University of Texas Press, 2000), 86–87.

9. *CA*, October 9, 1919; "High Court Sets Execution Date; Upholds Verdict," *NS*, June 26, 1920.

10. "Silent One Now Is Posing as Lone Blackhand," *NS*, December 1, 1919; "Faints at Death Verdict," *Chicago Tribune*, July 27, 1920; "Seeks Return of All Petitions Out," *NS*, July 15, 1920; "McNamara's Sentence Commuted to Life Term," *NS*, September 2, 1920; "Isham G. Harris III Is to Get a Pardon," *CA*, January 3, 1922; "Allen McNamara Appeals," *CA*, March 14, 1925; "Nab S.D. Head as He Tells on McNamara," *CA*, August 18, 1925; "McNamara Makes Bond," *CA*, August 27, 1925; "Allen McNamara Held," *CA*, September 16, 1925.

11. "Hold Werkhoven Again," *CA*, May 2, 1924; "Returns from Navy," *NS*, December 5, 1918; "Finds Wife in the Arms of Another; Shoots to Kill," *NS*, November 9, 1920.

12. "Posse Battles River as Boat Upsets," *CA*, December 29, 1923; "Werkhoven Acquitted," *CA*, February 13, 1924; "Hold Werkhoven Again," *CA*, May 2, 1924; "Ignore Liquor Charges," *CA*, May 7, 1924.

13. "Werkhoven, in Chains, Breaks for Freedom," *CA*, May 20, 1924.

14. "Butts Werkhoven Captured in Swamps," *CA*, June 13, 1924.

15. "Liquor Violations Have Day in Court," *CA*, June 18, 1924.

16. "Werkhoven in Second Flight from Officers," *CA*, June 22, 1924.

17. "Werkhoven Gets Twenty-One Years for Assault," *CA*, February 25, 1925.

18. "Veteran Policeman to Be Buried Today," *CA*, June 10, 1925; "Roadhouse Raided," *CA*, May 10, 1928.

19. "Scalds Prove Fatal to R.C. (Dick) Rather," *CA*, June 17, 1923.

20. "Scalds Prove Fatal to R.C. (Dick) Rather," *CA*, June 17, 1923: "Rather Held Guilty; 3–10 Year Term," *CA*, April 20, 1922.

21. Edna Bechtold Rather, State of Tennessee, State Board of Health, Bureau of Vital Statistics, Death Certificate, file no. 381 (June 17, 1922); "Gladys Rather Sues," *CA*, March 13, 1923; "First Wife Ties Up Dick Rather Estate," *CA*, June 21, 1923; "Mrs. Edna M. Rather Held in Los Angeles," CA, July 21, 1923.

22. "Scalds Prove Fatal to R.C. (Dick) Rather," *CA*, June 17, 1923; "Bury Rather Tuesday," *CA*, June 18, 1923.

23. "Police Persecuting Him, Says Popeye in Tale of Woe," *PS*, July 23, 1930.

24. "In Police Court," *CA*, October 22, 1925.

25. "N.K. Pumphrey Used Pistol on Two Friends," *CA*, March 4, 1923; "Indict Popeye Again," *CA*, March 28, 1923; "Supreme Court Rules 1923 Booze Law Valid," *CA*, December 16, 1923.

26. "Pumphrey Pardoned," *CA*, December 18, 1923; "Raid Dice, Poker Games," *CA*, December 24, 1923.

27. "Joe Carter Believed Man Slain in Attack," *CA*, June 18, 1924; "Carter Cases to Grand Jury Friday," *CA*, June 26, 1924; "Body of Joe Carter, Weighted with Iron, Found in Wolf River," *CA*, June 24, 1924.

28. "Two Arrests Fail to Solve Carter Case," *CA*, June 20, 1924; "Carter Cases to Grand Jury Friday," *CA*, June 26, 1924; "Pumphrey In Again," *CA*, June 20, 1924; "Pumphrey and Pal Freed of Hijacking," *CA*, March 4, 1925.

29. "Popeye Just Sowing Some of His Wild Oats," *PS*, June 25, 1929; "N.K. Pumphrey Held as Safe Blower," *CA*, December 19, 1926; "Girl Declares Pumphrey Not Payroll Thief," *CA*, February 11, 1927; "Police Fail to Link Pumphrey," *PS*, July 21, 1930.

30. "Told to Leave, Popeye Obeys," *PS*, October 14, 1930.

31. "Police Persecuting Him, Says Popeye in Tale of Woe," *PS*, July 23, 1930.

32. "Mother's Faith Follows Popeye to the Grave," *PS*, October 29, 1931.

33. Ray Robinson, "Machine Gun Kelly's Wife Lost Chance for Freedom Thwarted Deal Sealed Convictions," *The Oklahoman* (Oklahoma City), August 3, 1986, accessed September 1, 2015, http://newsok.com/machinegun-kellys-wife-lost-chance-for-freedom-thwarted-deal-sealed-convictions/article/2155463/?page=2.

34. "Yesterday's Developments," *CA*, September 28, 1933; "Gangster Denies Guilt Fights Return West in Urschel Kidnapping Case," *CA*, September 27, 1933.

35. Ibid.

36. "Memphians Recognize Barnes Despite Kelly's Blonde Hair," *CA*, September 27, 1933.

37. "Kelly Played Hooky to Peddle Whisky," *CA*, September 29, 1933.

38. "Memphians Recognize Barnes Despite Kelly's Blonde Hair," *CA*, September 27, 1933.

39. Freedom of Information and Privacy Acts, Subject: George "Machine Gun Kelly" Barnes Summary (Washington, DC: Government Printing Office, 2004), 7.

40. Robinson, "Machine Gun Kelly's Wife."

41. "Gangster Denies Guilt Fights Return West in Urschel Kidnapping Case," *CA*, September 27, 1933; "Kelly Confesses to Urschel Kidnapping," *CA*, September 28, 1933; "Kelly Confesses to Urschel Kidnapping," *CA*, September 28, 1933; "Sentence Kelly and Wife to Life in Penitentiary," *PS*, October 12, 1933.

42. "I'll Get Out," *PS*, October 14, 1933.

43. Robinson, "Machine Gun Kelly's Wife."

44. Mark Thornton, "Alcohol Prohibition Was a Failure," *Cato Institute Policy Analysis* 157 (July 17, 1991), accessed September 21, 2016, http://www.cato.org/pubs/pas/pa-157.html; "You Can't Make Flaming Youth Be Good, Says Judge," *CA*, November 23, 1928.

CHAPTER 12. ROADHOUSES AND PIG STANDS

1. "Mystery Slaying Puzzles Police; Hotel Man Is Held," *PS*, October 7, 1932.

2. "Hotel Slaying Baffles Police," *PS*, October 8, 1932.

3. Ibid.

4. "Any Bellhop Will Get You Whisky, Says Gore," *CA*, August 8, 1925.

5. "Arrest Pig Stand Man in Fight Over Hootch." *CA*, August 26, 1925; "Man and Girl Killed in Auto Liquor Party," *CA*, January 14, 1925; "Two Face Court after Arrest at Barbecue Stand," *NS*, October 8, 1920; "Man and Girl Killed in Auto Liquor Party," *CA*, January 14, 1925.

6. "Zanone Renews Fight to Operate Pig Stand," *CA*, August 21, 1925; "Hear Zanone Case," *CA*, February 11, 1926.

7. "Handing Police Liquor Seems to Be Bad Luck," *CA*, September 13, 1923; "Liquor Under Board," *CA*, October 9, 1924; "Police Find Home Brew Concealed Beneath Sand," *CA*, July 4, 1925.

8. "Little Grandi Held in Gunplay," *PS*, October 17, 1933.

9. "Shooting Ends Liquor Spree; Woman Held," *PS*, June 17, 1929; "Doctors Have Hope for Bellomini's Life," *PS*, June 18, 1929.

10. "Law Must Be Obeyed, Track Backers Told," *PS*, July 4, 1930; "Introducing Spec Horton, Caterer Extraordinary to the Public," *PS*, July 31, 1931.

11. Ibid.

12. Ibid.

13. "Detectives' Booze War Will Continue," *CA*, April 21, 1922; "Flying Squadron in Raids on Bullet Row," *CA*, June 4, 1922; "Jury Busy on Dry Law Violation Charges," *NS*, December 13, 1922; "$2,000 Sugar Theft Charged to Two Men," *CA*, August 1, 1923; "Two Waive Hearings," *CA*, August 2, 1923; "Caught for Liquor," *CA*, October 29, 1924; "Knight Fires Five of Squire's Deps," *CA*, January 14, 1926; "Harry Kiersky Arrested," *CA*, January 19, 1926; "In City Court," *CA*, August 24, 1926.

14. "Federal Men Made Raid," *CA*, August 26, 1927; "Club Padlocked in Police Raids," *PS*, April 7, 1930.

15. "Sheriff Starts Padlock Drive," *PS*, April 14, 1930; "Barn Proprietor Faces Pen Sentence," *PS*, April 18, 1930; "Anderson Frees Barn Operator," *PS*, April 26, 1930.

16. Ibid.

17. "Reno's Nightclub Opens Wednesday," *PS*, January 18, 1932; Joseph Blotner, *Faulkner: A Biography* (Jackson: University Press of Mississippi, 2005), 99–100.

18. "Sheriff Stages Lone Raid on Club House," *CA*, April 21, 1924; "Will Arraign 115 on Prohibition Charges," *CA*, November 8, 1925; "Sheriff In on Raid on County Roadhouses," *CA*, January 2, 1928.

19. "Racket Revenge Believed Behind Night Club Fire," *PS*, December 3, 1929.

20. "Firebug Gang Leader Know, Officials Say," *PS*, December 4, 1929.

21. "Reno Devaux's Arrest Sought by Chancellor," *PS*, August 11, 1931; "Devaux Awaits Court Hearing," *PS*, August 15, 1931; "Yes? No? Maybe," *PS*, September 21, 1931; "Club to Re-open," *PS*, October 17, 1931; "Reno Devaux Back at Old Stand; Spec Horton Will Open New Night Club Soon," *PS*, October 28, 1931; "Friends Say Reno Back in Memphis," *PS*, January 2, 1932.

22. "Another Nightclub Padlocked," *PS*, April 2, 1932; "Roadhouses Called to Time by Sheriff," *CA*, March 6, 1933.

23. "Barn Proves a Good Fellow," *PS*, December 15, 1933; Owen Payne White, *The Autobiography of a Durable Sinner* (New York: G. P. Putnam's Sons, 1942), 282–92; Owen P. White, "Sinners in Dixie," *Collier's*, January 26, 1935, 44.

24. "Fire Destroys Barn Resort," *PS*, November 13, 1934; "Party at Barn Tonight Opens Santa Benefits," *PS*, December 10, 1936; "Barn Raided Owner Fined," *PS*, January 8, 1937; "Seize Liquor at Barn Club," *PS*, March 5, 1937.

25. "Three Are Indicted on Liquor Charges," *PS*, April 20, 1937; "Car at Bellomini Inn Yields Liquor," *PS*, April 6, 1937; "Liquor Brings Fines for 12," *PS*, November 5, 1937.

26. "Prohi Raiders Throw Fear in Liquor Circle," *PS*, January 16, 1935; "Eyewitness Says Keenan Fired Shot Killing Baw," *PS*, November 19, 1936; "Keenan Waved Pistol at Me," *PS*, November 18, 1936.

27. "Prober Indicted for Inn Slaying," *PS*, February 8, 1935; "Indicted Prohi Agent Finally Going to Trial," *PS*, September 3, 1936.

28. "Keenan Hazy Over Gunplay at Roadhouse," *PS*, November 20, 1936; "McLain and Mooney Clash in Court," *PS*, November 21, 1936; "Keenan Trial Up Next Term," *PS*, December 30, 1936.

29. "Bound by Three Men; Shot Through Brain," *PS*, November 7, 1936; "Did Cianciola Fall Victim to Memphis Foes?" *PS*, November 9, 1936.

30. "Confessions Solve Nightclub Slaying—4 Face Murder Charge," *PS*, November 10, 1936.

31. Ibid.

32. Ibid.

33. "Bound by Three Men; Shot Through Brain," *PS*, November 7, 1936.

34. "Did Cianciola Fall Victim to Memphis Foes?" *PS*, November 9, 1936; "Confessions Solve Nightclub Slaying—4 Face Murder Charge," *PS*, November 10, 1936; "Jury Convicts 4 For Slaying of Cianciola," *PS*, March 13, 1937.

35. "Silver Slipper Will Be Closed," *PS*, November 24, 1930.

36. "Bob Berryman is Paroled by U.S." *CA*, December 9, 1924; "Roadhouses Ordered Padlocked by Judge," *CA*, May 6, 1926; "Grand Jurors Indict 3 in Gaming War," *PS*, July 17, 1929; "Berryman's Offer of Guilty Plea Refused," *PS*, December 11, 1929.

37. "Order Arrest of Gamblers," *PS*, December 29, 1937; "Gaming Cleanup Awaits Desoto Probers," *PS*, February 14, 1938.

38. "Lakeview Cars Turn Back at City Limits," *CA*, January 4, 1925.

39. "Laughter Raided Again," *CA*, May 23, 1926; "Giant Still Seized in Horn Lake Bottom," *CA*, November 7, 1926; "New Inquiry in Border Gaming," *PS*, March 2, 1938.

40. "Trio Captured As Still Is Destroyed," *NS*, October 6, 1922; "Clerk Is Arrested in Dancehall Shooting," *CA*, August 4, 1923; "Crime Carnival for Week a Bloody One," *CA*, August 7, 1923; "Notorious Resort at Lake View Is Closed," *CA*, August 14, 1923; "Kirkman Bound Over," *CA*, June 19, 1925.

41. "Bouncer Phillips Shot; An Accident He Insists," *PS*, August 8, 1938; Roger Biles, *Memphis in the Great Depression* (Knoxville: University of Tennessee Press, 1986), 38–39.

42. "Women Beaten at Night Spot; Bouncer Sued," *PS*, August 9, 1938.

43. "Gaming Cleanup Awaits Desoto Probers," *PS*, February 14, 1938; "Gaming Raiders Visit Tom Cat," *PS*, February 9, 1939.

CHAPTER 13. LIQUOR AND OTHER VICES

1. "Downtown Gaming Houses Dark—Police Lid Goes On," *PS*, July 19, 1934.

2. "Raid Craps Game," *CA*, September 7, 1924.

3. "Alleged Assailant Held," *CA*, February 10, 1925; "Craps Game Protests Cause Investigation," *CA*, July 5, 1925.

4. "Mountain Sleuth Leaves after Work," *NS*, September 11, 1920.

5. "Joe Conley Jailed; Made Bet on Peay," *CA*, August 4, 1926.

6. "Place, Facing Gaming Writ, Remains Open," *CA*, February 28, 1927; "City Files Suit for Injunction Against Place," *EA*, February 19, 1927; "Stage Uptown Raids on Games," *EA*, December 13, 1928.

7. Owen Payne White, *The Autobiography of a Durable Sinner* (New York: G. P. Putnam's Sons, 1942), 290.

8. White, *Autobiography of a Durable Sinner*, 287–88.

9. White, 287–88.

10. White, 287–88.

11. William D. Miller, *Memphis During the Progressive Era, 1900–1917* (Memphis: Memphis State University Press, 1957), 90; "Underworld Queen Says Easiest Way Is the Hardest," *PS*, April 24, 1930; "Old Rounder Finds Memphis All Right," *CA*, July 27, 1928.

12. "In City Court," *CA*, July 23, 1927; "U.S. Nabs Florence," *CA*, May 4, 1923; "Nab Three Whites in Raid," *CA*, June 24, 1923.

13. "Chief Plaxco Raids Ida Simmons' Place," *CA*, July 22, 1927.

14. "In City Court," *CA*, July 23, 1927.

15. "In City Court," *CA*, July 27, 1927; "Old Rounder Finds Memphis All Right," *CA*, July 27, 1928.

16. "Wanted—A Bartender," *CA*, November 18, 1922; "Police Paragraphs," *CA*, February 14, 1930; "In City Court," *CA*, February 16, 1930.

17. "U.S. Opens Vice Ring War Here," *PS*, September 20, 1932.

18. *CA*, October 24, 1926; "Purity Squad Arrests 16 as a Starter Today," *NS*, March 16, 1928.

19. "Old Rounder Finds Memphis All Right," *CA*, July 27, 1928; "Cape of White on Sinful City," *PS*, March 2, 1935.

20. "Federal Grand Jury Returns 8 True Bills," *PS*, November 23, 1932; "Nine Jailed in Slavery Drive," *PS*, September 20, 1935.

21. "Girls Tested in War on Syphilis," *PS*, June 9, 1937; "U.S. Funds Syphilis War," *PS*, September 8, 1938; "TB, Syphilis Lead in State," *PS*, April 3, 1939.

22. "John Revinsky Again in Toils of the Law," *CA*, June 28, 1927; "Underworld Queen Says Easiest Way Is the Hardest," *PS*, April 24, 1930; "Going Straight Not Worthwhile, Tries Suicide," *PS*, May 12, 1930.

CHAPTER 14. KING OF PRESIDENT'S ISLAND

1 "Twice Told Tales," *NS*, September 11, 1919.

2. "United States Census, 1910," database with images, FamilySearch.org, accessed April 27, 2016, https://familysearch.org/ark:/61903/1:1:MGFF-LW1, Joseph Sailors, Memphis Ward 10, Shelby, Tennessee, United States, citing enumeration district (ED) ED 169, sheet 2A, NARA microfilm publication T624 (Washington, DC: National Archives and Records Administration, n.d.), FHL microfilm 1375533.

3. "Booze not Hardware; Two Men Under Arrest," *NS*, November 19, 1918; "55 Are Indicted by Federal Grand Jury," *NS*, November 30, 1918; "Three Cases Heard," *NS*, December 12, 1918; "Marshal Denies Threat Charge," *NS*, December 13, 1918; "Berryman and Gold Fined $1000 Each," *NS*, December 14, 1918.

4. "The Adventures of Pete," *NS*, October 29, 1919.

5. "Pete Sailor Held on Liquor Violation Charge, *NS*, April 7, 1919; "Pete Sailor Indicted," *NS*, April 11, 1919.

6. "Pete Sailors' Dog Makes Bad Error," *NS*, September 8, 1919; "Pete Sailors Free of Liquor Charges," *NS*, December 2, 1919; "Sailors' Dog Is Still Enjoying Life," *NS*, September 9, 1919.

7. "Ropes Close In on Two Suspects in Sailors Case," *NS*, March 8, 1919; "Negro Found Guilty," *NS*, April 8, 1919; "Big Six Will Have New Day in Court," *NS*, May 17, 1919; "Joe Sailors Buys Farm," *NS*, October 7, 1919.

8. "Seize 7 Stills on President's Island," *CA*, December 16, 1921.

9. "Federal Net Bags 3 Former Officers," *CA*, September 23, 1921.

10. "Detectives' Booze War Will Continue," *CA*, April 21, 1922.

11. "Grand Jury Frees 19 Caught in Big Raids," *CA*, April 29, 1922.

12. "Seize Mammoth Still in Island Canebreak," *CA*, September 9, 1922.

13. "Moonshiner Wounded as Posse Raids Still," *CA*, May 14, 1923; "Still Operator Nabbed," *CA*, May 15, 1923.

14. "Ring Leaders Escape," *CA*, June 7, 1923.

15. "Sailors Out on Bond," *CA*, June 9, 1923; "Joe Sailors Indicted by U.S. Grand Jurors," *CA*, June 13, 1923.

16. "Joe Sailors Indicted by U.S. Grand Jurors," *CA*, June 13, 1923; "One of Missing Pair Appears," *CA*, June 15, 1923; "Missing Witnesses List Continues to Swell," *CA*, June 22, 1923.

17. "Police Board to Hear Liquor Scandal Case," *CA*, July 5, 1924; "Another Man Sought in Tamble Mystery," *CA*, September 11, 1923; "Charge Oliver Tried to Kill Sheriff," *CA*, March 23, 1924.

18. "Get Big Island Still, 10,000 Gallons of Mash," *CA*, August 25, 1923; "Tuesday Mighty Blue for Makers of Booze," *CA*, March 12, 1924; "Seize Big Stills," *CA*, May 21, 1924; "Charge Liquor Violation," *CA*, September 6, 1924.

19. "Dry Officers Hunt Slayer of Informer," *Miami (FL) News*, October 29, 1926; *CA*, January 2, 1927.

20. "Arrest Joe Sailors in Island Raid," *CA*, August 11, 1927; "Bootleggers Are Hit as U.S. Attack Opens," *CA*, October 4, 1927; "Joe Sailors' Jury Hung," *CA*, October 21, 1927; "Will Dismiss Charge Against Joe Sailors," *CA*, September 28, 1928.

21. "Judge Breaks Bootleg Clan," *PS*, June 22, 1934; "Raid Huge Still on Mississippi Island," *PS*, October 23, 1934; "Judge Shows Mercy to Help at Still," *PS*, November 15, 1934.

22. "Liquor Boat Held; Six Under Arrest," *PS*, September 17, 1935.

23. "Agents Trailed Still on Island by Mule Tracks," *PS*, June 11, 1936.

24. "Wiretapping Evidence is Admitted under Decision which Brandeis Opposed," *PS*, June 16, 1936; "Sailors's Phone Talk Is Bared," *PS*, June 10, 1936; "U.S. Grand Jurors Indict Joe Sailors," *PS*, April 15, 1936.

25. "Argue Legality of Wiretapping," *PS*, June 8, 1936.

26. J. K. Peterson, *Understanding Surveillance Technologies: Spy Devices, Privacy, History, and Applications* (Boco Raton, FL, CRC Press, 2007), 131; "Wiretapping Evidence Is Admitted under Decision Which Brandeis Opposed," *PS*, June 16, 1936; Olmstead v. United States, 277 U.S. 438 (1928).

27. "Sailors Dubbed Bootleg Brains," *PS*, June 18, 1936.

28. "Joe Sailors Acquitted by Federal Jury," *PS*, June 19, 1936.

29. Ibid.

CHAPTER 15. JOHN BELLUOMINI

1. Patrick O'Daniel, *When the Levee Breaks: Memphis and the Mississippi Valley Food of 1927* (Charleston: History Press, 2013), 106.

2. "Still Supply Launch Sinks Officers' Boat," *CA*, March 29, 1924.

3. "Bellomini Out, In Again," *CA*, April 1, 1924.

4. "Bellomini Pleads Guilty," *CA*, June 21, 1924; "Lawyer Knocks Out Narcotic Indictment," *CA*, March 14, 1925.

5. "Prosecution Scores in Police Hearings," *CA*, October 12, 1927; "Capt. Lee is Acquitted by Police Trial Board," *CA*, October 18, 1927.

6. Ibid.

7. "Allen's Probe Strikes 38," *CA*, September 23, 1927; "Prosecution Scores in Police Hearings," *CA*, October 12, 1927.

8. "Prosecution Scores in Police Hearings," *CA*, October 12, 1927.

9. "Police Bribe Story Stirs Paine to Act," *CA*, June 28, 1927; "Veteran Officers to Face Charges," *CA*, September 23, 1927.

10. "Paine Defends U.S. From McLain's Slur," *CA*, July 2, 1927; G. Wayne Dowdy, *Mayor Crump Don't Like It: Machine Politics in Memphis* (Jackson: University Press of Mississippi, 2006), 45–46.

11. "Paine Defends U.S. From McLain's Slur," *CA*, July 2, 1927; "Just Gang Politics Paine Fires at Fatty," *CA*, July 3, 1927.

12. "Paine Forces Bribery Issue in U.S. Capital," *CA*, July 8, 1927; "See the Prosecutors Anderson Tells Paine," *CA*, July 11, 1927.

13. "Prosecution Scores in Police Hearings," *CA*, October 12, 1927; "Police Bribe Story Stirs Paine to Act," *CA*, June 28, 1927; "Allen's Probe Strikes 38," *CA*, September 23, 1927.

14. "Grand Jury Returns Seventy-One Bills," *CA*, July 20, 1927; "Jury Will Not Pry Into Charges Today," *CA*, July 19, 1927.

15. "Allen Sues City Club Probers for $100,000," *CA*, August 3, 1927; "John Bellomini Held on U.S. Warrant in Payoff Book Probe," *CA*, August 16, 1927; "Seek More Evidence in Police Bribe Probe," *CA*, August 28, 1927; "Veteran Officers to Face Charges," *CA*, September 23, 1927.

16. "Allen's Probe Strikes 38," *CA*, September 23, 1927; "John Bellomini Held on U.S. Warrant in Payoff Book Probe," *CA*, August 16, 1927; "Police Realignment Brings Department to a Stable Footing," *CA*, September 24, 1927; "Herrington Will Take Capt. Lee's Command," *CA*, September 25, 1927.

17. "Police Trial Board to Convene Tuesday," *CA*, October 8, 1927; "Police Hearing Will Begin This Morning," *CA*, October 11, 1927; "Capt. Will Lee Seeks Immediate Hearing," *CA*, September 28, 1927; Dowdy, *Mayor Crump Don't Like It*, 52.

18. "Veteran Officers to Face Charges," *CA*, September 23, 1927; "Quianthy Is Arrested," *CA*, September 27, 1927; "Dismiss Quianthy Case," *CA*, October 13, 1927.

19. "Prosecution Scores in Police Hearings," *CA*, October 12, 1927; "17 More Police Cases Are Heard by Board," *CA*, October 15, 1927; "Officers Get Clean Bill by Board," *CA*, October 16, 1927.

20. "The Results in Figures," *CA*, November 11, 1927; "Allen Orders Sixteen Policemen Restored," *CA*, November 19, 1927; "Allen Orders Sixteen Policemen Restored," *CA*, November 19, 1927; "Officers Get Clean Bill by Board," *CA*, October 16, 1927.

21. "Allen Face-to-Face with John Bellomini," *CA*, July 8, 1927.

22. "John Bellomini Held on U.S. Warrant in Payoff Book Probe," *CA*, August 16, 1927; "Allen's Probe Strikes 38," *CA*, September 23, 1927.

23. "John Bellomini Held on U.S. Warrant in Payoff Book Probe," *CA*, August 16, 1927; "Nation Searched for Bellomini Partners," *CA*, August 17, 1927.

24. Ibid.

25. "Veteran Officers to Face Charges," *CA*, September 23, 1927; "Bellomini's Partner Expected Tomorrow," *CA*, October 2, 1927; "Nation Searched for Bellomini Partners," *CA*, August 17, 1927; "Allen's Probe Strikes 38," *CA*, September 23, 1927.

26. "Alan McNamara Involves Self in Police Scandal," *CA*, August 26, 1927.

27. "Seek More Evidence in Police Bribe Probe," *CA*, August 28, 1927.

28. Ibid.; "Bellomini Sentence to Start Monday," *CA*, October 22, 1927.

29. "Bellomini's Partner Is Denied Arrest," *CA*, August 8, 1928; "Bellomini Pal Bids Fair to Crash U.S. Jail Gate," *CA*, August 9, 1928; "Bellomini's Partner Fine of $1000," *CA*, September 28, 1928.

30. "Bellomini Indicted in Payoff Book Probe," *CA*, October 6, 1927; "Bellomini Sentence to Start Monday," *CA*, October 22, 1927; "John Bellomini Goes Free on Liquor Charge," *EA*, November 23, 1928.

31. "Bellomini Wounded in Store Gun Battle," *CA*, January 8, 1937; "Ex-Baron, 'Leggers Shot in Gun Battle," *PS*, January 8, 1937; "John Bellomini Gets Week Off From Jail," *CA*, February 10, 1928; "Louis Bellomini Is Hurt in Auto Wreck," *CA*, February 10, 1928; "Tragic Ending in Triangle of Life, Love, and Death," *CA*, February 16, 1928; "Bellomini Back in Jail; Leaves Infant and Grave," *CA*, February 22, 1928.

32. "Old Rounder Finds Memphis All Right," *CA*, July 27, 1928; "Bootleg Pair Shot Down by Angry Pal Fired by Jealousy," *CA*, May 30, 1928; "Fearing Bootleg Vendetta, Berjiacchi Estops Pacini," *CA*, June 17, 1928.

33. "Bellomini Is at Home," *CA*, June 5, 1928; "Old Rounder Finds Memphis All Right," *CA*, July 27, 1928.

34. "Bootleg Pair Shot Down by Angry Pal Fired by Jealousy," *CA*, May 30, 1928.

35. "Release Berjiacchi under $5000 Bond," *CA*, June 2, 1928; "Liquor Ring Barred in Bargiachi Trial," *CA*, February 19, 1929.

36. "Feud Is Temporarily Halted After Joe Pacini Is Arrested," *CA*, August 13, 1928; "Bootleg Pair Shot Down by Angry Pal Fired by Jealousy," *CA*, May 30, 1928; "Fearing Bootleg Vendetta, Berjiacchi Estops Pacini," *CA*, June 17, 1928; "Bargiachi Fined on Assault Charge," *CA*, February 20, 1929.

37. "Iron Bars and a King a Prison Make, Sighs Mitchell," *CA*, September 10, 1933; "250 Rum Cases Awaiting Trial," *PS*, September 15, 1930; "Agents Destroy Monster Still," *PS*, October 10, 1930.

38. Ibid.

39. "Bellomini Wounded in Store Gun Battle," *CA*, January 8, 1937; "Ex-Baron, 'Leggers Shot in Gun Battle," *PS*, January 8, 1937.

40. Ibid.

41. Ibid.

42. Ibid.

43. "Lenzis Go Free in Bellomini Death," *PS*, February 2, 1937.

44. "John Bellomini Dies of Bullet Wounds," *CA*, January 30, 1937.

CHAPTER 16. FALL OF THE LIQUOR BARONS

1. G. Wayne Dowdy, *Mayor Crump Don't Like It: Machine Politics in Memphis* (Jackson, MS: University Press of Mississippi, 2006), 57-58.

2. "Old Rounder Finds Memphis All Right," *CA*, July 27, 1928.

3. "Democrats on Beale Keen for McAlister," *CA*, July 30, 1928; "Ex-Rounder Thinks Boys Made a Blunder," *CA*, July 31, 1928; Elizabeth Gritter, *River of Hope: Black Politics and the Memphis Freedom Movement, 1865–1954* (Lexington: University Press of Kentucky, 2014), 96.

4. "Police and Thugs Run Election; Blacks Go to Polls Like Cattle," *CA*, August 3, 1928; "Indict Dynamiters; Free Willie Gerber," *CA*, August 29, 1928.

5. "Ex-Rounder Hears of Police Station Skit," *CA*, July 28, 1928.

6. Ibid.; "Moonshiners Will Stabilize Industry," *CA*, August 17, 1928.

7. "Bootleggers Glad Howe Transferred," *CA*, August 16, 1928; "Dry Forces to Drive on Inland—'Leggers," *CA*, July 17, 1928.

8. Ibid.

9. "Moonshiners Will Stabilize Industry," *CA*, August 17, 1928; "Indict Dynamiters; Free Willie Gerber," *CA*, August 29, 1928; "Knight Hits Another Trail of Dynamiting," *CA*, August 21, 1928.

10. "Former Bootlegger, Hijacker, Racketeer Heaps Scorn on Prohibition Joke," *PS*, July 7, 1932.

11. "Gunman Snipes at Jack Loague," *PS*, July 4, 1932.

12. Ibid.

13. Ibid.

14. Ibid.

15. Dowdy, *Mayor Crump Don't Like It*, 55; "Arrests Stop Liquor War, Sheriff Claims," *CA*, August 18, 1928.

16. "Crime in Memphis Arouses Legislators," *CA*, February 23, 1929; "Crime Investigation to Begin in Memphis," *CA*, March 11, 1929; "Crime Probers Proclaim War on Pool Halls," *PS*, March 11, 1929; "Ministers to Appear Before Crime Probe," *PS*, March 12, 1929; "Speedy Justice Aim of Crime Committee," *CA*, March 12, 1929.

17. "Bring 'Em In Only Orders to Booze Raiders," *PS*, June 25, 1929; "City Booze Leader Missing Tuesday," *PS*, June 25, 1929.

18. "Mills of Law Grind Slowly in Rum Cases," *PS*, October 12, 1931; "Dry Squad, 20 Strong, Goes On with Drive," *PS*, June 28, 1930.

19. "New Rum Boat Is Baptized," *PS*, October 21, 1929; "Federal Prohi Men Capture Four Stills," *PS*, October 22, 1929.

20. Joseph Y. DeSpain, John R. Burch Jr., and Timothy Q. Hooper, *Images of America: Green County* (Charleston, SC: Arcadia Press, 2013), 124.

21. "Dry Raids Send Booze Price Up," *PS*, November 6, 1929; "Still Captured," *PS*, November 7, 1929; "Bootleggers Fare Badly in September," *PS*, October 3, 1929.

22. "Ask New Boats to Seek Booze," *PS*, November 12, 1929; "Police River Dogs May Be Organized," *PS*, November 13, 1929.

23. "Liquor Quarrel Brings Arrests," *PS*, November 13, 1929.

24. "Federal, City, and County to Open Drive," *PS*, November 27, 1929; "New Offense in Rum Battle," *PS*, November 27, 1929.

25. "Probers Hint Law-'Legger Alliance Here," *PS*, November 26, 1929; "Dry Chief and Big Boss Plot New Offensive," *PS*, November 28, 1929

26. "Prohi Spies So Good Shiners Thought U.S. Badges Phoney," *PS*, July 3, 1930.

27. "Mills of Law Grind Slowly in Rum Cases," *PS*, October 12, 1931; "Prohi Shake-up Seen as a Boon to Rum Trade," *PS*, July 4, 1930; "Dry Squad, 20 Strong, Goes On with Drive," *PS*, June 28, 1930.

28. "Three Agents May Be Added to Dry Force," *PS*, June 25, 1930; "Shakeup Won't Touch Wilson," *PS*, June 27, 1930.

29. "Mystery Slaying Puzzles Police; Hotel Man Is Held," *PS*, October 7, 1932.

30. "Liquor Barons Facing Assault for Tax Fraud," *PS*, April 10, 1931; "Rumor 50 Rum Barons Named in Indictments," *PS*, April 16, 1931; "Federal Men Open Cleanup on Big Shots," *PS*, June 27, 1930; "Lawyers Battle Payoff Records," *PS*, February 26, 1932.

31. "Rumor 50 Rum Barons Named in Indictments," *PS*, April 16, 1931; "Leggers Fight to Save Selves," *PS*, April 13, 1931; "Booze Payoff Charges Fail to Stir Davis," *PS*, February 26, 1932; "Lawyers Battle Payoff Records," *PS*, February 26, 1932.

32. "Evidence in Rum Case Outlawed," *PS*, February 27, 1932.

33. "Acquit Marino, Ricci in Federal Court," *PS*, July 7, 1932; "Marino Is Dismissed in Conspiracy Case," *CA*, July 7, 1932.

34. "Mystery Slaying Puzzles Police; Hotel Man is Held," *PS*, October 7, 1932.

35. "Citizen Is Refused Pair Once Indicted," *PS*, November 30, 1932.

36. "500 Gallons Found," *CA*, August 1, 1922; "6 Police Raids Yield 48 Men and 4 Women," *CA*, August 27, 1922; "Free Liquor Suspects," *CA*, February 22, 1929; "16 Make Bond, 24 Sought by U.S. Officers," *PS*, April 17, 1931.

37. "16 Make Bond, 24 Sought by U.S. Officers," *PS*, April 17, 1931; "2 More Stills Taken in Raids," *PS*, April 18, 1931; "Order Arrest of Indicted Leggers," *PS*, April 22, 1931.

38. "Order Probe in Strange Death of Rum Runner," *PS*, March 10, 1932.

39. "Costello Conspiracy Ends in Guilty Plea," *CA*, June 2, 1932.

40. "Seven Men Facing Conspiracy Charge," *CA*, June 21, 1932; "Liquor Sale Menaces Liberty of Ten Men," *CA*, June 28, 1932.

41. "4 Men Held in New Year's Raids," *PS*, January 1, 1932.

42. "Atkins in Court Monday," *CA*, February 18, 1933.

43. "U.S. Deputy Prohi Administrator and Aide Shot at Still," *PS*, September 22, 1932.

44. Ibid.

45. Ibid.

46. "Truck Shotgun Ambush Clews," *PS*, September 23, 1932.

47. "U.S. Prohi Raiders Clean Warehouse of Liquor Supplies," *PS*, September 24, 1932; "Arrests Near in Ambush Attack," *PS*, October 21, 1932.

48. "Spoils of Rum Raid Ruined," *PS*, December 10, 1932.

49. "Three Arraigned in Liquor Roundup," *PS*, June 9, 1933; "U.S. Indicts 21 on Liquor Conspiracy," *PS*, May 25, 1933; "Liquor Conspiracy Case Nears Court," *PS*, June 23, 1933.

50. "Marche Denies Liquor Charge," *PS*, May 22, 1933; "Marche, 11 Others Draw Prohi Fines," *PS*, June 1, 1933.

51. "Special Agents Win Another," *PS*, June 2, 1933.

52. "Disposition of Dry Law Cases Puzzles Court," *PS*, December 21, 1933; John J. Guthrie, *Keepers of the Spirits: The Judicial Response to Prohibition Enforcement in Florida, 1885–1935* (Westport, CT: Greenwood Press, 1998), 124; "Leniency Extended to Five by Martin," *PS*, July 5, 1935.

53. "Probers Hint Law-'Legger Alliance Here," *PS*, November 26, 1929.

54. "Federal Men Open Cleanup of Big Shots," *PS*, June 27, 1930.

55. "District Prohi Chief Due Here," *PS*, August 29, 1930; "Booze Conspiracy Cases Involve 200, U.S. Agent Says," *PS*, April 7, 1931.

56. "25 Police Linked in Booze Traffic by Federal Drys," *PS*, February 25, 1932; "Leggers Fight to Save Selves," *PS*, April 13, 1931; "See No Federal Trial of Police," *PS*, May 2, 1931.

57. "Kehoe Believes in Payoff Lists," *PS*, March 4, 1932.

58. "Chief Admits Some Officers Taking Payoff," *PS*, February 27, 1932; "Police Probes Point Toward New Shakeup," *CA*, July 8, 1929.

59. "Was Policeman Offered Bribe?" *PS*, March 8, 1932.

CHAPTER 17. REPEAL OF THE EIGHTEENTH AMENDMENT

1. "Mike Haggerty, Once Political Chief, Dies," *CA*, December 30, 1929; "Jim Kinnane is Dead After Colorful Life," *CA*, November 12, 1930.

2. "No Chance to Repeal Dry Law, Says Fisher," *CA*, July 28, 1923; "Dry Law Is Best Gift, Declares Wheeler," *CA*, December 25, 1923; *CA*, March 15, 1926.

3. "Memphis People Real Americans, Said Billy," *PS*, November 7, 1935; *CA*, March 30, 1926.

4. Ibid.

5. "Preacher Billy, Fiery as Ever, Scathes Sin, Then Puts OK on Memphis," *PS*, December 28, 1931.

6. "Dry Workers Enter Schools," *PS*, November 29, 1930; "New WCTU President," *CA*, September 30, 1928.

7. "Failure of the Home the Cause of Crime Wave," *CA*, January 21, 1926.

8. "State WCTU to Pick Officers Today," *CA*, October 14, 1927; "Drinking Girls Cause Problem," *PS*, December 6, 1929; "WCTU Rally Urges Vigilance," *PS*, November 2, 1929.

9. E. Lewis Evans, "WCTU Crusade Against Tobacco Next, It is Said," *The Tobacco Worker* 23, no. 1, (1919): 1–2; "Plan Amendment to Outlaw Tobacco," *New York Times*, August 3, 1919; "WCTU Plans War on Cigarette," *PS*, March 22, 1929; "WCTU Rally Urges Vigilance," *PS*, November 2, 1929.

10. "WCTU Plans War on Cigarette," *PS*, March 22, 1929; Mattie Duncan Beard, *The WCTU in the Volunteer State* (Kingsport: Kingsport Press, 1962), 67.

11. "WCTU Will Celebrate Prohibition Anniversary," *CA*, January 13, 1926; "State WCTU to Pick Officers Today," *CA*, October 14, 1927.

12. "Dry Workers Enter Schools," *PS*, November 29, 1930; Herbert Hoover, "Message to the Annual Convention of the Woman's Christian Temperance Union," November 14, 1930, online at the American Presidency Project, edited by Gerhard Peters and John T. Woolley, http://www.presidency.ucsb.edu/ws/?pid=22436.

13. "National Prohibition Experts Gather Here," *CA*, May 1, 1928.

14. "Anti-Saloon League Founder Heard Here," *CA*, June 5, 1928; "Dry Violation Laid to Taste Not Distaste," *PS*, August 5, 1929; "Dry Law Here to Stay, Says Bishop DuBose," *PS*, September 29, 1930.

15. "Give Leggers Life in Prison, Says Minister," *PS*, January 25, 1932.

16. "Anti-Volstead Boys Nabbed for Vagrancy," *CA*, November 24, 1926.

17. Michael A. Lerner, *Dry Manhattan: Prohibition in New York City* (Cambridge: Harvard University Press, 2007), 191; Kenneth D. Rose, *American Women and the Repeal of Prohibition* (New York: New York University Press, 1996), 78–79; "Woman Named Anti-Dry Envoy," *PS*, May 16, 1929.

18. "Sheriff Gave Jury Whisky Says Member," *PS*, March 13, 1929; "Dr. Curry Strikes at Liquor Patrons," *CA*, January 20, 1930.

19. "Dry Violation Laid to Taste Not Distaste," *PS*, August 5, 1929.

20. "Wickersham Prohi Plan Is a Bombshell," *PS*, July 17, 1929.

21. "Wets Charge Gain in Liquor Drinking," *PS*, August 13, 1929; "Gailor Hits at Prohibition," *PS*, March 19, 1930.

22. "Washington Letter," *Southeastern Missourian* (Cape Girardeau), April 28, 1930.

23. "Local WCTU to Vote in Poll," *PS*, March 19, 1930.

24. "Memphis Wets Leading in Polls," *PS*, April 15, 1930; "Wet Voters Still Lead in Prohi Poll," *PS*, April 16, 1930.

25. "Memphis Votes Wet in First Day of Polling," *PS*, April 17, 1930.

26. "Poll Reveals Sentiment for Prohi Repeal," *PS*, April 24, 1930; "Wets Take a Four to One Lead over Drys in Poll," *PS*, April 19, 1930.

27. "Does Prohibition Deserve to Succeed?" *PS*, April 24, 1930; "Lawyers Asked Liquor Views," *PS*, July 3, 1930.

28. "U.S. Seeks to Poll Opinion on Prohibition," *PS*, October 15, 1930; "Poll Shows Most Papers for Prohibition, but Wet Journals Lead in Circulation," *PS*, January 15, 1931.

29. "Local Women Join Dry Law Reform Move," *PS*, May 29, 1930.

30. "Crump in Race as Wets' Champ," *PS*, June 10, 1930.

31. G. Wayne Dowdy, *Mayor Crump Don't Like It: Machine Politics in Memphis* (Jackson: University Press of Mississippi, 2006), 59–60; "Wets of State Rely on Crump," *PS*, March 15, 1932.

32. "Wets of State Rely on Crump," *PS*, March 15, 1932; "Organize Here to Push Prohi Repeal Move," *PS*, April 4, 1932.

33. "Mayor Overton Out for Dry Law Change," *CA*, June 17, 1932; "Tennessee Supports Plan for Legal Beer," *CA*, June 28, 1932.

34. "Hoover Approves Dry-Wet Prohibition Plank," *New York Times*, June 14, 1932; Herbert Hoover, "Address Accepting the Republican Presidential Nomination," August 11, 1932, in *Public Papers of the Presidents of the United States: Herbert Hoover*, vol. 4 (Washington, DC: Government Printing Office, 1974–1977).

35. "Wets and Drys Enter Campaign," *PS*, July 8, 1930; "Wet Cohorts Push Campaign to Modify Law," *PS*, May 17, 1932.

36. "Plates for and against Prohi Law Given Free," *PS*, July 12, 1932; "Wet Cohorts Push Campaign to Modify Law," *PS*, May 17, 1932.

37. "WCTU to Start Anti-Repeal Drive," *CA*, June 28, 1932; "WCTU Dry List Increases," *PS*, July 1, 1932; "25 Girls to Aid in WCTU Drive," *PS*, July 7, 1932; "WCTU Pledge Signed by 1500," *PS*, July 9, 1932.

38. "Making Plans for Prohi Rallies," *PS*, October 24, 1931.

39. "Businessman, Dry Attacks Repeal Move," *PS*, July 11, 1932; "Rally of Drys Comes Via WNBR," *PS*, July 11, 1932; "2200 Applaud as Prohi Group Assails Wets," *PS*, July 12, 1932.

40. "Drys Center on Young People," *PS*, August 9, 1932; "G.J. Burnett in Dry League Job," *PS*, March 5, 1932.

41. "Mrs. Searles Re-Elected President of WCTU, New Union is Formed," *PS*, September 24, 1932; "Charges Misleading Wet Propaganda," *PS*, November 2, 1932.

42. "WCTU Protests Against Convention for Dry Law Repeal," *CA*, March 30, 1933.

43. "Beer Bill Is Offered Tennessee Assembly," *CA*, February 28, 1933; "Cry of Beer Presages Bitter Battle in Tennessee House," *CA*, March 8, 1933.

44. "WCTU Group Prays Before Beer Hearing," *CA*, March 16, 1933; "House to Pass Beer Proposal as Sought by Roosevelt Today," *CA*, March 14, 1933; "House Speeds Beer Bill to Senate 316 to 97," *CA*, March 15, 1933; "House Speeds Thrift Measure to Passage of 373 to 19," *CA*, March 17, 1933.

45. "Beer Flows Today in Missouri, Kentucky," *CA*, April 7, 1933; "Great Thirst Assuaged As Beer Flows Freely Again," *CA*, April 8, 1933; "How Dry I Am Will Change to Sweet Adeline on Trip," *CA*, March 24, 1933.

46. "Dry Tennesseans Fill Coffers of Kentucky," *CA*, April 10, 1933.

47. "Babe Prefers Golf to Quiet on Farm," *PS*, April 1, 1933.

48. "Babe May Not Have Known It, but He Delayed Beer Bill," *CA*, April 5, 1933.

49. "Passage of Beer Bill in House Assured," *CA*, April 6, 1933; "Beer Bill Is Passed by House, 53 to 42," *CA*, April 8, 1933; "Tennessee Beer Sales Legalized Effective May 1," *CA*, April 13, 1933.

50. "Tennessee Beer Sales Legalized Effective May 1," *CA*, April 13, 1933.

51. "Convention in Tennessee Might Ratify Repeal Act," *CA*, February 21, 1933; "Leaders Favor Early Action on Repeal in Tennessee," *CA*, February 22, 1933; "Argument on Repeal Bill to Start Today," *CA*, March 22, 1933.

52. "J.P. Norfleet Will Lead W. Tennessee Fight for Repeal," *PS*, June 20, 1933; "Shelby Ticket for Repeal Is Filed," *PS*, June 20, 1933; "Repeal Campaign Swings into Full Force in Shelby," *PS*, June 30, 1933.

53. "Farley Arrives Today to Make Plea for Repeal," *PS*, July 15, 1933; "Big Jim Gets Noisy Welcome at Banquet," *PS*, July 16, 1933.

54. "Save Youth Is Farley's Plea to Dixie Democrats," *PS*, July 16, 1933.

55. Ibid.

56. "Drys Seeking York for Meeting Monday," *PS*, July 15, 1933; "Farley Denounced at Dry Meeting for Aiding Repeal Drive," *PS*, July 18, 1933.

57. "Repeal Forces Act to Get Out Big Vote," *PS*, July 18, 1933; "Repeal Chiefs Push Drive for Big Vote," *PS*, July 19, 1933; "Repeal Leaders Sight Victory in Ballot Today," *PS*, July 20, 1933.

58. "Repealists Win After Trailing in Early Count," *PS*, July 21, 1933; "Repeal Won by Scant 6,000 Votes," *PS*, July 26, 1933.

59. "Dry Forces Rally in Nashville Tonight," *PS*, July 27, 1933; "Dries Repeat Charge of Election Fraud," *PS*, July 28, 1933.

60. "Bishop DuBose Hits at Victory of Wets," *CA*, September 4, 1933.

61. "Fight on Tennessee Dry Laws Is Opened," *CA*, August 12, 1933.

CHAPTER 18. PROHIBITION AFTER REPEAL

1. "Tennessee Beer Sales Effective May 1," *CA*, April 13, 1933; "Memphis Beer Law to Be Fixed Today," *CA*, April 15, 1933.

2. "Licensing Trio Will Rule Sale of Beer in Memphis," *CA*, April 18, 1933; "Tate Pease Heads Beer Board with Chief Lee, Hicks Aides," *CA*, April 19, 1933.

3. "City Beer License Board Starts Today," *CA*, April 25, 1933; "No Beer to Be Sold Until 7 am Monday," *CA*, April 28, 1933; "County Issues First Beer Sale License," *CA*, April 27, 1933.

4. "Squires Adopt Plan for Beer Regulation," *CA*, April 18, 1933; "Beer Regulations Set," *CA*, April 20, 1933; "Beer Will Foam in County after Midnight," *CA*, April 30, 1933.

5. "Wins Wings," *CA*, October 28, 1929; "Carnival Aviatrix," *CA*, May 9, 1932; "How Dizzy That Frog Must Be!" *CA*, October 28, 1933; "Flying for Deaf Proves Popular," *CA*, March 2, 1932; "City and County Ready for Return of Beer," *CA*, April 23, 1933; "Millions of Pints of Beer Lift Memphis's Dry Lid," *PS*, May 1, 1933.

6. "Come On, Old Hot Weather, 3.2 Will Take Care of You," *CA*, April 13, 1933.

7. Ibid.; "Two Big Breweries Pick Dealers Here," *CA*, April 15, 1933.

8. "First Beer Truck Rumbles into Memphis and an Era Ends," *PS*, May 1, 1933; "12,000 Cases of Beer Consumed Here First Day," *PS*, May 2, 1933.

9. Ibid.

10. "200 Get Jobs Thru Return of Beer," *PS*, May 6, 1933; "Beer Revenue Enriches City," *PS*, May 3, 1933.

11. "12,000 Cases of Beer Consumed Here First Day," *PS*, May 2, 1933; "Stag Cafeteria Is Selling Beer," *PS*, May 11, 1933; "Distributor of Kingsbury Beer Has Big Demand," *PS*, June 1, 1933.

12. "Blatz Is Back in Front after Absence," *PS*, June 15, 1933; "8 Anheuser-Busch Beer Horses Here," *CA*, July 5, 1933; "Beer Demand Keeps Breweries on Jump," *CA*, July 14, 1933.

13. "3.2 Burgundy Wine Put on Sale Here," *PS*, May 9, 1933; "3.2 Apple Cider to Be Made in Memphis," *CA*, September 17, 1933.

14. "Pastors Won't Back Beer Ban," *PS*, May 1, 1933; "Church May Outlaw Beer," *PS*, May 11, 1933.

15. "Millions of Pints of Beer Lift Memphis's Dry Lid," *PS*, May 1, 1933; "First Beer Law Case Brings a $50 Fine," *PS*, May 3, 1933; "Drunk Driving Bonds Raised," *PS*, June 6, 1933; "Drunk Drivers Grow Scarce," *PS*, June 10, 1933; "County Pig Stand Beer Permits Lag," *PS*, June 9, 1933.

16. "Cost of Making Home Brew Up with Malt Hike," *PS*, May 16, 1933; "Come On, Old Hot Weather, 3.2 Will Take Care of You," *CA*, April 13, 1933.

17. "Radio to Give Dry Law Dirge," *PS*, December 5, 1933; "Repeal Wipes Out Sympathy for Violators," *PS*, December 6, 1933.

18. "Legal Liquor to Be Bootlegged in City During Christmas," *PS*, November 6, 1933; "Repeal Whisky to Flow Here," *PS*, December 2, 1933.

19. "How to Dry Up Tennessee Is Real Teaser," *PS*, November 10, 1933.

20. Ibid.; "$5,000 in Choice Liquor Hijacked," *PS*, August 2, 1935; "Truck Hijacked of $6,750 in Liquors," *PS*, December 11, 1936; "Hijackers' Bullets Cost Memphian Arm," *PS*, December 23, 1937.

21. "Ex-Dry Agent in City Jail," *PS*, March 26, 1936; "Four Indicted as Drunk Drivers," *PS*, April 4, 1936; "Former Dry Agent Tried as Hijacker," *PS*, April 28, 1936; "Former Dry Agent Is Given 12 Years," *PS*, April 29, 1936; "Jail Memphian as Hijacker," *PS*, September 8, 1936.

22. "Happy Days Hit Gamblers' Row As Dice Click Requiem to Lid," *PS*, January 10, 1934; "City Will Outlaw Strong Wine and Beer," *PS*, December 5, 1933.

23. "Want a Good Still? Now's the Time to Buy," *PS*, December 16, 1933; "Liquor Prices Here in Line," *PS*, June 22, 1934.

24. "Big Legal Liquor Bootlegging Joint Seized by Raiders," *PS*, December 16, 1933.

25. George W. Lee, *Beale Street: Where the Blues Began* (College Park, MD: McGrath Publishing Company, 1934), 102–3.

26. "Happy Days Hit Gamblers' Row As Dice Click Requiem to Lid," *PS*, January 10, 1934; "Police End Drive to Keep Lid On," *PS*, January 11, 1934.

27. "Liquor Gates into City Are Opened Wide," *PS*, June 9, 1934.

28. Ibid.

29. "Small Fry Leggers Flop in Police Rum Dragnet," *PS*, September 15, 1934; "Liquor Prices Return to Normal," *PS*, October 26, 1934; "City Won't Be 100% Pure," *PS*, March 6, 1935.

30. Owen Payne White, "Sinners in Dixie," *Collier's* 26 (January 26, 1935), 16, 43–44.

31. "Wicked Memphis Write-Up Paints Unfair Picture but Advertise City," *PS*, January 18, 1935; "Active Weekend for Police Raiders," *PS*, January 28, 1935.

32. "Social Clubs' Closed by Lid on Liquor," *PS*, April 14, 1937.

33. "Says Browning Should Call for Dry Law Repeal," *PS*, December 28, 1936.

CHAPTER 19. LAST BOOTLEGGERS

1. "Terms Policy Biggest Racket," *PS*, May 19, 1931.

2. "Policy Lures Small-Time Gambler with Dreams of Big Winnings," *PS*, January 26, 1931.

3. "Retired Merchant N.R. Grandi Dies," *CA*, March 4, 1968; "Detectives' Booze War Will Continue," *CA*, April 21, 1922.

4. "Bogus Cards Put Out by Williams to Fool Voters," *NS*, November 6, 1919.

5. "Detectives' Booze War Will Continue," *CA*, April 21, 1922; "Nello Grandi Raided," *CA*, August 17, 1924; "Total Nabbed in Raids, 72," *CA*, March 9, 1927.

6. "Professional Bail Men Hit by Judge Harsh," *CA*, January 28, 1927.

7. "Warerooms of Whisky Raided," *PS*, October 12, 1929; "Weekend Raids Cram City Jail," *PS*, October 14, 1929.

8. "Police Suspended in Game Holdup Probe," *CA*, January 7, 1929.

9. "Shakeup of Police Department Begun," *CA*, January 9, 1929.

10. "Liquor War? Well It's Not Impossible," *CA*, February 26, 1930; "Baldi Baldly Denies Owning Burnt Liquor," *CA*, February 27, 1930.

11. "Whisky Fires Start Raid," *CA*, February 28, 1930.

12. "Grandi Denies Liquor Charge," *PS*, March 21, 1934.

13. "Dice Game Raid Lands 9 in Jail," *PS*, March 26, 1930.

14. "Davis Orders Dice Raid Investigation," *PS*, March 28, 1930; "Police Nab 6 in Rum Raids Here," *PS*, March 29, 1930; "Wharton Here for Dry War," *PS*, September 25, 1930.

15. "Federal Officers Probe Citizenship of Nello Grandi," *PS*, March 29, 1932; "Grandi Grilled by Federal Officers," *PS*, August 17, 1932.

16. "Grandi Fined $60, Held to Grand Jury," *PS*, February 18, 1936; "Suit Names Grandi as Liquor Seller," *PS*, November 5, 1936.

17. "Retired Merchant N.R. Grandi Dies," *CA*, March 4, 1968.

18. Westbrook Pegler, "Pegler Finds Beale Street a Broadway in Burnt Cork and Dim Lights," *CA*, May 15, 1934.

19. Ibid.

20. Ibid.

21. Memphis, Tennessee, Burial Permit no. 7441 (February 14, 1905), Lillian Mulcahy, Shelby County Archives, Shelby County, Tennessee; Memphis, Tennessee, Burial Permit no. 20350 (May 9, 1910), William J. Mulcahy, Shelby County Archives, Shelby County, Tennessee; Memphis, Tennessee, Burial Permit no. 26563 (February 5, 1912), Thomas Mulcahy, Shelby County Archives, Shelby County, Tennessee; R. L. Polk and Company, *Memphis City Directory* (Memphis: R. L. Polk and Company, 1900–1915).

22. "Jim Mulcahy Arrested by Dry Raiders," *CA*, October 9, 1933.

23. David M. Tucker, *Lieutenant Lee of Beale Street* (Nashville: Vanderbilt University Press, 1971), 98.

24. G. Wayne Dowdy, *Mayor Crump Don't Like It: Machine Politics in Memphis* (Jackson: University Press of Mississippi, 2006), 101–2; David A. Jasen and Gene Jones, *Spreadin' Rhythm Around: Black Popular Music, 1880–1930* (New York: Routledge, 2005), 232; Paul Oliver, *Songsters and Saints: Vocal Traditions on Race Records* (Cambridge, UK: Cambridge University Press, 1984), 72.

25. "Jim Mulcahy Arrested by Dry Raiders," *CA*, October 9, 1933.

26. "6 Police Raids Yield 48 Men and 4 Women," *CA*, August 22. 1922; "Federal Raids Net 33 Liquor Arrests," *CA*, September 17, 1922; "Many Jury Trials Occupy Judge Ross," *CA*, January 4, 1923; *CA*, April 28, 1926; "Prohi Agents Make Raid," CA, April 14, 1928; "Mulcahy Given Time to Raise $1,000 Fine," *EA*, November 21, 1928.

27. "Two Negroes Slain in Pistol Fight," *PS*, February 29, 1932; "Jim Mulcahy Bound Over to Grand Jury," *PS*, March 2, 1932; "McLain Refused to Prosecute Mulcahy," *PS*, March 25, 1932; "Jim Mulcahy Arrested by Dry Raiders," *PS*, October 9, 1933; "Three Arrests Seal Lid Tighter," *PS*, October 10, 1933; "James J. Mulcahy Escapes Indictment," *PS*, November 10, 1933.

28. Jim Mulcahy Arrested by Dry Raiders," *CA*, October 9, 1933; Margaret McKee and Fred Chisenhall, *Beale, Black and Blue: Life and Music on Black America's Main Street* (Baton Rouge: Louisiana State University Press, 1981), 64.

29. "Beale Street Ghost of Past," *Spokesman Review* (Spokane, WA), May 12, 1940; McKee and Chisenhall, *Beale, Black and Blue*, 64; Shelby County, Tennessee, death certificate no. 3314 (September 5, 1940), James J. Mulcahy, Tennessee State Library and Archives, Nashville.

30. "King of Bootleggers Gone," *NS*, January 30, 1919.

31. "The Tennessee Liquor House are Hard Hit," *Hartford Herald* (Hartford, KY), January 26, 1916.

32. "King of Bootleggers Gone," *Hayti Herald* (Hayti, MO), January 30, 1919; "Nab Whiskey Boat and Nine Men in Tennessee," *Mixer and Server* 26, no. 9 (September 15, 1917): 53.

33. "King of Bootleggers Gone," *Hayti Herald* (Hayti, MO), January 30, 1919.

34. "Laughter Makes Plea for Delay," *NS*, February 13, 1919.

35. "Protection Too High in Memphis; Laughter Quits," *NS*, March 22, 1919.

36. "Laughter and Fisher Lose in Supreme Court," *NS*, April 21, 1919.

37. "Plans to Arrest Perry on Charge Kidnapping Fail," *NS*, April 15, 1919; "Laughter 'Bootleg King' Goes to Penitentiary," *NS*, March 2, 1920.

38. George W. Lee, *Beale Street: Where the Blues Began* (College Park, MD: McGrath Publishing Company, 1934), 83; "More Liquor Cases Up," *CA*, March 11, 1923; "Arrest Memphians," *CA*, March 11, 1924; "Car Runs Amuck," *CA*, November 1, 1924; "Giant Still Seized in Horn Lake Bottom," *CA*, November 7, 1926.

39. "S. Watkins Street Home Yields Booze Store," *CA*, May 26, 1923; "Laughter Pays Fine Under Nuisance Law," *CA*, July 10, 1923; "Sheriff Raids Giant Moonshine Plant," *CA*, October 14, 1924; "Harsh Fines Four," *CA*, May 16, 1925; "Affirm Laughter Case," *CA*, January 17, 1926; "Ha Ha, Laughter Bond Jumper Held," *EA*, April 1, 1927; "Gone After Laughter," *CA*, July 19, 1927; "Laughter Faces Prison Term Here," *PS*, June 25, 1931.

40. "Four Men Arrested," *CA*, November 3, 1923; "Laughter Raided Again," *CA*, May 23, 1926; "Indict 15 Defendants," *CA*, January 21, 1928.

41. "And They Call This an Election," *CA*, August 3, 1928; "Police and Thugs Run Election; Blacks Go to Polls Like Cattle," *CA*, August 3, 1928; "Election Boss Bound Over to Grand Jury," *CA*, June 18, 1929.

42. "Frisky Whisky Blows Up Houses," *PS*, June 12, 1929; "Whisky Blast Puzzles Cops as to Renter," *PS*, June 13, 1929; "Election Boss Bound Over to Grand Jury," *CA*, June 18, 1929.

43. "Laughter Clear in Liquor Blast," *EA*, June 13, 1929.

44. "Federal Dry Agents Renew War on Booze," *PS*, May 10, 1930; "Cap Laughter Out on Parole, Now Banished to Mississippi," *CA*, April 8, 1947.

45. Lester G. Fant to Ed Crump, March 19, 1945, W. J. Raney to Commissioner Boyle, March 11, 1941, E.H. Crump Collection, Series IV, General Correspondence, 1925–54, Box

185/337, Memphis Room, Memphis Public Library and Information Center; "Cap Laughter Out on Parole, Now Banished to Mississippi," *CA*, April 8, 1947.

CHAPTER 20. SIN AGAINST HIGH HEAVEN

1. "Repeal Faces Legislators," *PS*, January 1, 1935.

2. "Move to Tax Liquor Gains New Strength," *PS*, January 15, 1935.

3. Paul Johnson, Christopher Conrad, David Thomson, *Workers versus Pensioners: Intergenerational Justice in an Aging World* (New York: Manchester University Press, 1989), 118; "Local Option Liquor Bill and Three Percent Sales Tax Possible Thru Trades," *PS*, January 28, 1935.

4. "Local Option Liquor Bill and Three Percent Sales Tax Possible Thru Trades," *PS*, January 28, 1935; "Election Not Necessary by Liquor Bill," *PS*, February 11, 1935; "Liquor Bill Received in House with Lusty Cheer," *PS*, February 13, 1935; "Delay Sought in Action on Liquor Bill," *PS*, February 18, 1935.

5. "Methodists Assail Liquor Propaganda," *PS*, February 11, 1935; "Bishop DuBose for Browning," *PS*, May 13, 1938; "Demon Rum is Pastor's Topic," *PS*, July 2, 1938; "Bishop Hughes Lambasts Friends of Liquor Laws," *PS*, December 30, 1935.

6. "Church Rebukes Drinking Women," *PS*, May 19, 1936; "Drinks, Smokes Not For Girls," *PS*, November 7, 1935.

7. "Lunati to Discuss Effects of Liquor," *PS*, April 17, 1937; "Temperance WCTU's Job Now," *PS*, March 3, 1939.

8. "Five Percent Beer Is Refused by Senate," *PS*, April 20, 1935; "Five Pct. Beer Becomes Legal," *PS*, April 23, 1935.

9. "Smashing of Bootleggers Is Aim of Liquor Measure," *PS*, April 16, 1935; "Local Option Horse Racing Bills Offered," *PS*, July 23, 1935; "House Kills Legal Liquor Measure by 49 to 41 Vote," *PS*, July 29, 1935; "Budget-Wrecking Pension Bill Faces Senate Fight," *PS*, July 30, 1935.

10. "Bootleggers Smile," *PS*, July 30, 1935; "Expect Stores in W. Memphis," *PS*, March 16, 1935; "Liquor Stocks Are Enlarged," *PS*, March 25, 1935.

11. "House Favors Vote on Liquor," *PS*, August 2, 1935; "Senate Dooms State Repeal Referendum," *PS*, August 4, 1935.

12. "Can Governor Ban Election? Critics Say No," *PS*, August 5, 1935.

13. "Browning Is Not Pledged against Poll on Liquor," *PS*, December 17, 1936.

14. "Repeal Group to Delay Vote on Liquor Act," *PS*, January 4, 1937; "Liquor Bill Doomed to Defeat," *PS*, April 13, 1937; "Hotel Liquor Bill May Block Needed Revenue Program," *PS*, April 24, 1937; "Liquor Hopes Turn Toward Referendum," *PS*, May 12, 1937.

15. "Coup By Wets Turns Table on Dry Force," *PS*, May 14, 1937; "Senate Action Sets Election for August 12," *PS*, May 21, 1937; "Tennessee Dry Forces Plan Fight at Polls Sept. 23 in State Repeal Election," *PS*, May 22, 1937.

16. "Crump Cold to Referendum," *PS*, May 22, 1937; "Scant Interest in Referendum," *PS*, July 19, 1937.

17. "We Ask Our Assembly—Do People Rule?" *PS*, September 10, 1937; "Tennessee Plans Liquor Straw Vote," *Reading Eagle* (Reading, PA), September 20, 1937; "Wets Hopeful But Repeal Is Not Yet Sure," *PS*, May 6, 1937.

18. "Wets Confer on Enjoining Repeal Vote," *PS*, August 14, 1937; "Liquor Referendum Act is Held Valid," *PS*, June 25, 1937; "Drys Organize for Vote Fight," *PS*, August 18, 1937.

19. "Drys to Carry Fight to Polls," *PS*, July 6, 1937; "Drys Rally to DuBose's Call," *PS*, August 27, 1937.

20. "Browning Dry but Wants All to Vote," *PS*, September 1, 1937; "Wets Confer on Enjoining Repeal Vote," *PS*, August 14, 1937; "Referendum Called a Waste of Money," *PS*, September 1, 1937; "Appeal Taken on Referendum," *PS*, September 8, 1937; "No Hitch Yet on Referendum," *PS*, August 27, 1937.

21. "Tennessee Plans Liquor Straw Vote," *Reading Eagle* (Reading, PA), September 20, 1937; "Drys Prepare Death Blow to Liquor Issue," *PS*, September 10, 1937.

22. "Quorum Absent, Liquor License Bill Is Killed," *PS*, November 20, 1937; "Liquor Making in a Dry States," *PS*, January 15, 1938.

23. "State Liquor Income Taxes the Way Out," *PS*, December 14, 1938; "Liquor Vote OK with Cooper," *PS*, December 28, 1938.

24. "State Referendum Missing from House Liquor Measure," *PS*, February 14, 1939; "Revised Liquor Bill Calls for Referendum," *PS*, February 20, 1939; "Crump Calls for Repeal of State's Foolish Dry Law," *PS*, February 18, 1939; "Wets Line Up Repeal Votes," *PS*, February 23, 1939.

25. "Jubilant Wet Forces Ready for New Test," *PS*, March 1, 1939; "Legislature Quickly Kills Veto—Passes Liquor Bill," *PS*, March 2, 1939.

26. "State Map Will Go on Liquor Bottles," *PS*, March 27, 1939; "Stamp Liquor or Lose It," *PS*, March 30, 1939; "Liquor Stamps Order Switched," *PS*, May 16, 1939.

27. "Shelby Must Wait Until May 15 for Legal Liquor Sale," *PS*, March 3, 1939; "Liquor Move Started Here," *PS*, March 9, 1939.

28. "Locations in Demand for Liquor Stores in Memphis," *PS*, March 15, 1939; "First Liquor Store Charter," *PS*, March 18, 1939; "Legal Liquor Era Is Nearer," *PS*, April 7, 1939.

29. "Shelby Liquor Election Today," *PS*, May 25, 1939; "Liquor Vote on May 24," *PS*, April 11, 1939; "Shelby Liquor Vote Thursday," *PS*, May 24, 1939.

30. "Liquor Legal But Still No Legal Liquor," *PS*, May 26, 1939; "City Drafts Own Rules for Liquor Sale Control," *PS*, May 29, 1939; "State Liquor Inspectors to Enforce Law," *PS*, May 27, 1939; "State Liquor Inspectors to Enforce Law," *PS*, May 27, 1939; "Barney Plough Sells Drugstore; He's Going into the Liquor Business," *PS*, May 29, 1939; "Whiskey Blending Plant in Memphis," *PS*, May 31, 1939.

CONCLUSION

1. "Gangsters Escape Under Police Fire," *CA*, February 26, 1928.

2. "Al Capone's Brother Told to Leave Town," *EA*, February 6, 1928.

3. "Police Clean City Says Major Allen," *CA*, April 4, 1923; "Bacon Makes Plea for Legal Liquor," *PS*, January 4, 1935.

4. "How Will City Handle Liquor," *PS*, May 21, 1937; "Must Favor Local Option Liquor Sale," *PS*, November 28, 1935.

5. Perre Magness, "Bootlegging Thrived in Dry Time," *CA*, January 3, 2002.

6. "Moonshine Flows, High Taxes Blamed," *Sunday Morning Star* (Wilmington, DE), December 8, 1940; "Use Telescopic Lens to Trap Moonshiners," *Milwaukee Journal* (WI), February 15, 1941; "Occupational Hazard," *Sunday Herald* (Bridgeport, CT), April 15, 1951.

7. "WCTU Upset by Display of Stills," *Herald Journal* (Spartanburg, SC), September 26, 1965.

8. "Whisky Bill Is Discussed in Tennessee," *Times-News* (Hendersonville, NC), May 4, 1967; "Liquor by the Drink Defeated in Memphis," *Millwaukee Journal* (WI), September 1, 1967; "No Mixed Drinks Can Be Sold at Memphis Clubs," *Florence Times* (AL), July 27, 1968.

9. Magness, "Bootlegging Thrived."

10. "Moonshiners Still Their Stills; Find More Sugar in Pot," *Daytona Beach (FL) Morning Journal*, June 16, 1977.

11. Ibid.

12. Dan Baum, "Legalize It All: How to Win the War on Drugs," *Harper's Magazine* 332, no. 1991 (April 2016): 22–30.

13. "House Approves Bill to Block Nashville, Memphis Marijuana Laws," *The Tennessean* (Nashville), March 23, 2017; "Bill Haslam Signs Repeal of New Nashville, Memphis Marijuana Laws," *The Tennessean* (Nashville), April 13, 2017.

BIBLIOGRAPHY

LOCAL NEWSPAPERS

Commercial Appeal (Memphis, TN)
Covington Leader (Covington, TN)
Daily Avalanche (Memphis, TN)
Evening Appeal (Memphis, TN)
News Scimitar (Memphis, TN)
Press-Scimitar (Memphis, TN)

OTHER NEWSPAPERS

Arizona Journal-Miner (Prescott, AZ)
Boston Evening Transcript (Boston, MA)
Carroll Herald (Carroll, IA)
Chicago Tribune
Daily Mail and Empire (Toronto, Canada)
Daily Star (Fredericksburg, VA)
Daytona Beach Morning Journal (Daytona Beach, FL)
Deseret News (Salt Lake City, UT)
Eugene Daily Guard (Eugene, OR)
Evening Independent (St. Petersburg, FL)
Evening News (San Jose, CA)
Freelance (Fredericksburg, VA)
The Freeman (Indianapolis, IN)
Gazette (Montreal, Canada)
Hartford Herald (Hartford, KY)
Hayti Herald (Hayti, MO)
Herald Democrat (Leadville, CO)

Herald Journal (Spartanburg, SC)

Meridian Morning Record (Meridian, CT)

Miami News (Miami, FL)

Milwaukee Journal (Milwaukee, WI)

Nevada Daily Mail (Nevada, MO)

New York Times

The Oklahoman (Oklahoma City, OK)

Pittsburgh Press (Pittsburgh, PA)

Reading Eagle (Reading, PA)

Southeastern Missourian (Cape Girardeau, MO)

Spokesman Review (Spokane, WA)

Sunday Morning Star (Wilmington, DE)

The Tennessean (Nashville, TN)

Times Daily (Florence, AL)

Times-News (Hendersonville, NC)

Toledo Blade (Toledo, OH)

Toronto Daily Mail (Toronto, Canada)

Turtle Mountain Star (Rolla, ND)

Victoria Advocate (Victoria, TX)

PAPERS AND MANUSCRIPT COLLECTIONS

E. H. Crump Collection. Memphis Room, Memphis Public Library and Information Center, Memphis, Tennessee.

Hoover, Herbert. "Address Accepting the Republican Presidential Nomination," August 11, 1932, in *Public Papers of the Presidents of the United States: Herbert Hoover*, vol. 4. Washington, DC: Office of the Federal Register, National Archives and Records Services, General Services Administration, US GPO, 1974–77.

GENEALOGICAL RECORDS

Arkansas Marriages, 1837–1944, index. Digital images. FamilySearch.org, 2013.

Tennessee. Memphis. Burial Permits. Shelby County Archives, Shelby County, Tennessee.

Tennessee. Shelby County. 1870 US census, population schedule. Digital images. Family Search.org, 2013.

Tennessee. Shelby County. 1880 US census, population schedule. Digital images. Family Search.org, 2013.

Tennessee. Shelby County. 1900 US census, population schedule. Digital images. Family Search.org, 2013.

Tennessee. Shelby County. 1910 US census, population schedule. Digital images. Family Search.org, 2013.

Tennessee. Shelby County. Death Certificates. Tennessee State Library and Archives, Nashville.

Tennessee. Shelby County. Marriage Certificates. Shelby County Archives, Shelby County, Tennessee.

Tennessee. Shelby County. Marriage Certificates. Tennessee State Library and Archives, Nashville. Digital images. FamilySearch.org, 2015.

United States World War I Draft Registration Cards, 1917–1918. Digital images. FamilySearch. org, 2015.

SECONDARY SOURCES

Abadinsky, Howard. *Organized Crime*. Belmont, CA: Wadsworth, 2007.

American Marine Engineer 13, no. 1 (January 1918).

Bauman, Mark K., and Berkley Kalin. *The Quiet Voices: Southern Rabbis and Civil Rights, 1880s to 1990s*. Tuscaloosa: University of Alabama Press, 1995.

Beard, Mattie Duncan. *The WCTU in the Volunteer State*. Kingsport: Kingsport Press, 1962.

Bent, Silas. "Prohibition in the City of Memphis." *Mixer and Server: Official Journal of the Hotel and Restaurant Employees' International Alliance and Bartenders' Alliance League of America* 19 (January 15, 1910).

Biles, Roger. *Memphis in the Great Depression*. Knoxville: University of Tennessee Press, 1986.

Blotner, Joseph. *Faulkner: A Biography*. Jackson: University Press of Mississippi, 2005.

Burns, Ken. "Roots of Prohibition." *Prohibition*. PBS, 2011. http://www.pbs.org/kenburns/ Prohibition/roots-of-Prohibition/.

Coggins, Allen R. *Tennessee Tragedies: Natural, Technological, and Societal Disasters in the Volunteer State*. Knoxville: University of Tennessee Press, 2012.

Coker, Joe L. *Liquor in the Land of the Lost Cause: Southern White Evangelicals and the Prohibition Movement*. Lexington: University Press of Kentucky, 2007.

Coppock, Helen M., and Charles W. Crawford, eds. *Paul R. Coppock's Midsouth*. Memphis: West Tennessee Historical Society, 1985.

Coppock, Paul. *Memphis Memoirs*. Memphis: Memphis State University Press, 1980.

Davis, Marni. *Booze and Jews: Becoming American in the Age of Prohibition*. New York: New York University Press, 2012.

DeSpain, Joseph Y., John R. Burch Jr., and Timothy Q. Hooper. *Images of America: Green County*. Charleston, SC: Arcadia Press, 2013.

Dowdy, G. Wayne. *A Brief History of Memphis*. Charleston: History Press, 2011.

Dowdy, G. Wayne. *Mayor Crump Don't Like It: Machine Politics in Memphis*. Jackson: University Press of Mississippi, 2006.

Dowdy, G. Wayne. *On This Day in Memphis History*. Charleston: History Press, 2014.

Edwards, Richard. *Directory of the City of Memphis*. New Orleans: Southern Publishing Company, 1874.

Evans, David. *Ramblin' on My Mind: New Perspectives on the Blues*. Urbana: University of Illinois Press, 2008.

Evans, E. Lewis. "WCTU Crusade Against Tobacco Next, It Is Said." *Tobacco Worker* 23, no. 1 (1919): 1–2.

Farrell, Norman, and J. S. Laurent. *An Annotated Index to the Public and General Statutes of Tennessee from 1897 to 1911 Inclusive*. Nashville: Marshall and Bruce Co. Law Publishers, 1912.

Funderburg, J. Ann. *Bootleggers and Beer Barons of the Prohibition Era*. Jefferson, NC: McFarland, 2014.

Gately, Iain. *Drink: A Cultural History of Alcohol*. New York: Penguin, 2008.

Gritter, Elizabeth. *River of Hope: Black Politics and the Memphis Freedom Movement, 1865–1954*. Lexington: University Press of Kentucky, 2014.

Guthrie, John J. *Keepers of the Spirits: The Judicial Response to Prohibition Enforcement in Florida, 1885–1935*. Westport, CT: Greenwood Press, 1998.

Hammell, George M. *The Passing of the Saloon: An Authentic and Official Presentation of the Anti-Liquor Crusade in America*. Cincinnati: Tower Press, 1908.

Hildebrand, Bob. "The New Deal at Memphis, Tennessee." *National Police Journal* 5 (February 1920): 18–21.

Hofstader, Richard. "From the Age of Reform, Written by Historian Richard Hofstadter in 1955." *Playboy*, April 2006.

Honey, Michael K. *Going Down Jericho Road: The Memphis Strike, Martin Luther King's Last Campaign*. New York: W. W. Norton, 2007.

Industrial Refrigeration 27, nos. 1–6 (July–December 1904).

Isaac, Paul E. *Prohibition and Politics: Turbulent Decades in Tennessee, 1885–1920*. Knoxville: University of Tennessee Press, 1965.

Jackson, Kenneth. *The Ku Klux Klan in the City, 1915–1930*. New York: Oxford University Press, 1967.

Jasen, David A., and Gene Jones. *Spreadin' Rhythm Around: Black Popular Music, 1880–1930*. New York: Routledge, 2005.

Johns, Charles D. *Tennessee's Pond of Liquor and Pool of Blood: A Complete and Detailed Account of Our Shameless Condition in Tennessee*. Nashville: C. D. Johns, 1912.

Johnson, Paul, Christopher Conrad, and David Thomson. *Workers versus Pensioners: Intergenerational Justice in an Aging World*. New York: Manchester University Press, 1989.

Laska, Lewis L. *The Tennessee State Constitution: A Reference Guide*. New York: Greenwood Press, 1990.

Lauterbach, Preston. *Beale Street Dynasty: Sex, Song, and the Struggle for the Soul of Memphis*. New York: W. W. Norton and Company, 2015.

Lee, George W. *Beale Street: Where the Blues Began*. College Park, MD: McGrath Publishing Company, 1934.

Leinwand, Gerald. *1927: High Tide of the Twenties*. New York: Four Walls Eight Windows, 2001.

Lerner, Michael A. *Dry Manhattan: Prohibition in New York City*. Cambridge: Harvard University Press, 2007.

Linfield, H. S. "A Survey of the Year 5682." *American Jewish Yearbook* 24 (September 23, 1922–September 10, 1923): 24.

McKee, Margaret, and Fred Chisenhall. *Beale, Black and Blue: Life and Music on Black America's Main Street*. Baton Rouge: Louisiana State University Press, 1981.

Meyers, Frank, and Gennie Meyers. *Shelby County Sheriff's Department Annual Report*. Marceline, MO: Walsworth Publishing, 1976.

Miller, William D. *Memphis During the Progressive Era, 1900–1917*. Memphis: Memphis State University Press, 1957.

Miller, William D. *Mr. Crump of Memphis*. Baton Rouge: Louisiana State University Press, 1981.

Mohl, Raymond A. *The Making of Urban America*. Lanham, MD: Rowman and Littlefield, 2006.

Moore, Leonard J. *Citizen Klansmen: The Ku Klux Klan in Indiana, 1921–1928*. Chapel Hill: University of North Carolina Press, 1991.

Moss, Robert F. *Southern Spirits: Four Hundred Years of Drinking in the South, with Recipes*. Berkeley: Ten Speed Press, 2016.

National Provisioner Trade Magazine 31, no. 27. December 15, 1904.

Oakley, Giles. *The Devil's Music: History of the Blues*. London: Da Capo Press, 1997.

O'Daniel, Patrick. *When the Levee Breaks: Memphis and the Mississippi Valley Food of 1927*. Charleston: History Press, 2013.

Okrent, Daniel. "Prohibition Life: Politics, Loopholes and Bathtub Gin." Interview by Terry Gross. *Fresh Air*. National Public Radio, May 10, 2010. Accessed April 12, 2017. http://www.npr.org/2010/05/10/126613316/Prohibition-life-politics-loopholes-and-bathtub-gin.

Oliver, Paul. *Songsters and Saints: Vocal Traditions on Race Records*. Cambridge, UK: Cambridge University Press, 1984.

Patton, William. *A Guide to Historic Downtown Memphis*. Charleston: History Press, 2010.

Peters, Gerhard, and John T. Woolley. *The American Presidency Project*. http://www.presidency.ucsb.edu. 2017.

Peterson, J. K. Understanding Surveillance Technologies: Spy Devices, Privacy, History, and Applications. Boco Raton, FL: CRC Press, 2007.

Polk, R. L., and Company. *Memphis City Directory*. Memphis: R. L. Polk and Company, 1870–1939.

Postal Record: A Journal for Postal Employees 5, no. 2. February 1892.

Public Opinion 20. April 1896.

Raichelson, Richard M. *Beale Street Talks: A Walking Tour Down the Home of the Blues*. Memphis: Richard M. Raichelson, 1999.

Reisman, John M. *History of Clinical Psychology*. New York: Brunner-Routledge, 1991.

Roper, Daniel C. "Ruling of Internal Revenue Commissioner Roper on Manufacture, Sale and Distribution of Distilled Spirits." *Commercial and Financial Chronicle* 109 (July 1–September 30, 1919): 33.

Rose, Kenneth D. *American Women and the Repeal of Prohibition*. New York: New York University Press, 1996.

Sanchez, Juan O. *Religions and the Ku Klux Klan: Biblical Appropriation in Their Literature and Songs*. Jefferson, NC: MacFarland, 2016.

Schmeckebier, Laurence. *The Bureau of Prohibition: Its History, Activities, and Organization*. Washington, DC: Brookings Institution, 1929.

Sholes, A. E. *Directory of the City of Memphis*. Memphis: Boyle, Chapman and Company, 1876; Memphis: Southern Baptist Publication Society, 1877; Memphis: S. C. Toof and Company, 1878–79.

Szasz, Thomas Stephen. *Ceremonial Chemistry: The Ritual Persecution of Drugs, Addicts, and Pushers*. New York: Syracuse University Press, 2003.

Tapper, Josh. "Slivovitz: A Plum (Brandy) Choice." *Moment* 39, no. 2 (March–April 2014). Accessed April 4, 2017. http://www.momentmag.com/slivovitz-plum-brandy-choice/.

Thompson, Frank M. *Reports of Cases, Argued and Determined in the Supreme Court of Tennessee, Western Division*, vol. 8. Columbia, MO: E. W. Stephens Publishing Company, 1916.

Timbrell, John. *The Poison Paradox: Chemicals as Friends and Foes*. New York: Oxford University Press, 2005.

Trost, Jennifer Ann. *Gateway to Justice: The Juvenile Court and Progressive Child Welfare in a Southern City*. Athens: University of Georgia Press, 2005.

Tucker, David M. *Lieutenant Lee of Beale Street*. Nashville: Vanderbilt University Press, 1971.

US Department of Justice. *Department of Justice and the Courts of the United States*. Washington, DC: Government Printing Office, 1918.

Watson, James G. *William Faulkner: Self-Presentation and Performance*. Austin: University of Texas Press, 2000.

White, Owen Payne. *The Autobiography of a Durable Sinner*. New York: G. P. Putnam's Sons, 1942.

White, Owen Payne. "Sinners in Dixie." *Collier's*, January 26, 1935, 44.

Wright, Sharon D. *Race, Power, and Political Emergence in Memphis*. New York: Garland Publishing, 2000.

Young, John Preston. *Standard History of Memphis, Tennessee: A Study of the Original Sources*. Knoxville: H. W. Crew, 1912.

INDEX

References to illustrations appear in **bold**.

290